D1608593

Knowledge Engineering

Concepts and Practices
for Knowledge-Based Systems

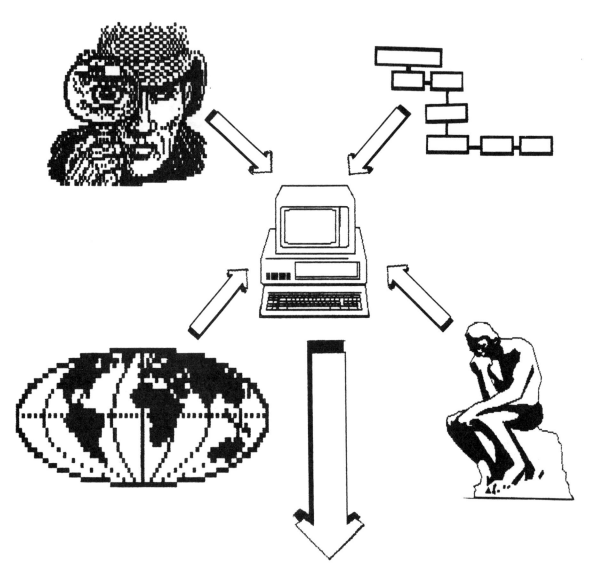

Knowledge Engineering

Knowledge Engineering

Concepts and Practices for Knowledge-Based Systems

G. Steven Tuthill, Ed.D.

 TAB Professional and Reference Books

Division of TAB BOOKS Inc.

Blue Ridge Summit, PA

HyperCard and **HyperTalk** are trademarks of Apple Computer, Inc.
Macintosh is a trademark licensed to Apple Computer, Inc.

TPR books are published by TAB Professional and Reference Books, a division of TAB BOOKS Inc. The TPR logo, consisting of the letters "TPR" within a large "T," is a registered trademark of TAB BOOKS Inc.

Published by **TAB BOOKS Inc.**
FIRST EDITION/FIRST PRINTING

Library of Congress Cataloging-in-Publication Data

Tuthill, G. Steven.
   Knowledge engineering : concepts and practices for knowledge-based
systems / by G. Steven Tuthill.
      p.   cm.
   Includes bibliographical references.
   ISBN 0-8306-9297-5
   1. Expert systems (Computer science) 2. Knowledge acquisition
(Expert systems) I. Title.
QA76.76.E95T88 1989   89-20285
006.3′3—dc20   CIP

TAB BOOKS Inc. offers software for sale. For information and a catalog, please contact TAB Software Department, Blue Ridge Summit, PA 17294-0850.

Questions regarding the content of this book should be addressed to:

TAB BOOKS Inc.
Blue Ridge Summit, PA 17294-0850

Larry Hager: Vice President & Editorial Director
John W. Young: Book Editor
Katherine Brown: Production
Jaclyn B. Saunders: Book Design
Lori E. Schlosser: Cover Design

Contents

Part II

Knowledge Acquisition and Representation

Part III
A Development Model

Foreword

There are many individuals moving into these highly technical fields that require knowledge engineering skills. However, as of this writing, there is no available formal training and there are no university degrees available. Perhaps the reason for this is that the knowledge engineer must possess knowledge and abilities from multiple fields of study, have computer skills, and possess a high level of communication skills.

Further defined, the composite skills of a knowledge engineer include computer science, cognitive psychology, behavioral psychology, and subject matter sensitivity. The knowledge engineer must be a quick study in technical areas, who can see the big picture and specify details. For this reason, the demand for knowledge engineers exceeds the current supply.

Knowledge-based systems are able to spread the knowledge wealth to those without the benefit of a resident expert. These resident experts are also scarce. Thus, the power of knowledge is in the hands of a relative select few.

The near-term future holds opportunities for knowledge-based systems that will impact our everyday lives. In fact, knowledge-based applications will probably transcend the information industry and become the backbone of the knowledge industry. In Japan, for example, the Fifth Generation Project is a government- and industry-funded effort to capture the "knowledge industry." This knowledge industry will produce a salable commodity like steel or oil. This new industry will cross geopolitical boundaries and become a force that can alter economies.

As a result of the potential global impact of knowledge-based applications, a solid start or stake in the ground needs to be established for a systematic approach to knowledge engineering.

This book is written for those of you who wish to become familiar with, or learn more about, the craft of knowledge engineering. This book presents and helps to establish a foundation for knowledge acquisition and representation.

While it does not have all the answers or cover all the bases, this book offers concentrated sources of "how to" information. With this information you can start to develop your own styles and procedures for knowledge acquisition.

The book limits its discussion to what knowledge engineers do to meet their responsibilities. It does not discuss in detail artificial intelligence, expert system tools, languages, accomplishments, etc. There have been many publications which cover these topics. What the marketplace has lacked is a guide that gathers and represents the essential expertise for knowledge acquisition and representation. This book contains basic information and options for learning how to harvest knowledge and extend our human decision-making capabilities.

There needs to be a caveat about replicating human decision-making capabilities. The processes currently employed by knowledge engineers will evolve as more is learned about human decision-making, and as the functionality of available hardware and software increases. The relationship of current and future knowledge representation schemes can be represented through an analogy: the early conceptualizers of manned flight envisioned flying machines as devices that flapped wing structures. Their logic was obviously based on the fact that birds flew and they flapped their wings. Current aircraft design and concepts have far outstripped the reaches of the imagination of those early pioneers. Designers of today's knowledge-intensive systems tend to focus on system designs and knowledge representation schemes that model the human brain and emulate human reasoning. The approach is a sound first-stage attempt, but most likely not the final form. As advances in technology and techniques transcend the current limitations, knowledge representation systems and knowledge dynamics will slip their present bonds.

The future of knowledge engineering is in the minds of current and near-term practitioners of knowledge sciences. The present belongs to myopic realists who adapt technology to meet current needs. The future belongs to visionaries who manage and anticipate technology to meet unrealized needs.

I wish to thank those that have helped in the preparation and review of this work. Special acknowledgement is gratefully given Terri Kubow for her editing; Susan Levy, Jim Quigley, Zhongmin Li, Boris Beizer, Ned Chapin, and Joe Hymes for their review comments; and my family—GayLa, Collin, and Chad—for their support and patience.

Introduction

The open society, the unrestricted access to knowledge,
the unplanned and uninhibited association of men for its furtherance—
these are what may make a vast, complex, ever growing, ever changing,
ever more specialized and expert technological world,
nevertheless a world of human community.

J. Robert Oppenheimer

The advent and proliferation of knowledge-based systems have produced both a wide range of applications and a wide range of quality. There is generally a collaboration between domain experts and knowledge engineers in the production of knowledge-based systems. The goal of these systems is to present the decision-making expertise of domain specialists in problem-solving situations.

Knowledge-based systems include expert systems, hypermedia systems, CASE engineering, and hybrid systems. While the most familiar of the knowledge-based systems are the expert systems, both developers and the marketplace are exploring many emerging technologies. Some of these technologies such as hypertext have been confined to laboratory or educational settings. Now these systems are beginning to emerge in the business world.

Knowledge-based systems are in daily use in most Fortune 500 companies. Applications of expert systems range from medical diagnostic systems to nuclear facility watchdogs, and from designing circuit boards to exploring for minerals. These systems are able to perform at levels that equal or exceed the decision making efficiency of human experts.

The reason that these systems are so powerful is that they contain the collective wisdom of successful practitioners in focused fields. There are too many changes in the domain, and, combined with the volume of data, too much opportunity to overlook needed information. However, knowledge-based systems that serve as intelligent assistants can leverage available information.

Herein lies the problem. The quality of the knowledge base has a direct correlation with the knowledge and heuristic rules of the domain expert and the skill of the knowledge engineer in extracting and representing that knowledge. Knowledge engineering is an art that uses science.

In addition, knowledge engineering is not restricted to expert systems. The function of knowledge engineering, to acquire and codify knowledge, is also needed in other endeavors. For example, those who create relational databases need to focus the contents of the database and compose the logical access links. Further, people involved in hypermedia attempt to supply the most logical modules and groupings with associated links. In both cases, the person creating the relational database or the hypermedia is usually not the content expert. Thus, there is a need to work efficiently with domain experts to acquire and codify knowledge.

Part I

Human Knowledge, Machine Knowledge, and Knowledge-Based Systems

Good sense is of all things in the world the most equally distributed,
for everybody thinks he is so well supplied with it,
that even those most difficult to please in all other matters
never desire more of it than they already possess.

René Descartes

The purpose of the first part of the book is to introduce selected terms and to establish a foundation from which to build and discuss knowledge concepts. These concepts are explored from the perspective of knowledge as it applies to humans and machine systems. Part I contains four chapters:

- The focus of chapter 1 is human knowledge, and the chapter provides a look at the different ways of examining human knowledge. The first chapter also directs the discussion of human knowledge toward considerations for knowledge-based systems.
- Chapter 2 explores knowledge sources for knowledge-based systems. These sources are analyzed and rated for several features, including availability and level of risk.
- Chapter 3 examines machine knowledge. This chapter discusses machine problem solving and offers a new classification scheme for expert systems.
- Chapter 4 reviews knowledge-based systems and provides a taxonomy for types of expert system applications.

1

The Nature of
Human Knowledge

Nature does nothing uselessly.
All men by nature desire knowledge.

Aristotle

INTRODUCTION

This chapter is the foundation for building the knowledge acquisition and representation content of this book. In order to convey the concepts of acquiring and representing knowledge, the connotations of knowledge are explored as they apply to knowledge-based systems. Thus, this chapter explores knowledge from various perspectives. Whenever possible, analogies are applied to relate concepts, and examples given to support concepts.

This chapter focuses on the knowledge of experts as it influences the performance of applications in knowledge-based systems. The manner in which knowledge is initially learned through formal education and training is not discussed. Thus, this chapter does not explore how a person assimilates aggregate learning. Rather, the focus of this chapter is to examine knowledge that has been acquired in a specific domain by an individual, and to provide an analysis of the structures and elements of knowledge.

Data, Information, and Knowledge

In this era, proclaimed as the Age of Information by various monitors of social evolution, society is besieged by mountains of data that require rapid sorting to be useful. Those who are able to sort, synthesize, store, and apply information become experts in a focused area. Because few of us have the time, interest, means, or wherewithal to become experts, we rely on the expertise of others for satisfying our information needs.

Without adequate sorting of the overwhelming amounts of data, and time to organize the information, we react as if we are in an Age of Data. Transforming data into information is the challenge of the 80s' postindustrial society. Transforming information into knowledge is the challenge of the 90s' postinformational society.

Information is part of a hierarchical process. At the base of the hierarchy are data. The next levels are information and knowledge. The top level of the structure is wisdom. Figure 1-1 illustrates the data-to-wisdom hierarchy.

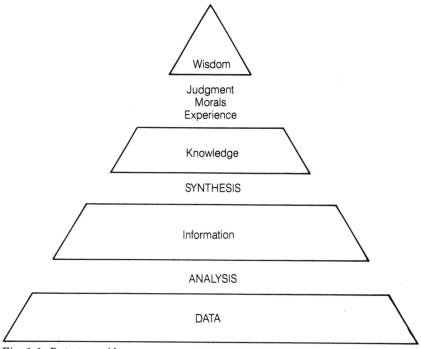

Fig. 1-1. Data pyramid.

Data denotes raw facts and concepts expressed in factual statements. Data consists of facts and figures. A receiver accumulates facts and figures for pro c essing. Data comprises the raw materials, the ingredients for information. These ingredients are collected, sorted, and interpreted. Without this further processing, data has little application.

The theorem that the sum of the squares of the lengths of the sides of a right triangle is equal to the square of the length of the hypotenuse, the Pythagorean theorem, is a factual data statement. Other data statements include:

- The length times the height times the width of a rectangle equals volume.
- Pi times the diameter of a circle equals the circumference of a circle.

One who knows these data statements cannot act upon them without additional focus and processing.

Processed data forms *information*. The difference between data and information at this point is the amount of "noise." The recipient analyzes data by separating significant messages from noise. This data analysis is a clarification process based on some established criteria. Information results from the clarification of data through analysis involving the interpretation of data in terms of locating elements and associations. The process of analysis reduces a large body of source material into smaller and related bodies.

For example, a general contractor has memorized many mathematical formulas, including job costing formulas; volume determination formulas; distance, rate, and time formulas; and others. Only some of these formulas are relevant to a particular application. Sorting the relevant from the total is an act of processing.

Thus, information is an accumulation of refined data that may be a short-lived commodity. For example, an individual can refine all of the available data about fasteners and become informed about a particular fastener in a particular application. After the application is complete, that particular body of information may not be used again. The information is used for a limited time and in a limited scope. Subsequent internal processing would be required for it to be of a longer-term benefit.

This internal processing is called *synthesis*. Synthesized information constitutes *knowledge*. During synthesis, information is compared to other information and combined in significant links to form a pattern of knowledge. The output of the synthesis process is an assimilation of relevant, concentrated information. This information undergoes a metamorphosis to become knowledge. Thus, synthesis builds information sets and complex structures from the element sets and relationships produced during analysis. Knowledge arises from the ability to create a model that faithfully describes the object and exemplifies the actions that can be performed on and with that object.

Information was noted as a short-lived commodity. There are forces of change that act upon information. Therefore, synthesis is required for intelligent decisions. We are moving through the Age of Information and into the Age of Knowledge.

Reconsider, for example, the general contractor with the profusion of formulas. From the collection of known formulas, the individual chooses examples that are most relevant to the task at hand. The information that can be applied to the task is further processed and weighed. Consider a requirement to lay out and construct a patio slab. Plotting the boundaries for the footing of the slab can be accomplished using a variety of methods, including use of a framing square, construction of a perpendicular, and use of the Pythagorean theorem. The contractor selects the quick, accurate tactic of the theorem as shown in FIG. 1-2 and then:

1. He selects a point.
2. He fastens a string to the point.

3. He measures 3 feet from the point, makes a mark, and fastens another string there.
4. He measures 4 feet along the first string and 5 feet along the second, and matches the two marks.

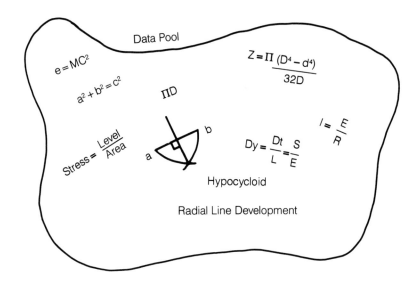

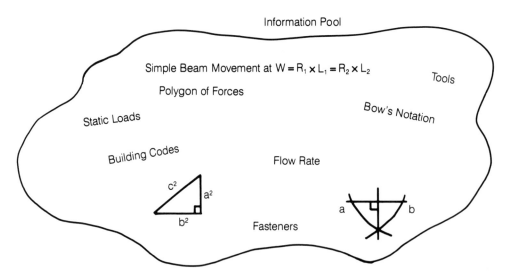

Fig. 1-2. Knowledge application.

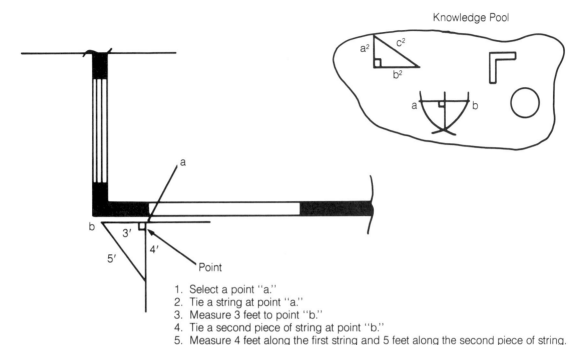

Fig. 1-2. Continued.

1. Select a point "a."
2. Tie a string at point "a."
3. Measure 3 feet to point "b."
4. Tie a second piece of string at point "b."
5. Measure 4 feet along the first string and 5 feet along the second piece of string.
6. A 90° angle is formed at point "a."

The contractor knows that a point can be established from which a 3-foot measure can be taken along a fixed line. A 90-degree angle results when a 4-foot measure and a 5-foot measure intersect. The result is a line that is 90 degrees from the original line.

This problem-solving algorithm is an information-driven process. The combination of possible solutions, thus the synthesis, of all the information is a knowledge-driven process. It is the use of the knowledge that results in selection of a solution approach and resolution of the issue.

Knowledge standing alone is more significant to the holder than information alone. The information evolution process can end with knowledge. However, the data evolution continues beyond knowledge. The highest order in the data evolution process is wisdom. The holder of knowledge taps into data and information pools to achieve resolution to challenges and opportunities.

Individuals, groups, and cultures collect and process information and output knowledge. This knowledge is then compared to other knowledge collections to provide insight and guide decisions. When the collected knowledge is evaluated against values, judgment, laws, and other higher-order standards, a knowledge system results, and over time wisdom is born. According to many, knowledge is, or should be, the outer limit of machine systems (Weizenbaum 1976).

Wisdom is a human system and should be limited to the human domain. Using algorithms and machine systems to place judgments on guilt or innocence, right or wrong, art or incompetence, truth or fiction, beauty or unsightliness, and love or disdain is morally wrong. Wisdom is the ability to apply common sense to facts, incidents, and circumstance. The limits of machine systems are now being discussed by sociologists, psychologists, and many other professional specialists. Machine intelligence is discussed in chapter 3.

How does the evolution of data begin? It begins with the acquisition of data. Figure 1-3 characterizes various sources of data.

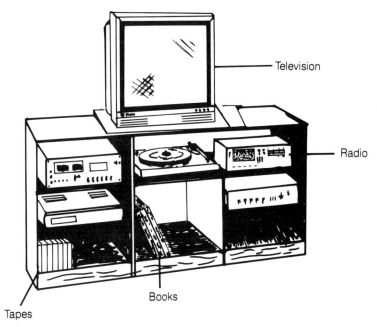

Fig. 1-3. Sources of data.

Data Acquisition

The acquisition of *data* is a passive activity, considering the sophisticated level of data-delivery systems such as television, newspapers, and magazines. Working with a data system can be a handicap or a benefit. For example, the stock market offers a deluge of data, which, on its own merits, provides the recipient with little useful input for decision making unless there is already a strong knowledge base. Stock market professionals provide their clients with *information*. With stock market information, the investors' future is in the hands of fate. With stock market *knowledge*, the investors' fate is in their own hands. This is because knowledge acquisition is an active process.

Others can inform us, but knowledge is an internal process. For example, a barrage of one person's knowledge upon another will not "sink in" until the recipient has been able to assimilate and synthesize the input. Thus, the receivers are integrating the input into an existing mental model, or they are forming a new mental model. Until the input is synthesized, it is information to those who are prepared, or merely data for others. (Mental models and memory are discussed later in this chapter.)

Consider a college student attending a physics lecture. This student and other students are receiving a deluge of statements from a professor. Until these students analyze and synthesize the input, the professor's lecture will affect different students in different ways. The input will range from data to information to knowledge depending upon each receiver's personal knowledge base, mental models, ability to analyze and synthesize, and internal "wiring," which accesses short- and long-term memory.

Relying on information for the decision-making process or not having an appropriate knowledge base results in a dependence on the output of others. For example, there are many books that explain the processes and procedures for buying, building, and repairing household devices and appliances. The purchase of a book for the repair of an appliance might supply the author's knowledge on the procedures, but if there are differences between the author's example and the homeowner's appliance there is a mismatch: the author offered knowledge, but the homeowner received information.

If the homeowner had a sufficient knowledge base or an ability to analyze and synthesize the author's example, the homeowner could have used the author's knowledge. Further, if the author's example was relevant, the homeowner could have repaired the appliance and possibly added to an understanding of the electrical and mechanical concepts. The homeowner's mental model could have matured as a result.

Thus, the acquisition, refining, and synthesizing of data is a hierarchical process. Those that are able to move through the data-to-knowledge process are experts. Their expertise is generally limited to knowledge in a specific domain. Experts with a knowledge focus are called domain experts. Experts are discussed later in this chapter.

THE NATURE OF KNOWLEDGE

We have just defined knowledge as the result of a process of synthesis in which information is compared to other information and combined into meaningful links. Is this view the only way of defining knowledge? No. Knowledge has been defined (Fischler 1987) as stored information called *models*, which are used by a person to interpret, predict, and appropriately respond to the outside world. Knowledge consists of the relationships formed by a combination of declarative (factual) and procedural (method) statements that are called upon for the performance of applications.

For example, a doctor needs to know more than the declarative names of instruments, their locations, and the concepts behind their design. There is also a procedural knowledge requirement that defines the appropriate use of the instruments. A large body of work (Newell and Simon 1972; Anderson 1976) has been done to explore the differences between declarative and procedural knowledge. This body of work includes findings that explore symbolic processing systems called *production systems*. Each production within a system is composed of a condition and an action. Thus, a production is like a rule or the steps used to do a task. This is called procedural knowledge.

Knowing rules by application is not the same thing as having the ability to state a rule. The ability to state rules requires declarative knowledge. This oral knowledge includes names and facts, as well as highly organized and complex, interrelated ideas. Thus, knowing rules implies performance—procedural knowledge. The ability to form ideas and to state those ideas is dependent on an individual's ability to tap long-term memory.

Much of the knowledge in a focused area is associated with intelligence. One view of human intelligence is that it is the ability to recognize a problem-solving opportunity as it relates to previous experience. The problem is represented in a form mapping to that prior experience. For example, a person learning a word processing program could compare the new program's functions to a previously known system. When the problem-solving situation does not appear in prior experience, an informed common-sense approach may work. For example, if a person knows how to drive a car, the knowledge of driving a car can be applied to driving a truck. If that person did not know how to drive a car or other carlike vehicle, there would be no other knowledge to build upon, compare, or use as an informed common-sense approach to the problem of driving a truck.

Knowledge Concepts

Humans react to and interpret the significance of events based on past experiences using mental models. Thus, new experiences are interpreted in terms of past intellectual and emotional experiences. The resulting representations become the realities of personal experience. A single personal experience can alter the reality of other experiences (Winograd and Flores 1987).

To some, the daily activities on the floor of the New York Stock Exchange are a jumble of nondirected activities and a profusion of meaningless numbers. To an experienced stock trader, the events that occur on the floor of the exchange are focused, complex, and significant. This latter person has relevant experience and interprets the activities according to that prior experience. Figure 1-4 represents the interaction between models and events with the influence of actions.

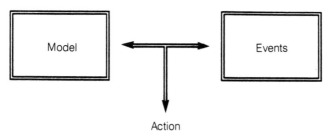

Fig. 1-4. Knowledge concept.

Two people can interpret the same event differently based on their past personal experiences: A large dog rushes out from the trees. Two people on a walk see the dog approaching them and react differently. One panics because of a bad childhood experience and visualizes Stephen King's dog Cujo. The other person puts out his hand and calls the dog. These people have different views or expectations of reality.

In each of these cases, the people interpreted the events under the influence of stored knowledge. In any knowledge domain, observable events are deciphered within an established knowledge framework. This knowledge framework forms a schema which serves as a model for matching and comparing the input of experiences with the current problem set. The output of the matching process is an action.

Mayer (1975) wrote that a mental model is a simplified knowledge structure that explains certain aspects of a topic or an experience. As a person becomes an expert in a domain, models are constructed to explain different aspects of that domain. The domain expert's understanding of the domain improves as the expert acquires many mental models defining its attributes.

Figure 1-5 symbolizes the forces upon a mental model and the mental model's influence on the world. Note the direction of the forces.

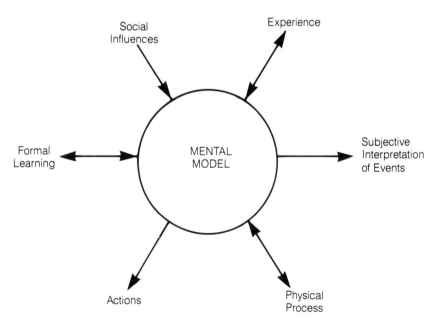

Fig. 1-5. Human knowledge functions.

Different realms of human experience interact with knowledge events using different models. For example, models used for physical processes such as manufacturing facilities depend on observable events which include instrument readings and visual observations.

Models used for making determinations of guilt or innocence, good art or bad art, and so on, have many variables. The criteria for judgment are not directly observable and objective. Sometimes subjective judgments are needed. The objective and the subjective require different types of models for representation.

Models for matching and comparing past experiences with current data are also used in computerized knowledge-based systems. The knowledge bases in these systems consist of machine representations of the human models of procedure and judgment. Both physical process models and subjective models influence the design and structure of knowledge bases for expert systems and other knowledge-based applications. These other knowledge-based applications include relational databases and hypermedia; they are explained in chapter 4. Model types and knowledge bases have two common links: the sources of knowledge, and those people who have the task of acquiring the knowledge and representing it in a computer.

Experts who own the knowledge are *domain experts*, as their knowledge is concentrated in a particular area. *Knowledge Engineers* (KEs) are computer scientists who acquire knowledge from the domain experts and other sources, and organize that knowledge into a knowledge base. Both domain experts and knowledge engineers require an appreciation of the need to understand human knowledge representation.

Knowledge Levels

Knowledge has levels. We have all experienced the acquisition and transfer of what we know in terms of easy to learn and hard to learn, or easy to explain and hard to explain, situations. One reason for degrees of difficulty in learning about things or teaching things is that knowledge has levels.

Facts. The lowest level of knowledge is facts. Facts are arbitrary relationships between objects, symbols, and events. Facts can be represented and displayed by data structures such as statements, lists, tables, tree charts, simple diagrams, and illustrations. Facts form the basis for groups of displayed available data to be organized visually to form clusters. These clusters play a role in recognition and pattern matching, and are used to begin formation of concepts about objects.

Concepts. The next level of knowledge is concepts. Concepts have greater detail than facts. Concepts are general in nature and address groups of objects, events, or symbols with common attributes. Concepts are conceived in the mind and result from abstracted ideas about classes of things. Concepts include example sets, models, and sophisticated elements. They can be concrete or abstract, and outline general characteristics defining a class of objects.

Concepts are hierarchical. A high-level concept encompasses a group of lower-level concepts. For example, the concept of "furniture" is a high-level concept. The concepts of "chair" and "couch" can be viewed as instances of member sets of the high-level concept of furniture. Thus, the general concept of furniture is at the top of the hierarchy with the lower-level concepts of chair and couch as linked concepts. The concepts of chair and couch serve as major categories of furniture, and each contains attributes such as number of legs and construction materials.

In order to avoid redundancy in the links (connections) and nodes (locations), the notion of *inheritance* is used. Inheritance makes the assumption that as the level of detail increases, there is no requirement to repeat the preceding information. For example, since "construction" is an attribute common to all types of furniture, it could be attached to that node, rather than being repeated for chair, couch, table, etc. Each of those would inherit that attribute from the common ancestor, furniture.

Figure 1-6 provides a hierarchical diagram of the concept of furniture with the instances of couch and chair. Furniture is at the top level as a node, and represents the high-level concept. Chair and couch are instances of furniture. The remaining nodes are attributes of chair or couch.

Locate the node in the lower right that contains "sofa." If sofa is traced upward, it connects to "types" which connects to "couch." The node "sofa" inherits the traits that are superior to it. As a result, the sofa node does not need to contain replications of the nodes construction, seats, legs, etc. Inheritance can save time and space when representing concepts. However, inheritance has a complex side too.

For the past ten years or so, those who have studied human knowledge found that while inheritance provides a compact representation of knowledge, attempts to symbolically characterize this knowledge using inheritance have resulted in difficulty creating these knowledge structures. This difficulty is the result of knowledge complexity.

Rules. Rules are the third level of knowledge. Rules are sets of operations and steps used to accomplish a goal, solve a problem, or produce something. They are displayed using decision tables, analogies, complex diagrams, and illustrations.

Rules develop from an analysis of facts and concepts. The facts are generally refined and linked; the concepts have a clarity of focus. Rules are composed of declarative and procedural statements and are guides for actions.

Rules represent knowledge as conditional assertions defined by IF-THEN statements. These statements represent conditions and actions, and are used in deductive problem-solving strategies. Rules are often associated with short-term memory and are a cornerstone of knowledge structures. Rules are used as a formal method of representing knowledge.

Higher-Order Rules, Problem Solving, Heuristic Knowledge. *Higher-order rules, problem solving,* and *heuristic knowledge* are terms used to depict the highest level of knowledge. Heuristic level knowledge arises from the invention of rules and their application to novel situations. Heuristic knowledge transcends rule knowledge. As problem situations are encountered, rather than using a rule algorithm, shortcuts and combinations of rule parts are applied. Thus, heuristic knowledge is the synthesis of facts, concepts, and rules previously learned.

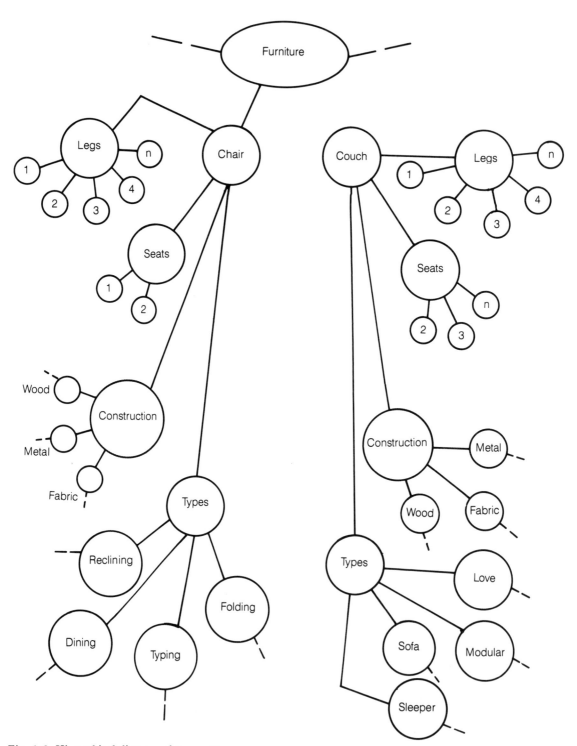

Fig. 1-6. Hierarchical diagram of a concept.

An example can be used to show the different knowledge levels. Consider the knowledge levels of facts, concepts, rules, and heuristic knowledge in terms of a hobby. Let's begin with facts. After selecting a hobby, facts are gathered. Suppose stained glass was selected. A fact pool is formed and may consist of time, space, cost, difficulty, and other features that enable an understanding of the hobby. Figure 1-7 shows a representative array of hobby considerations.

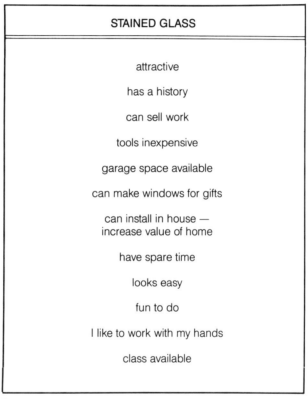

Fig. 1-7. Fact pool.

Next, concepts are established. These concepts enable the person to consider the hobby as an entity with collective properties called attributes. The facts are judged for accuracy and completeness. A deeper level of learning about the hobby is obtained at this point. The individual knows the scope of the venture. This is an early "ah-ha" experience of seeing "the big picture." This understanding is often established after the expenditure of a considerable amount of money on the hobby.

Figure 1-8 represents the original facts with judgment comments. The refined facts are conceptualized.

Rules are established from the concepts. This builds object class properties that enable further discrimination among similar object sets. Thus, the individual can judge for quality, decide if some form of the hobby has commercial

CONCEPTS

More attractive from a distance
    for larger pieces

Works are hard to sell —
    cannot break even for expenses

Tools need constant replacing

Garage is inadequate —
    bad light, too little table
    space, too hot or too cold,
    little pieces of glass on floor

Gifts are good ideas, but take
    too much time and effort

Lead channel is hard to work with

At my rate of production,
    it will take about two years to
    do the four windows I want to do

I have no spare time — starting
    is an effort

Looked much easier than it is

Quality soldering is tough

It is not as much fun as it seemed

My hands are all cut up and have
    little burns

Classes teach very little —
    too far to go, hard to transport work

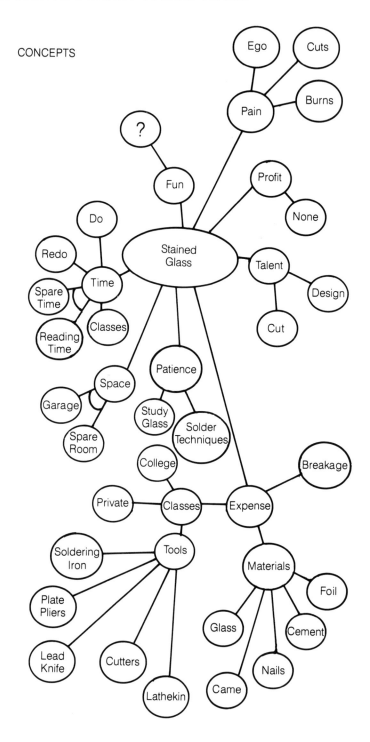

Fig. 1-8. Concepts.

potential, and can establish boundaries of the hobby. This level of knowledge is what separates the serious hobbyist from the professional. At this point, the person "understands" the hobby.

Figure 1-9 lists some of the rules that emerge from the concepts. The rules are personal interpretations of the concepts. Thus, rules tend to be informally stated.

RULES

If a window is X by Y in size, it needs no supports.

Rather than using the stained glass *as the* window, it should be placed against an existing window.

"Professional" quality soldering irons are needed for accurate temperature control.

The quality of the soldered joints is proportional to the quality of the types of flux, quality of the lead, and the temperature of the soldering iron.

Grain and other properties of glass must be understood for making cuts.

Glass scoring and breaking must be done with care and varying techniques.

There are classical designs that sell.

Making professional contacts is extremely important if one is considering making stained glass into a profitable hobby.

Never go over a score line twice.

Red and yellow glass separate better by tapping rather than pulling.

Avoid designing interior right-angle lines.

Fig. 1-9. Rules.

The highest level of knowledge has been called problem solving, higher-order rules, or heuristic knowledge. Heuristic knowledge is the synthesis of what has been learned and applied to problem-solving situations. This level of knowledge is what separates the professional from the guru. Knowledge of the hobby is complete, abstract, and inventive. At this point, the individual fully knows the hobby.

Figure 1-10 provides some heuristic understandings about the hobby. The heuristic knowledge in the figure lists words of "wisdom" and exhibits a maturity of understanding. It appears the hobbyist is "going commercial."

HEURISTIC KNOWLEDGE

- Purchase glass in daylight—preferably in sunlight.
- Multiple pieces need to be planned that consist of a central work and lesson works that can incorporate the "scraps."
- The most important tool is a well-lubricated cutter. A person who understands the properties of glass does not require "professional" tools.
- Smaller pieces can be sold to generate a cash flow.
- When I buy in quantity, I receive better selections of glass and better prices.
- Portions of the effort such as cutting the caming can be done by others who want to learn how to make pieces.
- Can teach techniques at a junior college.
- Works can be made for art galleries and sold on consignment.
- Patterns can be conceptual rather than on paper.
- A wet sponge can quickly alter the temperature of solder on the iron.
- Multiple irons are better than changing tips.
- Glass can be reused and obtained from other than commercial sources.
- A studio can be rented with subleases for others.
- I can become a supplier of glass, tools, lead, solder, flex, etc.
- Can grow into a business with employees.
- Can tie into craft centers, art stores for workers, sales, and displays.
- Stained glass will sell very well at swap meets.

Fig. 1-10. Hobby heuristic knowledge.

As you examine knowledge over the range of levels from heuristic rules to facts, you can see that at each level it can be organized into groupings of related concepts and attributes. As more is learned about the domain, these structures become finer-grained and more detailed, and the differentiations among them become clearer. The resulting complexity can become difficult for humans to grasp and machines to process.

Fluidity of movement between levels of knowledge is the challenge to the computer scientist designing and constructing the hardware and software of tomorrow's knowledge-based systems. While knowledge engineers can graphically construct models of fine-grained structures, the current state of technology often cannot emulate these models. With the advent of Compact Disc technologies such as CD-ROM, and Very Large Scale Integration (VLSI), increased storage ability and access speed have added dramatically to computer capabilities. Computer sophistication has doubled every two to three years since the early 1940s. Current research efforts are directed toward prototype parallel processing computers. Parallel processing may enable the fluidity of movement required of sophisticated knowledge-based systems. As these systems become available, a trend towards broader domains and common-sense knowledge inclusions will tax these system-enhanced capabilities.

Figure 1-11 symbolizes the four knowledge levels. Facts are shown in a fact pool. Collections of facts are clustered into concepts. Concepts are defined,

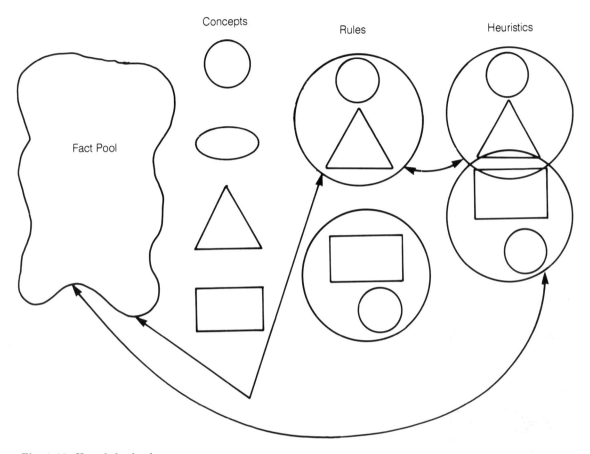

Fig. 1-11. Knowledge levels.

refined, analyzed, combined, and formed into rules. Facts, concepts, and rules are synthesized to form heuristic knowledge. There is fluidity between and among knowledge levels.

Knowledge Types

Knowledge about things can be divided into two groups. The first group contains the generalized concepts about objects in terms of "what things are," with a focus on categories of things and "how things work" in sequence. These knowledge types are called *declarative* and *procedural knowledge,* respectively. Procedural knowledge types consider the manner in which things work from a broader perspective. This broader perspective of "knowing how it all works together" is called *informed* common-sense knowledge and heuristic knowledge. Thus, declarative, procedural, common-sense, and heuristic knowledge types can be present in each of the levels of knowledge.

Declarative Knowledge. Declarative knowledge is a descriptive representation of knowledge. It consists of factual statements about people, places

and things. Domain experts with declarative knowledge can set forth synthesized relationships and classifications of people, places and things. However,
these domain experts do not offer explanations. Truths and associations of
truths are the principal assets of declarative knowledge domain experts.

Declarative knowledge is knowing "what." Declarative knowledge is the
strategic aspect of knowledge. However, declarative knowledge is surface
knowledge that an individual can verbalize. When a knowledge engineer starts
the knowledge acquisition process, verbalized knowledge is the place to start.
As the development of a system progresses, the expert cannot verbalize the
processes and procedures used in decision making.

Declarative knowledge statements include:

- Poison hemlock is a large, many-branched plant with finely divided, fern-
  like, dark green foliage and poisonous juice.
- Liquids can splash when poured from one container into another.

The poison hemlock example tells about the plant by relating facts. The liquids
example relates characteristics of liquids. The knowledge about each is surface
level and conceptual. Recipients of these declarative statements can add these
statements to their information pools.

Procedural Knowledge

Procedural knowledge is the intellectual skill of knowing how to do something. It might have both psychomotor and cognitive components. An example
of procedural knowledge is the diagnosis, break-down, and rebuilding of an
internal combustion engine; these are psychomotor tasks. Speaking a foreign
language is an example of a cognitive task.

Procedural knowledge is sometimes difficult for knowledge engineers to
acquire when it is second nature to its human source. The tasks might be so
well known that the individual cannot express the hows and whys. Consider an
individual using a map to chart a route to a specific destination. Each of the
streets is carefully noted. As the individual travels the route time and time
again, the route is learned. If the individual is then asked to draw a map requiring street names, some of them will not be recalled.

Procedural knowledge is prescriptive knowledge. It is explanatory and
employs declarative knowledge to determine an action. A course of action and
the associated procedures are the outputs of most domain experts. Procedural
outputs include step-by-step sequences and "how-to" types of instructions.
Procedural knowledge statements include:

- (Declarative) Poison hemlock has hollow, grooved stems spotted with
  purple. These plants stand about 2 to 6 feet tall and contain a very poisonous juice.
- (Procedural) Thus, when gathering this plant, take care to avoid contact
  with any plant secretions.

- (Declarative) When forming an acid solution, add acid to water to avoid corrosive splash. Wear appropriate eye protection and safety clothing. Do not lean over the solution. Avoid breathing fumes.
- (Procedural) First, calculate the acid to water ratio needed to form the appropriate solution percentage. Next, fill a calibrated beaker to the appropriate level. Add the acid solution to the water in a slow, steady manner. Thoroughly clean the transfer beaker. Label the solution.

Figure 1-12 depicts an action model with declarative and procedural knowledge inputs. The inputs are processed, resulting in various outputs.

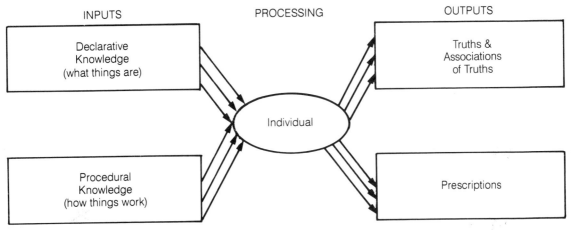

Fig. 1-12. Declarative and procedural knowledge types.

Procedural knowledge also can be represented through algorithms. These algorithms are often presented in flowcharts from such sources as books, technical manuals, and job aids. However, note that having a procedure to do something does not necessarily imply possessing the skill of performing that task. Consider common flowcharts such as tire-changing charts, and toy- or appliance-assembling charts. The presence of a flowchart and associated directions does not necessarily ensure rapid progress through a task.

Common-Sense Knowledge. *Common-sense* knowledge is composed of collected, general knowledge about the world and how it works. Common-sense knowledge is what is obvious to most people, such as judgment of right and wrong; knowing that driving over broken glass may cause a flat tire; awareness that still waters run deep. If the calendar reads "June 21" and there is snow on the ground, the calendar might be in error.

Common-sense is built up over time and is composed of accumulated declarative and procedural knowledge. Declarative and procedural common-sense statements include:

- Wood is smooth when sanded. Wood should be sanded in the direction of the grain with finer and finer grades of sandpaper.

- Barbecue charcoal requires about 45 minutes for maximum heating efficiency. If dinner is at 6:00 and the fish takes 12 minutes to cook, light the
  charcoal by 5:00.

In addition, common-sense knowledge requires massive storage facilities,
and it often involves understanding of a situation through rapid sensing. Thus,
common-sense knowledge is also called *world knowledge*.

Another aspect of common sense is *informed common-sense* in focused
domains. Informed common sense is the collective "should-know" information
in a particular environment. Thus, informed common-sense knowledge is also
called *generic knowledge*. In this level of knowledge are the procedures, practices, and processes that people use to complete tasks. For example, informed
common sense tells a person working on a computer that it is necessary to
make backup copies of work and not depend on hard disk storage. Those new to
computer use may depend on the computer's hard disk not to crash and destroy
data. Examples of informed common sense follow.

- Computer diskettes are sensitive to temperature extremes, magnetic
  fields, and improper handling. Do not expose diskettes to temperatures
  below 50 degrees Fahrenheit or above 125 degrees Fahrenheit. Keep
  diskettes away from telephones, magnets, and other devices that generate a magnetic field. Do not bend or touch the surface of a diskette. Do
  not spill liquids on a diskette.

Those familiar with computers know about diskette care as informed common-
sense. Those that do not work with computers are less likely to know these
common-sense facts.

- Cars that are older or out of tune are subject to electrical shorts or failure to start because of moisture. If a car will not start following damp or
  rainy conditions, and it has a distributor and rotor ignition system, there
  is a simple procedure. It is logical to first check battery connections for
  contact and then wipe the rotor and inside of the distributor cap with a
  clean dry cloth.

Those familiar with some attributes of automobiles as a result of study and
experience consider this procedure as one that everybody should know.

Although more general in nature, common-sense and informed common-
sense knowledge are composed of declarative and procedural knowledge readily
available when needed. There are concepts and sequences in the common-
sense domain. Common-sense knowledge can be, to a degree, taught, but it is
more commonly collected over time.

Heuristic Knowledge. *Heuristic knowledge* is not gained from books or
other external sources. Heuristic knowledge is an internal process. It is not
necessarily unique in the knowledge domain; it is unique to the individual.
Other people might have encountered similar situations and used similar heuris-

tic knowledge findings. Heuristic knowledge is usually presented at professional conferences designed for focused domains.

Heuristic knowledge consists of personal "rules of thumb." These rules evolve from strategies that provide assistance and orientation when devising solution to problems. There are many forms of problem solving using personal rules of thumb. The most common is the IF-THEN rule. IF-THEN rules work when explicit conditions have been met. Personal rule formation is based on knowledge about a particular obstacle to be resolved.

Another attribute of heuristic knowledge is systematic guessing. This involves selection of the best option from a group of alternatives. Each option that is not viable is removed from consideration. The purpose of systematic guessing is to reduce or limit problem solving attempts.

Heuristic rules are characterized as tactics employed in problem solving to assist in problem resolution. Heuristic rules are often associated with problems that have uncertain outcomes. However, heuristic approaches are not assured of being successful.

Thus far, heuristic knowledge has been discussed in terms of its overt effects. Polya (1973) described the heuristic reasoning process from an internalized viewpoint. He states that during the process of problem solving several approaches are taken including analysis processes to decompose a problem. Synthesis processes are then used to recombine the elements of the problem.

> Trying to solve a problem, we consider different aspects of it in turn, we roll it over and over incessantly in our mind; *variation of the problem* is essential to our work. We may vary the problem by *decomposing and recombining* its elements, or by going back to the *definition* of certain terms, or we may use the great resources of *generalization, specialization,* and *analogy.* Variation of the problem may lead us to *auxiliary elements,* or to the discovery of a more assessable *auxiliary problem.*

Polya approached heuristic knowledge as the methods and rules of discovery and invention. He stated that heuristic knowledge aspects are composed elements resting in the fields of logic, philosophy, and psychology. Heuristic rules were regarded as "provisional" and "plausible" approaches to solving problems, resulting in plausible guesses.

Figure 1-13 summarizes the four knowledge types.

Knowledge Reliability

Not all knowledge is created equal, nor is all knowledge accurate 100 percent of the time in 100 percent of the possible situations encountered. Therefore, systems should be developed to communicate the degree of truthfulness, certainty, or uncertainty of presented knowledge. Decisions are made by doctors, attorneys, career counselors, and others based on their best judgments using available information. The outcomes of their decisions are based on degrees of certainty through judgment indicators. These experts share the common problem of making decisions with incomplete or uncertain information. Knowledge-based systems need to explore and manipulate knowledge with attached uncertainty.

Knowledge Types	Concepts Relate to	Knowledge Levels	Knowledge Characteristics	Principal Attributes	Relationship to Knowledge	Output
Declarative	what things are	facts/ concepts	descriptive/ relational	truths and associations of truths	strategic/ verbalized	why to
Procedural	how things work	rules	psychomotor/ cognitive	rote knowledge/ algorithms	prescriptive tactical knowledge & action	how to
Common Sense	additional input factors	concepts	affective/ cognitive	conditions	judgment	when to
Informed Common Sense	experience learning	rules	cognitive	associations	tactics	know of
Heuristic	shortcuts	problem solving	meta-usage	discovery & invention	new concepts declarative/ procedural knowledge	why not

Fig. 1-13. Knowledge table.

Chapter 8 details various measures of confidence in knowledge-based systems. The intent here is to introduce the notion of uncertainty. The key consideration for the KE is that the higher the degree of certainty of the components about the knowledge base, the higher the degree of rule reliability output. There are two basic types of judgment indicators commonly associated with human everyday knowledge: certainty factors and probability.

Certainty Factors. Human decision makers operate in terms of probabilities associated with their conclusions and recommendations. With few exceptions, domain experts will not commit to a 100 percent confidence level in their decisions. Generally, domain experts make recommendations in the form of advisories. Using certainty factors and confidence rating factors, domain experts can accommodate uncertainty and ambiguity.

Certainty factors are used to create a numerical or graph-type measure of confidence in a conclusion. They permit the domain expert to work with inexact information and to offer counsel with a caveat. The users of the advice make decisions based upon criteria that include the certainty factors.

For example, an investment counselor states that if the real estate market is good and an investor requires a stable long-term investment, real estate is a good choice with a confidence rating of 80%. This confidence rating does not imply the truth of the statement. Rather, it denotes the statement's strength or weakness.

Probability. *Probability* is the numerical indication of the chance of an action occurring. It is the ratio of the number of times that a particular outcome takes place in relationship to the total number of attempts. In contrast with certainty factors used to designate a number on an arbitrary scale stating the extent to which a solution is valid, probability is mathematically obtained but not exact. A coin tossed in the air will land heads-up 50% of the time and tails-up 50% of the time. Thus, the odds of a fair coin landing heads-up is 1 out of 2, over time—a very long time.

Probability, with a range from 0 to 1, relates to the likelihood that an event will occur. Thus, certainty factors and probabilities are different. A certainty factor is a number on an arbitrary scale asserting the extent to which a statement is believed to be true. Probability is a mathematically derived ratio. Both confidence factors and probabilities are used in knowledge-based systems. Figure 1-14 summarizes these two methods of relating knowledge reliability. Chapter 8 explores measures of confidence in greater detail.

Types	Format	Representation	Nature
Certainty Factors	advisory	number graph	arbitrary
Probability	ratio	number	math model

Fig. 1-14. Knowledge reliability.

HUMAN KNOWLEDGE REPRESENTATION

In the quest for an understanding of human knowledge and thinking, many fields of study have evolved. One of these fields of study is knowledge engineering. Knowledge engineering is the process of acquiring and representing human knowledge for evaluation and incorporation into a computer system. Once in the system, this knowledge can be manipulated by symbolic processes within the knowledge base for problem solving and other human knowledge applications.

The process of knowledge engineering is undertaken by people called knowledge engineers. A knowledge engineer (KE) is responsible for the collection, organization, and machine representation of human problem solving. The knowledge collection process is called knowledge acquisition. Knowledge acquisition and knowledge organization procedures are discussed in depth in part II.

The remainder of this chapter establishes the concepts and declarative aspects of knowledge representation schemes. In addition, an exploration of some of the methods for understanding human thinking is undertaken.

The conduit for merging human knowledge and machine capabilities is understanding through modeling. One approach to modeling is the representation of human cognition. Cognition is the process of knowing, including both awareness and judgment. Human cognitive processes compose intelligent reasoning.

Machine representation of human cognitive processes is required to model complex problem solving. Thus, cognitive modeling is the selected tactic for representing human problem solving. Cognitive models approach problem solving by evaluating knowledge using humanlike strategies. This tactic is the recommended approach to representing human knowledge because it offers easier approaches to representation and communication.

Concept Set Elements

In order for knowledge to be discussed, acquired, and represented, a rigorous analysis of knowledge must be conducted. With the results from this analysis, knowledge can be described and organized into a concept set. Parsaye and Chignel (1988) refer to the *concept set* as a knowledge component. The purpose of a concept set is to define the objects in the set and their interactions. The Parsaye and Chignel set, and the derived set described below, are analogous to natural language classes and word functions.

A concept set can be used to help represent the interactions of knowledge. The concept set described here is also based on an analogy of the parts of speech and will be used in discussions relating to knowledge representations. Through this concept set, different knowledge domains can be represented; a single knowledge domain can be represented from different perspectives.

Knowledge-based systems use various knowledge representation strategies. Although these strategies will be discussed later, it is important to note a general fact about these knowledge representation systems. Knowledge representation systems do not use concept sets in a universal or generic manner. Thus, the representation system generally drives the concept set. The concept set elements are generic in nature and are presented to enable a model and display the "concept" of concept set elements.

The elements of the concept set are listed and matched to natural language components and parts of speech as follows:

Concept Set Element	Part of Speech
Label	Noun
Attributes	Adjective
Transaction	Transitive verb
Constraint	Conjunction
Depiction	Diagram

Label. The best representation of an object, thing, or entity requires a reference point or name. The name should be unique in the overall schema so there is no misunderstanding about the thing in question.

Whenever a child or adult becomes involved with a set of objects, a naming convention is established. In the professional world, domain experts are able to distinguish among similar objects by establishing naming conventions. These names are often given as a result of function; thus the concept behind the object set has an influence on object names. For example, a pump for liquids may be named "high-volume pump," "submersible pump," "high-viscosity pump," or any other name that helps convey an understanding of the object's function.

As expertise grows, the concepts related to the object and its functions are categorized in increasingly finer levels of detail. Names are given to those details representative of salient characteristics or functions.

Attributes. As adjectives are used to modify nouns, the attributes of an object are used to further define the label. Attributes are used to note the properties of the object in a knowledge set. Sometimes the attributes are given in an inexact or fuzzy manner, such as tall, old, or brittle. These attributes are most often used when comparing similar objects within a set. For example, the high-volume pump could have attributes such as equipped with three brass valves, or permanently lubricated as opposed to a model that requires periodic lubrication.

Attributes generally focus on the application environment. Attributes of a circuit board diagnostic system might focus on physical properties such as materials, amount of heat generated, or space required. A loan processing system would focus on credit history, income, job held, years on the job, property holdings, and other less tangible attributes. A medical diagnostic system about cardiac risk would be concerned with age, height, weight, smoking, family history, etc.

Part of the complexity of building a knowledge-based system is acquiring the knowledge for the application. The loan processing system and the medical system both deal with people, but from different aspects. The loan processing system would not be concerned about whether the person smoked, and the medical system would not look at property holdings.

Transaction. A *transaction* is a relationship between and among conceptual elements. The deeper the knowledge structure, the greater the quality and numbers of these links in the transaction. These transactions consist of such relationships as actions, structures, and affiliations.

- Action: Supersonic aircraft *break through* the sound barrier.
- Structure: The coaxial cable *is attached to* the VCR.
- Affiliation: George Bush *is a member of* the Republican Party.

Transactions help describe the internal structure of object sets. Object sets are described in terms of composition or in terms of actions and relationships to other object sets. Sometimes these descriptions are both an attribute and a relationship. For example, General Motors cars are available with a 350-cubic-inch engine. However, General Motors is related to a group of automobile manufacturers and a 350-cubic-inch engine is one of many engine types. Thus, the relationships between objects and the relationships among attributes of object sets can be very complex.

Another way to view these convoluted relationships is to think of them in terms of family relations. An uncle can be directly linked by blood, or be the result of a marriage event to a blood link. The uncle in the first situation is a member or attribute of a blood-linked family. The second situation places the uncle as a relation of the family.

Sometimes, transactions are the focus in an object set relationship. For example, supply and demand are two object sets. The transactions between these two sets form a variety of links. The system application is generally the driver of the transaction links. Various systems and their applications require different transactions including rules, frames, examples, etc.

Constraints. Constraints establish the limitations within which object set elements relate. These bounding devices, like conjunctions, express limits, values, and associations. Constraints are relationship rules. For example, a sign stating, ''All persons *except* those under 42 inches may enter this ride'' expresses a rule. This rule states, IF [the height of] person X is less than 42 inches, THEN person X may not enter the ride.

Constraints can also be prepositions, for example, ''Children *with* measles should not attend school.''

Some constraints are inherent to the nature of the object set: ''Fresh water freezes at 32 degrees Fahrenheit at sea level and boils at 212 degrees Fahrenheit.'' Thus, there are constraints on liquid water within a range.

Further, constraints can be layered. An individual is governed by a national body such as by national laws. This individual is also governed by state laws and local laws. Additional constraints can be imposed by religion, family, and education.

What is the value of constraints? They focus the application's scope. Constraints help identify out-of-range values for the system. By planning general constraints at the beginning of a development effort and relating specific functional constraints, the system will be focused. Constraints help differentiate concept set elements.

Depiction. Once objects are named and described, they can be sorted and grouped. Depiction establishes linkages between concepts to show which concepts can associate and which cannot. The process is similar to the diagramming of a sentence, providing a graphic representation of the components of the sentence set. Object groups are generally the result of conceptual categories that share attributes. In addition, links are often made between the groups. These conceptual categories are useful for long-term memory groups. For example, there are no surface connections between a festive meal and an estranged aunt. The festive meal requires some thought for meal preparation, decorations, and guest list. Its links include Aunt Bessy and her funny hats. Another conceptual category is strange relatives. Here, Aunt Bessy may be predominant and linked to events, one of which might be the festive meal. Thanksgiving is near and Aunt Bessy will wear her funny hat. (See FIG. 1-15.)

Fig. 1-15. Knowledge depiction.

Thus, these categories help recall information for humans and access to information by machines. The depiction of objects is represented by hierarchies, flow charts, diagrams, frames, mind maps, and other relational means. Figure 1-16 summarizes the five knowledge elements.

Knowledge Element	Analogies to Speech Element	Description
label	noun	name
attributes	adjective	properties of the object that differentiate it from other related objects
transaction	transitive verb	relationship between attributes; relations between object and related objects, rules, frames, examples, etc.
constraint	conjunction	conditions, limits, values, associations, If-Then
depiction	diagram	graphic representation of the attributes showing how they are related

Fig. 1-16. Knowledge element table.

Knowledge Longevity

There are other attributes of knowledge such as duration of knowledge. The focus of knowledge longevity is in terms of knowledge-based system application considerations. Included in these characteristics are the properties of being permanent, static, and dynamic knowledge.

- Permanent: Knowledge that is an integral part of an application that will not change (natural laws, physics, etc.)

- Static: Knowledge that remains constant over a period of time, but is likely to change at some point in the application (policies, procedures, etc.)

- Dynamic: Knowledge that can change from one application to the next or even during use (Return On Investment (ROI), patient information, etc.)

Given the characteristics of knowledge through its concepts, levels, and types, another definition of knowledge can be established. This definition of longevity will be the working definition for discussion of knowledge-based systems.

Knowledge is the composite of facts, rules, concepts, and heuristic rules applied to problem-solving activities. Knowledge results over time from education, training, and experience. Knowledge implies learning, awareness, and a mastery in one or more topics that are represented by mental models.

Figure 1-17 summarizes the three classes of knowledge longevity.

Knowledge Longevity	Descriptive	Example
permanent	never-changing	natural laws
static	long-term	policies
dynamic	variable	return on investment

Fig. 1-17. Knowledge longevity.

THINKING, PROBLEM SOLVING, AND REASONING

Now that knowledge has been explored from several perspectives, we can investigate the ways in which knowledge is used. The purpose of Thinking and Mental Models is to offer a conceptual or declarative view of thinking as it applies to human problem solving. Mental models provide process models from the scientific community and general problem-solving strategies.

Thinking

Thinking is the active, reflective process of developing or modifying general understandings that exist in mental models. Domain experts are generally unaware of the extent of the processes they use to make decisions. Focused thinking involves both inductive and deductive lines of reasoning that establish and test hypotheses. The domain expert manipulates these lines of reasoning through the application of intelligent processing. One way to simplify thinking is through models like the physical process models and subjective models introduced earlier. These models are also called *mental models.*

Mental Models. The concept of mental model was discussed by Bruner (1966) as a structure that permits people to predict, interpolate, and extrapolate further knowledge. He states that:

> Our knowledge of the world is not merely a mirroring or reflection of order and structure 'out there' but consists of a construct or model that can, so to speak, be spun a bit ahead of things to predict how the world *will* be or *might* be.

Bruner's work implies that models are personal expectancies. With a model, the individual not only deals with the available information, but also goes beyond that information. Because we use models of the world, we tend to organize experiences into categories.

According to Johnson-Laird (1983), mental models can be thought of as knowledge structures. These structures are schema-based and include perceptions of tasks in terms of demands and performance. Schemas are organizational structures. A schema can consist of a major factor and a list of attributes. A major factor might be the arthropoda. Attributes include: crustacea, arachnida, insecta, chilopoda, diplopoda, and onychophora.

Multiple schemas can be formed during the building of a model for a particular problem. These models are constructed and modified throughout the course of learning, and as greater levels of proficiency are acquired. Thus, mental models are constructed while learning and doing tasks. Experts are able to solve problems through intrinsic problem solving. Problems are not solved by merely matching a problem state against a model. Rather, the problem state is first simplified and matched to a model as an early step in the problem-solving process. While there is no single problem-solving model or an established series of linear steps that move to a conclusion, there has been research in problem-solving strategies.

The scientific community has developed a problem-solving paradigm known as the scientific method. This process offers a structure for intelligent processing which starts with a defined problem. Following the problem definition, there are five steps:

1. Review relevant literature.
2. Collect field data or conduct equivalent observational inquiry, and supplement this data, if necessary, by laboratory examination of specimens.

3. Itemize the problem in the form of specific questions.
4. Form hypotheses and make intelligent guesses to answer the questions.
5. Experiment to test the most likely hypothesis that focuses on the most crucial questions.

Each of these steps is repeated as often as necessary.

The scientific method is the logical basis used to form a physical process model in a knowledge-specific domain. From this scientific method, a generalized view of the process can be derived from which an individual can arrive at a conclusion in a problem-solving domain: the problem solver establishes a plan for a course of action using problem representation through a mental model and suitable knowledge to carry out that plan. Successful problem-solving efforts are predicated on success at each of these points.

The following is a problem-solving process model which can accommodate most problem states.

1. A problem-solving opportunity is present when the current state is not the desired state.
2. A gap is the difference between the current state and the desired state.
3. The problem solver responds to the problem state by doing the following:

   - Recognizes and bounds the state.
   - Forms hypotheses as potential resolution strategies.
   - Selects and mentally evaluates a hypothesis.
   - Tests the "best bet" hypothesis.
   - Modifies and repeats the process as required.

Figure 1-18 demonstrates a method for solving problems.

There are problem-solving strategies that can be helpful:

- Do not overreact. Gather sufficient data.
- Form a plan.
- Record facts.
- Analyze and synthesize the facts to form knowledge.
- Link knowledge to a model.
- Explore the model.
- Test in a controlled environment.

Mental models can be thought of as schema-based knowledge representation structures. These models contain the human perceptions of task requirements and outcomes. Models are built, used, and modified throughout their use. The scientific method and the problem-solving model are examples of two such models.

The purpose of the mental model is for inferencing during the problem-solving process. Experts in a focused field, also called domain experts, are able to integrate new information into their existing model of an area. As individuals

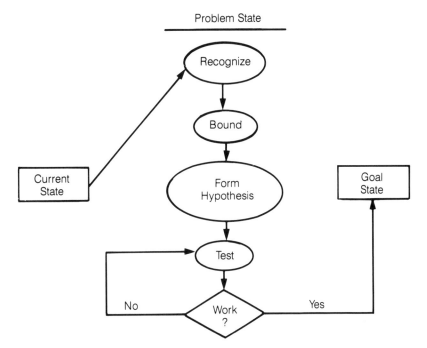

Fig. 1-18. Problem-solving process model.

grow in knowledge sophistication, their mental models also grow. These models have an element that is not usually present in the models of novices, viz. *metacognitive awareness*.

Metacognitive awareness is the experts' knowledge about the extent and limitations of their mental processes and output abilities. This awareness determines the degree to which levels of attention are applied to task demands, the nature of the resources, the performer's abilities, and the extent of task demands to meet the requirements. Included in high-level models are levels of awareness of the interactions of the established knowledge elements.

Research has shown that people who are successful at solving problems have models for doing so. These models generally entail recognizing that a problem exists, then representing the problem in a formal manner.

One model type is a *top-down model*. This model uses automatic internal processing where distinct connections are difficult to relate. For example, the processes of skiing, ice skating, and aiming a dart are difficult, at best, to describe in a step-by-step fashion.

Top-down processing can also call on a schema that processes experience and knowledge from old to new contexts. If a person hears someone say ''fixin','' top-down processing enables that person to recognize the word ''fixing.'' There is no need for heroic stretches of the imagination or to stare in disbelief at never having heard the word before.

A second model type is a *bottom-up model*. This model is a formative model where links need to be established. For example, learning a new language requires creating a new model, separate from old ones. The learner has no basis of comparison and needs to establish links and associations among the attributes of the new stimulus. Sometimes learning is impaired by attempting links with other models.

Some learning situations benefit from mixing attributes of top-down and bottom-up models. These learning situations are ones in which analogies can be drawn.

Human Thinking. The human brain has billions of nerve cells. The brain weighs about three pounds, and is probably the most complex and least understood phenomenon on the planet. The fields of study that investigate thinking and the workings of the brain are those having "cognitive" in their titles, such as cognitive psychology.

This chapter has defined thinking as an active, reflective process of developing and modifying general understandings that exist in mental models. Knowledge structures in the form of mental models were described. Thus, a concept of thinking in a declarative seting was established. Now, thinking will be described in more procedural terms that begin to focus on a transition to machine representations and processes.

Thinking can be defined as a directed, goal-oriented activity focused on problem solving. It is an attempt to move from a problem state to a goal state. The distinguishing characteristic of thinking is that the problem state is new to the individual, although there may be familiar elements. Thus, thinking is a problem-solving activity.

Bigge (1982) provides a Gestalt psychologist's view of thinking as a reflective process. Through this reflective thinking process, people combine inductive—fact finding—and deductive processes that find, elaborate, and form hypotheses. This process is similar to the scientific method, but provides a holistic approach. Bigge states that the principal steps in reflective thinking are:

1. *Recognition and bounding of a problem.* The problem solver is required to have an understanding of the current state, the goal state, and the gap. This understanding is the result of study, sensory input, experience, research findings, or provided data. The problem solver can survey the problem to gain a perception of its breadth and depth.
2. *Formulation of approach.* The problem solver generalizes the gap and formulates a hypothesis for resolution. A confidence rating or probability of acceptable resolution is assigned to the approach. A plan is also established to verify the hypothesis.
3. *Consequence of approach.* The problem solver explores the perceived consequences of the application of the hypothesis. This exploration of consequence is important to avoid "adding gasoline to the fire."
4. *Field test hypotheses.* The actual testing under controlled conditions is designed to verify the consequences of the approach. In this step, problem solvers are able to refine their understanding of the current state, the goal state, and the gap.

5. *Resolution*. Once a hypothesis is tested, it can be adopted, modified, or rejected. Problem solvers can further refine their understanding of the problem and repeat the entire process or relevant portions as needed.

Research studies about how we humans think and learn have uncovered several findings. For example,

- There are learner misconceptions about the relationship between the content (input) and expectations (output or behaviors) as a result of the content. These factors deal with the establishment and modification of mental models.
- Learning must go beyond what is taught—the learner needs to synthesize the input.
- Learning success correlates to prerequisite cognitive skills—the more a person knows before the learning experience, the more successful the learning.
- We learn through practice—interactivity and multisensory opportunities enhance learning.
- Motivation impacts learning—the higher the motivation level of the learner, the more effective the learning.

No current studies pinpoint how we think. The inductive and deductive holistic model offers insights into the design of learning materials and procedures to better accommodate learning. Most studies report that learners use mental models as a foundation for learning. These models tend to be modified over time and are used for learning transfer. In order to help learning and thinking, models are required to be correct and complete.

Studies also suggest that thinking involves the active integration of new knowledge with existing knowledge and skills. This suggests that it is necessary to understand which prerequisite knowledge and skills are most relevant to aiding the thinking process. Thus, there are many variations of tactically directed mental models used by domain experts. Often these models are built to meet a particular performance requirement. For example, cognitive skills such as learning a language, performing a complex operation, or playing a strategy game are best learned by doing. The process of thinking about a problem and effecting a solution follows the path of: recognizing of task performance requirements, addressing an internal knowledge base, locating a pattern match and line of reasoning, establishing a plan to implement an action, evaluating the success of the action, and modifying the plan and action in an iterative loop until complete. A follow-up of the process is modification of the model.

Experts and Novices. Domain experts are people who are successful at cognitive processing applied to solving problems. These people tend to have a "tuned" awareness. From a tuned awareness, experts can perceive, process, store, and recall information. They have strategies for storing information or knowledge sets in short- and long-term memory.

Awareness enables experts to select pertinent information and perform rudimentary processing that stores information in short-term memory. The process is analogous to a buffer in a computer. Unless the information is processed further, it will be purged. In short-term memory, information is used immediately in an input-output sense. For example, information is gathered to make a decision based on available data. Thus, short-term memory is working memory. Should the task at hand require comparisons or data retrieval, long-term memory is tapped.

Long-term memory consists of a large conceptual set of mental models called compressed symbols with many index stimulators. These index stimulators allow multiple access to the same data. For example, a person's dentist may be listed under his or her name, "dentist," "doctor," or other personally significant index.

Multiple-indexed systems are currently available for computers. These systems are called *HyperCard* and *hypertext*. The work with HyperCard and hypertext is analogous to the internal cognitive process. This kind of symbol manipulation is related to the concept of scripts. *Scripts* are scenarios of activities that are perceived by an individual. For example, a scenario of the procedures for cooking a holiday meal is a script. The script of one individual can differ from the script of another. Other researchers are working on the premise of memory chunks. These chunks are a hierarchical arrangement that unfolds into smaller and smaller chunks.

Both experts and novices are able to draw from both short- and long-term memory, and exchange information as desired. Long-term memory is analogous to a computer's hard disk mass storage device. A computer's hard disk stores information in organized sectors. The distinctive quality of experts may be in their ability to retrieve knowledge, not in their knowledge storage strategies.

Experts have developed complex strategies to process information, select what is relevant, use what they require immediately, and store what they may need to draw on at a later time. In addition, they have an ability to both store and link information, synthesize that information, and make new or additional links.

The ability to synthesize information is dependent upon the presence of the information to be synthesized, and the quality and quantity of the models. Experts acquire information as they gain experience in their craft. Information accumulates as the experience becomes more considerable. Thus, experience is composed of a comprehensive group of observed facts or events. Further experience gleaned from observation and participation in events enables experts to acquire knowledge.

Experience enables these domain experts to function at higher levels of abstraction than their colleagues. This abstraction level permits more rapid sorting and indexing between and among models. Further, the experts have very probably stored a larger number of compiled domain-specific links. Through these links, they are able to rapidly recognize patterns, eliminate possibilities, and form hypotheses. The knowledge engineer has the challenge of representing these domain-specific links in a knowledge-based system.

Experts reach their status from personal experiences, and because of an ability to apply their acquired knowledge. According to Hart (1986), experts can be characterized by the following features:

- Effectiveness: Experts apply their knowledge to problem resolution with a high rate of success.

- Efficiency: Experts solve problems rapidly and efficiently.

- Awareness of limitations: Experts are aware of what they know and the limits of what they can do. When these limits are reached, experts refer to someone else.

Experts are used in situations to fulfill three basic roles:

- Information source: Experts possess a wealth of information. Thus, the experts are consulted to "bounce ideas" around or play "what if's" with those in need of a sounding board.

- Solver of problems: Experts apply their knowledge to find causes or solve problems. If the problem cannot be solved, the expert states the conditions needed for resolution.

- Teacher: Experts explain their problem-solving strategies to those learning the techniques and tricks of the trade.

Novice Thinking. Those at the level of *novice* are in possession of a base set of knowledge and skills that is rich in breadth, but lesser in quantity and depth than that of the experts. Novices are "experts in training" while they gather experience and skills, and accumulate knowledge to a greater depth. In addition, novices lack two basic tools of an expert: the ability to quickly analyze a problem, and the vast array of models and problem-solving strategies.

Transition from Novice to Expert. Hubert and Stewart Dreyfus (1986) identified five stages of skills learning:

- Novice: Performs tasks using context-free rules; the novice "follows the rules" and is personally detached from the problem-solving situation.

- Advanced Beginner: Incorporates situational elements into the performance of tasks; decision making is rote.

- Competent: Applies goals, priorities, and planning in the management of skills; personal involvement in the outcome begins to show in the competent-level person.

- Proficient: Intuitive organization and understanding are evident; the level of understanding increases; use of pattern matching to approach a problem.

- Expert: Uses intuitive decision-making and is committed through the process; makes decisions from ''knowing'' rather than from an analytical process.

Novices construct models and encounter problem-solving opportunities as they gain experience. In addition, they interact with experts, read case studies, and gain a greater awareness of their domain. As a result of these experiences, novices gain heuristic knowledge and learn from their successes and failures. When failures are analyzed and models are altered, novices strengthen the organization of their knowledge, hone their analysis and thought processes, derive useful heuristic rules, and gain speed in solution strategies. This is the beginning of the development of heuristic knowledge. In addition, it is the learning of their limitations in concert with strengths that enable novices to make the transition to experts. When domain specialists learn the limits of their knowledge, they have achieved metacognition.

Thus, the characteristic of mature experts is a well-developed metacognitive awareness. These people show a greater awareness of the requirements needed to perform a given task, the materials to be acquired, and the activities essential to complete that task. As a result, they are aware of the interactions among the knowledge elements and form a plan according to the need. Novices, however, have a lesser awareness of the major factors and, where the experts have a sharp focus, novices only have an indication of the need.

Flavell (1976) wrote:

''Metacognition'' refers to one's knowledge of one's own cognitive process and products. For example, I am engaging in metacognition if I notice that I am having more trouble learning A than B; if it strikes me that I should double-check C before accepting it as a fact; if it occurs to me that I had better scrutinize each and every alternative in any multiple-choice type task situation before deciding which one is the best one;...if I sense that I had better make a note of D because I may forget it.... Metacognition refers, among other things, to the active monitoring and consequent regulation and orchestration of these processes in the service of some concrete goal or objective.

Metacognitive abilities are regulators of performance. Expert performers have greater levels of metacognitive awareness than novice performers. These regulators of performance include knowing what the performer knows or does not know, predicting the efficiency of one's performance to the task, planning required activities, and monitoring the effectiveness of the planned solution.

PROBLEM SOLVING

Problem solving is often associated with the performance output of thinking creatures. Animal behaviorists have expended years of time, resources, and money in the study of how animals react to changes in their environment. Pet owners often play with their animals by carrying out problem solving activities such as, "Let's see if Muffy can find where I hid the ball."

Further, most educational institutions are constructed around providing a foundation such that learners can solve problems. The process of human reasoning has been the subject of many studies. Three common reasoning approaches are deductive reasoning, inductive reasoning, and analogical reasoning. In order to understand these reasoning approaches, a foundation of human problem solving will now be established.

Human Problem Solving. Cognitive psychologists and others carefully assess and study human problem-solving techniques and attributes. While there are many theories, little has occurred that can readily transfer the problem-solving ability from those successful at the craft to those with lesser skills. However, efforts are continuing, and many generalizations and characteristics of problem-solving approaches are available for consideration.

The knowledge engineer (KE) has emerged as a behavioral scientist who focuses on human problem solving with the goal of emulating that knowledge in a computer program. The KE has an understanding of basic problem-solving strategies that may be employed in various forms by the domain experts. By understanding how problems are approached, the KE leverages problem solving to encompass the problem domain. Problem-solving strategies employed by domain experts provide insights into the domain itself. For example, by presenting simpler problems from a variety of perspectives, a better grasp of the extent, variety, and depth of a particular domain is obtained.

By having this knowledge, the KE better evaluates the current states of how things are, and the goal states of where things should be. The KE then forms a measure of the difference between the two states called a gap analysis, and establishes a strategy for filling that gap. The success of the gap analysis rests in the ability to perform the gap analysis.

Domain experts have a knowledge base that is an assemblage of related facts in a focused area. This personal knowledge base is a highly organized, formatted structure that the domain experts access to solve problems. The knowledge base is analogous to a data structure. Thus, it is not a program; it is the universe of knowledge in the focused area that is constantly evolving and expanding.

So, what is problem solving? Problem solving is an active mental activity in which recall is only a portion of the mental process. Taken further, problem solving implies finding solutions for problems or situations that are not apparent when first encountered. The result of problem solving is the modification of an initial state to a desirable goal state. For example, suppose that a person plans to drive from one location to another. Generally, there are a variety of routes; some are favored over others. Given the time of day, weather conditions, type and condition of the transportation, known and encountered road and traffic conditions, purpose of the trip, mood of the individual, and other factors, the route is subject to modification. This trip planner may simply recall an initial or favorite route, or add to it after considering other factors.

What most problem-solving activities have in common are perceptual sets of stimuli in the form of mental models about how things ought to be or what things are, and action plans for resolution when the model is not met. E.g., a herpetologist spots an approaching snake. The perceptual set of stimuli indicates that the snake is possibly of the viper family. Further observation reveals distinguishing characteristics showing it is not poisonous. The snake is captured by hand. Thus, a mental model and stimuli were processed, and an action formed.

Surface vs. Deep Structure Approaches. Successful problem solvers have some commonality of approach. General problem solvers tend not to probe deeply or look at long-term implications of a situation. Rather, a strategy is adopted that tests the waters by cursory attempts at resolution. Should any clues surface, the cursory approach becomes focused. This approach is also referred to as surface similarity, as on the surface the problem looks much like something that is familiar. For instance, an interior decorator experiments with color combinations that help define a theme. The decorator draws upon past experience to match similar clients and needs with successful resolutions. Once a likely theme is conceived, it is presented in an abbreviated fashion such as a demonstration model, photographs of similar "treatments," or computer simulation. If accepted, strategies for implementation are put into place.

If the problem does not have a readily available solution, a more serious approach is undertaken. This approach involves a more carefully planned and systematic attempt referred to as a deep structure approach, since it moves from the short-term memory processing of the original concept of the problem to symbolic representation of the problem in long-term memory. The problem is then match-processed with existing models termed "the problem space" by cognitive psychologists. In general, problem space has patterns of symbols that represent an ideal or normal state in which a task scenario flows. The second portion of the problem space is the links denoting changes or influences that migrate from one state to another.

Stages of Problem Solving. Although there is active discussion on the subject, problem solving does have recognized stages. One schema for problem solving cites three stages. The first stage is recognizing, followed by forming a representation, and then pattern matching in long-term memory for a solution.

- First Stage: A stimulus provides recognition of a problem situation or space. The stimulus may be the result of sensory stimulation such as a noise, smell, feel, or the result of a memo, progress report, budget analysis, etc. A co-worker, supervisor, or other individual may surface the awareness of the problem or problem potential.

- Second Stage: Forming a representation consists of accessing declarative knowledge and models that pattern match to a current, recognized problem situation. If the match is an exact one, the problem solver moves to the third stage with a precise plan of action. If there is a less than threshold match, the problem solver forms hypotheses and proceeds with an informed common-sense resolution approach.

- Third Stage: This stage involves the triggering of procedural knowledge that matches the stored algorithmic performance actions to the problem in order to resolve the problem state into a goal state. The algorithm is a well-defined tactical procedure for resolving exact matched patterns, and is more globally capable when the informed common-sense approach is used.

For example, a quality car mechanic has a "tuned ear" that provides a surface approach to solving a problem based on an engine sound. If the approach does not reap benefits, the mechanic tries to eliminate possibilities in a systematic fashion. The mechanic draws on experience, links the attributes of that experience (the model) with problem factors considered as a group, and outlines other considerations that require a synthesis of processing. The problem is generally represented in a mental flowchart or other symbolic fashion with links to possible resolutions.

Backward and Forward Chaining. Human problem-solving techniques also involve backward and forward chaining. Chaining and its uses in machines are discussed in chapter 3. However, there are distinctions that require understanding by the knowledge engineer. In brief, *backward chaining* involves links from the known to proofs that support the known, as in the identification of a captured insect. *Forward chaining* is the collection of clues and movement towards a conclusion, as in tracking an animal.

These two chaining techniques can be expressed conceptually in terms of an analogy. A college student enters his freshman year with the goal of becoming a world-renowned brain surgeon. He realizes that to become a world-renowned brain surgeon, a medical degree is a prerequisite, as is a graduate degree from a substantial university, good grades, out of school community service, and many other factors. Thus, the student has a goal in mind and plans a sequence of events that will lead to the goal. This is backward chaining.

Another individual enters college and pursues a general education curriculum, explores courses from several disciplines, works various summer jobs, takes more courses, evaluates what has occurred, and then realizes that the courses taken meet the requirements for a major. This person discovers that this was where she was heading all the while. This process is an example of forward chaining.

Reasoning

Humans reason in patterns similar to backward and forward chaining, using deductive and inductive reasoning. *Analogical reasoning* is a method that relates an unknown to a known. A fourth form of reasoning is *common-sense reasoning*.

Deductive Reasoning. The purpose of deductive reasoning is to identify or formulate a chain of assertions. These assertions lead from one "true" statement to another. The forged chain of deductive links leading to a solution forms a rule.

Deductive reasoning is a powerful formal system because symbols are established, validated, and transformed into a logic chain. Conclusions follow premises in deductive reasoning. These premises move from the general to the specific. Sets of logic chains form a rule base that defines true statements of related factors, their attributes, and meaning. This rule base contains declarative and procedural knowledge in a focused area.

Deductive reasoning uses facts and rules. The process generally begins with a syllogism consisting of the premise(s) and the inferences. This process involves three basic factors in its premise:

1. Knowledge can be stated in the form of facts and rules. This is a major premise.
2. Newly discovered facts are added to a fact pool. These newly discovered facts are minor premises.
3. Combining existing facts and rules with newly acquired facts and rules enables a deduction of additional facts and rules. This is the conclusion.

- Major premise: I wind the 31-day clock on the first of the month.
- Minor premise: Today is the 26th day of the month.
- Conclusion: Therefore, I will not wind the clock today.

To use deductive reasoning effectively, the problem statement is divided into major and minor premises that lead to a conclusion. The addition of facts leads to new knowledge gleaned from previous knowledge. Domain experts work with their knowledge which is composed of mental models, rules, and other internalized strategies for solving problems. *Inference* is a deductive reasoning process that an expert uses to arrive at a conclusion or course of action.

Inductive Reasoning. Inductive reasoning starts with a given data set and has a goal of finding the attributes that formed the set. For example, a doctor learns that a patient has a pain in the knee. As a result, the doctor begins an inductive process to determine the cause. Inductive reasoning moves from the specific to the general. Thus, the major distinction between deduction and induction is that inductive reasoning has a set of observed attributes to which to conform.

Inductive reasoning tends to be less precise than deductive reasoning. While deductive reasoning proceeds through exact links, inductive reasoning makes best-guess logic leaps. Further, inductive problems tend to have more than one justifiable solution. Premises are supported but do not always denote an indisputable truth. For example, an archaeologist may find evidence of a civilization that disappeared as a result of some cataclysmic event. Through evidence gathered, the inductive chain of logic may conclude that a disease killed the entire populace. A second "expert" might conclude that the people were killed by a marauding horde, and might have a case that supports the conclusion. In fact, it may have been a loss of water supply that caused the mass exodus. An earthquake may have disrupted a burial ground and provided the appearance that people died en masse. Because no one from the era is available to supply the facts of the event, the inductive solution is all that there is. The rules established by inductive reasoning do not provide a manner in which to verify proposed links.

A distinction between deductive reasoning and inductive reasoning is the gap from one link to the next. Because deductive chains have consistency and "small" steps, they tend to have many rules or statements that define and set parameters around the conclusion. Thus, many deductive statements can be used to identify a course of action. However, the strength of deductive reasoning is also its burden.

Deductive reasoning sometimes presents a myopic view of reality. Reasoning chains generally do not make logic leaps to reach a conclusion. Thus, global viewpoints and quick action are not characteristics of deductive reasoning. In contrast, inductive reasoning uses shorter logic chains, thus requiring larger logic leaps to reach a conclusion. These shorter chains contribute to the possibility of bogus logic paths. Inductive systems generally use as much information as possible, but depend on what seems right through a consensus of view. As a result, inductive systems function at a global perspective.

Analogical Reasoning. *Analogical reasoning* is a logic system that works from what is known and understood as a standard, and compares the problem in question to that standard. Thus, two systems are compared or contrasted to arrive at a premise or conclusion. This reasoning base requires insight and understanding to form an appropriate analogy.

Analogical reasoning is a type of verbalization of an internalized learning process. An individual uses processes that require an ability to recognize previously encountered experiences. This type of reasoning is beyond the reach of today's expert systems. Because analogical reasoning relates the present with the past in an attempt to relate unrelated objects or concepts, analogical reasoning is similar to common-sense reasoning. For example, a fisherman hooks a fish that fights in a familiar manner. The fisherman recalls the way a fish once ran and the feel of its tail against the line. The fish circled the boat and severed the line in kelp. As a result the fisherman has an idea of how the present fish will fight, anticipates its actions, and lands the fish. Thus, the fisherman was able to relate a "feel" on the line to a past experience and a current condition.

Another example of analogical reasoning is the teacher who tells the class that the structure of an atom is similar to the structure of the solar system. The structures have vast size differences, but can be illustrated in the same manner. It is only a matter of scale that differentiates the concepts.

Common-Sense Reasoning. Common-sense reasoning, as discussed earlier, is based on the collection of personal experiences and facts that humans acquire over time. If a person is in location A and needs to be in location B at a certain time, his common sense considers time of day, traffic conditions, weather, mode of transportation, and other factors to determine the best departure time and ensure a timely arrival. Once again, knowledge-based systems are not capable of common-sense reasoning at this time because of the complexity of the relationships involved, the massive database that would be required, access time, and other factors. Much research in this area is underway, however.

There is a form of human common-sense reasoning that is applicable to knowledge-based systems. It is called *heuristic search reasoning*. Recall that heuristic knowledge consists of rules of thumb and shortcuts acquired over time. A heuristic search tries to find the most promising possibilities before formulating an approach. The search technique uses rule of thumb methods to effect solutions. For example, the lights suddenly go out in a home. There are many possibilities for the cause: short circuit, breaker switch, general power outage, etc. The human involved would consider the possibilities and act on the most likely candidate. Each potential cause would not be physically explored.

The heuristic search technique eliminates alternatives that have a low possibility of occurrence, or low certainty factor. Thus, there is an internalized scheme that organizes, calculates the odds, and arrives at a best approach. Often, those persons using heuristic reasoning cannot verbalize their reasoning—they just "know." It is the heuristic rules of thumb that the knowledge engineer and the expert explore.

Knowledge engineers use an expert's heuristic knowledge on two levels. The first level is used for pruning and optimizing the search. This level of search works on major factor chunks by eliminating options without exploration of the major factors' details. After the problem is of a manageable size, a more focused, detailed level or exploration ensues. Thus, the KE employs finely honed problem-solving techniques. Note, however, that heuristic rules are not accurate all of the time in all of the possible situations. When heuristic knowledge is applied, the expert places high confidence in the success of the action, or has reasoned that there are no guaranteed solutions and the heuristic is the best alternative.

Each of the human reasoning methods presented here will be compared with its machine reasoning counterpart in chapter 3. Figure 1-19 provides a conceptual illustration of four common reasoning styles used by humans.

INTELLIGENCE IN HUMANS

While it is not possible to hold, define, or completely understand, intelligence does have certain characteristics. Awareness of the characteristics of intelligence can help to clarify the considerations and components for constructing knowledge-based systems. These systems contain knowledge bases com-

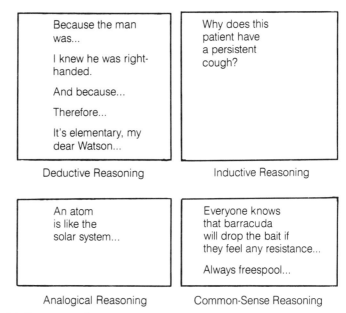

Fig. 1-19. Four reasoning styles.

posed of the knowledge of one or more experts. Knowledge-based systems cannot contain wisdom.

According to Douglas R. Hofstadter (1979), there are essential attributes of intelligent behavior. These attributes include the ability to:

- Respond to situations very flexibly. Humans tend to approach problems with a variety of solutions. For example, we alter our travel routes, change our eating habits, and vary our habitat.
- Make sense out of ambiguous or contradictory messages. Ambiguous references made to past experiences are often sufficient to stimulate total recall of places and events. This is a form of analogical reasoning.
- Recognize the relative importance of different elements of a situation. The veritable explosion of information that besieges us daily is processed, sorted, prioritized, and acted upon in an efficient manner.
- Find similarities between situations despite differences that may separate them. We have a need to attempt recognition of an existing situation in light of past experience. By conducting a compare/contrast analysis, future actions are calculated.
- Draw distinctions between situations despite similarities which may link them. We are able to note differences when confronted with near-identities.
- Synthesize new concepts by taking old concepts and putting them together in new ways. We have the ability to evolve concepts and objects by using creativity and innovation.

It is noteworthy to point out that Hofstadter's list of intelligent attributes is dependent upon common-sense abilities. An individual is able to synthesize the fact that a container intended for soda pop can also hold orange juice. Common sense is an area in which machine intelligence is challenged. A machine would need to be told what is appropriate for the container.

Martin A. Fischler and Oscar Firschein (1987) state that additional attributes of intelligence include:

- Mental attitudes of beliefs, desires, and intentions
- Ability to learn (the ability to acquire new knowledge)
- Ability to solve problems, including the ability to break down complex problems into simpler parts
- Knowledge of the limits of one's knowledge and abilities
- Ability to perceive and model the external world
- Understanding and use of language and related symbolic tools

Rudolf Arnheim (1969) provided a cognitive treatment for inputs and a person's thinking process that calls for operations including:

Active exploration	Analysis and synthesis
Selection	Completion
Grasping of essentials	Correction
Simplification	Comparison
Abstraction	Problem solving
Combining, separating, and putting into context	

Arnheim contends that whether active participation is a problem-solving activity or just thinking, humans use this process.

There are many theories of intelligence that involve performance, structure and function, context, and other abilities. The exploration of these theories is the domain of the psychological researcher. The application of these theories is the domain of the knowledge engineer. Those interested in knowledge engineering are encouraged to remain current on the development and progress of these theories.

A KE should maintain an awareness of the development and progress of theories of intelligence and other relevant areas by reading professional journals. In addition, the KE should join professional organizations and attend meetings to exchange information and views. These organizations often present conferences where professionals gather from widely diverse geographic areas.

KNOWLEDGE ENGINEERING CONSIDERATIONS

Knowledge-based systems are immersed in cognitive theory, which constitutes a psychological approach to human knowledge. Thus, KEs must have an understanding of cognitive theories in order to produce a quality knowledge base. While the KE does not need a degree in cognitive psychology, she or he needs a familiarity with learning theories and concepts.

The following discussion includes some of the terms and areas that a KE must grasp. These areas are not explored in depth; the section is intended to encourage the experienced or aspiring KE to consider certain aspects of cognitive theory. These areas are important and should therefore be explored through formal classes or texts focusing on cognitive areas.

Cognitive Theory

The emphasis of cognitive theory for knowledge-based systems is in the process of *human cognition*, the acquisition of information for an understanding of the world. This world understanding is based on an individual's subjective experience, which is composed of basic data sources, motivational concepts, conscious experience, unconscious material, external stimuli, and a sociocultural context.

Basic Data Sources. Basic data sources are derived from observed behaviors, and form or modify mental models. They are the personal experiences, analysis, and synthesis of the individual. Other basic data sources are physical processes and subjective mental models.

Cognitive theorists recognize that the conscious experiences of an individual are deduced from overt behaviors. The internal processing of the experiences by the individual involves careful evaluation; experiences are not taken at face value if they would make the mental models inaccurate. Perceptions of personal experience are often delusionary. Thus, those involved in the acquisition of knowledge or codification of patterns of performance must evaluate a variety of situations.

Motivational Concepts. Cognitive theory focuses on a motivational force within humans that results in a quest for structure and order. This quest is the source of motivation that energizes and directs behavior used to form or augment mental models. The individual organizes, synthesizes, and stores experiences in short- and long-term memory. These experiences must make sense and have structure and organization. It is important to make a distinction between this form of motivation and motivation as viewed by behavioral psychologists. The concern of cognitive psychology is not with the motives, drives, or needs that psychologists such as Maslow have studied. The knowledge engineer explores the motivations of experts in their quest for domain knowledge, as these motivations influence their mental models.

Conscious Experience. Conscious experience is composed of attitude, structure, and balance. Attitude is the perspective from which an individual views events. Structure is the interplay of the mental models and experiences of the individual. Balance consists of the forces of change from society, values, and other "soft" influencers of mental models.

Cognitive psychologists subscribe to the belief that conscious experience is the most essential aspect of human psychological activity. Conscious experience is the way in which an individual organizes experiences and creates privately coherent interpretations. An awareness of the types of experiences that influence mental models assists the knowledge engineer during development of the knowledge base.

Unconscious Experience. An individual's experiences outside the range of cognitive awareness may have an impact on the process of cognitive organization. This influence of outside factors suggests that a person may make assumptions and inferences, and draw conclusions that trigger cognitive order. The resulting cognitive order may not benefit solely from internalized experiences, because of factors of which the individual is not immediately aware. These factors are called *determining tendencies*; they influence mental models. Thus, the synthesized knowledge storehouse of mental models may be the product of learning and past unconscious experiences. This is the heuristic processing that characterizes a domain expert.

Forces related to determining tendencies include:

- Proximity: Elements of experience that occur adjacent or near one another, constituting a pattern of organization

- Continuity: Elements of experience that are continuous in either space or time

- Similarity: Elements of experience that share common properties and thereby constitute a pattern of organization

- Closure: Elements of experience that serve to bring a series of experiences to completeness in good form, and thereby constitute a pattern of organization

The heuristic knowledge level and problem-solving prowess of the expert also include an ability for perceptual selectivity. This selectivity is the ability to direct awareness within an environment. There are two forms of selective awareness: perceptual vigilance and perceptual defense.

Perceptual vigilance refers to a selective alertness. Perceptual defense refers to selective inattention. These perceptual sets work systematically, often without the awareness of the subject. Perceptual vigilance and perceptual defense work to provide maximum opportunity to pattern match previous experiences, reduce surprise, minimize inconsistency, and contain conflict within previously produced models.

External Stimuli. External stimulus conditions (noise), are regarded as important only if they are represented in experiences. An expert needs to correctly separate the "nice to know" from the "need to know" stimuli. Only the individual who experiences the noise can determine if it exerted an influence on the experience by influencing the mental model. An outside observer, such as a knowledge engineer, may anticipate that a noise will influence the subject being observed. However, this noise may have been a projected influence. The noise may have influenced the observer and not the observed. By the same observational error, an influence may pass by the observer and have a profound influence on the subject. This diversity in the impact of noise is a separation of experience and actuality, or reality and truth.

Sociocultural Context. Cognitive theory does not differentiate between the social and cultural elements of environmental context and the nonsocial or physical elements. Thus, an expert may be from a culture different than that of the KE. As a result, the mental model of the expert and KE may be substantially different.

Sociocultural context is the basic area where classical Gestalt theory and Lewinian field theory begin to diverge. The Gestaltist does not call attention to the significance of social and cultural determinates of behavior. Lewinian field theory is explicit in these elements of behavior. The knowledge engineer understands and allows for the sociocultural influences on the expert's knowledge and mental model.

KNOWLEDGE ENGINEERING TOMORROW

Besides the knowledge acquisition and representation strategies introduced in this chapter, there are considerations for future systems. These considerations include further attempts to alleviate knowledge acquisition bottlenecks, improve hardware, and produce more capable software.

Psychologists, sociologists, computer scientists, and others are attempting to learn more about human thinking. Their hope is to eventually understand human knowledge processing, storage, and retrieval. Until human expertise is understood, we can only attempt to emulate human knowledge through successive approximations. Thus, knowledge acquisition is the present and likely the future bottleneck to the construction of efficient, effective, and wide-ranging knowledge acquisition applications.

Some future knowledge engineering tools may assist in the creation of more sophisticated knowledge acquisition techniques and representation strategies. These computer system tools are alleged by some AI researchers with computer science backgrounds to solve "world problems." More realistically, these systems will be used for solving problems in specific domains as opposed to systems built as general problem solvers (GPS).

The hardware of tomorrow will differ from today's hardware. Speed and storage are two common problems in the hardware of today. Knowledge systems that serve the needs of tomorrow will require vast amounts of storage that accommodate common-sense knowledge. Along with this knowledge storage requirement is a need to process in a simultaneous fashion, rules, frames, or whatever knowledge structures are utilized.

In order to accomplish the simultaneous processing of knowledge, parallel processing will be required. These parallel processing giants are one form of supercomputer. According to DeWitt in the March 28, 1988 edition of TIME Magazine, supercomputer research is underway by such groups as Cray, IBM, Hitachi, Fujitsu, and NEC. For example, the Cray-3 series will use chips based on gallium. IBM is experimenting with at least six different entries in the supercomputer market. One machine, the experimental TF-1, has 4,000 miles of internal wiring, 33,000 high-speed processing units, and a single switching device measuring 80 feet in diameter. The TF-1 is expected to run 2,000 times as fast as the supercomputers of today.

Speed is the name of the game, and speed is the goal of parallel processing, where the measure of speed is in floating-point operations per second, or *flops*. Flops is the measure of the speed at which elementary operations, like addition, can be performed on numbers which can be very large or very small. Current machines are measured in gigaflops, or billions of operations per second. Tomorrow's machines will work in teraflops or trillions of operations per second. It is a widely held view that supercomputers are the enabling technology for artificial intelligence.

The software of tomorrow will react to changing input or function dynamically. In addition, the software will learn from experience and update its knowledge bases. Thus, the software will require what is called machine learning. The merging of the supercomputer and the software of tomorrow will be the leap towards today's concept of artificial intelligence.

By using supercomputers and software advances, knowledge acquisition techniques will evolve into an automated process. Because knowledge engineers are expensive and scarce, each expert system developed will not have the sufficient budget for or access to a human knowledge engineer. Larger development efforts will continue using the services of a knowledge engineer. Smaller efforts, such as general office applications, will take advantage of automated knowledge acquisition software.

This automated software will contain the expertise of knowledge engineers with an interactive interface able to present multiple approaches for knowledge acquisition. The interview results will be able to present back to the user a hierarchy of rule sets or other appropriate knowledge representation.

The user interface for this software will likely be through speech recognition. The knowledge representation portion will correlate the knowledge type and select an appropriate representation scheme. The system will take advantage of peripheral links with sophisticated data-knowledge bases and will be able to communicate with target users in their choice of native language.

The next chapter explores sources for data, information, and knowledge. In addition, it investigates the size, complexity, stability, and form of these sources.

SUMMARY

Knowledge was objectively discussed in terms of facts and actions taken by domain experts. These experts have created subjective and physical process models to serve as matches for input stimuli in order to form action plans. Intelligence tends to be discussed from a subjective position. Further, even a universally accepted, definitive definition of intelligence is elusive, debated, and the focus of several disciplines. Thus, the nature of intelligence is the subject of an academic debate.

PRACTICAL APPLICATION

1. Weizenbaum's premise was that knowledge should be the outer limit of machine systems.

   a. Technology has made it possible to impart wisdom to a machine. What factors must be considered in the ''go/no go'' decision?

   b. Using the same scenario, what if it were possible to instill emotion plus knowledge into the system? Also, consider that the machine might be in the form of a robot—an android.

2. Just as there are many ways of defining knowledge, there are probably many ways of representing the levels of knowledge. Consider the graphics below or devise one of your own that could represent an alternative knowledge structure.

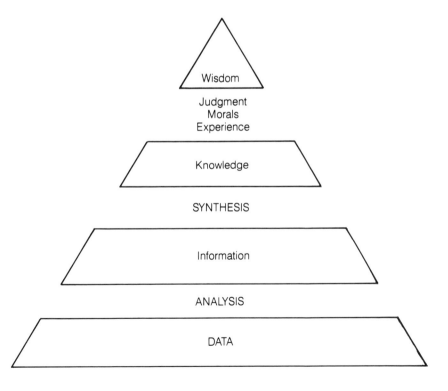

Note: The graphics represent the conceptual level in varying positions. A justification might be that concepts are a higher-level order given the amount and type of experiences and information input required, e.g., the concepts underlying the theory of relativity.

3. Given the information regarding thinking, problem solving and reasoning in this chapter plus knowledge you may have acquired in other fields of study, give thought to these "popular" premises:

   a. He is well-versed with much experience in the field, therefore he should be a trainer.
   b. He has many years of study and degrees; therefore he can teach.
   c. It's really an easy program to use. Why do we need to add menus, prompts, and helps?
   d. "Trial by fire" is the best way to gain experience and knowledge.

4. Consider the data pyramid presented in this chapter. Can data, information, and knowledge be represented using a Venn diagram? Make a drawing and explain the rationale for the degree of overlap.

5. Create a representation of a mental model about a topic such as voting. Ask a friend to make a model on the same topic. Compare and contrast the models.

6. Consider the levels of knowledge associated with a job, hobby, or area of knowledge. List major points as they relate to facts, concepts, rules, and heuristic aspects of the selected job, hobby, or area.

7. Knowledge can be thought of as having types such as declarative, procedural, common-sense, and heuristic knowledge. Consider the fluid-

ity of knowledge. What are the thresholds that divide the knowledge types?

8. Use concept set elements to define a system such as an automobile, a neighborhood, or a working environment.

9. There are times when a KE would prefer a novice level performer over an expert. When and why might this be?

10. When might deductive or inductive reasoning be the preferred approach to a problem-solving situation? Are analogical reasoning and common-sense reasoning ever a first choice over deductive or inductive reasoning?

11. Design and support a problem-solving process model. In what situations is the model effective? Is it more effective in a discernible problem type?

12. Compare the mental model in FIG. 1-5 with the influences of cognitive theory including basic data sources, motivational concepts, conscious experience, unconscious experience, external stimuli, and sociocultural context. Can these influences be linked with the concept set elements? Why or why not?

2

The Knowledge Sources

The longest journey is the journey inwards
of him who has chosen his destiny,
who has started upon this quest
for the source of his being
(Is there a source?).

Dag Hammarskjõld

INTRODUCTION

In order to build an effective knowledge base, it is essential to become as familiar as possible with the domain. While the primary source of knowledge for most knowledge bases is the domain expert, there are other sources that can both help expedite the development process and contribute to the knowledge base. These sources include information ranging from the informal notes of a novice, books, case studies, empirical studies, databases, records, etc., to professional research papers and computer databases.

Knowledge engineers benefit by preparation prior to interacting with domain experts. Besides familiarization with new terminology, rapport must be established between the knowledge engineer and the domain expert. There is a direct correlation between the knowledge engineer's subject matter familiarity, and the depth and quality of the knowledge base. After preparation, the KE can more easily assimilate the information derived from the domain expert. In addition, there is a smaller likelihood the KE will become lost or confused. The prepared KE will be able to ask more focused, pertinent questions.

KNOWLEDGE TYPES REVISITED

The focus of a study of knowledge types is to determine the sources of information that an expert uses to reach solutions, and their availability. For example, if the expert renders decisions based upon data that can be gathered from reports, interviews, or electromechanical means, the expert's primary task is one of logical analysis. If the expert's data is derived from one of the senses such as touch or smell, or from "intuition," the development of a knowledge-based application will be of minimal help.

In addition, data collected from news reports, feature articles, or other unstructured sources is not easily subjected to knowledge-based system analysis. The data and information for analysis needs to be quantifiable for possible inclusion in a knowledge-based system. The data must be available and be able to be interpreted.

The expert's knowledge cannot be of a common-sense nature. Early discussions with experts determine the presence or extent of common-sense knowledge. If common-sense knowledge plays a major role in the decision-making process of an expert, a knowledge-based system application will not work.

Once again, there is a difference between common-sense and *informed common-sense*. Common-sense knowledge says that if it is cool outside at 4:00 P.M. and you are going outside, by 7:00 P.M. it will be cooler, so it would be a good idea to take a jacket or sweater.

Common-sense awareness is learned over time and cannot be programmed into a knowledge base because of inability to represent its breadth and complexity, and because of limitations of storage space and search time. Informed common sense is the body of knowledge that is common to those experienced in a particular area. Informed common-sense tells nurses what instruments will be required for a particular procedure, or tells an insurance agent the types of coverage needed by the owner of an apartment complex. To those in the areas, the knowledge is common. To those inexperienced in the areas, knowledge of this nature is limited or absent.

ADDITIONAL CHARACTERISTICS OF KNOWLEDGE

Chapter 1 discussed different ways to look at human knowledge in terms of levels, types, and other foci that pertain to human knowledge attributes. Now it is important to begin to view knowledge as it may affect knowledge-based systems. These views include size, complexity, stability, and form.

Size

The estimate of knowledge base size may influence the manner in which the knowledge is captured or represented, in addition to determining the requirements for storage. The size of a very large knowledge base affects development time and complexity. The delivery system and options become limited as the knowledge base increases in size.

For example, a knowledge-based system designed to assist in the identification of trees would have an immense knowledge base. If a knowledge base of this design were to be pursued, it would be subdivided into reasonable parts. A knowledge base of this size would be approached by partitioning it into logical divisions. These divisions could be based on regions, climates, elevations, or key identifying attributes such as size or leaf type.

Complexity

The complexity of knowledge is another consideration for the knowledge engineer. Complexity issues are similar to size considerations because the knowledge base might have to be divided according to some convention. The strategies and tactics employed by the experts can provide clues about the requirements for capture, and representation of the knowledge to users.

Rarely will a KE find a knowledge base that cannot be divided. However, partition might not solve all the problems. The KE should keep in mind that, when a very large knowledge base is involved, much time will be expended in the acquisition and testing of the knowledge. In addition, search time of the knowledge base by the control program will be severely impacted.

Stability

Dynamic knowledge can be difficult to capture, represent, and codify into an efficient and cost-effective application. Problem situations that require dynamic knowledge have some elements that are stable. In this manner, modification of the knowledge base is minimal, thus, having a lesser impact on costs.

Dynamic systems include knowledge-based applications that focus on such rapidly changing topics as tax laws, fish locations, or weather events. The KE finds the stable portions of the knowledge areas and then creates provisions for data tracking or user input opportunities.

Form

Knowledge is available in many forms. The knowledge engineer and the expert consider the most efficient form for the knowledge about the problem type. Knowledge can be in the form of facts, such as "212 degrees Fahrenheit is the boiling point of water at sea level." Knowledge can also be represented in other forms:

- **Numbers and mathematical relationships:** $5 \times 10 = 50$
$$or \ 3 \times 2 = 6$$

- **Symbols:**   Chair, green, little, etc.

- **Relations:**   X is subordinate to Y

- **Patterns and shape recognition:**   A passenger aircraft versus a military aircraft, or a constellation that resembles a dipper.

SOURCES OF KNOWLEDGE

The range of knowledge sources is vast, however, the availability and value of each type varies according to the scope and focus of the individual KE and knowledge-based system project.

In general, knowledge can be considered as public or private. Public knowledge is acquired from books and guides, empirical writings, video and audio recordings, and presentations. These sources of knowledge contain general concepts and theories of a domain. Knowledge from sources such as books is generally declarative in nature but can contain some procedural applications. Private knowledge is refined and synthesized to influence events in a domain. A job aid created by a domain expert, for example, contains both public and private knowledge. The private knowledge results from performance analysis of the domain by the domain expert. Thus, the job aid may appear procedural in nature, but it contains the heuristic knowledge of the domain expert. Heuristic knowledge is the most private knowledge. It is the heuristic knowledge that makes the expert an expert. These general categories of knowledge can be further broken down into more specific types, each having its benefits as well as limitations.

Books and Guides

Books and guides provide information which ranges from basics to advanced concepts. The biggest limitation of these types of publications relates to the timeliness of the information. Often, the information on which the text is based is obsolete by the time the reader sees it. This is particularly true in the case of technical research and development. However, books and guides do provide the KE with a good general overview of the knowledge domain.

For the KE with little to no background in the knowledge domain, textbooks, encyclopedias, and specialized dictionaries provide basic concepts, an introduction to terminology, and a bit of history and insight into the development of the topic. Keep in mind that dictionaries range from general to topical information, and new editions can appear frequently.

While the importance of the domain expert is heavily stressed, some small system applications can be constructed solely from existing books. These books are not standard text books, but focused, technical publications in a particular field. They can provide background information or actual material for the knowledge base. Additional sources of this type include troubleshooting guides, topical and professional reference books, documentation, and manuals.

For example, field guides can be used in a knowledge-based system to classify trees, plants, animals, fish, and insects. Information from sources like these can provide a foundation for a knowledge base. Knowledge engineers must be aware that there might be copyright implications; it is the responsibility of the knowledge engineer and the company involved to investigate these.

The same types of books are available for medicine, nuclear power plants, automotive repair, and other areas. One heuristic in this area is to have an initial interaction with domain experts and ask about their sources of reference.

Empirical Data

Empirical data consists of experiential writings. These writings include research writings, periodicals, computer-based information, information or data from memos and job aids, formal documentation such as policies and procedures, records, and files, i.e., any printed "informed knowledge" about the domain. Empirical data is particularly helpful for the design and development of expert systems that focus on diagnosis and control.

Empirical data is generally informal. For example, it is not unusual to see handwritten notes that served as job aids when a person first learned a task. It may be necessary to have the expert fill in missing steps and interpret them for a task or related ideas for a concept. Sometimes empirical data helps to remind the expert about thought processes before they become automatic. Thus, the KE can use empirical data to act at the level of informed common sense.

Once data of this nature has been accumulated, characterized, and organized, it is referenced during the design phase of the knowledge base. This data provides clues not only about the problems that can be encountered, but also the types of knowledge required to interact in the particular domain.

Research

The surveys, questionnaires, studies, and statistical documentation produced by ongoing research is a valuable source of current information and knowledge. The limitations of this source include accessibility, reliability, and the level of the information. If the KE is a novice in the knowledge domain, the data collected may be acquired as factual information rather than knowledge.

Computer-based Sources

With the growing number and usage of computers, data and information is increasingly available in the form of databases, bulletin boards, periodical information such as NEWSBANK, and other computer means, some of which are intended to be used in conjunction with published works, microfiche, and other information sources.

Databases offer a source of compiled, empirical data since they are assembled to address specific topics or store a range of information. The knowledge in a database is primarily declarative because general facts about objects and things are stored.

A knowledge engineer should consider the ease of access a database program might provide, although not all knowledge-based application system tools are able to link with outside programs. Database systems make it easy to use a personal computer to create, organize, store, and retrieve information. Using a database, a knowledge-based system can tap into:

- The analysis of relationships
- A manipulation of commonalties and differences among declarative groups

- The organizing of information
- The listing of files
- The structuring of information
- The updating of information

Formal

Knowledge and information may be acquired from formally produced documents and materials, such as policies and procedures, rules and regulations, laws and propositions. As with books and guides, the information may be outdated. It is the responsibility of the KE to check not only the validity of the information with responsible sources (who are often the administrators of the information), but also the reliability of the information. Although formal sources of knowledge may offer procedural information, there is a good possibility that those procedures are not the same as those that are practiced. What is said and what is done may differ greatly.

Informal Information

Informal information is information found in the hand-written notes of the apprentice, office memos, job aids, and other data that is not formally published. Currently, technical job aids are increasing in number and application as publishers realize the value of simple, concise information about common technical tasks.

The limitation of this type of resource is that it is limited to factual and procedural information, and not ordinarily designed for use in problem-solving situations. However, informal knowledge sources that contain heuristic knowledge can be the most important source of knowledge next to domain experts. Job aids, tailored to specific operations and procedures are an example of this valuable informal knowledge source.

Periodicals

Probably the most up-to-date versions of current knowledge can be obtained from periodicals such as newspapers, reports, pamphlets, brochures, magazines, and professional journals. In addition, periodicals often contain information regarding minor topics that are difficult to locate in books, contemporary options and varied viewpoints, and recent events in many fields of study.

The KE must be aware, however, of the purposes and biases of the publishers and writers who might be putting forth information to "prove a point" or "make a sale" rather than furnishing useful information that is both reliable and valid. Additionally, locating past issues of newspapers and journals might prove difficult as libraries sometimes retain them only for a limited time.

Records

Records are another form of empirical data that can point to weak links in a system, aiding repair or service. They might also document design considerations, or contain in-house comments that stimulate the memories or options for the domain expert. This information can help the KE identify questions that address major factors and attributes of those factors. Information from records can also provide case studies for system validation. These records include: repair orders, patient health records, title information, case studies, logs, professional files, charts, and abstracts. Records focus on historical data for a particular object or class of objects.

Prior to and following the construction of the knowledge base, the use of documented problem resolutions can be beneficial. Before the construction of a knowledge base, the knowledge engineer and the expert can acquire a "feel" for the real-time system requirements. Research in this area can also provide information about target users. Using records such as case studies, auxiliary investigations can provide information regarding the education, knowledge, experience, and other relevant characteristics of the target users.

After the construction of the knowledge base, the case studies can be used as test inputs for validation purposes. These validation exercises can be conducted by the knowledge engineer before unveiling the system for public evaluation, criticism, scrutiny, or ridicule. This strategy is beneficial for both the knowledge engineer and the domain expert.

Mechanical Recordings

Like books and guides, videotapes, audiotapes, CD/ROM, movies, slide presentations, and interactive recordings can be sources of all levels of knowledge. As with the prior types of resource, the biggest limitation of these mechanical recordings is the timeliness of the information. Often, the information is obsolete by the time the reader sees or hears it. This is particularly true in the case of technical research and development.

Like books and guides, mechanical recordings do provide the KE with a good general overview of the knowledge domain. A distinct advantage of mechanical recordings over print materials is their ability to present visual and/or audio aspects of the domain. This is particularly valuable to the KE who is working in a knowledge domain that includes physical skills such as the assembly of equipment or diagnosis on the basis of visual or auditory evidence.

Mechanical recordings are currently available in such areas as training, troubleshooting, marketing and promotions. For the KE with little background in the knowledge domain, these knowledge sources can provide not only an introduction to terminology and basic concepts, but also a realistic or animated "picture" of the topic under study.

Presentations

Presentations often combine some of the preceding sources and add the element of a "warm body." Hands-on training, workshops, lectures and seminars, courses and classes, forums, meetings and roundtables, and conferences provide the KE with knowledge that can range from mere data to invaluable information.

A problem with this source type is the unpredictability of the level and applicability of information presented. Often, these attributes are unknown until well into the session. Further, presentations often cost money and involve travel.

A good presentation can offer a KE useful knowledge by means of a lecture accompanied by visual aids, discussion, a question and answer period, handouts that reiterate and expand on the information, references to other sources, and so on. Worst case is a presentation from which the KE acquires no new knowledge.

Visits

Like presentations, tours and visits to sites can range from worthless to invaluable. Again, the most valuable visits are those in which useful knowledge is acquired, preferably by means of additional sources such as written materials and personal interactions. In addition, visits might allow the KE to observe people at work, speak to personnel about their jobs and tasks, and peruse the resources of the facility, such as documentation and topical libraries.

Humans

Instructors and teachers of the domain, researchers in the field, persons whose daily work requires knowledge of the domain, and human experts are another source of knowledge. The opportunity for free communication between them and the KE can provide not only the basics of the knowledge domain, but also a window into declarative and procedural information that leads to understanding and perhaps even the ability to analyze, diagnose, and problem solve. The interchange of information and the ability to formulate questions that can be presented at the moment they're conceived is a condition not offered by the other knowledge sources.

Although there are other forms of data available to fill the knowledge base, the domain expert offers the highest quality of knowledge. The domain expert may also be an instructor, researcher, worker, or combination of these.

The hardest job of the knowledge engineer may be the identification, acquisition, and "buy-in" of the "best" qualified expert. At this point, it could be asked, "What is an expert?" An expert, in this book, is an individual who is a competent problem solver in a focused domain and who has techniques and abilities better than the problem-solving skills of his peer group.

RANKING SOURCES

As the KE is becoming familiar with the knowledge domain, there are criteria by which the value of each type of knowledge source is judged. These judging criteria include the accessibility of the source, reliability and validity of the information, level of risk (as in visits to research sites), breadth and depth of information required, type of information (procedural or declarative), use of the information during the expert system's design and development cycles, date of the information—be it historical or the latest developments—and completeness of the information.

The criteria can be ranked in terms of the type of expert system under development. Prior to a search for the sources, the KE performs a secondary ranking of the criteria. This secondary ranking takes into account such factors as accessibility given the time frame, geographic location of the project, budgetary constraints, etc. Chapter 5 provides additional information about ranking sources of knowledge and contains a table for assessing knowledge sources.

PROCURING THE SOURCES

Once the KE ranks the sources, the search for those sources begins. Where does one begin? There are several means by which sources of information can be located. Among them are the following:

- Ask human experts what they use as references and sources of information.
- Ask resource personnel such as librarians, instructors, etc., what sources they recommend.
- Research documentation references such as bibliographies, endnotes, footnotes, quotes, etc.
- Make use of public and private libraries. Within libraries:
  - Scan through the appropriate sections (this requires that the KE become familiar with the library's classification system).
  - Do subject, title, and author searches through the card catalog.
  - If available, search through computer catalogs and services such as INFOTRAC, NEWSBANK, etc.
  - Scan through fiche collections, and files containing clippings, pamphlets, etc. (''vertical files'').
  - Utilize periodical indexes.
  - Check abstracts of articles in the knowledge domain for bibliographic information.

- Visit general and topical bookstores.
- Request information from public information services from federal down to local levels.
- Seek information from community services and businesses.
- If possible, request information from research facilities.

It is the task of the KE to locate sources from which to acquire knowledge for the knowledge base. But what about the human expert? How does the KE select an expert, and what is the role of the client in expert selection?

Expert Selection

Given the working definition of an expert, there is one very important aspect to consider in the selection of an appropriate expert. An expert more than "knows" about a particular subject. This expert is also able to perform in the area and apply that knowledge. An expert who has all of these characteristics can interact with a KE to produce a fabulous database.

Fortunately or unfortunately, knowledge-based systems rely on knowledge bases. These knowledge bases contain declarative knowledge and procedural knowledge. Thus, the expert must possess both the "know" declarative elements and the "do" procedures in order for them to be acquired by the KE. So, how is a domain expert selected?

If the choice of an expert is not supplied or obvious, there are techniques the KE can use. One of these techniques tends to be overlooked. That technique is to ask several people involved in the problem domain who it is that tends to "get the job done." This person is likely to be the one that others turn to when a problem appears to be unsolvable.

Involving this individual as the expert for the project could result in a problem for those depending on the expert. The expert's diverted attention might result in a time crunch or cause a production bottleneck which could place internal task completion at risk. If this happens, there must be a sales pitch to management to justify the diversion of the expert's time. Others' belief in the expert is also important for that expert to want to participate.

For now, assume that the expert has been identified. The next step is to interview the individual. It may be that the expert has domain knowledge, but can that knowledge be communicated? The identified expert is more than the person who can "fix" the problem. This expert must be able to explain the "fix" to others. The requirement of being able to communicate is a very quick way of paring down the expert pool.

Can you accept the prospect of working very closely with this person in a potentially stressful arena? Is the expert willing to impart the wisdom gained over time through education, training, and experience? Can you trust this individual to be completely honest, helpful, and complete? Do you need to ask all the "right" questions to surface the necessary knowledge?

It is interesting to note that an inadequate knowledge base reflects more on the knowledge engineer than on the domain expert. The acquisition of knowledge is the domain of the KE, not the domain expert. If the process is not working and the cause is communication, consider selection of another expert. If the process is not working, and the cause is the technical nature of the information, consider selection of another knowledge engineer. One way to know if the process is working is to construct a rapid prototype that provides a flavor of the solution.

Sometimes one expert is not in control of all of the knowledge, or politics dictates that multiple experts participate in the project. This places the KE in a high-risk situation. Groups of experts tend to have different problem-solving techniques, competitive personalities, hidden agendas, "one-upmanships," and the like, thereby adding distracting elements to the process. Once again, it is not the expert(s) at risk, it is the reputation of the KE and the efficiency and effectiveness of the knowledge-based system that are at risk.

If a situation arises in which multiple experts are participating, a chief expert should be designated to make all final decisions. This individual may have seniority or other license to control the group. Placement of this control can stem from the output goals, politics, or job responsibility. A heuristic is to make the experts responsible for the accuracy of the knowledge base content.

The accuracy and completeness of the knowledge base is, by contract, the responsibility of the designated expert(s). Unless the contract specifies who is responsible for the accuracy and completeness of the knowledge base, the KE may be open for malpractice law suits. Thus, it is the job of the expert(s) to supply the knowledge to build the knowledge base. The KE is the facilitator of the process.

A final word on expertise and experts. Important as it is to fit the tool to the problem type, it is also important to match the expertise to the problem. The purpose of knowledge-based systems is to leverage expertise. If expertise alone cannot solve the problem, or the nature of the expertise is too esoteric, or if expertise is tied to common sense or physical prowess or dexterity, experts and knowledge-based systems may not be the answer.

Detailed techniques for selecting experts, and other information pertaining to working with domain experts are presented in chapter 9.

Expert Knowledge Limits

Expert knowledge is limited in terms of breadth and depth. Both experts and KEs need an awareness of them. These bounds should be discussed up front. The experts are not required to reveal every fact or procedure they know. Instead, a focus is identified, set, and maintained.

Expert Ego

The expert ego and the KE need to recall why they are together and to focus on the goal. It is not unheard of for an expert to provide false or misleading data. This misinformation is sometimes a smoke screen to protect a power position. If the KE suspects conflicting, incorrect, or cursory information, a short testing cycle is recommended. This test cycle builds knowledge segments that can be validated against test cases. The testing reveals inconsistencies. If the expert cannot be focused, a higher level of authority needs to become involved, and the expert replaced.

Sometimes this situation can be avoided by the rapport established between the knowledge engineer and the expert. It is not uncommon for a fiduciary relationship to become established in which the KE becomes a sounding board for frustration or insecurity. Resolution and interaction is solely dependent upon the interpersonal skills of the KE.

LANGUAGE AND COMMUNICATION

Human language is a system of communication involving speech, body language, and writing to convey thoughts and ideas. Language is a still-evolving evolutionary process. By using language, humans have formed organizations of syntax and semantics to organize and express thought.

Language is not designed—it is the result of attempts to convey meaning. Those who dedicate their efforts to the study of what language is and how it is used are called *linguists*. Language study concerns itself with the use of symbols, words, phrases, and grammatical rules of present-day languages.

Linguists concentrate on the meaning of what is stated or written. One strategy used to accomplish this search for meaning focuses on context and pragmatics. Context is the completeness of thought associated with a sentence in a spoken paragraph, a paragraph in a paper, or any smaller portion of a whole document or speech. When a portion of a statement or written document is looked at in isolation, it is subject to interpretation that may be out of context. Thus, when the collective thoughts are in context, meaning is clarified.

Pragmatics is the study of what is meant by what is said, as people can say or write one thing and mean another. Both context and pragmatics are used to imply meaning and foster understanding when communicating with others. The process of decoding the meaning of another person's communication is also within the domain of the knowledge engineer.

Often communication is out of context because the whole of the communication is known only to the domain expert. The knowledge engineer works with bits and pieces in an attempt to form a whole. According to Hofstadter (1979), there are three layers to any message: the inner message, the frame, and the outer message. The inner message is the meaning intended by the sender. The frame message is the message to be decoded. The outer message is the information that is implicit from the context and pragmatics which tells how to decode the inner message. Hofstadter states, "to understand the outer message is to build, or know how to build, the correct decoding mechanism for the inner message."

Hofstadter writes that the outer message is an implicit message, and that the outer message is a set of triggers for the decoder. The knowledge engineer should understand native language from the perspective of the expert to analyze the meaning that the message carries.

Selecting Sources

For the knowledge engineer, the correct knowledge source or knowledge source set is critical for the knowledge-based application. The optimal knowledge-based application is one in which the knowledge has been structured over time as in a book. Examples of knowledge sources of this nature include field guides, electronic troubleshooting guides, and process-type books such as cookbooks.

The more dispersed the knowledge, the more difficult it is to organize in terms of accuracy, reliability, and focus. The KE should be cautious and avoid singular sources or approaches.

SUMMARY

Paul D. Leedy (1980) likens the researcher and resources to a craftsman and a tool kit. Much like the craftsman, the researcher—or knowledge engineer—soon realizes that the solution to a given problem depends not upon a single tool, but depends on the assistance of several or even all of those tools.

During the course of identifying and selecting sources of knowledge, it is the responsibility of the knowledge engineer to consider not only the knowledge domain, but also the availability and intrinsic value of each source as it relates to the project at hand. In later chapters, we will discuss the impact of the project's design, particularly the determination of the mission statement, on the selection of those knowledge sources.

In the next chapter, we will review machine knowledge and artificial intelligence and determine its relationship with that of humans.

PRACTICAL APPLICATION

1. In this chapter, we discussed the sources of knowledge for knowledge-based systems. In *The Search for New Intellectual Technologies*, Andrew R. Molnar makes a reference to some thoughts of Dr. Robert Glasser:

   > . . . we now expect individuals to not only master beginning skills but to also be able to learn from reading and make inferences and solve problems with verbal and mathematical input . . . today in many subject domains, attainment of comprehension and problem solving skills is now a greater problem than mastery of elementary skills.

   Consider how Dr. Glasser's views relate to the selection and values of sources of knowledge for development of a knowledge base.

   a. Do sources of knowledge tend to relate information that is for the mastery of skills or for analysis and problem solving?

    b. What is the current trend in the fields of education and training? What role should knowledge engineering play in each of those fields?

2. A common problem among those who are "new" to research is their failure to consider the consequences that the pursuit of their domain entails as to the availability, collection, and interpretation of data. How can this be avoided?

3. One of the most difficult tasks an individual faces when investigating a domain is recognizing which individuals posses the appropriate problem-solving strategies. Consider a problem and the sequence and desirability of knowledge sources to solve the problem. Evaluate your rationale for these decisions. Match the knowledge sources to knowledge types discussed in chapter 1.

4. Complete the table on the facing page with a specific topic or problem in mind. Formally state the topic or problem and secure a second opinion.

KNOWLEDGE SOURCE	Availability and Accessibility	Level of Risk	Type of Info	Dated-ness	Depth and Breadth	Level of Detail	Validity and Reliability	Format	Level of Inter-action	Range of Use
Books/Guides										
Empirical										
Research										
Computer										
Formal										
Informal										
Periodical										
Records										
Mechanical Recordings										
Presentations										
Visits										
Humans										

Key:
Knowledge
Source

Attributes	Descriptions	
Availability/ Accessibility	0	The knowledge source is unavailable.
	1	The knowledge source is available but may not be accessible to the KE.
	2	The knowledge source is available. There are criteria that must be met or constraints that must be dealt with in order to exploit the source.
	3	The knowledge source is available and accessible.
Level of Risk	0	There is a high level of risk involved in procuring/securing the knowledge source, e.g., going on-site at a nuclear test.
	1	There is a medium level of risk involved in procuring/securing the knowledge source, e.g., interviewing inmates at a local prison.
	2	There is a low level of risk involved in procuring/securing the knowledge source, e.g., visiting a post-op ward in a hospital.
	3	There is no risk involved in procuring/securing the knowledge source.
Type of Information	D	The majority of information available from the knowledge source is **D**eclarative in nature.
	P	The majority of information available from the knowledge source is **P**rocedural in nature.
	DP	The information available from the knowledge source is both **D**eclarative and **P**rocedural.
Currency	H	The information available from the knowledge source is **H**istorical in nature, that is, it is less than current. This information is often viewed as background and ''nice to know'' data.
	C	The information available from the knowledge source is **C**urrent but probably not ''the latest.'' This applies particularly to technological domains.
	R	The knowledge source has the most **R**ecent information available in the domain.
Depth/Breadth	DN	The knowledge source has **D**etailed knowledge of a **N**arrow slice of the knowledge domain.

Attributes	Descriptions	
	DW	The knowledge source has **D**etailed knowledge over a **W**ide area of the knowledge domain.
	BN	The knowledge source has **B**road, general knowledge of a **N**arrow slice of the knowledge domain.
	BW	The knowledge source has **B**road, general knowledge over a **W**ide area of the knowledge domain.
Level of Detail	O	The knowledge source's information provides a good **O**verview of the knowledge domain.
	B	The knowledge source's information is composed mostly of **B**asic terms, concepts, facts, etc.
	T	The knowledge source's information is **T**opical in nature; that is, it is focused on and limited to the knowledge domain as it is defined for the expert system.
Validity/ Reliability	0	The information imparted by the knowledge source might be invalid as well as unreliable.
	1	The information imparted by the knowledge source is reliable but may be invalid. This is of particular importance in technological domains that are in the midst of new developments.
	2	The information imparted by the knowledge source is valid but may be unreliable. This pertains particularly to domains in which research findings have not been fully tested.
	3	The information imparted by the knowledge source is both valid and reliable.
Format	1	The knowledge source's information is available in print.
	2	The knowledge source's information is available in audio format, as in cassette tapes; visual format, as in slide presentations, illustrations, etc.; or both audio and visual as in movies, interactive video, etc.
	3	The knowledge source's information is available in both print and audio/visual format. An example is an interactive video that is available with its script and additional print materials such as job aids, references, etc.

Attributes	Descriptions	
Level of Interaction	0	Interaction with the knowledge source is not possible. An example is print materials.
	1	Interaction with the knowledge source is limited. This type of interaction is often one-sided, as in accessing information from a database.
	2	Interaction with the knowledge source is available at an intermediate level, for example, in the form of a discussion following a workshop presentation.
	3	Interaction with the knowledge source is available at a high level. The highest level would be a one-on-one interview and discussion with a human knowledge source.
Range of Usability	1	The information imparted by the knowledge source is most applicable to the KE during preparation for knowledge base acquisition.
	2	The information imparted by the knowledge source is applicable during development of the knowledge base.
	3	The information imparted by the knowledge source is applicable during both development and testing of the knowledge base.

3

The Nature of
Machine Knowledge

So it is that the gods do not give all men gifts of grace
—neither good looks nor intelligence nor eloquence.

Homer

INTRODUCTION

Human knowledge was characterized in chapter 1 through a variety of perspectives including knowledge levels, knowledge types, element sets, and mental models. Human knowledge was presented as an ascending process based on a hierarchy. The base of the hierarchy was data and the top of the hierarchy reached into the realm of intelligence.

One focus of machine knowledge is to emulate the decision-making processes of humans. Because of this emulation, many knowledge-based applications use human mental and physical attributes. Machine knowledge can be presented through a variety of focuses in artificial intelligence.

Computers and Thinking

Alan Turing, according to Firebaugh (1988), was a mathematician and part of a British team that broke the German Enigma machine cipher during World War II. Among Turing's other accomplishments were several papers about the theoretical aspects of mathematics and computing. One of these papers, entitled "On Computable Numbers," described in 1937 a hypothetical machine that could perform algorithmic operations.

In 1950, Turing wrote a paper entitled "Computing Machinery and Intelligence." In this paper, Turing asked "Can machines think?" As a result of this paper, Turing is credited as being the conceptual father of artificial intelligence.

In the field of computer science, artificial intelligence is said to have begun at Dartmouth College in 1956. A group of scientists met to discuss the potential of computers for simulating human intelligence. These scientists represented fields including mathematics, psychology, neurology, and electrical engineering. Each of these participating scientists used the computer to conduct research in attempts to simulate aspects of human intelligence.

The principal conference organizers were: John McCarthy, Marvin Minsky, Nathaniel Rochester, and Claude Shannon. Of these organizers, John McCarthy was credited with coining the term "artificial intelligence."

As of this writing, machines do not think, but even now they can perform human-like problem-solving tasks in specific domains. These machines are computers that are executing knowledge-based software programs. The field of knowledge-based systems is expanding with developments and achievements occurring daily. While Arthur C. Clark's anthropomorphic computer in *2001*— the HAL 9000—is not real, supercomputers and new concepts for computers are being developed. Sometime in the not so distant future, a computer might say, "I think, therefore, I am."

The Human-Machine Contrast

Human intelligence consists of facts, concepts, rules, and heuristic knowledge. Facts and concepts can be thought of as structures that house symbols. Rules and heuristic knowledge can be thought of as manipulators of the symbols. Mental models are formed using facts, concepts, rules, and heuristic knowledge in ever-changing arrays.

The field of machine intelligence can be viewed as the pursuit of emulating human intelligence. Simon (1981) stated that the root of intelligence is symbols with denotative power subject to manipulation. Human thinking can be viewed in terms of categories of thinking. These categories are cognitive, associative, and philosophical.

Human cognitive thinking involves the gathering of input data and the manipulation of symbols. The manipulation of symbols takes place through mental models. Machine thinking does an admirable emulation of the cognitive process. Both the human and the machine are able to process input and reach decisions for action of project future events from that input.

Associative thinking consists of the concepts of vertical and lateral thinking. According to deBono (1973) there are two basic thinking styles, vertical and lateral. Vertical, or logical, thinking involves movement from state to state through a series of justified steps. Lateral thinking uses information not for its own sake, but for its side effects. Vertical thinking is selective and lateral thinking is generative.

Humans are able to think laterally and machines cannot. Lateral thinking is associated with creativity and the ability of the mind to be self-organizing and self-maximizing. Edward deBono wrote that logical thinking is incomplete without lateral thinking.

> The mind is a patternmaking system. The mind creates patterns out of the environment and then recognizes and uses such patterns. . . . Because the sequence of arrival of information determines how it is to be arranged into a pattern, such patterns are always less than the best possible arrangement of information. In order to bring such patterns up to date and make better use of the contained information one needs a mechanism for insight restructuring. This can never be provided by logical thinking which works to relate accepted concepts not to restructure them.

Maximally efficient problem-solving uses both vertical and lateral thinking to address and resolve problem situations. While machine systems are adequate for certain tasks, there is still room for improvement in their capability for this kind of reasoning.

Philosophical thinking involves rhetorical query. It can encompass a pattern-matching attempt such as, "Is there a correspondence between the breadth of a tree's branches and the breadth of its root system? If so, is this correspondence consistent across species? What could I do with this information?" Philosophical thinking can also involve pondering one's existence. It is the realm of original thought and involves self-consciousness. At this time, philosophical thought is the sole domain of humans.

Machine intelligence shares many attributes with the human capability as we strive to improve human emulation. However, there are aspects of human thought that may be among the last to be incorporated into machines. Among these are human understanding, consciousness, language, and mind.

Understanding is composed of more than declarative and procedural knowledge; it also contains wisdom and intuition. Wisdom is judgment based on right and wrong and other factors. Intuition is a "feeling" for or against an action. Machine intelligence can possess limited understanding, but is many generations away, if ever, from attaining understanding on a human level.

Consciousness is an awareness composed of perception, thought, memory, emotion, and ego. Consciousness is a holistic state of being in which imagination and planning a future are mental activities. Machine intelligence, at least until the advent of biochips, does not possess an ability for consciousness.

Language is related to thought, and thought is related to images and image-based reasoning. Human language and thought has a malleability. Further, they can be formed, revised, and purged. Machine intelligence basically operates in a self-contained state. The events surrounding the machine have little impact on the mechanism itself. The knowledge that is resident in a machine is generally the total universe from which it can draw.

According to Minsky (1988), the mind is the process that transports the brain from state to state. However, minds are not things. Minds have none of the usual properties associated with descriptions such as: size, shape, color, or weight. In addition, minds remain beyond the senses of sound, touch, sight, smell, or taste. Minds may be the "wiring" of the brain that serves as the conduit between states. They can set goals and be proactive. Minds can daydream and brainstorm. In contrast, machine intelligence is reactive and cannot set high-level goals.

The collective input for both humans and computers is converted into symbols. The interactions of the symbols give rise to knowledge. This knowledge is the result of multiple perspectives in a focused area. The *Bhagavad Gita*, translated by Juan Mascaro (1962), states, "In the idea of work there is a knower, the knowing, and the known. When the idea is work there is the doer, the doing, and the done." The reference to work designates knowledge. The knower, the knowing, and the known denote knowledge, intelligence, and consciousness in an interrelation. Humans support all three legs of this triangle. Machines currently support only the knower leg that denotes knowledge. The other two legs are the future of AI.

Machine intelligence is represented by a variety of applications spawned from artificial intelligence. With the preceding as the basis for an understanding of human and machine capabilities and limitations, artificial intelligence can be explored.

WHAT IS ARTIFICIAL INTELLIGENCE?

Artificial Intelligence (AI) is the branch of computer science that focuses on the development of computer systems to simulate the processes of problem solving and duplicate the functions of the human brain. According to Elaine Rich (1983), "Artificial intelligence is the study of how to make computers do things at which, at the moment, people are better." This simple, but eloquent, statement captures the essence of the pursuit.

AI comprises hardware and software systems and techniques that attempt to emulate human mental and physical processes. The mental processes emulated include thinking, reasoning, decision making, data storage and retrieval, problem solving, and learning. The physical processes include human senses and motor skills. AI is also called machine intelligence. Artificial intelligence is a serious pursuit, but most of its components are currently limited to the status of research and theory-based laboratory goals.

Cognitive theories by gestaltists, Lewin, and others are the antecedents of AI. Their theories encompass the process of human perception and inference, or cognition. AI's concern is with the concepts and methods of symbolic inference by a computer, and the symbolic representation of the knowledge used in making inferences. Thus the objective of AI applications is to enable computers to process information, gain knowledge, and understand their environment.

At present, conventional computers process data and produce information. These conventional systems can transform, amplify, modify, and distribute this information. With the addition of AI, the essence of the computer changes to the processing of information and the production of knowledge in the form of recommendations. With sensory links and robotics, computer systems have the ability to gather data, analyze that data, and effect actions without human interaction. The task of the AI pioneer is to redefine the computer from a data processor into a knowledge processor. Therefore, an intelligent computer will be one that can collect, assemble, choose, understand, perceive, and know.

While research continues in the area of machine intelligence, several other branches of AI research have received attention and achieved varying levels of success. These areas include research into communicating with computers using human communication languages such as English, rather than a programming language such as C or Fortran; expert systems; speech recognition; computer vision; robotics; and other endeavors. Figure 3-1 provides an AI tree with its many branches.

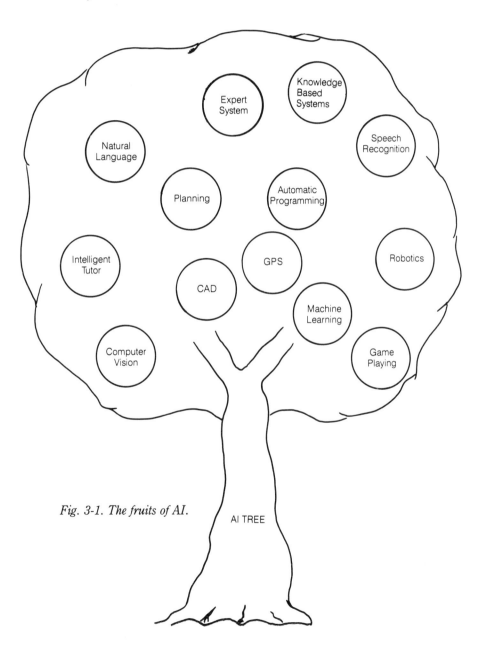

Fig. 3-1. The fruits of AI.

Expert Systems

An *expert system* is a narrow slice of computer intelligence and knowledge-based application. Its programs are designed to emulate human decision-making expertise in a particular domain. Expert systems belong to a group of systems known as knowledge-based systems. Knowledge-based systems contain the facts and procedures representing the rule of thumb (heuristic) decision-making processes of an expert. That collection is kept in a knowledge base that is separate from a control program. These systems are discussed in detail in the next chapter.

Expert systems are used to improve productivity, preserve knowledge, cultivate understanding and human performance, and help evolve information into knowledge. Most expert systems in current use were developed as in-house or custom systems. There are very few generic applications available as of this publication. However, the near future will offer a variety of off-the-shelf systems for both business and home use.

Expert system applications are made to supplement the supply of experts, not replace them. Because the knowledge bases of the current group of expert systems cannot automatically update themselves, the knowledge they contain is static. If conditions change or new information is required, the knowledge bases are manually revised.

Expert systems are, as of this writing, the most successful members of the AI family. There are many commercial applications of expert systems serving the medical industry, manufacturing, the computer industry, and many others.

Some of the reasons for expert systems are:

- There exists a decided lack of experts.
- Procedures are becoming complex and burdensome.
- There is little time to groom new experts.
- There is a growing flood of information.
- The competitive edge is difficult to maintain.
- Rapidly made judgments are becoming necessary.

Some of the reasons that expert systems will be pervasive in society are:

- Most of the contents of expert knowledge can be programmed into rules or examples that form the heuristic knowledge.
- The IF-THEN statements can be rank-ordered according to likelihood of occurrence.
- Most experts work on an iterative, branching basis.
- Most experts work within a narrow band of situations which can be replicated by a sophisticated knowledge-engineered expert system.

Natural Language Processing and Human Interfaces

Next to expert systems, *Natural Language Processing* (NLP) is the most commonly explored branch of AI. A natural language is a spoken or written human language. Natural language programs are designed to accept language input, interpret and process the input, and output natural language results.

Natural language processing is divided into two subbranches: understanding and output. Natural language understanding explores methods of computer comprehension of human language stimuli. Natural language output is the ability of a computer to communicate verbally with a human.

Computers, like people, speak many languages. At the base level, computers understand and process in machine language. This language is difficult to program. Thus higher-level languages were developed to ease programming requirements. The drawback still exists for communicating with a computer; a user still must speak the computer's language.

Natural language programs are composed of a parser, a knowledge base, and a control program. The parser receives the natural language input and decomposes it into the various elements of speech. Each word of the input is analyzed to determine the function of the word and how it relates to all of the other words. The output of the parser is a variation of a sentence diagram that graphs the words according to their meaning and purpose.

The knowledge base contains a dictionary that comprises the computer's range of understanding. The dictionary constitutes the universe of words that are in a specific domain. Any input that is not in the dictionary is likely to receive a "no data" interpretation.

The control program receives input and uses the knowledge base to try to understand it. The syntax, semantics, and context of the input are considered. If the program understands the input, it outputs a statement derived from that understanding. This statement can be directed at the user, a peripheral computer device, or a program.

Natural language programs are currently being used to provide an interface with other computer applications such as database management programs. At their best, database programs tend to require service requests to have a complex structure. The natural language interface receives language input and then converts it into the required form.

Natural language front-ends are used on spreadsheets, operating systems, and other programs. One interesting (but only partially successful) application of natural language processing is to translate input from English to another language. The future of natural language may offer an information processing capability in which mass data is scanned, interpreted, and abstracted.

Speech Recognition

Whereas natural language processing receives commands in text format, speech recognition allows a computer to respond to voice input. The goal of speech recognition research is to simplify the process of interactive communication between humans and computers.

Speech recognition is accomplished by use of an electronic process which converts analog voice input into signals that can be understood by the NLP system. A process involving search and pattern recognition, and pattern matching is used. The speech recognition ability is typically accomplished through hardware, although the use of software processes is gaining. By using a software approach, speech recognition and NLP can be combined.

Computer Vision

Another of the human senses that AI is attempting to emulate is vision. *Computer vision* is achieved by adding to the system a camera that collects analog input which is then converted into digital signals that the computer can interpret. The computer uses prestored pattern-matching techniques to recognize real life or photographic images. These pattern-matching techniques allow computers to identify key targeted features that escape the human eye.

Computer vision systems have many potential applications, such as the inspection and exploration of areas that are of high risk to humans. The goal of those involved in the development of computer vision is to provide computers with the same primary input sense that humans have—the sense of sight.

Robotics

In contrast to AI efforts to emulate human mental abilities, robotics is concerned with engineering attempts to duplicate human physical attributes. *Robots* are electromechanical machines that are programmable and perform manipulative tasks. These tasks range from delicate to heavy-duty. A typical robot is a manipulator arm used in manufacturing to weld, paint, insert screws, lift, and move parts.

There are two basic classifications for robots: dumb robots and smart robots. Dumb robots are mechanical devices that do functions in a repetitive manner and cannot adjust to their environment. These robots are preprogrammed by software or mechanical means. For example, a common household appliance like a dishwasher is a type of dumb robot. Robots of this nature are controlled by computers or other controller devices that send signals effecting a repetitive, tireless performance.

Intelligent robots have sensory input devices such as computer vision, pressure sensors, sight sensors, and other devices which feed environmental data to an AI computer control device. The intelligent robot can respond to changing conditions. The computer can accept input and alter its routines to adapt to new conditions.

Other AI Areas

While the major directions of AI work have been classified and briefly discussed, there are additional ones worth mentioning. One of these is computer learning. An outstanding attribute of human intelligence is the ability to learn. Researchers are investigating methods of enabling computers to learn from experience or from new data. Once this computer learning barrier is traversed, growth in the industry will be astronomical.

Machine Learning. Machine learning is a focus of current research in AI. Some of this is in an attempt to imitate sensory-type learning and to produce systems that can learn new constructs and rules and perform at higher levels. According to Bowerman and Glover (1988), most machine learning in AI systems can best be described as deduction, rather than the type of inductive process associated with learning new skills. As human learning is not yet understood, emulating this process at other than rudimentary levels is beyond the technology of today. More about machine learning is presented in chapter 4.

Computer-Assisted Instruction. Computer-Assisted Instruction (CAI) has been used in training and education for many years. This application brought the power of the computer to the aid of learning. With the advent of AI methods applied to instructional techniques, intelligent tutoring offered a way to provide computerized tutors.

An AI-equipped computer that can interact with a student can diagnose that student's learning level, compare that level to a given goal state, and prescribe a course of study to fill the gap. This course of study is tailored to the student's individual requirements and allows for periodic reevaluation of the study plan.

Automatic Programming. Automatic programming is a logical outcome of NLP. The ability to communicate with a computer in a natural language, tell the computer what is wanted, and have the computer output programming code is a worthy goal of AI. The development of a quality, bug-free, on time, on budget program that meets performance objectives is a program developer's dream.

Intelligent programming tools will help programmers in the development of new applications that are faster getting to the market and cheaper to produce. Consumers would greatly benefit from high-quality, low-cost software.

Computer-Aided Design. Computer-Aided Design (CAD) is associated with automatic programming. CAD is used with current levels of technology to design applications in the automotive industry, electronic industry, and others. The addition of AI will enable these systems to take advantage of the experience of experts to influence designs. The problem-solving abilities of AI-CAD can help designers and developers to engineer superior designs.

Planning. Planning, especially business plans and decisions, can have positive and negative impacts on the lives and livelihoods of many people. The aid of AI systems as powerful consultants can help those in decision-making roles. While the systems may not carry the final word, they can help in a big picture approach and simulate many potential ''what if'' scenarios.

General Problem Solving. General Problem Solving (GPS) systems are designed to solve classes of problems expressed in a formal language. These problems are beyond the realm of algorithmic computer processes. GPS systems are custom-made to fit a specific application such as planning power facilities.

Game Playing. Game playing and puzzle solving were among the first applications of AI. The early researchers felt that producing computer programs that had the ability to play games was an excellent way to demonstrate an emulation of human intelligence. These games and puzzle solvers included chess, checkers, tic-tac-toe, backgammon, and Rubik's cube. While the systems were interesting, they were of little use.

Most programs are designed to improve performance and productivity. Game-playing programs did, however, help to illustrate the limitations of hardware and software technology. Memory size imposed a limit on search strategies, and speed on game rules, strategies, and procedures. Because of these limits, many human chess experts can still outplay a computer. This should change in the next decade through the advent of parallel processing and improved search strategies.

The various areas of artificial intelligence are designed and developed, not discovered. Each probe into another human mental or physical emulation is debated and theoretically explored before commitment of the extensive funds required for development.

MACHINE PROBLEM SOLVING

Given that humans solve problems using various strategies, it is easy to compare and contrast problem-solving techniques for machines. The knowledge engineer is familiar with the problem-solving abilities and limitations of machines. These have impacts on the options for knowledge representation, and affect how speed and machine efficiency will be achieved.

Computers, like humans, require search strategies to solve problems. These strategies involve matching search techniques with application types. The objective is to find an expedient path through the knowledge base to reach a solution. Machine problem solving is composed of a collection of search methods, control strategies, and reasoning techniques.

Conceptually, machines deal with three basic elements in searching their knowledge bases in order to reach solutions. These elements are problem states, goal states, and operators. The initial state of the problem is supplied by the user through the user interface. The initial goals are predetermined and stored in the knowledge base as results. (See FIG. 3-2.)

Problem State

1	2	3
4	5	6
7	8	

Operators

Moves required
to transform
the problem state
to the goal state

Goal State

8	7	6
5	4	3
2	1	

Fig. 3-2. State space representation.

Operators are the procedures used by a system to move from one state to another within the space. These operators move the problem from one state to another state which (one hopes) more closely matches the goal. The operators follow the master control strategy set by the system's inference engine. An operator can be as simple as an algorithm, or as complex as a sophisticated search technique.

Search Tree

A *search tree* is a tree whose nodes represent possible states for the expert system, and whose arcs correspond to operators that change the system from one state to another. The system's initial state is the root of the tree, and the leaves represent final states for the system. As described in the previous section, the system's control program starts at the root and tries to find a path through the tree (i.e., a sequence of states) that will reach a leaf corresponding to a (or the) desired state or goal. Often it attempts to find the path that is optimal by some criterion like length or tree search time.

Sometimes the nodes connected to a given node are referred to as its parents, ancestors, and children. All of these tree and genealogical terms have been developed to create a conceptual framework representing an existing model. Another attribute of the search tree is the notion of levels. The root node(s) is at level 0; the levels of the descendants start at 1 and increase to the deepest level. An upper level node is called a predecessor of the nodes that lie below it.

In many cases (including chess), the search tree is much too large to exist in its totality anywhere in the computer at any one time. When this is true, the system must generate whatever part of the search tree it needs for its immediate concern. In the case of chess, after the first pair of moves is made, the system need worry about only the possible successor states to the opponent's move—it doesn't have to concern itself with all the positions that could have resulted if the first moves had been different. In order for the developer to understand what is going on, however, it is often advantageous to construct selected nodes and chart their relationships.

Figure 3-3 shows an infinitesimal piece of a search tree for a chess-playing program. The root represents the beginning state of the board, the operators are the legal moves, and the nodes at the other levels in the tree represent the possible board positions after a move by one of the players. (If you're not familiar with chess, don't worry—the labels on the arcs are just the conventional notation for specifying a move.) The control program, during its turn to play, tries to find a move that will improve its situation. It takes into account both the current state of the board and its opponent's probable reactions to its moves (and its responses to those reactions, and its opponent's . . .!). If the program plays first, the system will move from the root state to one of those on the next level; the human opponent then will make a move that will take the system to a third-level state, and so on.

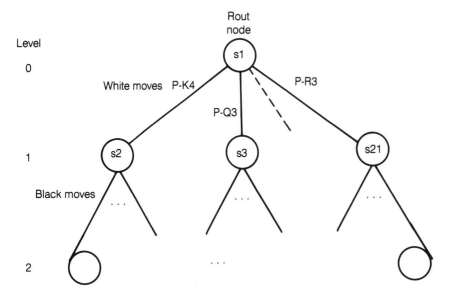

Fig. 3-3. Search tree.

Search Methods

Search is the process of exploring the set of possible solutions within a knowledge base to resolve a problem. This process is a trial-and-error approach to matching a solution to a given problem.

Machine problem solvers such as expert systems, use a control program called an *inference engine* to decide how and in what sequence the knowledge base is searched. The inference engine controls and executes the reasoning strategies used by expert systems. The search techniques are contained within the inference engine of the selected language or tool. The KE is aware of the options for the match between the search techniques and knowledge representations. The field of AI is constantly seeking new and better search techniques.

There are two basic methods for searching *state space* representation of the knowledge base. These methods are blind search and heuristic search. In either case, the system's objective is to find a solution, or at least a node that seems closer to a solution. Blind search can be used in those cases in which the system is unable to determine how close it is to a solution (traversing a maze, for example), and therefore must search the state space according to some pattern that potentially passes through every node, and therefore will certainly bring it to a solution eventually. If there is a way of evaluating the "quality" of the various exits from a node, heuristic methods can be used. Blind search consists of exhaustive, breadth-first, and depth-search models. According to Wolfgram, Dear, and Galbraith (1987), heuristic search methods consist of hill-climbing, best-first, branch-and-bound, the A* Algorithm, and generate-and-test.

Blind Search. A blind search is a brute force method that searches every node of the tree in an effort to find a solution. The typical blind search starts with the root node and then systematically explores the entire tree until a solution is found.

Exhaustive Search. The exhaustive-search technique involves the examination of the first state and its associated paths. If this search does not find a solution, successive paths are generated in an arbitrary fashion, and searched. In problems that offer many state alternatives, a phenomenal number of new states are generated and many alternatives are considered. This search technique is conducted in the memory of the computer. Each time a potential match or intermediate state is considered, the volume in memory grows.

In large state searches, the computer can run out of memory. Should a computer's memory not be exhausted, large state searches can take a considerable amount of time. Even with today's personal computers working at 20 to 33 megahertz, unacceptable delays may occur. One solution to this problem is faster computers or multiple processors. Another solution is methods that limit the search. It might be that the KE does not find an exact fit, but an approximate one.

These drastic increases in numbers are called "combinatorial explosions" and can be calculated mathematically. Suppose that each node in the search tree has B branches to other nodes and that there are L levels in the structure. The total number of nodes in the search space is

$$N = \frac{B^L - 1}{B - 1}$$

Suppose that there are three branches and three levels. This combination results in a total of 13 nodes. Should this search tree be expanded to 10 branches that reach 9 levels, the result is approximately 100 million.

Consider that some problems can expand to an extent that would make a blind search unacceptable. As a result, there are several techniques to limit the possibilities. Figure 3-4 shows an abstract search tree which will be used for examples.

Breadth-First. A breadth-first search begins at the root node and continues across the nodes at each level before moving to the next lower level. It stops when it finds a solution or gives up. A breadth-first search will find the shortest path between the given initial state and the goal state.

The computer is not intelligent, and does not know where best to begin conducting the search. For this reason, the breadth-first search usually begins at the root node and moves across from left to right. Figure 3-5 illustrates a breadth-first search.

The breadth-first search explores all of the steps at a given level before moving to the subsequent level. A breadth-first search explores a problem in a general manner.

Depth-First. A depth-first search begins at the root node and continues down through successive levels of the left-most branch. When it gets to a leaf, it backs up to the last previous node where there is an unexplored path, and takes it. This search process continues until a solution is reached or the search reaches a dead end and is forced to backtrack.

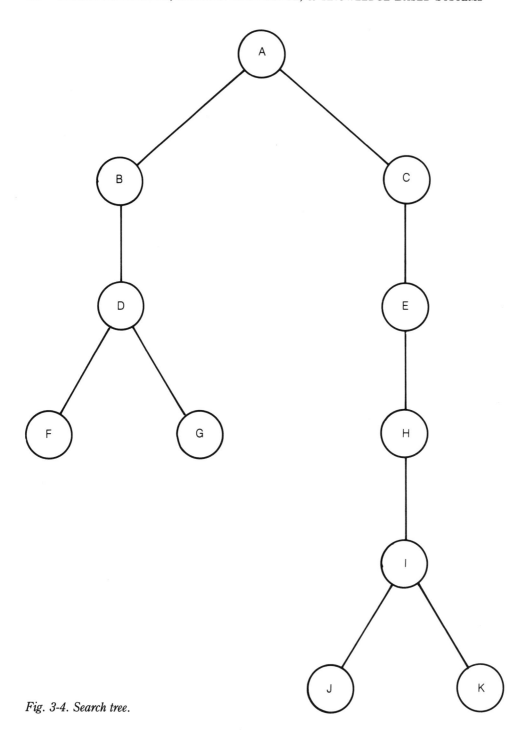

Fig. 3-4. Search tree.

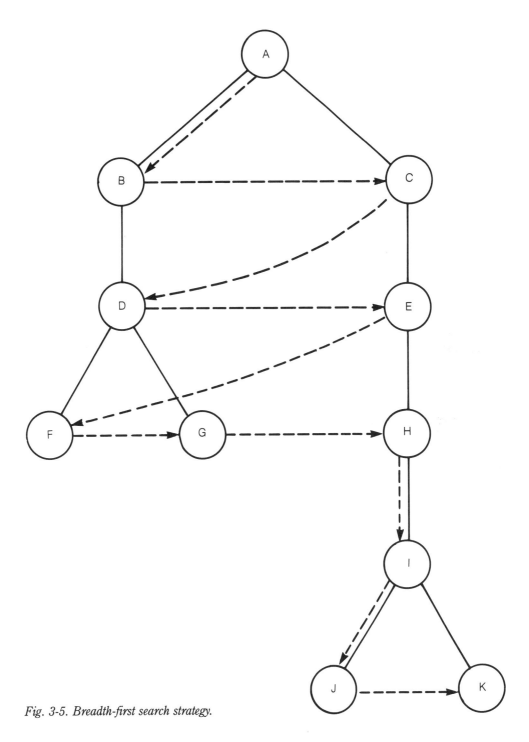

Fig. 3-5. Breadth-first search strategy.

The depth-first search will eventually reach a conclusion, but the search can be time consuming and even run the computer out of memory. In an effort to prevent this, some depth-first systems have a depth limitation established. This depth limitation establishes a maximum depth before it is forced to backtrack. Using a system with a depth qualification is faster, but the appropriate depth setting is experimental. Trial and error by the KE is required to establish a usable search cut-off level.

Thus, the depth-first search focuses on the details of the problem. If an employee was leaving as the result of a money problem, the system would move down through nine levels to support the new pay rate. Figure 3-6 illustrates a depth-first search.

Heuristic Search. None of the previous search techniques discussed offers an intelligent search method, so they are called blind-search techniques. If the search space is limited, very fast computers are used, or if the information is not time-critical, blind searches are adequate. For more complex situations, a more sophisticated search approach is needed which limits the search area.

One technique to reduce the size of the search tree is to prune the nonvital nodes. Even though some viable solutions may exist, they may not be appropriate. For example, when the Coast Guard searches for a lost ship at sea, every square mile of the ocean is not searched. Tides, currents, weather, and other factors are used to prune the possibilities. The term for this pruning of the search tree is a *heuristic search*. The heuristic techniques all require that the system be able to evaluate how "good" a given node or path is.

Heuristic-search strategies are presented with the intention of providing an overview of the techniques. There are texts available that review these search strategies in depth. If the reader is interested in more information, Firebaugh (1988) and Winston (1984) are excellent references.

Heuristic searches focus on the portions of the tree that are likely to yield results. The function of the heuristic is to eliminate the low probabilities and focus on accelerating the search. There are two classifications of heuristic techniques: general purpose heuristic rules and domain-specific heuristic rules.

A typical general purpose technique is a depth-bound set that limits the search down the tree and forces backtracking. Domain-specific heuristic rules are created to apply to a specific application. One type of domain-specific search uses special rules called metarules that establish methods for how the knowledge rules can be used. Either or both heuristic techniques can be used to limit the search depending upon the problem. The objective of using a heuristic-search technique is to provide knowledge that reduces combinatorial factors and search time.

Note that heuristic techniques are not 100 percent accurate or consistent. Neither are they foolproof nor do they guarantee solutions. The techniques are designed to provide an intelligent approach to prune the search space and improve the odds over the use of blind search techniques.

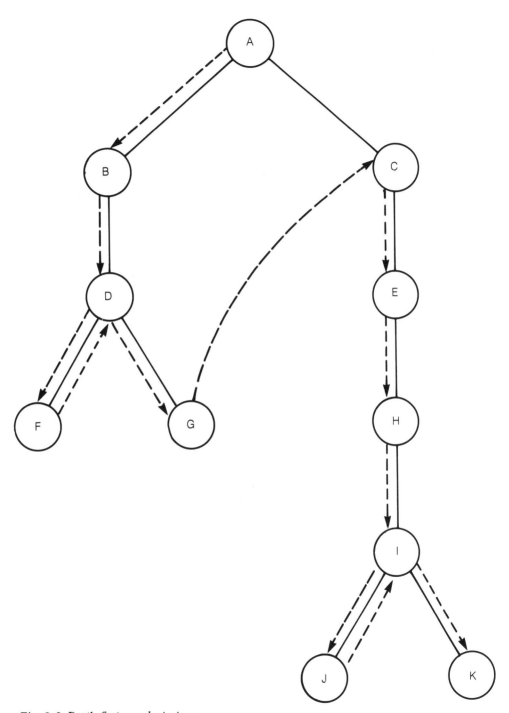

Fig. 3-6. Depth-first search strategy.

Hill-Climbing. Hill-climbing is similar to depth-first techniques with one major difference. Among the current node's successors, that one is chosen whose estimated distance to the goal is the smallest.

Best-First. Best-first searching uses heuristic rules to determine the best path to take as it moves through the knowledge base nodes. The system's selection of the next state is the best open node whatever its location, i.e., it does not have to be a successor of the current node. A best-first search is analogous to crossing a stream by locating and leaping onto rocks that make progress across that stream.

Branch-and-Bound. The branch-and-bound search evaluates all remaining uncompleted paths from the present location. More paths are generated after traveling from one state level to the next. This branch-and-bound procedure is repeated and all paths are reevaluated. The search is terminated when the shortest incomplete path is longer than the shortest complete path.

A* Algorithm. The A* algorithm adds an estimate of the distance to the goal from the current node and the cost of getting to the current node. The use of proximity estimation replaces the shortest path evaluation. A* uses pruning techniques when distances between states are too great. The use of different estimation functions yields a whole family of A* algorithms.

Generate-and-Test. Wolfgram, Dear, and Galbraith (1987) describe generate-and-test or hypothesize-and-test as a procedure composed of 5 steps:

1. Add a specification criterion (e.g., a known symptom).
2. Try a path that satisfies the specification.
3. Determine whether the path is plausible; "prune" that path if it is not plausible.
4. Move to the next path.
5. When complete, check to see if all specifications have been mentioned. If not, add the next specification criterion and reiterate the above steps by returning to Step 1. If all specifications have been resolved, the process is complete.

Search Strategies for Control

In a rule-based system, another kind of search must be carried out to choose the next rule to be tried. There are four basic control strategies: forward chaining, backward chaining, means-end, and least-commitment. Forward chaining is effective for planning and design-based applications. Backward chaining is effective for diagnostic and control-based applications. Means-end strategies are effective for synthesis activities. Least-commitment strategies are effective for large knowledge bases.

Forward Chaining. Forward chaining is also called *forward reasoning.* Forward chaining is a way to emulate human deductive or data-driven reasoning. The data provided by the user enables the search to begin at an appropriate entry point. A classic problem for which forward chaining is appropriate is de-

The Nature of Machine Knowledge   *91*

termining the correct configuration for a computer system, given a customer order. Typical (oversimplified) rules in such an application are:

IF there is a printer
THEN make sure there is a printer controller for it

IF there is a remote terminal
THEN make sure there is a modem for it

IF there is a printer controller
THEN add 87 watts to the power requirement

IF TRUE
THEN number of power supplies = power required/1200

The system starts with a known fact like "There is a printer" and looks to see if there is a rule with this as the IF condition. If there is, it carries out the THEN clause, and so in this case adds the fact "There is a printer controller" if that is not already in the knowledge base. It then looks for another rule in which the IF condition is true, and repeats the process until there are no more rules whose IF conditions are true. (In this application, that will happen when the entire computer configuration has been generated.) Of course there must be special provisions to avoid infinite loops—after you have added the fact about the printer controller once, you don't want to repeat that action unless a rule somewhere else adds another printer.

Rules that may be available to the system, but do not apply, are eliminated from consideration by the system. This method of reasoning is known as fact-driven or data-directed reasoning.

Forward chaining is generally associated with knowledge bases that have large numbers of possible solutions. Further, these systems are frequently used when data is the starting point for solving a problem. Examples of applications that are associated with forward chaining are planning, designing, and forecasting.

The efficiency of forward search is dependent on the KE's efforts to both represent the knowledge appropriately, and provide a user interface that enables the user and the system to focus on the problem.

Backward Search. Backward search is also called *backward reasoning* or *backward chaining*. The backward search is a way to emulate human inductive reasoning or goal-directed reasoning. Backward search starts with the goal node and works backward toward initial states. The strategy of backward search is for the user to assume a particular event outcome and search for evidence that supports the assumption.

The user is charged with selecting one of several possible goal nodes and attempts to reach an appropriate match to validate the assumption. By providing a backward-chaining option, fewer nodes may require searching. This type of system employs either a depth-first or breadth-first strategy. Should the initial assumption prove false, the system search continues by selecting another goal and attempting to locate a pattern match that supports the selection.

A backward-chaining system starts with the goal to be proven and works its way back through the rules to establish the required facts. The assumption is that the answer or object is correct and it is to be supported by gathering rules and testing them along the way.

For example, suppose our application is car repair, a parallel classic illustration of backward-chaining systems. The rule base has such contents as:

IF the battery is dead
THEN no voltage reaches the coil

IF the battery is dead
THEN the lights will not light

IF no voltage reaches the spark plugs
THEN the engine will not start

IF the distributor rotor is missing
THEN no voltage reaches the spark plugs

IF no voltage reaches the coil
THEN no voltage reaches the distributor

IF no voltage reaches the distributor
THEN no voltage reaches the spark plugs

The system starts with the fact that the car will not start, and searches for a rule in which this is the conclusion. When it finds one, it attempts to verify that rule's IF clause by looking for the condition as a given fact. If that strategy fails, it may look for the IF condition as a conclusion and continue the process (corresponding to depth-first search), or it may ask the user if the IF condition is known to be true. On the other hand, if the system uses a breadth-first strategy, this line of attack will be temporarily dropped and another appropriate rule sought. This cycle continues until the system has either constructed a chain of reasoning from some known or discovered fact (e.g., "The distributor rotor is missing") to the goal ("The car will not start"), or has run out of possibilities.

Backward chaining is generally associated with diagnostic applications and knowledge bases with a limited number of rules. Backward chaining is also called hypothesis-driven or goal-directed reasoning. This chaining strategy is often associated with applications such as diagnosing, controlling, and monitoring.

The KE selects or participates in the selection of the best search strategy, as there are direct impacts on the form of knowledge representation. The basic consideration is this: if there are more possible outcomes than initial states, backward chaining may provide the fastest search, because the shortest path is taken by the control portion of the program. Another aspect of considering a backward-search strategy is the target user group. If the users have little knowledge, a backward-search organization may prove futile.

Forward reasoning is best used when there are more initial states than goal states. As each path leads to a goal, a particular attribute may clue the user. This results in a very quick initial to goal state transition. Whether a backward or forward technique is used, the drivers are the problem to be solved and the target user group.

Bidirectional. The current trend is for the incorporation of a combination of forward- and backward-chaining opportunities within a system. The control program begins at one end and moves either forward or backward. As the succeeding state or node is reached, a heuristic algorithm provides direction to the next state. This technique provides a fast path for users who are familiar with the content and options for other users. This bidirectional approach can prove effective in many problem and user situations.

Means-End. Means-end analysis is simultaneous forward and backward chaining. The control program begins at both ends and converges at the goal state. Means-end is designed as an iterative process that reduces the difference between the current state and the goal state until the difference has been eliminated.

Least Commitment. A problem, found particularly in planning applications, arises when an action seems to be desirable at one time but turns out to have been counterproductive, e.g., trying out the ceiling paint on the step of the ladder. Least commitment is an information-driven strategy that tries to avoid these situations by postponing decisions as long as possible. To do this, the system needs to know when sufficient information is present to make a decision, when to await more information, and how to combine progress to date with previous incomplete attempts.

Wolfgram, Dear, and Galbraith (1987) report that the system will deadlock if partially solved problems are waiting for more information, thus forcing the system into a guess. The guess may lead the system into conflict where a solution can never be reached. The least-commitment strategy is stalemated when there are many options and no compelling reasons for choices, as when there is an equal probability weighing on all paths.

Additional Reasoning Techniques

There are less-used techniques that provide intelligent problem-solving strategies. Most knowledge-based systems are built around reliable data sets with static data relationships. This model is the paradigm of knowledge-based systems. Exceptions to this paradigm are handled through a series of techniques including disjunctive facts, constraints, abstraction, blackboarding, and plausible reasoning.

Disjunctive facts are ''third cousin'' relationships between apparently unconnected facts. The relationship may be a common-sense or other intangible factor known by the expert. Inclusion of disjunctive facts into a knowledge base can benefit search time by allowing state changes which would not normally occur.

Constraints are delimiters among the search spaces. These constraints are generally in the form of limiting the number of paths in selected areas. Constraints can be shifted or lifted if no solution is reached.

Abstraction facilitates rapid goal state attainment by leaving out unnecessary details, e.g., planning a cross-country trip by using a sketch of the interstates rather than a collection of street maps.

Blackboarding maintains the problem-solving knowledge in a global knowledge base shared by independent knowledge processes which cause changes in the blackboard contents.

Plausible reasoning is also called guessing. It occurs when knowledge is incomplete or the system exhausts other problem-solving techniques. This reasoning technique is also used for rapid search. The system uses this technique by randomly selecting a path or by selecting a path based on a heuristic algorithm.

Wolfgram, Dear, and Galbraith (1987) attempted to construct a model for selection of data representation, search strategy, or line of reasoning. For each technique, such as exhaustive search, this model specifies the characteristic(s) of applications suited to the use of that technique:

Exhaustive Search	Knowledge base is static Reliable knowledge
Certainty Factor	Unreliable knowledge
Fuzzy logic	Unclear knowledge
Generate-and-test	Large, factorable solution space
Abstraction	Large, factorable solution space Noneffective pruning rules for generate-and-test
Top-down Refinement	Large, factorable solution space Noneffective pruning rules for generate-and-test Variable amount of detail per abstraction level Variable amount of data per abstraction level
Guessing	Incomplete knowledge Large, factorable solution space Noneffective pruning rules
Disjunctive facts	No clear relationships for reasoning
Constraints	No clear relationships for reasoning
Blackboarding	Several independent knowledge processes

THE COMPUTER "THINKING" PROCESS

Although there can be a very technical discussion of the hardware involved in today's computers, this discussion will be kept at a conceptual level. Humans are not "wired" like computers, and computers do not possess the synaptic connections of people . . . as of this writing. Therefore, it will be easier to stay at a conceptual level. Because it is the most visible area in AI, expert systems are the best example for discussing computer "thinking."

Earlier discussions of expert systems provided general background information about these systems. This discussion goes into greater detail. Given that artificial intelligence is embodied in a computer system that can simulate human reasoning and intelligence, expert systems are one application of artificial intelligence.

Expert systems simulate the reasoning of a human expert in a particular subject. The functioning of expert systems relies upon large bodies of knowledge. They have a knowledge base stored independent of a control program. As a result, expert systems are knowledge-based systems. Their general applications are in the service of a human expert, or instead of one. As a result, expert systems are also called intelligent assistants.

Expert systems contain the heuristic problem-solving knowledge of one or more experts. They follow the same problem-solving strategies as most experts and include various types of knowledge: formally trained, experiential, judgmental, and heuristic.

The evolving technology of expert systems has resulted in a variety of approaches and configurations. As a result, there is no system standard that governs components, developer screens, or other developmental or user concerns. However, most expert systems share three common components: a knowledge base, a control program, and a conjecture component. In addition to the three common components, expert systems have two additional aspects: the hardware platform and the software environment. Figure 3-7 illustrates the components of a typical expert system.

Knowledge Base

The knowledge base is the key support element to the expert system. The worth and effectiveness of an expert system are largely determined by its knowledge base. This knowledge base embodies the problem-solving identification and solution strategies of those who are recognized as superior in their field. These problem-solving strategies are represented by heuristic rules. The domain expert and a knowledge engineer are able to transfer into those rules the facts and actions that the expert uses to solve problems.

The facts possessed by an expert are collectively called declarative knowledge. The actions constitute the procedural knowledge. Together, the declarative and procedural statements are the codified representation of the expert's skills, experience, education, and training.

The knowledge engineer can represent the domain knowledge using many knowledge representation alternatives. These alternatives include production rules, semantic networks, frames, and other forms of knowledge representation. For example, the combination of declarative and procedural knowledge forms rules. A completed knowledge base can contain from a few to several thousand rules.

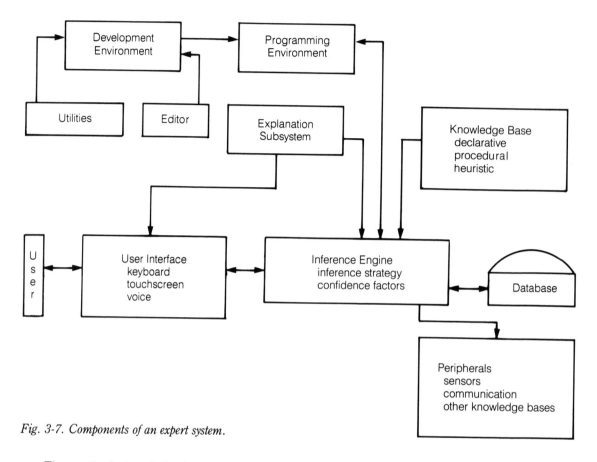

Fig. 3-7. Components of an expert system.

The worth of a knowledge base, like the worth of a book, lies in the quality of the contents, not the quantity. Like any software endeavor, one programmer can say in one line what another programmer says in several lines. The completed knowledge base is accessed by an inferencing program. The knowledge base is the single largest concern for the knowledge engineer. In addition, the knowledge base is not static. The knowledge base will require attention for modifications and enhancements as conditions change in the problem domain. In the future, the maintenance requirements of expert systems will change with the advent of self-learning systems.

Control Program

The control program, also called an *inference engine*, is the reasoning component of the conceptual group mentioned earlier. Once the knowledge base is in place, a rich resource exists. However, the resource is of little value without a program to access the knowledge. Once the knowledge is accessed, it is channeled to problem-solving. This program is the algorithm that controls the reasoning process. It has many names including inference engine, control program, and rule interpreter.

The control program directs the search through the knowledge base for a particular needed fact or rule, or to decide which rule should be tried next. The search techniques might eliminate alternatives or search for a match. They include forward and backward chaining, heuristic search, breadth-first, and depth-first methods, or a combination of these search techniques. The pattern-match function of the program effects the search. After one cycle of the reasoning process is complete, the system might generate an option or solution for the user, or if there is more than one plausible one, a ranked list.

The control program can interact with the user at the beginning of a session, or when a fact or rule is needed and is not found in the knowledge base. The control program directs the expert system by determining which rules are used, assessing those rules, executing them, and determining the display options. This entire process is conducted by the expert system in a manner that is transparent to the user.

Conjecture Component

The third of the conceptual components of an expert system is the conjecture component. The conjecture component in many expert systems has three parts: the user interface, a database, and an explanation subsystem.

User Interface. The user interface is responsible for interactions with the user. These interactions are accomplished through a variety of input devices such as keyboards, mice, and touchscreens. The input devices activate selections in displays of graphics icons, windows, and forms. Outputs to the user include explanations, displays of the rules, on-line helps, graphic representation of critical components, solutions, and traces. Through the user interface, the user must be able to communicate the problem, provide required and requested information, and interpret the system's advice.

Questions for users are often presented in selection menus in which the user is asked a multiple-choice question. Some input requirements are best satisfied by a fill-in form, on which the user inputs multiple data values at one time. Outputs from the system are generally sent to a monitor. However, some systems are linked to control programs which activate outside devices including valves, switches, warning devices, computer peripherals, and robots.

In addition, an external interface may be present to conduct a data exchange with other sources. These sources include: databases, spreadsheets, other programs, other computers, and measuring instruments and sensors. The data calls and exchanges can be automatic or invoked by the user.

Database. Expert systems have auxiliary components, one of which is the database. The system's database is its working memory similar to a human's short-term memory. This database tracks and stores inputs, internal processing, and outputs during a session and stores them in a "notepad" memory area. Sometimes this database is called a global database, fact base, or working store.

The database receives the initial problem description which the system is to solve. This information is received from user interaction with, for example, a system-presented menu. The initial input starts the pattern-match pruning algorithms. The control program matches the information in the database against the rules in the knowledge base. The database content is altered as the match procedure progresses.

The database in the expert system is different from a database known to data processing. Expert system databases are a temporary storage that is purged at the end of a session. A data processing database is designed as a long-term storage facility for repeated access.

Explanation Subsystem. Expert systems are designed to present options to users so that they can arrive at reasonable solutions as rapidly as possible. Sometimes the options presented to the user are unclear. At other times, a user may question why a particular question is asked. At still other times, a conclusion can be questioned by a user.

As a result, knowledge engineers provide explanation options that are built into the system. The system preserves an audit trail that can provide interim "why" reasoning for the user. Thus, the system can also act as a training aid. Additionally, the system can show the rules by which a conclusion was reached.

Some systems provide an ability for the user to replay the session so that the system's reasoning chain is displayed. In this manner, the advice is supported and justified for user acceptance or education. Another value in this is that the system acts as a colleague. However, note that the use of an explanation subsystem is a design issue. There may be cases in which the result is policy, and management does not care to justify the conclusions, or the recommended action takes precedence over education.

If an explanation subsystem is constructed, care should be taken to use a language level suitable to that of the users. When a system has a variety of users that perform at different levels, a good choice is to use a hypertext-based explanation subsystem. This facility enables the user to probe deeper for an understanding, without the burden of receiving more information than is necessary.

Hardware

The foundation of an expert system rests with the hardware and software platforms. The hardware provides the physical storage and speed of operation of the system. These issues of storage, speed, and other characteristics are addressed in the early stages of a development effort. Another fundamental decision is the form of hardware processing, viz. conventional computing or symbolic processing. Symbolic processing hardware uses an AI language such as LISP.

Developers consider the possibilities for peripheral devices and upgrading the hardware platform. Hardware can include mainframe computers, workstations, and personal computers. It also includes cables, modems, printers, and other input and output devices.

Software

Software considerations go beyond selecting a programming language or shell. The issues include operating environments such as DOS and versions of

DOS, OS/2, or UNIX. The selection of software includes considerations of compatibility with existing software and hardware.

CLASSIFICATION OF EXPERT SYSTEMS

Whenever a group of "things" is discussed, it is easier to discuss and think about them if a method to discriminate among "things" is established. In an attempt to classify expert systems for discussion purposes, schemas have been devised that are based on the number of rules.

These classification systems suggest that there are three basic classes of expert systems: small, medium, and large. A small system has been defined as one that uses a knowledge base comprising fewer than 500 rules. A medium system consists of up to 10,000 rules, and a large system has in excess of 10,000 rules.

The technology of expert systems has evolved to the point at which these early lines of separation blur. Most available systems are capable of chaining together thousands of rules, have a knowledge base of over one megabyte, and can perform very similar functions. There are many new tools on the market that have communication links with mainframe computers, contain new capabilities, offer a variety of knowledge representations, and provide search options. Some of the smaller systems are not properly described by the existing rule size classification. Highly complex systems can be used to produce applications with only two to three hundred rules, provide access to multiple users, and retrieve data by way of a satellite link. A system of this nature should not be called small. As a result, a rethinking of expert-system classification is in order.

Human professionals are classified in terms of their level of performance, ranging from novice to expert. The proposed schema is based on function and performance rather than rule quantity. Each level of the system provides the functionality of its preceding level or levels.

Level 0

The base-level system is self-contained. This system makes no calls outside its knowledge base, but can display explanations. A Level 0 system has restricted reasoning methods such as backward chaining, forward chaining, inductive reasoning, a rule-based method, or example-based reasoning.

Any Level 0 system has an automatic display of the rules it has used. In addition, a Level 0 system has global attributes including the ability to produce reports, an ability to offer control over user interface colors and screen locations, and the provision of window size and placement options. These systems are able to print their rules and simple reports. Systems that do not meet these criteria are probably not suitable for commercial application.

Level 1

Level 1 systems can make use of external program calls. These systems are used for a wide variety of popular applications such as intelligent databases, diagnostic systems, and other applications that can effect a two-way flow of communication. These systems have a free exchange of data between the user and peripherals.

In addition, Level 1 systems have the following options: forward- and backward-chaining selection, math ability, control over peripherals, data interface options, an explanation subsystem that describes the line of reasoning upon request, inference cut-off, window definition, import of text, learner control, line positioning options, and user interface control.

Level 2

Level 2 systems can serve as closed-loop or modified closed-loop systems. They are typically used to perform such functions as diagnosis and prescription, and then to effect the prescription through communication links. For example, a system could be located in a manufacturing facility. This system would be designed to monitor a control process and detect out-of-range limits through sensors. Once an out-of-range situation is detected, the system sends messages that modify operations by shutting valves, altering a flow, etc.

In addition, Level 2 systems have the following options: user interface control (control over field placement), frames, incorporation of sophisticated graphic displays into the user interface, dynamic math calculation and recalculation, hypertext explanation subsystems, control over all output formats, import/export of portions of the knowledge base such as a major factor and its attributes to a single frame, and the ability to send user-generated inputs such as window descriptions or call codes to a file.

Level 3

Level 3 systems offer higher-level functioning across a variety of applications. In addition, these systems operate in a variety of operating systems and environments such as OS/2 or UNIX, and they can execute on mainframes or PCs. The developer has control over the type of output code generated such as LISP, Prolog, C, or Pascal. Level 3 system developers also have control over search selection: hierarchical search, depth-first, breadth-first, etc. Level 3 systems are found in applications that typically involve over six person-years to develop.

Level 4

A Level 4 system is a system that can automatically add to and thereafter alter its knowledge base. This is a system that can learn. Level 4 systems are found in research labs and are not available for commercial use at this time.

WHY PURSUE INTELLIGENT MACHINES?

The difficulty that users of data and processors of information face is a general lack of experts to meet the demand for someone to synthesize information for focused needs. The synthesized information—knowledge—is the missing piece in many businesses, educational institutions, and government agencies.

Intelligent machines are one answer to the knowledge shortage. One class of intelligent machines is composed of knowledge-based systems. While the next chapter explains these systems as a whole, this discussion will continue with the most visible of the knowledge-based systems, called expert systems. We will build on the information about expert systems presented earlier.

Expert-system applications are able to synthesize data using some of the same kind of reasoning that underlies the experts' methods, thereby placing a tool in the hands of the less experienced. Expert systems are constructed using languages such as C, LISP, and Pascal. Expert systems are also produced by shells. Shells are computer software systems that provide a knowledge representation mechanism, an inference engine to process the represented knowledge, and a user interface.

The expert-system languages and shells, containing synthesized information in a machine knowledge base, offer the same kind of reasoning experts use to arrive at decisions through their human knowledge base. Users of these shells interpret data through their analytic criteria and interact with the expert system to synthesize the information for prescriptive actions. The expert systems consult various knowledge bases as a result of user input. Thus, the expert system becomes the conduit for knowledge applications in focused areas. Because expert systems solve problems by using the reasoning patterns of human experts, these systems can be said to use human thought processes to reach their solutions.

Expert systems are constructed using several strategies that will be discussed in more detail in the next chapter. However, the most common systems use the same rules and examples as human experts use to solve problems. Expert systems also use problem-solving strategies of backward and forward chaining as well as inductive and deductive reasoning. These systems often use shells that are either rule-based or example-based.

Rule-based Systems

Rule-based systems are also called *production systems*. These systems represent the knowledge of an expert through a series of rules. These rules include IF-THEN and other types of rules. These rule sets will be discussed in depth later in the book.

In general, rule-based systems center on IF conditions and THEN action statements. A successive group of IF-THEN rules used to reach a conclusion are called an *inference chain*. The system may move from condition to condition by interfacing with the user. Thus, the processing in a rule-based system can react to a changing environment.

Rule-based systems are very effective for knowledge that can be represented in a rule format. Knowledge that can be coded in a rule format can be declarative or procedural, with associated certainty factors.

Induction Systems

Example-based systems are also known as *induction systems*. These systems generate rules or conclusions from examples of past cases or histories from the knowledge base. Induction systems can develop a knowledge base from information sources that typically exist in many business organizations. These information sources include databases, spreadsheets, billing, and other records. Example-based shells generate rules from the example data with the assumption that they are independent rather than interdependent. Thus, an inference can be reached based upon a limited example set.

The risk for the user is that situations may interact. For example, if a diagnostic system concludes that the reading on a temperature valve requires shut down and stops the operation, the resultant heat generation may do more damage to the system. Knowledge engineers and domain experts must consider every reasonable alternative and consequence.

As just described, example-based systems place users at risk. However, when rules are not known, example-based systems are the best choice. For instance, systems dealing with prediction or judgment might be best developed in an example-based environment. An example-based system can take advantage of the heuristic knowledge implied when an expert gives processes and procedures with many caveats.

Integrated systems use a variety of techniques. These systems can move the user through the interaction with backward and forward chaining, deductive and inductive approaches.

Expert Systems and Reasoning

Expert systems function by emulating two basic reasoning approaches listed earlier under human reasoning: deductive reasoning and inductive reasoning. While both reasoning approaches function within the framework of cognitive theory, they differ in approach. One of these systems represents the knowledge base as rules and evaluates in a deductive sense. The other represents the knowledge base as examples and evaluates in an inductive sense.

In general, the *deduction-based system* uses rules to reach decisions. Deductive systems reason from general assumptions to a specific conclusion. To accomplish this, a process of backward chaining is initially used. "IF-THEN" rules express relationships between facts. The system processes the knowledge base by examining the goals and then working backward to determine if there is sufficient data to conclude that one or more of the goals is true. One or more goals can be recommended by the system depending upon the database. Common applications of deductive reasoning are:

- **Design:** The movement from theory to something new
- **Planning:** The establishment of a sequence of events to reach a goal
- **Configuration:** The collection and integration of individual parts to form a whole

In general, the *induction-based system* derives facts and relationships from examples and from a system-generated decision tree of queries to the user. Inductive systems reason from the particular to the general. The value of this system is its processing parsimony. It eliminates unnecessary factors and arranges questions in an optimal order.

Inductive reasoning is a process similar to analysis. With analysis, a large problem is broken down into its components to foster better understanding. Inductive reasoning starts with a set of observations and tries to find a generalized explanation for them. Inductive reasoning attempts to reach a general conclusion by the examination of facts moving from the specific to the general. Common applications of inductive reasoning are:

- **Classification:** Categorizing by examining attributes
- **Diagnosis:** The identification of causes
- **Prediction:** The extrapolation from knowns to possible outcomes
- **Testing:** The matching of items against existing criteria

WHERE ARE EXPERT SYSTEMS FOUND?

The number of expert system tools and applications is doubling each year. These systems are predominantly in the PC environment, but are growing in the mainframe environment as well. The range of expert system locations is limited only by imagination, budgets, human experts, resources, and knowledge engineers who can acquire, codify, and integrate knowledge into systems.

In order to evaluate applications of expert systems, their benefits must be considered. Current expert systems can be used to:

- Transfer expert knowledge to nonexperts
- Perform diagnostic and prescriptive tasks
- Recommend intelligent alternatives based on a list or input data

Expert systems are of two types: stand-alone and embedded. The stand-alone system is one that runs on a personal computer, minicomputer, or a mainframe. While the computer is running the program, it is dedicated to the application. The embedded system is a portion of another program. This other program is usually a conventional program that accesses the expert system on an as-needed basis. Another type of embedded expert system may be transparent to the user and run concurrently with another application.

Current uses of expert systems are clustered around applications that provide long-term monetary benefits, decision-making policies, or accurate decisions. Knowledge engineers tend to become entrapped in a particular type of knowledge domain and to make a series of systems of limited variety. The following list merely scratches the surface of expert systems applications, and is intended to stimulate thinking about the possibilities.

- Education and training expert systems are used for development and delivery of instruction. Development systems can be used to advise the developer on levels, media selection, and quality instructional design. Delivery systems include tailored testing models, diagnostic systems, and prescription.
- Manufacturing expert systems help firms to produce goods, archive knowledge, and perform diagnostic, monitoring, and prescriptive tasks. Systems can help managers plan return on investment, expedite repair, help in design, aid in the management of information systems, and provide efficiency for all phases of an operation.
- Financial expert systems are involved in all aspects of money management. Systems are found in banks, accounting firms, brokerage firms, insurance companies, and financial planning concerns.
- Medical expert systems are used for diagnosis of diseases, analysis of symptoms, evaluation of X rays, triage, and other applications.
- Military expert systems are used for strategic and tactical purposes. Applications include situation assessment, automating weapons, personnel efficiency, and troubleshooting and repair.
- Government agencies including NASA, the FBI, CIA, and other groups that have been using conventional computing programs have developed and continue to benefit from knowledge base applications.

There are many potential uses for expert systems ranging from accounting to zoology. Expert systems can be used in any field where expert knowledge can be captured and applied.

WHEN ARE EXPERT SYSTEMS DESIRABLE?

There are a number of situations in which the applicability of expert systems needs to be investigated.

There Is a High Payoff

The degree of payoff can be determined by considering alternative solutions. These alternatives include hiring more experts, creating more experts, or eliminating the problem source. The hiring of more experts impacts the budget. If the nature of the problem is such that the experts will have idle time, an expert system has a high payoff.

Additional experts can be created by providing training or education. Both education and training are long-term strategies, as they do not alleviate the immediate problem. In addition, training and education are expensive and the value devolves to the recipient of the training or education. Should the recipient leave the job, the training and education cannot be transferred to others.

Consideration of eliminating the problem at the source includes changing a product line, purchasing new or additional equipment, modifying a mission statement, or other actions that may affect the profit statement.

Human Experts Are Unable or Unavailable to Do the Job

Expert system development can be justified when existing human experts have reached their knowledge limit or are scarce. Experts cannot be expected to know everything about everything. Thus, experts can use expert systems as intelligent assistants.

Expert systems can also be used in environments that place human life at risk, such as nuclear power plants, war zones, ocean depths, and outer space. Human experts may be too expensive or too much at risk to be on-site in these environments. Expert systems in these locations can help nonexperts who make critical decisions.

Human Experts Are Scarce

Human experts are both expensive and scarce. Until cloning is perfected, experts cannot be in two physical locations at one time. However, problems that require expert advice often occur simultaneously in multiple locations. An effective, justifiable way to solve this problem is an expert system.

Expertise Is Being Lost; There Is a Need for Institutional Memory

Expert systems can be justified when a few individuals have the majority of the knowledge. If any of these individuals retire, quit, or die, knowledge is at risk. This could result in grave disruptions which could impact performance and revenues.

THE ANTICIPATED IMPACT OF EXPERT SYSTEMS

Quite simply, expert systems will have a greater impact on business than the advent of the computer. The computer alone is an employee of the business, the computer equipped with an expert system is a business partner.

The intent of this discussion is not to detail expert systems, as there are many publications that are dedicated to the internals of expert systems. The intent is to provide an overall view of expert systems and how the attributes of these systems affect knowledge engineering.

It has been established that expert systems constitute one of the branches of AI dedicated to reasoning and problem solving. Expert systems are in the group of knowledge-based systems and are considered as advisors. These systems are capable of organizing data in a specific area and providing the best answer or options. These systems provide expert advice to nonexperts and can help the expert. Decisions made by experts can earn or lose money, save or lose lives, enable success or failure. Because human experts are always a limited commodity, expert systems will be used in every field.

CONSIDERATIONS FOR THE KNOWLEDGE ENGINEER

There are two main points about expert systems that a knowledge engineer must keep in mind. First is that expert systems contain the problem-solving strategies of experts in the form of heuristic rules. These strategies are acquired by the expert through time, experience, and formal education or training. Second, the knowledge engineer strives to understand the domain, distill the knowledge, and represent that knowledge in a manner that is accurate and that works with the selected tool. It is to this knowledge base that the knowledge engineer devotes the most time and effort.

The knowledge base is composed of two basic knowledge types. The first type of knowledge is declarative. This knowledge comprises the facts and general attributes of the major groups of factors. The second knowledge type is procedural. Once the general set of circumstances has been identified, the procedural knowledge expresses what actions to take or conclusions to make.

Collectively, the knowledge types used in the knowledge base are called the knowledge structure. This knowledge structure is the representation of the collective expertise of domain professionals. The selection of the manner in which knowledge is represented has many implications. Among these implications are evaluation for accuracy by reviewers and the types of inferences that can be made.

Thus, the KE pays careful attention to both the acquisition and representation of knowledge. Expert systems currently use a variety of knowledge structures including rules, semantic networks, frames, and others. Descriptions of each of these structures are provided in the following chapters.

SUMMARY

With computers came the information revolution. The first impact of this revolution was on automatic data processing. The current wave of the revolution is using computers and knowledge-based software and is directed at decision making. These revolutionary computer and knowledge-based systems are used to improve human productivity.

Artificial Intelligence (AI) was officially born at the Dartmouth Conference in 1956. Firebaugh (1988) states that the 1956 conference attendee John McCarthy is credited with giving this computer discipline the name "artificial intelligence." Since that time, many researchers in universities and privately funded efforts have pursued AI.

To this day, there is no universally accepted agreement on the definition or parameters of artificial intelligence. The various definitions focus on various applications and branches of AI. One reason for this may be the mix of disciplines that participate in AI. These disciplines include computer science, cognitive science, medical science, and manufacturing sciences.

Machine intelligence is another term for artificial intelligence. Those involved in AI use the term ''intelligent'' when referring to computer systems as they perform behaviors. If a system behaves in a fashion that if performed by a human would be called intelligent, the system is called intelligent. The intelligence performed by the system is simulated intelligent behavior.

Simulated intelligent behavior was the focus of studies by Alan Turing in the early 1950s, resulting in the Turing test. This test challenged a person to interact through a terminal, ask questions, and determine if the responses to those questions were made by another person or a computer. If no determination can be made that identifies a human or a machine, and it was the latter, then the machine is said to be intelligent, like the former. The system that can do this is actually displaying intelligent behavior.

The pursuit of intelligent machines will continue. This pursuit will be carried out on parallel processing hardware working at extraordinary clock speeds in personal computers, minis, and mainframe computers. Languages and software programs will progress with improved user interfaces and greater abilities to perform intuitively. Additional technologies such as neural networks will blossom. The first decade of the next century is likely to have an intelligent machine that will mimic Arthur C. Clark's vision of the HAL 9000.

PRACTICAL APPLICATION

1. Consider for a moment, your chosen field of study.

   a. How could current/future machine knowledge be beneficial to the domains within that field?

   b. Which areas of AI could be useful and in what ways?

2. Then select a narrow slice of one of those domains. Identify a common problem within that slice. Determine the advantages and disadvantages of various search strategies that could be applied to a system designed to address that problem.

3. In this chapter, it is said that the computer alone is an employee of the business, the computer equipped with an expert system is a business partner. Consider the "average" business person's knowledge of expert systems. Anticipate that person's questions about this statement and prepare responses to them.

4. Review chapter 1. Develop a chart, grid, or table that compares and contrasts human and machine knowledge in terms of thinking, problem solving, and reasoning.

5. Consider the areas of artificial intelligence. How are these areas likely to impact other technologies currently in use?

6. Construct a search tree for troubleshooting an appliance or other tangible minisystem. Make the rules into the nodes of an efficient search tree. Note the conditions under which a breadth-first, depth-first, or other search strategy would be most effective.

7. Defend or contest the model for selection of a data representation, search strategy, or line of reasoning listed under "Additional Reasoning Techniques."

8. Why or why not use a performance-based classification system for expert systems rather than a system based on quantity of rules?

9. What are the necessary ingredients to enable an expert system to reason using analogical or common-sense approaches?

10. Defend or refute the notion that expert systems should be used to bridge the performance gap between American and Japanese workers, as opposed to training or education.

11. Evaluate the shortcomings of using heuristic knowledge in an expert system.

12. Comment on the business prospects of "off the shelf" knowledge bases as an item available in your local computer store.

4

Knowledge-Based Systems

Our little systems have their day.

Alfred, Lord Tennyson

INTRODUCTION

Currently, there is a range of potential knowledge-based system applications. The numbers of knowledge-based system applications are flourishing as technology and the market permit. The evolution from a society of agriculturists to industrialists, to information technologists, to knowledge brokers is on track and accelerating.

Hardware advances, software technology, and the cognitive sciences are merging to produce the next generation of knowledge-based tools and techniques. The systems discussed in this chapter are the vanguard of this emerging knowledge-based generation.

KNOWLEDGE-BASED SYSTEMS

Chapter 1 explored human knowledge and chapter 2 discussed a variety of knowledge sources. Chapter 3 explored machine knowledge and provided a contrast to human knowledge. The link between human thinking, problem solving, and reasoning on the one hand, and the machine processes on the other is the knowledge engineer. The product created by a knowledge engineer is the computer-accessed emulation of human knowledge. This computer emulation is through access to stored knowledge bases. These knowledge-based systems are of five basic types:

- Expert systems from the field of artificial intelligence
- Database management systems from the field of information systems

- Hypertext—hypermedia from the area of linked-knowledge systems
- CASE—computer-aided software engineering development systems
- Intelligent tutoring systems—computer-controlled training and educational systems

The knowledge engineer selects the appropriate knowledge-based tool to fit the situation and perceived requirements. In order to make intelligent decisions, an understanding of knowledge-based systems is required. In this chapter, five tools are explored from a conceptual perspective.

EXPERT SYSTEM APPLICATIONS

Expert system is a generic name assigned to a class of software programs that have the ability to interact with a user to define a concern, and will then tailor a solution. These systems use knowledge and reasoning techniques to solve problems that normally require the abilities of human experts. The term expert system is overused and overdefined to the point of nebulousness. Better terms for expert-system software focus on what the software does. Thus, names like decisionware or advisory systems are more appropriate. However, for the sake of commonality of terms, *expert system* will be used to identify the branch of artificial intelligence software applications that uses knowledge bases and human expertise.

There are many publications that offer a list of expert system application classifications. For example, Waterman (1986) listed ten generic categories of expert system applications:

- **Interpretation:** Inferring situation descriptions from sensory data
- **Prediction:** Inferring likely consequences of given situations
- **Diagnosis:** Inferring system malfunctions from observable events
- **Design:** Configuring objects under constraints
- **Planning:** Designing actions
- **Monitoring:** Comparing observations to expected outcomes
- **Debugging:** Prescribing remedies for malfunctions
- **Repair:** Executing plans to administer prescribed remedies
- **Instruction:** Performing diagnosis and prescribing instruction
- **Control:** Governing overall system behavior

Other expert system classification strategies have added further functional descriptions such as decision making, knowledge-fusing, identifying, interpreting, and explaining. With no great effort, the number of system types could be expanded much further. However, it is the intent of this discussion to provide only a conceptual overview of expert systems. Therefore, the variety of expert systems will be compressed into categories expressing the spirit of their functions. These categories are: Analysis, Synthesis, Instructional Systems, and Memory-Resident Aids.

Analysis-Based

Expert systems designed for analysis have the characteristics of an *optimizing* system. *Diagnostic systems* are a type of analysis-based system. They are systems that isolate the probable cause of system malfunctions. Input sources for these systems can be mechanical or human. A variety of diagnostic systems can be constructed to diagnose failures in such complex systems as aircraft, communications, ecologies, and the human cardiovascular system.

Diagnostic systems tend to have knowledge bases containing range limits and relationships. They explore out-of-range parameters. Diagnostic systems are often linked to interpretation devices that gather sensory data for input.

These inputs are generally pressure readings, temperature readings, flows, etc. Input devices can be located in situations that are hazardous for humans such as areas with radiation dangers, undersea depths and the void of space. Input devices must function every minute, twenty-four hours a day.

Diagnostic systems also serve in the inductive arena of analyzing quantities of data, interpreting the data, and outputting a recommendation or interpretation. Humans tend to suffer from information overload when storing more than seven items in short-term memory. Mental manipulations that are challenging to a human are easy for an expert system. Examples of these types of applications are testing and classification.

Input for analysis data is from a human or peripheral link that can be manipulated by the expert system. Selected inputs trigger the control program to access databases. Based on the available data, recommendations are provided or additional data is requested.

Prescriptive systems are often linked to diagnostic systems. Prescriptive systems advise or execute the remedies or solutions for the maladies identified by the diagnosis. These remedies may be in the form of reparation procedures. When a diagnostic expert system is linked to electronic switching devices, it can achieve corrections for out-of-limit values identified by the sensing devices. A system of this nature is called a closed-loop system. Very few closed-loop systems exist at this time because of the complexity required. However, closed-loop systems are a vision for the near-term future.

Analysis-based systems perform through inductive reasoning. These system applications start with the solution, then try to accumulate facts that support and prove it. A general conclusion is reached through the examination of specific facts or premises. Thus, analysis-based system applications reason from the specific to the general.

Synthesis-Based

A *synthesis-based* application has a knowledge base that contains rules and heuristic knowledge about assembling components for applications. The knowledge base contains specifications about the options and the resulting impacts of the selected options in combination with other factors. An example of a synthesis-based application is one that is dedicated to design. A design-based expert

system is generally used to configure a system based upon specific requirements. Users interact with the system by specifying selected attributes and
constraints. The expert system application then designs the system or assists
in the design.

The design process typically requires an extensive knowledge base linked
to a system such as one for Computer-Aided Design (CAD) in the manufacturing arena. CAD systems are used to help engineers in the design of a wide
range of manufactured products.

Design systems can provide specifications for motherboards and other
electronic components that have a variety of functions integrated to form a system. During design, for example, the use of a particular component imposes
constraints on other components with respect to heat generation, space, and
other attributes.

The design process is generally thought of as a creative-intensive process.
However, designers are able to construct their selection criteria based on rules
and procedures. This is an area in which an expert system is of particular benefit. Design-based expert systems can be used for applications ranging from the
medical field to home construction, where laws, variances, and other restrictions make design challenging.

Another type of synthesis-based application system is a planning system.
Planning applications are characterized by advising on actions. A planning
expert system sets or helps to establish the sequence of events that form a
plan. Planning systems do not carry out the plan. Rather, they advise based on
data supplied from an interactive session with a user, perhaps supplemented by
a database or other input source.

Expert systems used for planning can review data and form an approach to
achieve a stated goal. Typical planning systems are given a goal state, timeline,
resources, and other inputs to provide the basis for a plan. Planning systems
can be used to decide company growth direction, investments, and overt
courses of action such as acquisition. These systems can help determine the
market feasibility of a product or service.

Planning systems become more complex as the time frame of the plan
lengthens. For example, if a course of action extends over several days, the system must be able to adapt. The ability to adapt is to be able to accept or reject a
line of reasoning at a specific point in the plan. For example, the system lays out
a course of action based on its input. As the system progresses and plans are
advised, an event of "show-stopping caliber" may cause the system to halt.
The system then adapts the plan to a point such that the knowledge base constraint is not violated.

In order to avoid this situation, the KE and the domain expert do a quality
job of analysis to ensure decomposition of the problem to the simplest possible
set of subproblems. The sequence that the system uses to address these subproblems can eliminate costly adaptations.

The primary consideration for synthesis-based systems is that synthesis is
achieved by deductive reasoning, so that the systems work with facts and

attempt to build up to a solution to reach a goal. Synthesis-based systems use broad premises to draw a conclusion. Thus, reasoning is achieved by moving from the general to the specific. An additional example of a synthesis-based application is a configuration system.

Instructional Systems-Based

Instructional application systems perform diagnostic, prescriptive, and monitoring functions. These instructional applications are similar to the analysis-based systems. The performance of a student is diagnosed and assigned a prescriptive recommendation. Previously described systems are involved with diagnosing the performance of things rather than the performance of people.

While the function is much the same, these systems are separated because they are becoming a branch of AI on their own. The knowledge base is created to house the heuristic knowledge of professionals who are able to recognize trends or patterns and set limits. The reasons for incorrect answers are deduced and corrective measures prescribed.

Today, most schools use a computer in the learning process. Both computer-aided instruction (CAI) and computer-based training (CBT) are used in many school and business systems. An expert system can be linked to CAI and CBT software to function as a front-end assessment instrument for tailored testing. This front-end is used to assess each student's current state and the goal state, to output prescription to fill the gap. With expert systems serving as intelligent front-ends for an instructional system, instruction can be optimized.

An instructional expert system can rapidly analyze the level of the students' knowledge or understanding, and prescribe a plan for correcting out-of-range values. These instructional systems repair overt student performance behaviors by prescribing appropriate corrective action or enrichment activities.

Memory-Resident Aids or ShadowWare-Based Systems

These expert systems are designed to function in the background of another program. When the user of the program violates some range limit or requires help, the program surfaces. The selected programs can include word processing, database programs, number crunching programs, etc.

Each memory-resident expert system is designed and tailored to meet specific requirements. Like any memory-resident program, the memory capacity of the host machine and the requirements of the main program must be considered before using a program of this nature.

ShadowWare systems can be used for training purposes, or as aids that increase user friendliness. As developers become more sophisticated in the use of expert systems of this nature, they will fall into common use. Many software applications will contain memory-resident expert systems that will function totally transparently to the user.

DATABASE MANAGEMENT SYSTEMS

Database management systems (DBMSs) are an outgrowth of conventional databases. In order to understand these systems, the foundation of a general database will be presented. An understanding of the present form of these systems will allow a leap in logic, to foresee the future of these systems. The present role of these systems in data and information manipulation; they map to the data pyramid presented in FIG. 1-1 in chapter 1. The future of these systems is migration to knowledge-based management systems, which will take the form of decision support systems and databases with expert system query front-ends.

Databases

Conceptually, a database is a repository of information used for various functions in business and industry. The data in these bases can be retrieved, revised or added to, and placed back in the database.

A database is a collection of interrelated data stored together for multiple applications. Generally speaking, a database can be any organized collection of data. It can be as simple as a file cabinet or a published catalog of goods. All parts of a database are capable of being used together in each application. Data storage is independent of the programs that access the data. An example of a data structure for a small application is a collection of records used for a mailing list. Figure 4-1 provides an illustration of a flat file data structure. Flat file structures are characterized by all records having the same simple structure.

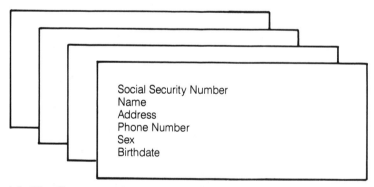

Social Security Number
Name
Address
Phone Number
Sex
Birthdate

Fig. 4-1. Flat file.

Typical application areas for flat file systems are banking, universities, and insurance companies. Flat files were used prior to the late 1960s and in the early 1970s. A drawback was their limited flexibility in terms of outputs. Programs were connected by interface files using conventional data processing approaches such as sequential access. These approaches required the development of one or more programs for each application, for example, the airline applications of flights, crews, passengers, maintenance, and reservations.

These programs were soon outgrown. Users demanded and developed more complex logical data relationships. The new systems that emerged were called database management systems.

A *database management system* is a computer program, designed to organize, store, retrieve, and perform data entry and updating of a database. A database management system enables access to integrated data as required by the functional, organizational, and operational elements within an enterprise.

There are database terms that are useful to know. These terms relate to the attributes of a database structure. At the top of the hierarchy is the *file* which is a unit of storage containing related items or records of information. A *record* is a group of related fields that are stored and retrieved together from the data file. A *field* is that part of the record where a single item of data is stored. An *entity* is a person, place, thing, event, or concept for which data is entered.

DBMSs operate at three levels of description. The highest is the *conceptual schema*, which describes the enterprise's information independent of any particular database structure, i.e., the description is in terms of entity types like employees and departments, attributes like name and age, and relationships like "works for," not in terms of records, fields, and pointers. The next level is the *logical schema*, which contains the four conventional database models: inverted file, hierarchical, network, and relational; these will be described in the next few sections. The final level is the *physical schema*, which specifies the actual physical layout of the data on the media. The hierarchical, network, and inverted file data models have been used as the foundation structure for DBMS since the early 1960s. The fourth, the relational data model, was proposed as a foundation structure for DBMS in the early 1970s. The main difference among the four data models is the way the relationships among the records are represented.

DBMSs are often designed by programmers rather than users. Thus, the design driver is convenience of design and what appears to be logical from the perspective of the programmer. A knowledge engineer can be useful in assisting in designing the structure of the records. Interactions with an expert can help to structure the system in order to optimize flexibility, integrate new records, facilitate search strategies, and design new levels of data relationships.

Hierarchical Data Model

In the *hierarchical data model*, each record type corresponds to a node in a set of one or more trees, with each type in a tree, except the root, having a single parent (superior) type, and each having zero or more child (dependent) types. The root might be "division," which has "department" and "project" as children; "department" could have "employee" and "branch" as dependents; and so on. Each record type has fields corresponding to the attributes of the entity type which it represents—name, age, and so on for employees, for instance. Figure 4-2 shows a hierarchical data structure.

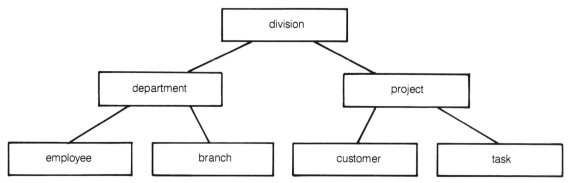

Fig. 4-2. Hierarchical data structure.

Network Data Model

It is often difficult to force application data into a hierarchical structure— e.g., an employee might work for one department but on several projects, and each project might be supported by several departments. To overcome this kind of problem, the *network data model* was developed. In it, record types can be freely connected by any number of named relationships, with one type owning any number of others and in turn being owned by another set of one or more types. Thus in a network version of our previous example, a project reports to one or more departments, and an employee works for a department and one or more projects.

Although it is not inherent in the network model, many implementations impose the restriction that a single relationship cannot be many-to-many, i.e., a record type can both own, and be owned by, multiple record types, but within a given relationship a child can have only one parent—Sue Jones cannot work for both Accounting and Personnel. (Of course, a relationship can be one-to-many—Accounting can have as many employees as it can afford.) This limitation is solved by setting up an intermediate entity type, say, "assignment," such that Sue Jones is assigned to assignments 173 and 174, and Accounting is charged for assignment 173 and Personnel for 174. In this way, none of the assignments has more than a single parent in one relationship.

Martin (1988) states that network data models can store multiple hierarchies simultaneously, when records have more than one link. For example, Martin states, record type A has a one-to-many relationship with record type B if some occurrences of A are related to more than one occurrence of B, and all occurrences of B are related to a unique occurrence of A.

Network systems vary in their ability to respond to inquiries that move from relationship to relationship within the system. These systems can have configurations of one-to-one, many-to-one, and many-to-many. Designers are sometimes confused by the linking, interweaving, and networking of records. Figure 4-3 shows a network data structure.

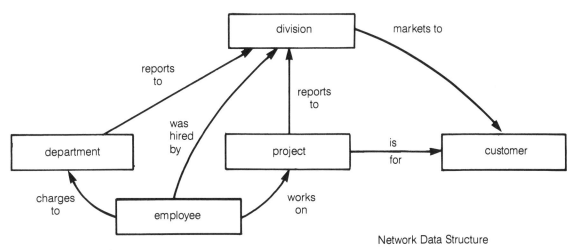

Network Data Structure

Fig. 4-3. Network data structure.

Inverted File Data Model

The *inverted file data model* represents each entity type by a file. Each attribute of the entity becomes a field. The file is called "inverted" because at least one field has an associated index. Each file record represents an occurrence of the entity type. If and only if two files have one or more fields in common, a relationship exists between the entities represented by the files. While the names of these fields do not need to be the same, the data values come from the same *domain* (value pool). The nature of the mapping, one-to-one, one-to-many, or many-to-many, is determined by the data values.

The inverted file data model allows data access methods that provide users with efficient access to individual files. An index file is constructed containing all of the values for the inverted field. These values are maintained in order for ease of access to the index file. Record pointers are stored with each value. The inverted file data model allows one or more inverted fields in each file.

Atre (1988) states that one of the major advantages of the inverted data file is its simplicity. The inverted file model allows data independence. Further, new entities and attributes in the form of files and fields are easily added. It is also easy to remove or create an index to change relationships. For each of the inverted fields, an index file is constructed containing, for each value of the field, a list of pointers to the records in which that field has that value.

Figure 4-4 shows a data file inverted on part name.

Relational Databases

In the network model, relationships are between conventional record types. Also the relationships are explicitly named (like "works-for") and a program references them by name ("Find the department record that this

Index		Record	Inverted File		
Part Name	Record List		Part Number	Date of Purchase	Part Name
Bracket	102	101	3105-2	02-09-88	Support
Filter	103	102	2120-5	07-11-87	Bracket
Hanger	106	103	4621-9	03-03-89	Filter
	107	104	3105-2	04-02-89	Support
Strap	105	105	6742-7	06-06-88	Strap
Support	101	106	3535-4	09-30-87	Hanger
	104	107	3535-4	10-01-88	Hanger

Fig. 4-4. Inverted file data structure.

employee record works-for''). The *relational data model* differs in both these regards. In this model, the analogue of a file is a *relation*, which corresponds to a certain entity type (e.g., ''employee'') and consists of a two-dimensional array of rows and columns, where each row (often called a *tuple*) contains the set of attribute values for an instance of the entity type, and each column corresponds roughly to a field in a record. Thus one tuple in the employee relation would represent Sue Jones. Each tuple in a relation has the same structure; no item can be multiple-valued (i.e., no row-column intersection can contain more than one value); no two tuples in a relation can be identical; and the order of tuples in a relation is arbitrary (i.e., the user cannot use that order to represent, say, seniority).

The key structural feature of the relational data model is that interentity relationships are represented and specified by equality of values in the corresponding tuples. The fact that Sue Jones works for Accounting is indicated by its department number appearing as the value of the ''department'' column in her tuple. A program finds out the name of her department manager by looking for the tuple in the department relation that has her department number in its ''number'' column, and taking the value in the ''manager name'' column.

The advantages of the relational data model are that it is both simple and easy to understand, and the data structure is easy to modify since there are no built-in interrecord relationships (as there are in the hierarchical and network models) and most implementations allow to be added or deleted without disrupting the existing data. This means that the model can accommodate unanticipated uses of the data. Its disadvantages, however, are that multiple-valued items require a proliferation of relations, interrelation referencing is awkward, and access is often slow.

Figure 4-5 shows a relational data structure.

Knowledge-based Management Systems

Each of the DBMSs discussed represented a strategy for structuring, processing, and presenting data. Each of the database types possesses strengths and weaknesses in terms of hardware and software requirements. These systems have two basic shortcomings in common. The first problem is the acquisi-

Relation
Employees

No.	Name	Age	Dept.	...
1795	Sue Jones	27	143	
1102	Maria Hernandez	46	128	
1359	Chan Nguyen	31	144	
...	...	...	...	

Fig. 4-5. Relational data structure.

tion and structure of the databases, and the second problem is their inability to accommodate present-day data.

A programmer is usually responsible for developing the links and using techniques for improving speed and efficiency. Neither the programmer nor the domain expert generates the content of the databases. However, the domain expert is usually accountable for quality input and an accurate database. Therein lies the first problem.

One solution is to use a knowledge engineer who has the responsibility of interacting with both the domain expert and the programmer to ensure a complete and accurate knowledge base. To a knowledge engineer, acquisition of the content, and arrangement of that knowledge in the knowledge base, is crucial. The content source, or expert, is subject to knowledge acquisition techniques and practices in forming a content-rich knowledge base. The knowledge engineering techniques, combined with a programmer's expertise, produce a sound knowledge base.

The second problem is that present-day data includes video, graphics, images, and symbols. Tomorrow's systems will evolve to accommodate these new data. One way to begin the move toward tomorrow's Knowledge-based Management Systems (KBMSs) is to separate the control structures from the knowledge base.

The use of sophisticated inference strategies, rules and facts for relevancy of search elements, and heuristic linking of elements will produce powerful systems. Perhaps these systems will be able to monitor electronic data sources for possible inclusion into the knowledge base.

HYPERMEDIA

Conceptually, *hypermedia* is present data linked in logical paths to produce knowledge. Hypermedia comprises hypertext, HyperTalk, and a growing number of applications. The content and form of the knowledge, and the delivery vehicles are lesser considerations than the interrelatedness of the knowledge. Hypermedia includes the integration of text, pictures, sounds, data, and knowledge. This integration provides the multimedia capability of hypertext. Hypermedia may become the database structure of tomorrow.

Goodman (1987) wrote that HyperCard has relational capabilities with an additional ability. HyperCard allows navigation to other stacks for viewing. Relational databases, on the other hand, restrict their relational capabilities to information retrieval from a fixed set. Goodman also contrasts hypertext with DBMS software by viewing the display of the retrieved information. Goodman stated, ''A DBMS report usually consists of columnar data that lists some or all elements of a form . . . HyperCard, on the other hand, is not designed for generating reports of that nature . . . it is optimized for quickly looking through existing cards—browsing in search of desired information. Therefore, while a DBMS program might produce a report listing based on desired selection criteria. HyperCard very quickly finds cards matching your criteria.''

The vehicles of hypermedia include CD-ROM, videodisc, and hard disks combined with sophisticated retrieval software that explores the knowledge base through associative links. Thus, the contents of the storage devices becomes information space awaiting exploration.

The practical application of hypermedia will increase a person's ability to approach a complex problem situation, gain comprehension within the problem parameters, and derive paths to problem solutions.

In corporate society, problems are becoming more complex. In addition, urgency can dictate the manner of problem address and resolution. Decisions need to be responsive to an increased rate of domestic activity and global influence. To this end, knowledge systems store data and enable its assimilation through interrelated links.

Hypermedia and Expert Systems

You may be thinking, ''What is the difference between hypermedia and expert systems?'' Expert systems are defined as programs designed to emulate human expertise in a particular area. This expertise takes the form of knowledge composed of facts and procedures. Knowledge is represented in various forms such as rules, triggered by user input. When a sufficient number of triggers are activated, a recommendation is made. The rules are stored in a knowledge base. An expert system has a knowledge base as one of its components.

Hypermedia, on the other hand, can contain a highly sophisticated textual, graphic, or image knowledge base. Hypertext has the ability to present stored text nonsequentially. In both the expert system and hypertext, a user navigates through a knowledge base. The principal difference between hypermedia and expert systems is in the methods used to navigate through the knowledge base.

Hypertext environments have no special programming that guides a user through major points or over a prespecified path in the system. As a result, a user has complete freedom to navigate or meander through a system. The quality of the results depends on the goal of the system. If the goal is for a discovery learning process, the system is excellent. If there are essential points to be addressed, the user can inadvertently navigate around them and miss crucial knowledge, i.e., a user can explore the "nice to know" information and miss elements of the "need to know" knowledge.

Expert systems explore knowledge bases by presenting a user with options or by evaluating user input. The system then branches to an appropriate portion of the knowledge base, and presents other options to the user. This process continues until a conclusion is reached or a recommendation options list is presented. In this way, all the critical knowledge components are touched with pre-pathed, mapped, or guided navigation.

The hypertext system can allow a user to miss critical knowledge points and an expert system restricts tangential exploration. The near-term future is obvious: a hybrid system will evolve from a merger of the attributes of the two systems. The users of such a merger of systems will be knowledge workers. Knowledge workers are people in decision-making positions. These workers, to be effective, are able to recognize links among seemingly unrelated pieces of information. Therefore, there is a requirement to provide a system for interrelating data under which a user defines parameters that influence navigation. The navigation decisions are prompted and have the benefit of an expert's guidance.

Systems of this nature are useful in education and training by providing a Socratic learning method. In this system, an expert system tailors user options with advisories and alerts. A system of "bookmarks" can allow ancillary exploration and a return to the "main path." The knowledge base is embodied in hypermedia and searched with a custom search system. An education and training system designed in this manner is a knowledge processor.

Researchers, designers, developers, and others who do investigative work can benefit from a knowledge processing system. Data is grouped into user-defined knowledge frames which contain the links for inference. These frames also contain individual slots, or data areas, for values. The slots can contain facets for auxiliary information. Figure 4-6 illustrates a knowledge frame.

CAR FRAME

	Facets	Slot
Engine size		
Wheel base		
No. of doors		
2- or 4-wheel drive		
Transmission type		
Gross handling weight		
Weight of vehicle		

Fig. 4-6. Knowledge frame.

This automobile frame is a blueprint or control frame. The facets are defined for the frame set. This frame represents one of a number of frames. The user fills in the slots for each of the frames. Unlike databases that can just list each vehicle with a specified wheelbase, this system can do that and more. This system contains an intelligent user interface that queries the user requirements and supplies results to meet those needs. For example, a person could specify a requirement for a vehicle that can operate in inclement weather, carry 1200 pounds gross weight, etc. The system would select on such labels as four-wheel drive and truck or truck-type vehicles. The relationship between a requirement and the corresponding characteristics could be defined by facets.

One strategy to realize a knowledge processor is to conceptualize and refine a system that combines the benefits of an expert system with the storage ability of CD-ROM and other memory peripherals with hypertext links. The expert system is used to create the frame parameters with desired depth of content and linkages. The search methods and inferencing are provided through the expert system. The expert system also provides the control over the user interface. CD-ROM provides a mass media storage facility for the selected hypermedia. DVI or videodisc devices provide access where motion video is required. The expert system links these devices as peripherals. The hypermedia links provide access to the knowledge pool stored in the memory peripherals. The expert system can manage storage areas and download data from larger-capacity storage media to other facilities.

CASE TOOL APPLICATIONS

Computer-Aided Software Engineering (CASE) tools are an evolving class of software tools. These tools are the implementation systems of the structured software development strategies and techniques created in the 1970s. CASE software tools are composed of software and hardware with support through methods and management to meet the growing demands for more and better software. CASE technology is a combination of integrated software tools and methodologies that automate the traditional "waterfall" software life cycle (FIG. 4-7). This life cycle consists of five phases.

McClure (1988) placed CASE tools into five categories:

- Diagramming tools for pictorially representing system specifications
- Dictionaries, information management systems, and facilities to store, report, and query technical and project management system information
- Specification-checking tools to detect incomplete, syntactically incorrect, and inconsistent system specifications
- Code generators to generate executable code from system specifications
- Documentation generators to produce technical and user documentation required by structured methodologies

CASE technology can be compared to the five generations of software technologies. Figure 4-8 shows the generations of computer evolution and the overlap of CASE.

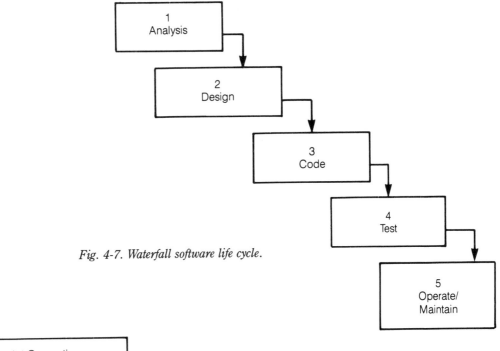

Fig. 4-7. Waterfall software life cycle.

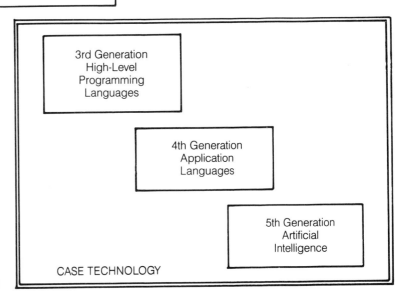

Fig. 4-8. CASE technology.

CASE technologies use a combination of third-, fourth-, and fifth-generation software tools and techniques. From the third generation, CASE uses compilers, program editors and libraries, and test data generators. The fourth-generation aspects of CASE include the capability of writing nonprocedural code that generates report programs. The fifth generation of CASE is on the drawing board.

Intelligent CASE tools will probably be geared towards a methodology repository. This methodology repository is an expert system that carries out the software development steps. The system will receive input from a user to define the solution, draw from a knowledge base, and then create the integrated application. The knowledge base will contain the basic principles of software technology, rules and facts of accepted software development practices, software development strategies, and heuristic knowledge of selected experts.

INTELLIGENT TUTORING SYSTEMS

Intelligent tutoring systems offer an application of artificial intelligence in education. These systems are similar to the expert system applications of instructional systems, but tend to be linked to larger databases. Intelligent tutoring systems are becoming their own branch on the AI tree. This branch will be shared by expert system applications and those originating from this fertile area. These systems, if accepted by educators and conformable to their budgets, will demonstrate significant impacts on the efficiency of education.

Within intelligent tutoring systems, the term *tutoring* implies that some level of teaching and learning will occur. Skinner (1968) characterizes a good tutor as possessing the following attributes:

1. Constant interchange between program and student
2. Occupies the student with sustained activity
3. Insists that a given point be thoroughly understood before the student can move on
4. Presents just the material for which the student is ready
5. Helps the student to come up with the right answer
6. Reinforces the student for every correct response

Intelligent tutoring systems satisfy these attributes and represent the next step in the evolution of computer-assisted instruction. Burns and Capps (1988) assert that computer-assisted instruction bridges this evolutionary gap by passing three tests of intelligence.

First, the subject matter, or domain, must be 'known' to the computer system well enough for this embedded expert to draw inferences or solve problems in the domain. Second, the system must be able to deduce a learner's approximation of that knowledge. Third, the tutorial strategy or pedagogy must be intelligent in that the 'instructor in a box' can implement strategies to reduce the difference between expert and student performance.

Burns and Capps also state that more experience is required to make the transition to knowledge-based educational systems. They offer seven kinds of expertise that pertain to the components that form the foundation for intelligent tutoring systems:

1. Content expertise in the expert subject matter module
2. Diagnostic expertise (understanding what learners know and need to learn) in the student diagnostic module
3. Instructional and curriculum expertise in the instructor module
4. Expertise in creating instructional environments
5. Human-computer interface expertise
6. Implementation expertise
7. Evaluation expertise

These seven components relate to one aspect of knowledge-based systems, that of expertise. The quality of intelligent tutoring systems, like expert systems, resides in the knowledge sources and the ability to acquire and represent that knowledge. With the full complement of expertise, intelligent tutors can help students learn through tailored interactions.

LOGIC

Expert systems, DBMS, hypermedia, CASE, and intelligent tutoring systems have been introduced. Each of these systems has strengths and weaknesses. Collectively, these systems are evolving into knowledge-based applications that will overlap each other. This overlap will produce hybrid systems with attributes of two or more of these systems. The following introduces one possible hybrid system.

- Name: Laser Optical Generated Intelligent Communicator (LOGIC)

- Purpose: Knowledge-based processing system that contains hypermedia links and is paired with an expert system search facilitator connected to appropriate, rapidly accessed, accurate knowledge sources.

- Features: A PC-based workstation system which contains an erasable/writable optical storage subsystem accessed through the guidance of an expert system. If required, there is an initial link through a mainframe to a mass storage device.

- Functions: A knowledge-parsing expert system is accessed in a mainframe storage facility. The user's requirements are explored, search parameters are defined, and knowledge bases searched. The selected knowledge is prioritized, summarized, and downloaded to an optical disc. This knowledge is in the form of text, audio, video, and graphics. The user's expert-system-driven personal computer presents an intelligent interface to further optimize the knowledge to meet the user's needs. The system then structures the knowledge base to meet the user's requirements and stores the resulting linked information.

- Benefits: Selected industries and people require knowledge for processing, established knowledge bases, and information pools. An expert system screening and search aid, in concert with a mass storage facility with PC portability, is the solution to the needs of information managers.

A LOGIC knowledge processor system can approach knowledge in a modular fashion. It builds knowledge frames that have a topical organization. These frames are linked and relinked into structures that meet the user's needs.

While this system does not yet exist, it is suggestive. Systems similar to LOGIC will be created in the near term. The hardware and software components exist today. It is likely that there are individuals draped in money and shrouded in secrecy actively developing systems with the performance capabilities of LOGIC.

SUMMARY

This chapter provided a conceptual review of five knowledge-based tools. Several important issues were discussed:

- The acquisition and structure of databases and the roles of the KE, domain expert, and programmer
- The growth potential of today's systems in terms of ease of adding hardware and software
- The need for guiding users through critical knowledge points and yet providing tangential information as and when desired

The development of more sophisticated tools is well underway. The selection of appropriate tools to meet identified requirements will become increasingly critical. A taxonomy for expert system applications was suggested. Part 2 provides further exploration in the areas of knowledge acquisition and representation.

PRACTICAL APPLICATION

1. Professionals in the fields of education and training may look upon knowledge-based tools as adversaries. Some currently feel that ''noth-

ing can take the place of a warm body," be it in the classroom, lecture hall, or training site. Respond to this issue, focusing on potential "hot" debate items as well as the features and benefits of the tools and the redirection of those professionals into other avenues or the redefining of their current job responsibilities.

2. How will knowledge-based management systems be used differently from today's database systems such as relational databases?

3. Will hypermedia be used most in education or business? Why?

4. Construct a series of knowledge frames on a selected topic. What type of system would be required to drive the application? Who would use it? What would it be used for?

5. Will CASE technologies migrate into other industries such as financial? Why or why not?

6. Under what conditions would you accredit intelligent tutoring systems? Why?

7. How could a system such as LOGIC be used in education or business? What events must occur in technology and society before a system of this nature is possible?

PART I—SUMMARY

In Part I, a foundation and structure was established for knowledge concepts as they relate to humans and machines. Further, a relationship was built to link human and machine knowledge with knowledge-based systems.

The importance of familiarization with cognitive theories of thinking, reasoning and problem solving on the part of the knowledge engineer was stressed. Further, considerations for developing a mental structure regarding knowledge, its definition, components, and structure were discussed. This is important to the knowledge engineer whose task it is to represent knowledge domains in structures—structures that will be discussed in other chapters in this book.

Adequate preparation for development of not only a sound knowledge base but also a foundation for developing client-KE relations was discussed. The relationship of the knowledge-based domain and structure is critical to the effectiveness of the system. The latter element is based on the careful selection of a system of problem-solving strategies and tools.

Appropriate representation of appropriate knowledge is vital to a successful system as is evidenced by the efforts of knowledge-base-tool research and design to maximize system potential without risking critical information or the opportunities for tangential learning.

PART II—PRACTICUM

1. Given the various types of data sources and an overview of knowledge, reasoning, thinking, and problem solving, consider your reaction to the following situation:

   A prospective client comes to you and expresses an interest in having a KE develop a knowledge-based system that will enable system engineers to spot potential mechanical problems in a particular line of equipment. In your discussion, you make mention of the fact that several of your KEs have backgrounds in learning theories and cognitive psychology. The client looks straight at you and asks why that's so important and how will that help in designing and developing a system that deals with highly technical equipment.

2. Given what you've read and thought about knowledge-based tools in part I, design a course of study for a person interested in pursuing a career as a knowledge engineer.

   a. What kinds of classes, experiences, and background would you require?

b. How would you determine or assess the individual's abilities before granting the "title" of KE?

c. What kinds of careers could such a person pursue if, upon reaching the conclusion of the course of study, he or she decides against a profession as a KE?

d. What about the experienced programmer or domain expert? Would on-the-job training be sufficient?

Part II

Knowledge Acquisition and Representation

The first precept was never to accept a thing as true until I knew it as such without a single doubt.

René Descartes

Part II expands on the basis of understanding knowledge as it applies to knowledge-based system applications that were established in part I. For those that have a firm understanding of the concepts of knowledge and machine intelligence with respect to knowledge-based systems, part II discusses the process of knowledge acquisition and representation.

The focus of part II is the people, the process, and the structures of gathering and representing knowledge. The people include domain experts, knowledge engineers, managers, and users. The process portion of part II deals with knowledge acquisition techniques. Knowledge representation is discussed in terms of strategies and structures.

Questions located at the end of each chapter help to address a variety of interests, domains, and strategies for understanding and applying the material presented in this part of the book. Because of the diverse natures and backgrounds of the readers, the variety of knowledge-based applications, and the number of possible approaches to example sets, I chose to provide readers with an opportunity to participate in the assimilation of the material. This participation is in the form of optional exercises at the end of each chapter which are designed to encourage introspection. The level of interaction is in the hands of the reader; it can range from sublime to pedestrian.

Examples in this part of the book have the flavor of general human experience. The examples may appear as extensions of the previous text; however, they are intended to provide a different declarative perspective of the topic at hand. The procedural aspects of these materials can be derived through participation.

5

Knowledge Acquisition: Discovery

Knowledge is of two kinds.
We know a subject ourselves,
or we know where we can find
information upon it.

Samuel Johnson

INTRODUCTION

This chapter provides guidance on the aspects of preparation for a knowledge-based application development. Preparation involves defining the application, gaining familiarity with the content and resources, selecting the team, and developing detailed design specifications.

The intent of this chapter is to focus on the development of the application following the project "go ahead" stage. Part III of this book presents a development model which explores the issues and requirements for all phases of a project.

PREPARATION

Preparation activities include: establishing the project's mission statement, forming the team, locating the knowledge-base sources, and formulating the plan for the system's development.

The Mission Statement

The mission statement is a written declaration of the purpose of the application under development. This statement is similar to an instructional behavioral objective. Behavioral objectives were designed to lay out a planned route that helps maintain a focus for teachers and learners. Typical behavioral objectives include statements pertaining to the following factors:

- Audience:　States who is expected to perform the desired behavior
- Behavior:　Provides the verb in the sentence that describes what is observable or measurable
- Standards:　Denotes the givens and the constraints used to set the scope of the objective
- Degree:　Specifies the level or criteria of acceptable performance for the task

Like a behavioral objective, the mission statement of the project is also intended to maintain focus and direction. A typical mission statement includes:

- Users:　States who is included in the target audience; similar to the audience in a behavioral objective
- Function:　States what the application is designed to do; knowledge-based systems perform behaviors; similar to behaviors of a behavioral objective
- Scope:　Defines the application in terms of functional limitations; similar to conditions of a behavioral objective
- Outcomes:　Specifies system outputs in terms of recommendations, tips, reports, etc.; additionally, outcomes can state the expected length of user interaction with the system; somewhat similar to a behavioral objective.

The mission statement helps hold the team on track. It also provides a clear understanding of the inputs and expected outputs for the application. The overall statement focuses the scope of the application and ensures that managers, developers, and users are aware of the nature of the project and are working in parallel.

The mission statement also serves as a validation guideline during the discovery stage of system development. By maintaining attention and focus on the mission statement, the KE can assure a successful development effort.

A final note about the mission statement. The mission statement is the guiding force during the development phase, and may require slight modification as development progresses.

THE TEAM

The team is composed of people with various roles, responsibilities, and agendas. The development team expands and contracts at different stages of the development effort. In addition, the team is formed into configurations to meet the application. Sometimes a configuration stems from internal resources, and at other times there is a mixture of internal and external participants. In the final analysis, the team is likely to consist of four groups of people: knowledge engineers, experts, management, and users.

Knowledge Engineer

Knowledge engineers are not plentiful, because of the unique complement of required characteristics and skills. If a classified ad were to be run for a potential position, the description of the qualified knowledge engineer (KE) candidate might look like the following:

WANTED: Knowledge Engineer: Immediate opening for a Knowledge Engineer to acquire, organize, and codify the heuristic knowledge of domain experts in general business and manufacturing industries. Must show proof of skills, attributes, and education as listed below.

General Skills and Professional Skills. The ability to: analyze, appraise performance, clarify roles and expectations, communicate, coach, conduct meetings, define goals and objectives, delegate, design, develop, have discussion skills, edit, evaluate, form concepts, identify problems, implement, have interview skills, have leadership qualities, listen effectively, make decisions, manage time, manage stress, manage conflict, market, motivate, persuade, plan, have presentation skills, prioritize, process information, set goals, write proposals, write reports.

Technical Skills. Possession of computer skills: systems, main frame environment, PC environment, word processing, database, spreadsheet, computer languages, expert systems, utilities, CAD-CAM, graphics, peripherals, computer-based training, design, development, evaluation, LAN, laser-optical media, optical scanners, telecommunication, knowledge-based system software for both PC and mainframe environments (rule-based systems, forward chaining systems, backward chaining systems, object oriented systems).

Informed About/Contacts In: Accounting, advertising, agriculture, art, astrosciences, banking, biotechnology, broadcasting, chemistry, communication, construction, education, electronics, entertainment, farming, fishing, food, geology, government, health, high-tech manufacturing, horticulture, human resources, insurance, journalism, law practice, law enforcement, lumber, manufacturing, marketing, medical, military, petroleum, pharmaceutical, photography, physics, production, publishing, real estate, research and development, retail, sales, security, small business, social services, sports, textile, training, transportation (automotive, rail, air, mass transit), travel, zoology.

Observable Behavior Characteristics. The subject is: aggressive, professional in appearance, attentive, big-picture-oriented, aware of business politics, creative, detail-oriented, idea-oriented, imaginative, informed, innovative, capable of juggling tasks, loyal, positive in attitude, quick study, able to react well to change, equipped with a sense of humor, socially skilled, supportive, task-oriented, tenacious, capable of working in a team environment, willing to work long hours, able to meet deadlines, zealous.

Other. Advanced education degrees (e.g., computer science with cognitive psychology emphasis, behavioral psychology emphasis, and/or artificial intelligence), 5 years knowledge base design/development experience, willing to travel, 3 years consulting experience, knowledge of multiple computer languages, security clearance, publications in the field. Apply in person. Be prepared to supply references and work samples.

The KE analyzes the problem, conceives the knowledge acquisition strategy, acquires the knowledge, represents that knowledge, and constructs and tests the system. Additionally, the KE specifies the breadth and depth of the knowledge that an expert uses to solve problems, the strategies used, and required outside sources. The focus of the KE is the interpretation and interrelationships of the knowledge and the options for making that knowledge available to others.

Realize that knowledge engineers are not from a singularly unified holistic community. Among knowledge engineers there are different approaches, variance in depth and breadth of knowledge and experience, and different levels of skill. One of the most important qualities of a knowledge engineer is metacognition. Knowledge engineers must know and understand their limitations.

In addition to the knowledge engineer, there are other people to consider for the development effort. These people include management teams, a project leader, and a person in the role of project champion. The positions for the other project members are generally filled on the basis of their formal training and job experience over time. The knowledge engineer is the position that is critical to the effort and hails from an almost unknown origin.

Management Team

The management team controls the budget. The KE should keep this fact in mind. This group of people ought to have an opportunity to become involved in the project, be kept informed, and be called upon if required. The management team must be committed to the work effort or the project is doomed.

The KE should have formal, agreed to, written agreements for the milestones and deliverables in the contract. The project scope is carefully defined, and a sign-off process established for the deliverables.

Another member of the management team is the *Project Champion*. This person is usually in a leadership role, technically capable, and will benefit from the success of the project. The project champion and the KE usually become close friends, as this individual serves several functions. First, this person makes events happen including providing personnel, equipment, resources, and working areas. Next, this person usually knows the ''right'' person for the job.

Finally, the project champion buffers problems from most directions. Commitment to the project by the project champion seems automatic; however, the KE should maintain an awareness of any other projects that this person is also backing.

The *Project Manager* usually reports to the Project Champion. This manager handles the day-to-day business of the project and its personnel. The Project Manager has an adequate technical level of knowledge-based systems. This is important so that as a member of the management team he or she can verify that milestones have been met, or intercede if there is a lack of support or schedule slippage is occurring. The Project Manager may be a domain expert or represent the target user audience. It is beneficial if the Project Manager has experience with the problem area addressed by the application.

Users

Since any knowledge-based system application is developed for a specific group of users, it makes good sense to involve them. Obvious statement, but often overlooked. The target-user group should be involved from the start. Selected users should participate in the determination of system requirements, interfaces, and outputs. The users should see a demonstration of a knowledge-based system similar to the system under consideration. These people are to be informed about the purpose of the system. User understanding of the features, functions, and benefits of the system serves to alleviate rumors and suspicions. The development effort will be a waste of time if the intended users do not accept or cannot use the completed system. Figure 5-1 illustrates the members of the development team.

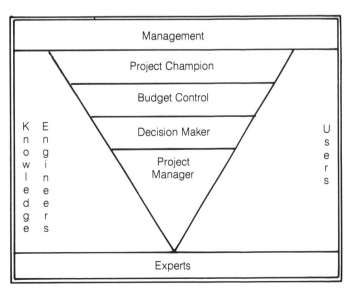

Fig. 5-1. The team.

Knowledge Base Categories

There are two categories of knowledge in the knowledge base: domain-independent knowledge, and domain-dependent knowledge. Domain-independent knowledge is derived from the education, past experience, and general information that an expert draws upon to solve problems. This knowledge may not be directly related to the specific problems that are addressed on the job. The second category of knowledge, domain-dependent, consists of the knowledge which reflects the expert's special capability in the subject domain. This knowledge is refined so as to apply to specific problem solving aids.

Expert systems require a greater proportion of domain-dependent knowledge than domain-independent knowledge. The KE has a greater chance of success with a development effort that resides in the domain-dependent knowledge area. An awareness of these two knowledge base components as they apply to the development effort enables the KE to save time in the knowledge acquisition tasks. The KE can consult with domain experts and target users to gain a "big picture" view of the project. Within the project's problem domain are the stated problem, subproblems, and any subdomains that may be intrinsic to the overall effort. In addition, there may be considerations that focus on the interrelations among the members of the problem domain.

The KE takes care not to be too quick to embrace a particular approach as a result of these initial contacts. The purpose of this initial exploration is to gain insight into the problem. For each of the subproblems and any subdomains, the KE establishes the problem type, its characteristics, the types of knowledge required to meet the problem, and any other strategies that can help to ensure a successful effort.

Chapter 2 provided information regarding general purpose sources for knowledge-based systems. Chapter 4 presented four general categories of expert systems that encompass the broad range of current applications. Three of the systems listed have slight differences in prime knowledge sources. The fourth category, memory resident, has its knowledge sources as application dependent. Each of the other three systems have a different set of advantageous knowledge sources. By comparing the target application with one of these three knowledge sets, you can help focus the knowledge search. The practical application at the end of this chapter challenges you to address the knowledge sources for analysis- and synthesis-based systems.

THE PROCESS

Previous chapters have addressed knowledge from broad perspectives. The KE focuses his efforts in pursuing the knowledge sources and support resources. The knowledge focus explores the domain knowledge needed to solve the identified problem. The resulting domain knowledge is considered for inclusion in the knowledge base.

Gain Familiarity

There are a series of activities in the preparation process. These activities overlap and they are iterative. In addition, these activities have attributes that require careful consideration. Time, money, and energy is heavily spent in each activity. These activities are shown in FIG. 5-2.

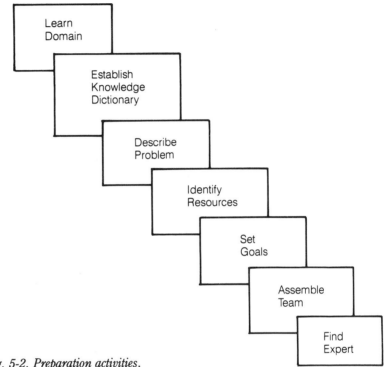

Fig. 5-2. Preparation activities.

Domain

In order to comprehend the magnitude and scope of the realm of the domain expert, the KE makes a concerted effort to learn about the domain and tasks done by the experts in that domain. A domain is a restricted field of concentration associated with knowledge and expertise. Examples of industry domains include law, medicine, and manufacturing. Domains also include the work done by law researchers, tax specialists, doctors and technicians, efficiency investigators, and marketeers, as examples of domain positions held by people. The KE gains familiarity with both the domain and the expert(s) in the domain. In order to work effectively, the KE prepares by gaining familiarity with the subject area to be explored. This preparation is very important for the KE, as it will provide working knowledge and a means to communicate. The sources for a knowledge area were discussed in chapter 2, and include books, case studies, empirical data, and records. The knowledge gained from these initial sources is cursory when compared to the knowledge level at the project's completion. However, a start needs to be made.

There is a secondary benefit to gaining a familiarity with the domain content. This benefit is that of a common ground which can be used to educate the domain expert in the process to follow. By presenting a model, the KE can illustrate how knowledge is captured and represented. From a base of operations in the familiar, the KE and the domain expert can establish a test case. In the test case, a step-by-step protocol is established for solution resolution by which to judge efficiencies and progress of applications.

The reasoning process of the domain expert will become evident. The confidence and rapport within the team is established. There are some early-on tasks that are initially addressed following the start of a knowledge-based system development effort.

The knowledge engineer becomes familiar with jargon and other terminology in order to communicate effectively with the expert. This understanding of terms and jargon both facilitates rapport and provides a means by which information can be understood and evaluated. Further, an understanding of the terminology sometimes helps eliminate superfluous information in the knowledge base, because a clarity of focus can be maintained. In addition, the terminology may suggest a requirement for non-experts to receive supplemental training or job aids to help their understanding.

As discussed in chapter 2, the best source knowledge for the domain is vested in the domain expert. The KE establishes a rapport with the expert to create a team bond. Together, the KE and the domain expert agree on and establish the general characteristics of the system and the composition of the development team. At this point, the problem parameters, resources, goals, and team are defined, established, and built. (Waterman, 1986)

Knowledge Dictionary

Just as many instructional design and software development projects establish common usage for terms, a knowledge dictionary is established for a knowledge-based project. This dictionary of terms can also be used in the application by way of user help screens. Candidates for the dictionary are words unknown to the KE, words with multiple meanings, jargon, key terms, acronyms, models, charts, maps, and any other meaningful items.

Along with the knowledge dictionary, there are additional required pieces of documentation for the project effort. A project book is kept. Included in the project book are:

- The Mission Statement
- A list of the project personnel, their roles and their responsibilities

- A description of the target users
- The system's performance expectations
- A description of the problem as it evolves
- A list of all of the subproblems or subdomains
- A list of all reference sources

Problem

Gaining familiarity results in a conceptual understanding of the problem's breadth and depth. The KE gathers information from available data sources and preliminary discussions with the domain expert. Together, the KE and the domain expert compile a "first-pass" problem description as a model. This model is modified and expanded as the team refines the problem description. The model is sometimes represented by strategy constructs.

The purpose of *strategy constructs* (SCs) is to specify typical problems that arise and the typical successful strategies that are used to solve them. Each problem type that is identified in a strategy construct contains a solution approach.

The benefit of SCs is the visual relationship of problem types and their solutions which can be displayed graphically using tables, hierarchical charts, flowcharts, or decision trees. By studying these visuals, the KE and the domain expert may work together to establish pattern matches between portions of the problem and the knowledge base. The strategy constructs also include the sources required to solve the problem and a description of the user community. Strategy constructs are illustrated in chapter 7.

Resources

Resources include knowledge sources which contain the written references and knowledge of one or several domain experts. The knowledge base for the problem is derived from the knowledge acquired from these sources.

Goals

The goals of the system were established before the project "go ahead" and are continually reemphasized and posted as the project rallying cry. By using this approach, the KE, the domain expert, and the development team maintain a common focus. It is very easy in a development effort to move beyond the identified scope in discussions or generate additional requirements. These goals are woven into a statement of the focus of the project—a goal or mission statement.

The statement of the system goals includes identification of the problem task, problem domain, problem scope, and the appropriateness of the application to solve the problem.

Team

The output of the defining tasks is an enriched understanding of the requirements by all of the key participants. When this phase is properly executed, the KE gains insight as to the:

- Abundance and reliability of the knowledge sources
- Structure of the knowledge
- Reliability of the knowledge
- Consistency of the knowledge
- Presence or absence of commonsense knowledge
- Strategies for acquiring the knowledge
- Problem-solving tactics of the domain expert

With this information, the KE and a representative from the organization can begin to assemble a development team. The Project Champion is generally the person that assumes this role. The team members and their responsibilities, titles, and decision-making boundaries are established. These team members generally come from a talent pool derived from the employees of the organization and employees of the developer or vendor. The KE considers personalities, motivations, and individual talents for the best team "mix."

THE DOMAIN EXPERT

The domain expert is a major key to the success of the system. We turn now to acquiring and utilizing that central personage.

Find the Expert

Because the knowledge-based system is both composed of and dependent upon an accurate, rich collection of heuristic knowledge, the source(s) of that knowledge undergo strict scrutiny. The quality of the system is dependent on the quality and structure of the knowledge base. The principal knowledge source, the domain expert, has the declarative knowledge (facts about objects, events, and things) and procedural knowledge (the link between stimulus and response) to provide reasoning and heuristic rules in a specific domain. The domain expert acquires the declarative and procedural knowledge through education, training, experience, and a basic ability to synthesize the process.

While the combined sources of human domain experts, books, databases, and other information sources provide the knowledge, the knowledge engineer harnesses the sources into a knowledge environment for the system. To do this, the KE is very selective about the sources of the knowledge base information.

A heuristic rule in this area is that the KE interviews several potential experts, if available, and selects one. One domain expert is best to work with because two or more experts are likely to have two or more problem-solving strategies and sets of tangible knowledge. The system will be validated at a later time with other experts. By using one expert, time will be saved and egos will not be bruised.

However, the more technical or extensive the knowledge domain, the more the KE needs to consider if multiple knowledge sources are required. If this is the case, the KE starts with the knowledge source which provides a general overview or a person who offers control over the "big picture" with its vital elements, attributes, and structures. The system validation is even more critical in situations having large or very technical knowledge bases.

In addition, the stated purpose of knowledge-based systems is to emulate the reasoning of the human expert. Because two experts will probably reason in different ways, the KE expends time and effort attempting to unify the diverse tactics. The resulting data can be reviewed by another domain expert. While one expert is desirable for development purposes, multiple experts may be required for political purposes or when there are gaps in the principal expert's knowledge.

Should multiple experts be required or desired, the following technique may prove effective. The technique is based on the Delphi Method. The purposes of the Delphi Method are to narrow divergence of opinion and eliminate the untoward effects of position, seniority, etc. Isolated experts are given a problem to solve and are debriefed using any of the techniques previously discussed. The solutions are collected, compiled, and redistributed anonymously for comment and revision. After two to four iterations, solutions converge and consolidate into a composite form. The disadvantage of the Delphi method is that it is more time-consuming and expensive than using a single expert for system development.

Find the Expert: The Process. The knowledge engineer is the outsider who coexists with the selected expert(s). Therefore, it benefits the knowledge engineer and the project when the KE is able to participate in the selection of the expert. Sometimes the expert comes along with the project; this person may be a somewhat reluctant participant or not really an expert. Selection of a candidate for the expert requires care. This care is in the form of seeking certain qualities in the expert, and, if these qualities fall short, of having a fallback plan. The principal attributes of a project expert, as mentioned earlier, are:

- Knowledge that fits the demands of the project
- An ability to communicate that knowledge
- Commitment to the success of the project
- Time to dedicate to the project

The time factor is the hardest to achieve of the four listed attributes of a candidate for the position of project expert. The most common tendency for selection of the Project Expert is to use the designated guru or a person in an administrative role. Save the big guns (gurus) for the big projects or have them serve in the role of knowledge base validator. The more expert the experts, the greater the demands on their time. Administrators tend to be removed from the deep knowledge of the problem that is to be solved. However, watch out for politics. If the boss says, "I'm it," then the boss is it.

Smaller projects and even portions of larger projects can be staffed by lower-level experts (if there is such a thing). These lower-level experts are easily identified by their peer group. One place to look for these experts is among the target users for whom the system is being designed. Lower-level experts tend to have fewer demands placed on their time. These experts tend to have the application knowledge without the theoretical background. For these experts, the project may not be their prime interest, but it should be close to their hearts.

One way to locate an expert is to ask, "Who is it that makes the day-to-day decisions—not policy decisions, but decisions made 'in the trenches'?" It is often more efficient to enlist the sergeant who knows how-to rather than the lieutenant with the when-to knowledge.

The Needed Expertise for the Problem. Even experts have limits to their expertise. These limits are in terms of breadth or depth of knowledge. For example, doctors who are general practitioners may recognize a broad range of symptoms. However, the depth of their knowledge may be insufficient to solve a particular problem. In that case the doctor refers the patient to a specialist. General practitioners recognize the limits of their knowledge.

Further, experts are selected for the extent of their knowledge about solving problems of the type to be solved. This knowledge match needs to be sufficient in breadth and depth to meet the project requirements. It is extremely important to carefully define the problem to be solved prior to interviewing experts.

Exploring the Expertise. In exploring the problem with potential expert(s), KEs are interviewing the field of candidates as well as applying knowledge engineering skills. The KE investigates the qualifications of the experts as they compare to project needs. The KE's role is that of selling the job of project expert, selling himself or herself and doing an initial screening of candidates.

The KE is prepared to provide general information about knowledge-based applications in terms of features, functions, and benefits. In addition, the KE helps to establish the mission statement for the project and describes the intended users of the completed system. This description is followed by projected features, functions, and benefits of the development effort.

Management contributes a list of experts with some type of justification or biographical information, and a place to have informal discussions. The expert candidate pool should be given information about the KE and the project under consideration. Management needs to communicate confidence and enthusiasm in the project to the project's potential personnel.

In the initial contact, the expert may raise issues that indicate hesitations and a shaky comfort level about knowledge-based systems. If so, the expert could be expressing discomfort about being put on the spot to produce precise knowledge and have all of the answers to every situation. The KE needs to alleviate these fears.

Another facet of the initial contact is energy and signs of support. The expert indicates verbally or non-verbally an interest or non-interest in the effort. Reluctant experts can ruin the day of a KE. The initial contact should reveal the general breadth and depth of the expert's knowledge, as well as ability and willingness to communicate. This contact should also yield an indication of the expert's personality and levels of cooperation.

The preceding may seem very one-sided in that the KE is "expert shopping," while the expert has little or no voice in the choice of a KE. The KE is staking the success of the project and perhaps a professional reputation on the expert and the anticipated working relationship. The KE exhibits prudent judgment in the selection of the expert for the project. While there are many areas to evaluate that focus on unique aspects of a problem or project requirement, there are some general attributes that can be considered. Attributes of a likely candidate include:

- Expertise:
  The expert is able to dispense accurate, quick, and timely solutions to problems. This requires high-level analysis skills and a wealth of mental models from which to draw.

- Confidence:
  The expert should demonstrate self-confidence about his knowledge in the domain.

- Communication:
  The expert should be able to communicate his knowledge from various perspectives in varying degrees of breadth and depth.

- Perception:
  The expert needs to differentiate among knowledge sources and select those relevant to the application under development.

- Perseverance:
  The expert needs to have worked on long-term projects that were iterative in nature, exhibited team and personal milestones, and challenged the expert.

- Humor:
  The knowledge acquisition process is an intense, sometimes frustrating experience. The expert and the KE will profit if the expert can maintain a sense of humor.

- Commitment:
  The expert needs to express commitment to development efforts, and understanding of the project's probable demands on personal time.

Experts who have these seven attributes as well as levels of competence, credibility, and peer recognition for these attributes are top-notch candidates.

Everyone has heard about first impressions. There are some first impressions that can make experts less than desirable candidates. The negative attributes—those of an unlikely candidate—include:

- Expertise: The expert flaunts vast book or theoretical knowledge, but has too little practical experience. The breadth and depth of knowledge required to meet the application is questionable.

- Confidence: The expert exhibits an attitude of total knowledge, superior to the local peer group (usually identified by name), and takes on the status of the Oracle of Delphi.

- Communication: The expert communicates knowledge from one perspective, does not display appropriate breadth and depth for the application, and speaks in a didactic manner. Direct questions tend not to be answered, or responded to by war stories.

- Perception: The expert fails to differentiate among knowledge sources that are relevant to the application under development. The expert perceives that the application is inappropriate, inadequate, and incomplete in concept, scope, and design.

- Perseverance: The expert is accustomed to rendering a quick opinion and handing off the work to someone else. A conversation about perseverance is turned into a discussion of the expert's self-importance. This expert is quick to say, ''That's not in my job description.''

- Humor: The expert's picture is in the dictionary next to the word *stoic*, or is on a poster at the local comedy auditions. In either case, this expert may wear thin the patience of team members over the course of the development effort.

- Commitment: The expert verbalizes commitment, but is unable to schedule a time to meet again, needs to constantly consult a schedule, or talks about juggling appointments . . . these are signs of an unwillingness to commit.

These attributes do not necessarily preclude selection of an expert with one or more of them, but it is often easier to rule out a choice than make the perfect selection. The KE may need to justify the choice for or against selected candidates for project expert. Establishing sound selection criteria will save time, effort, and possibly face.

Multiple Experts. Sometimes projects need the services of more than one expert. Multiple experts can be profitably utilized when there is a large application that can be decomposed into logical chunks to be worked on separately. Distributing the work load among experts eliminates time burdens on a single expert.

Multiple experts can also participate on smaller projects. In small project situations, there is a lead expert who focuses on the creation of the knowledge base. Other participants serve as rule validators and testers after prototype production. The KE needs to realize and communicate that too many experts participating in a project are likely to delay project completion by a factor proportional to the number of excess experts.

Sometimes (fortunately, rarely) management assigns multiple experts to a project that does not need the extra bodies. If management cannot be convinced of the time and cost savings which could be achieved by removing one or more experts, the assignment was probably political in nature. In cases like this, problems can be minimized by deciding on a lead expert and assigning validation, testing, and research roles to the other participants.

Disagreements are likely to arise among the experts, as backgrounds and problem-solving approaches differ. Sometimes, the disagreements are the result of semantic problems. The KE helps to clarify the issues by rephrasing statements or by making statements such as, ''Can you rephrase that so I can understand what you said?'' Another question that works well is, ''Can you give me an example of that?''

Disagreements also take place as a result of deviating from the project mission. Some individuals have ideas or make comments that broaden the scope of the effort. The KE maintains the scope of the project. A mission statement that is posted is one way to maintain scope. However, if there are valid reasons for broadening the scope, a formal approach to management is in order. It is often better to regroup and hit the mark, than to move ahead and have an ineffective application.

What Candidate Pool? It would be an understatement to declare that some projects offer little, if any, choice in experts. In this situation, the KE is a diplomat and is prepared to dig in his or her heels. The critical attributes mentioned earlier can be boiled down to three requirements:

- Expertise: The expert has demonstrated expertise in the problem space of the targeted application. This expert is able to cite typical problem states and resolution tactics. There are general problem-solving strategies that allow for quick diagnosis. These strategies are not to be found in books, but reside in heuristic knowledge.

- Communication: The expert is willing and able to communicate expertise. This expert is sometimes found in a teacher or mentor role. The problem-solving strategies, tactics, and knowledge sources are shared in an articulate fashion. The KE sometimes challenges points of conflict in statements, approaches, or rule sets.

- Commitment: The expert wholeheartedly accepts the effort, and commits to it. This commitment includes a willingness to work in a team environment. Commitment is often evidenced by enthusiasm expressed about the benefits of the proposed application and its role in the "big picture" of the company's growth directions.

If this portrait does not fit any of the available expert personnel, the KE and management need to have a serious discussion. The company can supplement its experts by using consultants. These consultants can provide or augment missing breadth or depth of the knowledge required for the application. The KE can tactfully express to management that the knowledge-based application under consideration is intended to close the gap that is currently filled by a consultant.

Communicating with the Expert

There is one basic rule for success in working with the expert. That rule is mutual respect through communication. This mutual respect does not imply intense friendship, but rather a relationship that is a marriage of convenience. Success is dependent upon teaming where a win is a win for the team and a loss is unacceptable. One way to help establish this respect is to clarify roles. The expert has the responsibility of providing the knowledge and the KE is in charge of making the expert look good.

One way to quicken rapport is for the KE to become familiar with the expert's jargon. The first step in learning the jargon is to develop a dictionary of terms. Consider this dictionary as a beginning. The KE "rolls up his sleeves" and experiences the terms even if it is a vicarious experience.

Motivating the Expert

Each person has different sources of motivation. Often motivation is related to acceptance of the project. Motivational techniques are different for willing and resistant participants. Some dimensions when considering motivation include the approach taken to introduce the project, the person's commitment to the job and company, internal motivation, attitudes toward technology, and interest in growing in terms of exploring new ground.

Most knowledge engineers are familiar with basic motivational principles and theories. These principles and theories include: Maslow's hierarchy of needs, Herzberg's motivational theories, and other popular motivational approaches.

Ritti (1969) studied professionals including scientists, engineers, and other technical people. These people were labeled as *local* or *cosmopolitan* with respect to their working motivations and loyalties. A local worker was described as an individual whose loyalty is directed to the organization. A cosmopolitan worker's loyalty transcends the immediate organization and is oriented toward peer workers, academic circles, and other professional communities. Ritti wrote,

> Locals are more interested in application, working on technology that is applicable to the business aims of the company. The "local" type is expected to pattern his behavior and to measure his success against internal or company standards; the "cosmopolitan" is expected to measure his success against the standards of his entire profession or field of specialty.

Local workers tend to be motivated by increased pay or internal recognition. Cosmopolitan workers tend to be motivated by professional recognition, autonomy, and an ability to publish findings or attend conferences. The KE might increase the odds of project success by being aware of the motivational needs of the project expert(s).

The Domain Expert in Summary

Selection of the expert(s) was covered in detail in the sections on knowledge sources and their ranking in chapter 2.

Selling the Project

Given that management has agreed to the initial candidate pool, it is time for the KE to gain acceptance from the expert(s). It is likely that one or two of the experts stand out in the mind of the KE. Now is the time to sell the project to the experts with the objective of gaining commitment.

A memorandum might be sent to the expert from management, stating that the expert has been selected to play a role in an upcoming project requiring expert knowledge. This memo serves two purposes. It provides a vote of confidence in the abilities of the expert, and it offers an opportunity for the expert to decline the honor before meeting with the KE in a mood of less than joyful anticipation.

Selling the project requires a seller and a buyer. In any sales situation, the seller is prepared. This preparation includes learning more about the expert from such available sources as managers. Selling also includes providing information, focusing the purpose, persuading, and gaining commitment. According to Hersey (1985), selling and selling styles are behaviors that are matched to buying readiness. His book presents a model that knowledge engineers would do well to read and study.

Selling is not successful without a buyer. The expert should gain interest in and commitment to the project and want to become involved. Most good salespersons are able to demonstrate their wares. Therefore, the KE should be prepared to put on a miniclinic. This clinic presents various knowledge-based applications to the expert. The KE makes comments about each of the systems shown. These comments are directed at question types, user interfaces, and the "feel" of the system.

The KE hopes that the expert begins to ask questions about the applications and offers suggestions. These suggestions for improvements may need prompting. The conversation is steered toward the processes used to acquire the knowledge inside the applications.

With an expert system shell, a KE can build a sample application that demonstrates what a knowledge engineer does, the role of the expert, and a little insight into the process of building an application. The subject of the application can be part of a hobby, wine selection, or a small piece of relevant technical knowledge. The small amount of time invested in the construction of a so-called toy system can be very telling.

The reaction of the expert to the completed toy system should be positive. If the expert is underwhelmed, the KE had better find out why this is the case. The KE probes the expert's apprehension. This apprehension may be the result of doubt or misunderstanding about the larger application. The sales skills of the KE come into play to overcome these objections.

It is likely that the expert is looking beyond the toy problem and surveying the future. Typical concerns include the possibility that the developed application will replace the job of the expert or change the exact nature of what the expert is expected to do. A weakening of the expert's confidence level may begin to surface.

The KE anticipates these and other concerns and is prepared with responses to the concerns. The selection of the expert is one of the crucial aspects of the project. The KE needs to remember that the expert should be exceptional and well-balanced—not merely acceptable.

There are some techniques and questions that a KE can use with an expert during pursuit of a sale:

- Find out what the finished system can accomplish that is beneficial to the expert. Examples are: save the expert time, archive the expert's knowledge as a living legacy, allow the expert to grow into other areas.
- Communicate how the system will meet the requirements of the expert.
- Probe for interest from the expert. For example, "If we can make the system do X, would this be a worthwhile project for you?"
- Be prepared to answer typical questions with examples from success stories.

- Pursue an agreement that the system performance target is important to the expert.
- Avoid questions that can be answered with a yes or no.

Preparing the Expert

While the expert might be a master of the domain, there might be little familiarity with knowledge-based systems development efforts. A description of how those proceed is presented to the expert. More importantly, the domain expert(s) should have a complete understanding of the requirements and performance expectations for the project.

Specify Performance Expectations

The domain expert and those who are subsidizing the financial aspects of the development require performance specifications. These specifications are generally linked to system performance during the validation tests. They might be in the form of a comparative problem resolution in which a novice uses the system and an expert uses heuristic knowledge to solve a specified problem.

If the establishment of the performance criteria is jointly organized by the KE, domain expert, and other team members, a common goal is established which can bond the development team. The performance criteria help to focus the development as a physical embodiment of the mission statement that was created in the predevelopment stage.

The KE, expert, and team members need to establish a plan by which the development effort will proceed. This plan contains the expected outcomes of the system, the performance criteria that will validate the outcomes, and a strategy for knowledge acquisition. Some or all the outcomes were specified in the contract; however, the team needs to further refine the project while in the midst of it.

The problem was identified and parameters established at the points of project inception and first pass. Following the identified limits, the KE begins the task of graphically depicting the problem, outputs, conditions, and exceptions. The purpose of these tasks is to launch the decomposition of the problem into subproblems.

During the course of graphic depiction of the problem and its subproblems, the team may begin to question and rethink the exact nature of the problem. This is not an uncommon occurrence. The knowledge acquisition process and knowledge base system building process are iterative. At this stage, the KE and the domain expert are forming an understanding of the problem and listing its key concepts and parameters.

The KE and the domain expert are also gaining an understanding of the correlation between the knowledge and the performance rules of the system. An early rule base is beginning to emerge, albeit in crude form. The benefit of this rule base is an understanding of the exercise by the domain expert. This understanding concerns the relationship between the questions and the outputs.

The output of these tasks is an established validation strategy for the completed system. It is easier to acquire knowledge and develop a system when the KE and the domain expert are aware of and agree on the criteria by which the completed system will be judged.

The criteria are detailed in behavioral terms with little left that is subject to interpretation. By stating the validation criteria in measurable terms, judgmental calls can be minimized. As a result, contractual agreements can be consummated with other ideas such as "why not . . . ." "Should the system be able to . . ." type comments also fall out of contract scope. These additional considerations can be topics for system modifications or additional systems.

A heuristic rule in this area is that without criteria for closure, the system can and will be in the development stage for eternity. For this reason the system is field-tested for a significant period of time—six months to one year—before revision. The validation of the system is accompanied by "bug" sheets, a formal reporting structure, and the gathering of sufficient evidence before taking action.

Here are examples of performance criteria statements:

> The target audience will be able to reach the same conclusion that the domain expert reached on a specified number of documented cases. A designated user of the completed system will be able to reach the same conclusion as the domain expert on a certain number of simulated or hypothetical situations.

Essentially, the KE specifies and gains agreement on performance criteria that meet the intent of the system. The criteria are based on a *gap analysis*. A gap is the difference between the outcome state and the initial state. The KE and the domain expert detail and build to the initial states, anticipate the outcomes, and construct a knowledge base that contains the "gap" specification.

A part of establishing the performance criteria is to establish a preliminary knowledge breakthrough. Some of the preliminaries include: the establishment of the data dictionary, the beginning of the Project Notebook, a listing of the first-pass determination of inputs and outputs for the system, selection of typical solutions, and beginnings of identifying problem-solving strategies.

THE PREPARATION

There are many actions that a KE performs in order to meet the responsibilities of the position. The actions include:

- Gain familiarity; review the content
- Specify performance expectations
- Select the tool
- Refine the demonstration prototype

- Develop the detailed design specification
- Identify the outcomes
- Identify considerations
- Capture the knowledge
- Select the domain expert
- Select the strategy
- Perform the knowledge acquisition
- Organize the knowledge
- Encode the rules and examples

FORMS, REPORTS AND WORKSHEETS

The last step in the preparation process is to establish the data gathering and reporting methodologies for the project. These forms, reports, and worksheets establish a reference and audit trail for the project's progress and can be recorded on hard copy or on-line.

It is recommended that the KE make maximum use of available or developed computer-based tools for as much of the process as possible. These tools enable data preparation and analysis to be done with minimum heroic effort and memory strain. Tools that can output reports save another necessary but time-consuming task.

Team Forms

Team forms are comprised of a combination of typical personnel information and interview forms. When there are multiple experts on a project, the work load is divided. However, not everyone is assigned to an area of strength, has the same ability to communicate, or shares the same spirit of the effort. The team forms can be used for initial screening of experts or during a session to learn the level of expertise needed to perform selected tasks.

The form is multipurpose and might or might not apply in every situation. However, consistency of forms can save set-up time, reduce confusion, and benefit the effort.

Team Form

Name _____   Title _____

Phone _____   Office No. _____

Primary Job Responsibilities   ### Education or Training Needed

1 = less than 2 years

2 = more than 2 years

1. _____   1   2

2. _____   1   2

3. _____   1   2

4. _____   1   2

5. _____   1   2

With 1 = low and 5 = high, rate the performer on the following:

Interest in the Project   1   2   3   4   5

Ability to Communicate   1   2   3   4   5

Session Form

The session form is used to document interactions between the KE and the domain expert(s) or documented sources. These forms can be keyed to problem components such as the overall problem, subproblems, or subdomains.

The session form lends an air of organization and provides a structure that is more productive than casually run meetings.

Session Form

Date _____   Session Number _____

Time _____   Location _____

Participants:

1. _____   Responsibility _____

2. _____   Responsibility _____

3. _____   Responsibility _____

4. _____   Responsibility _____

5. _____   Responsibility _____

Session Objectives:

1. _____

2. _____

3. _____

Session Notes:

Session Accomplishments:

Examples:

Factors   **Results**

       1:_____   2:_____   3:_____   4:_____   5:_____

Attributes:

    a.

    b.

    c.

    d.

An agenda is established for sessions. The agenda helps to maintain focus and utilize time to everyone's advantage. Meetings or sessions that extend into more than one encounter should use a session form with newly defined session objectives.

Session Agenda

Introduce personnel:

Introduce agenda:

List intended outcomes:

Notes for highlights:

Session summary:

Action Items:

Reports

Reports are used to keep the lines of communication open and to follow the progress of the project. If reports are completed weekly, there will be few surprises and caution flags raised. This is preferable to operating in a crisis management mode.

A typical weekly report contains a heading detailing the date, project name, vendor contact person, and the project manager for the host company. A section for "tasks to be performed" discusses vendor plans for the week such as milestones, production expectations, etc. This section also discusses tasks for the buyer such as reviews. The "questions/remarks/issues/flags" section identifies concerns and unresolved issues, and presents reminders for tasks that were not completed by the buyer.

WEEKLY REPORT

Date:

Project:

Vendor Contact:

Project Manager:

Task Performed: Vendor/Buyer

Tasks to be Performed: Vendor/Buyer

Questions/Remarks/Issues/Flags

WORKSHEETS

Worksheets are visual documents that record the substance of thought. Examples include those that define the problem domain, subdomains, and subproblems; explore rules; sketch physical and logical layouts; and serve as working documents during sessions. Much of the data collected on worksheets can be transferred to the appropriate session form.

Worksheet

Problem Domain Description:

Subdomains Identified:

Subproblems Identified:

Rules Derived:

Sketches:

    Title:

    Purpose:

FACT SHEET

A fact sheet is established at this stage of the process summarizing the project plan to date. This fact sheet becomes a part of the Project Notebook and is updated as changes occur.

Fact Sheet

Mission Statement:

User Description:

Performance Expectations:

Team Members:

Schedule:

Setting:

Resources Required:

Knowledge Acquisition Strategies:

SUMMARY

This chapter focused on the initial development of a knowledge-based application from *kick off* through design. These initial stages are potentially time- and energy-consuming, and therefore costly.

Agreement on the problem, mission statement, and project goals; development of a team and its members (in terms of roles and numbers); identification and bounding of the domain; creation and upkeep of project documentation; and identification, review, and acquisition of resources are the critical tasks at this stage. One of the most difficult tasks in terms of client-KE relations and the relative "ease" of project development and success is the selection of a domain expert. Here is where a KE's human relations and professional/technical expertise are tested. Politics, motivation, information versus working knowledge, time, cost, communications skills, and other variables are considered. Based on a solid foundation consisting of a well-designed plan of action that includes both a log of project progress and acceptance by the team of each milestone and critical decision point, the KE can move the project into its next phase: prototype development.

PRACTICAL APPLICATION

1. Develop a chart, grid, table, or other graphic aid to display knowledge sources and their attributes. (A suggested framework is shown on the facing page.) Then select a narrow domain area for which you must acquire knowledge. Choose either an analysis- or synthesis-based type of application as the structure for your system. Now fill-in your chart, assessing the quality and need for the various sources of information that should be acquired. Prepare a report for a hypothetical client, summarizing your findings.

2. A common dilemma of project engineers in any field is that once management has signed-off an agreement to develop a system, they want to move immediately into development. The danger lies in bypassing a detailed analysis of the project's mission and a well-thought-out design and development plan. What are some of the ways you would address this problem in terms of prevention (before it happens), meeting it "*head-on*" (when it happens), and prevention of reoccurrence (after it's happened)?

KNOWLEDGE SOURCE	Availability and Accessibility	Level of Risk	Type of Info	Dated-ness	Depth and Breadth	Level of Detail	Validity and Reliability	Format	Level of Inter-action	Range of Use
Books/Guides										
Empirical										
Research										
Computer										
Formal										
Informal										
Periodical										
Records										
Mechanical Recordings										
Presentations										
Visits										
Humans										

3. Create a mission statement with the attributes presented in the chapter.

4. Create your own Help Wanted ad for a knowledge engineer. What is the single most important attribute of the candidate?

5. A knowledge dictionary is commonly used in knowledge-based development efforts. What other industries can benefit by using a knowledge dictionary? Why?

6. Select a domain that is familiar to you. List the major factors of that domain that a knowledge engineer would need to know about in order to construct a knowledge-based application. What would the application do? Who would use it? How would it benefit the organization?

7. Think of someone that you consider an expert. What separates the skills and knowledge of this individual from those of the expert's peer group? How would you confirm this expertise?

8. What are the parameters you would consider in project selection? Describe a perfect project for a knowledge-based application.

9. Map strategy constructs for problems for which you can hypothesize solutions, such as a lamp that will not work. Use a table, a flowchart, and a decision tree to graphically represent each of your selected problems.

10. Generalize a knowledge-based application example. With a small group, use the Team Form to select your team. Prepare a Session Agenda, complete a Weekly Report, and establish a Fact Sheet. This exercise can be used as your personal case study and can be further addressed in chapter 6.

6

Knowledge Acquisition: Preparation

I am but a gatherer and disposer
of other men's stuff, at my best value.

Sir Henry Wotton

INTRODUCTION

From inception to maintenance, knowledge engineering is a task-rich challenge. This challenge should be considered a marathon rather than a sprint, as the tasks involved take time, care, and iterations. There are two main participants in the knowledge acquisition process—the knowledge engineer (KE) and the domain expert. The KE has the task of acquiring the required knowledge to develop the knowledge-based system. The domain expert provides the information needed to form the knowledge base.

The knowledge acquisition process is the result of a well thought out but iterative plan that requires vigilance and patience. This chapter is designed to cover the declarative aspects of knowledge acquisition preparation. The procedures for the tasks introduced in this chapter are discussed in part III.

THE DEFINITION DOMAIN

The "discovery" efforts discussed in chapter 5 will have produced a design framework that the KE and the domain expert can examine like a joint-effort sculpture. They can look at it from different angles, request the opinion of others, discuss options for display, etc. The output is a good points/bad points list.

The KE and the organization have bounded the project effort and assembled a team to effect a knowledge-based system solution to the problem. The next step ought to involve the team. If the team creates a bond, they can ensure a successful effort. This can be accomplished by sharing information and knowledge to enhance the full team's understanding of the domain and acceptance of the development effort.

The KE has explored a variety of knowledge base sources and has probably developed a mental model of the problem and its domain. However, other members of the team also have mental models. Each team member is compelled to put his model ''on the table.'' The models should merge into a single reference. Mental models were discussed in chapter 1. Consider a group of people given the task of drawing a map for a visitor. This map starts from their present location and goes to a destination of the visitor's choice. Each person in the group has a ''best route'' to achieve the visitor's goals. Seven people are likely to produce five or six different maps. These maps are different because some of the cartographers considered different parts of the problem including the visitor's knowledge of the area, the method of transportation, the time of day, the season, road conditions, etc.

The same ''best route'' views and opinions are present in a knowledge-based development effort. The KE manages the effort to define the system and domain concepts. The knowledge immersion should have produced a structure which is also called a concept framework. Instructional designers refer to this framework as the skeleton that is to be fleshed out. The framework consists of shallow knowledge. The flesh is the deep knowledge that is laid out in this chapter. Chapter 7 presents tactics to effect the strategies.

The principals on the team begin to establish answers to questions that explore a system concept. These questions include:

- Does the original mission statement stand or does it require modification?
- What is the composition of the main problem group?
- What are the subproblems?
- What data and information types are required? What is their availability?
- What are the primary concepts being explored?
- What are the problem's solutions, ranges, quick fixes, early warning indications, options?
- Are there any sources required outside of the team?
- How much time will be required to elicit the knowledge to form the knowledge base?
- How rigorous a schedule can be set up to accomplish the development effort?

Through these types of questions, the KE, the domain expert, and the team can refine the design specification. A heuristic rule in this area is to carefully review the possible problems that are to be confronted by the system and the list of possible solutions to those problems. In order to conduct this investigation, additional experts, manuals, documents, etc. may be consulted. It is critical that the link or links between the possible problems and acceptable solutions are achieved. A management representative signs off once these links are formed. This sign-off is used to protect both the developer and the management personnel. It is a communication device as well as recognition of achieving a project milestone.

Following the detailed list of outcomes comes a list of required inputs necessary to achieve the outcomes. This list includes all of the choices that the user considers, along with any facts, numerical data, and other information that the user will be required to input.

In order to achieve the conceptualization of the domain, the KE rapidly focuses the attention of the team. First, the KE applies proven techniques to blueprint this conceptual knowledge. Next, the KE assesses the results and plans the knowledge acquisition nucleus. The concept set elements described in chapter 1 can be surfaced through common facilitator communication techniques. The results of the concept set can be analyzed and built into a working mental model.

Hart (1986) states that the conceptual model depends upon the domain under consideration, and is the result of agreements on some conceptualizations of the problem. Hart includes issues such as:

- What are the inputs or problems?
- What are the outputs of the solutions?
- What types of inputs cause difficulties for the expert?
- How are the problems characterized?
- How are the solutions characterized?
- What sort of knowledge is used?
- How are problems or methods broken down into smaller units?

More detailed questions include:

- What data are input; in what order and form?
- What are the interrelationships between the data items?
- Which data might be missing?
- What assumptions does the expert make?
- What constraints are there?
- What sort of inferences are made?
- How are concepts or hypotheses formed?
- How do these relate to each other?
- How does the expert move from one state to another?
- Which evidence suggests particular goals or concepts?
- What are the causal relationships?
- Are there any logical constraints on the system?
- Which problems are easy, common, hard, interesting, etc?

RESOURCE POOLING

The team members have the breadth and depth of knowledge to address and identify the domain. The contributions from this team help to establish the focus of the knowledge acquisition efforts. The team members provide a collaboration of opinion to form the problem state—goal state differentials, the inputs required to meet these state changes, the interface needs, the primary group of major factors, and some of the attributes required to effect the change.

Chapter 1 discussed aspects of knowledge including knowledge levels composed of facts, concepts, rules, and heuristic knowledge, as well as concept sets. Pooling the resources allows exploration of the levels of knowledge required for the system. The team can easily establish the facts or the relationships between the objects, symbols, and events. They can also construct the concept level of the knowledge requirements by structuring the factual relationships into concept groups or low-level models. Finally, the team can contribute basic declarative and procedural statements to form the third level of knowledge, that of rules.

In addition, the team can identify and sort out any commonsense knowledge requirements which might have surfaced from these discussions and which could influence the solution sets. While common sense should be acknowledged and explored before the project starts, this is not always the case. The KE carefully investigates any of the commonsense requirements that may surface, and weighs the alternatives.

There are four basic alternatives used to address the commonsense issue. The first alternative is to fashion a team decision that the commonsense knowledge is trivial and not a factor. Secondly, the commonsense knowledge may actually be informed common sense which can be trained. Third, the target user base of the system may require elevation in talent or experience. Lastly, this factor may be strong enough to be a ''show-stopper'' requiring the project to be terminated.

The likelihood of suffering a show-stopper at this juncture is slight but not zero. Each discovery is graphically represented. One effective representation medium is a whiteboard. It is an easy to view, easy to modify medium that does not offer permanence or hard copy. Transparency projectors with light pen computer screen links are another effective, albeit expensive, medium.

The outputs of the resource pool are:

- The principal facts, concepts, and rules
- An idea of the higher-order rules and heuristic rule targets for the knowledge acquisition process.

THE WORKING MENTAL MODEL

The outputs from the pooled resource effort help to form a working mental model according to which the team orients its thinking for solving a particular domain problem. Mental models where characterized as schema-based knowledge representation structures containing the strategies for effecting the satis-faction of task requirements.

This working mental model focuses on key information and relationships of the schema within the domain. Problem-solving activities and the ultimate per-formance of the knowledge-based system emerge into focus following the estab-lishment of the working mental model. This focus emphasizes the gap formed by the difference between the problem state(s) and the goal state(s).

The working mental model is forged by concept clusters and cognitive map-ping. Michalski (1988) discussed concept clustering as one of the characteris-tics of human learning. Concept clustering is a part of learning by induction which includes the processes of concept acquisition, stimulus-response, and descriptive generalization. Concept clusters aid in the depiction of the primary elements in a domain and the drawing of conclusions based on interactions of the elements.

A cognitive or mental map can be constructed to represent the concept hierarchy and the interrelationships in the domain. A cognitive map is formed by listing the identified major factors in the domain. Each major factor spawns attributes which supply detail to the map. The attributes can be cataloged by order of occurrence, hierarchy or importance, or interrelationships. The cogni-tive map provides structure for the yet-to-be-scheduled knowledge acquisition sessions. Mapping strategies are discussed in chapter 7.

DEVELOPMENT OF THE DETAILED DESIGN SPECIFICATION

A detailed design specification is the KE's plan that describes the system's functionality and the manner in which it will be accomplished. Estimates are made about the total number of outcomes and the number of rules to support those outcomes. The plan, the schedule, and the budget are verified.

The detailed design specification builds on the functional specification. This specification is the project delineation. It tends to be more fluid for knowledge-based projects than for conventional software projects. This is because the domain of the project and the problem to be solved tend to solidify early into the project rather than at its onset. The procedures for developing functional and detailed specifications are discussed in chapter 9.

The functional specification starts with the mission statement. This mission statement is refined and supported by the development of various documents including flowcharts and logic diagrams. The document also contains answers to questions like those listed previously in the Definition Domain segment.

TOOL SELECTION

The tool selection process is critical. Tool options tend to have advantages and disadvantages tied to functionality. The breadth and depth of the knowledge base requirements are usually realized by this time. As a result, the KE is gen-erally adept at understanding the system requirements in terms of the know-ledge structure and interface requirements. In addition, the options for knowledge acquisition and knowledge representation are dependent on the tool. Some tools can accommodate performance requirements that others cannot. Under no circumstances should an entire design and knowledge acquisition effort be bent in an attempt to match a tool bias of the client or the KE.

Selection of a tool is based on identified requirements. These needs include knowledge representation requirements, user interface, expense, development skills and experience, RAM and storage requirements, and performance. The key factor for the tool to be selected is the match of the knowledge base structure, size, and control search strategies requirements. The selected tool is tested during the demonstration prototype effort. At that time, the tool, strategy, expectations, and form will begin to take shape.

Following the efforts at defining the problem, the next most difficult task a KE has is that of selecting the ''best'' tool. The selection task is difficult because of the fact that most tools and languages were not developed to support a particular problem type. For any given problem type, it is likely that there are several tools that can support it. Thus, the numbers of possibilities for selecting a tool places the burden of final selection on the KE.

Knowledge-based systems are software programs that run on a variety of hardware. In addition to the selection of software, the KE makes other selections in constructing the complete system. To select an appropriate tool for a knowledge-based application, the KE considers the available characteristics of the hardware, the tools, and the many ways the various pieces of the applications under construction can be linked. The following provides general information about hardware and software considerations and some questions to consider for the selection of the tool.

Hardware

This may come as no surprise, but hardware is at a more advanced technological stage by far than software. We are living in the era of the supercomputer. Machines such as the Cray 3 with it gallium arsenide chips, IBM's experimental TF-1, and other supercomputer research efforts have been aimed at multiple processors. It is the advent of these multiple processors that will stimulate the software of artificial intelligence.

The AI hardware in use today includes LISP machines and some contemporary machines that are dedicated workstations. Most knowledge-based system applications and languages can operate on almost all of the various hardware available. There are four basic hardware options for knowledge-based systems: mainframe computers, minicomputers, workstations, and microcomputers.

Mainframe Computers. Mainframe computers exhibit both benefits and drawbacks for knowledge-based systems. The benefits include large data storage and access to databases. Knowledge-based system applications, such as planning and design systems, require access to databases. If the user has a mainframe available and a software tool or language that is supportive of the application, a mainframe system could be extremely effective. In addition, multiple users at remote locations can benefit from a mainframe-based application.

If the organization has a mainframe computer in place, a mainframe may need to be considered for the end product. There are many more reasons not to use the mainframe than to use it. Some of the plus sides of the decision were mentioned. Some of the negatives follow.

The drawbacks of mainframes include low-quality graphics, some inefficiency in running problems in LISP, and a narrower group of knowledge-based system tool options. Further, cost-effectiveness is generally low for applications. Usually, applications that are to be run on a mainframe system are developed on a mainframe. This could place a burden on the developer or on time resources on the mainframe. The demands on computing activities can slow response time of either the knowledge-based system application or other applications on the system. The developer and the organization must carefully weigh the potential benefits against the negative aspects of mainframe applications. Nowadays, there is one additional factor that plagues multiuser facilities, viz. the problem of computer viruses. Once a virus is introduced into one of the user programs, all of the users and all of the programs are potential victims.

Minicomputers. Minicomputers are medium-sized computers with many of the attributes of mainframe computers. Technology is improving the bandwidth between the terminal and the host so that graphic interfaces will improve in the near-term. The advantages of minicomputers are their connectiveness and sharing of databases. For an application requiring searches of dynamic data sources, this could be a good choice. The purchase of these machines and their software is becoming more cost-effective. Many of the features, functions, and benefits of minicomputers combine the strengths of mainframe computers and microcomputers.

Workstations. Workstations are presently of two basic types: List Processor (LISP machines), and conventional technology machines. LISP machines and conventional technology machines are usually single-user machines. LISP machines are dedicated to LISP processing and development. While the dedicated nature of these machines offers some advantages, there are also disadvantages. LISP workstations are, as of this writing, difficult to link with conventional software systems. Thus, LISP machines are isolated, or require added expense when there are requirements for data from outside sources. To supply the LISP workstation with the required data, added programming expenses are incurred. The linking of LISP workstations involves overcoming many obstacles.

Conventional processing machines are capable of being linked with other systems, and have a variety of knowledge-based system languages including LISP, a variety of tools, and a powerful development environment. The LISP options on a conventional machine are not as powerful as on a dedicated LISP machine.

In either case, dedicated workstations are expensive.

Microcomputers. Microcomputers are the fourth category of current hardware. Microcomputers are also called personal computers. With recent advances in technology, today's microcomputer has the power of yesterday's minicomputer. Its processing speeds and memory capabilities are improving almost daily. In addition, the 80386 chip and its successors, the advent of OS/2, and the reductions in terms of cost have made microcomputers attractive and available.

Microcomputers are capable of being interfaced with other microcomputers, minis, and mainframe computers. The current trend in computer architecture is to link unlike computers together to form a communications network. In addition, there is a vast quantity of knowledge-based system languages and tools available for microcomputers.

With microcomputers, the proliferation of knowledge-based system applications throughout industries, including entertainment and education, will be phenomenal. The more systems that are developed, the more feedback will be provided to the software developers. This loop will bring about higher quality development software and commercially available systems.

The primary hardware considerations for knowledge engineers are the operating system, the interfaces, and the configuration of the hardware components. The operating system is generally a software issue. However, if the application requires multitasking with an 80386 chip, the operating system works in tandem with the hardware. Knowledge-based systems that are designed to monitor and control manufacturing environments may need to run under UNIX and carry out multitasking. OS/2 can also do multitasking.

Software

There is a basic software choice to be made when building a knowledge-based system application. The choice is between use of a programming language such as C or LISP, on the one hand, and an expert system shell, on the other. An expert system shell contains all the components of an expert system except the knowledge base itself. This includes the user interface, an inference engine, and knowledge base support facility. Users of expert system shells can concentrate on structuring and representing the knowledge, and need no knowledge of programming, and, if the application is simple, limited AI expertise. Users of languages must create the expert system components as well as the knowledge structure and representation. However, there are expert system development languages emerging that provide some of these components.

Software for knowledge-based system applications is of secondary concern to the considerations of problem and user requirements. The use of conventional software, AI languages, and knowledge-based system tools is a function of the application, not the bias for a particular tool by the developer. In addition, no single tool, be it algorithmic conventional languages, symbolic AI languages, rule-based tools, object-based tools, or any hybrid, is inherently superior. The matching of the problem, the users, the hardware, the available experts, and the quality and competence of the KE determine the superiority of the system.

One consideration in the use of a shell or a language in a DOS environment is internal memory. The maximum amount of random access memory or working memory in the DOS environment, without expanded/extended memory, is 640K. Because memory is sometimes used dynamically by a program, it is easy to exceed the memory limit. This limit can be rapidly reached when a system makes outside calls to other programs that also require memory. The limit is also easily reached by embedded applications where the knowledge-based system resides in the background. Such operating systems as OS/2 and UNIX have a memory ceiling larger than 640K. RAM is one of many considerations for the developer during selection of a language or shell.

No matter what vehicle is chosen, the developers and financiers must realize that the knowledge-based system is built to give advice and serve as an important link in the decision-making process. Knowledge-based systems are electronic consultants or "black boxes," leaving the users and their input with control over the final decision. The knowledge engineer considers the knowledge-based system tool also as an instructional tool. If the system is properly designed with explanation subsystems, users can improve their skills to the level of recognized experts. There are many characteristics and features of the problem that the KE carefully considers when pairing the software with the application.

Tool Questions: Considerations

There are many characteristics and features of the problem that the KE carefully considers when pairing software with the application.

- What tools are available?
- Which knowledge representation schemes match the tools?
- What are the tools' abilities in terms of user interface flexibility, structures, and functions?
- What level of peripheral reach does each tool have?
- What are the levels of vendor support?
- What are the hardware requirements for the tools?
- What are the initial costs of the tools?
- What are the licensing restrictions?
- What training is available?

Tool Questions: Selection

- What is the knowledge representation scheme to be used for the problem?
- Which tools support this scheme?
- What are the interface requirements: graphics, inputs, outputs?
- Which tool(s) supports these interface requirements?
- What is the project's budget and does the tool(s) meet the budget?

The project team needs to become familiar with the capabilities and limitations of the selected tool.

SOFTWARE TOOL CHECKLIST

Product name

Manufacturer name

Address and Phone Number

Contact Person

Price

List of available utilities or libraries

Classification level

Hardware compatibility

RAM requirements

Operating system options

Language of the tool

Usability of external procedures

Compiler needed/not needed

Disk requirements

Chaining abilities

Explanation subsystem

Graphic interface

Database interfaces

Screen and report generators

Language output

Knowledge representation structure

Management of uncertainty

Interfaces

The knowledge engineer considers the user-machine interfaces as well as the machine-machine interfaces. The user-machine interfaces include input and output capabilities. The input interface could be a keyboard, mouse, touch-screen, or, soon, voice. The output interface may be a screen, data files, printer, or voice.

The user-machine interface is all that the user sees of the knowledge-based system. The knowledge base and development process are all transparent to the end-user. If the system is difficult to operate or understand, fails to behave as expected, or does not "feel" right, all of the expense and effort go to waste. The user-machine interface is designed with a focus on the target users with consideration given to the users' expectations, and how comfortable they are with computers and keyboards.

The user-machine interface must also be appropriate. The selection of the user-machine interface is important because some interfaces work better with some applications than with other applications. Further, a combination of user-machine interfaces may be a better solution. The KE must assess the requirements and wants of the end-users.

Machine-machine interfaces entail data exchange and equipment control. In these data exchanges, many technological challenges are encountered, such as fiberoptics, robotics, satellite communications, and other real-time, high-tech opportunities.

Operating Environment

The operating environment is the computer on which the developed program is designed to run. Considerations for computers include internal storage, speed, mass storage types, compatibility, and monitor types. In addition, the program is designed to run under the same specific operating system used by other applications on the computer.

The KE must be cognizant of the computer's storage capabilities, since some programs require massive amounts of storage. The knowledge base and inference program must be able to be accommodated by the computer. The KE investigates the intended computer. If there is a mismatch between requirements and what is available, the KE not only makes this fact known, but also follows up the mismatch until it is resolved. Random access memory (RAM) is the memory storage area used by application programs. It is the area in which the program is "brought up" for the user. Included in RAM are the computer's operating system, executive files, and other files that are required to run the program. The RAM portion is the volatile portion of memory that is lost when power is turned off.

Some applications of knowledge-based systems are accessed by a *hot key*. A hot key provides one-key access to an application like a training program, help function, or knowledge-based application. These applications are memory-resident programs, and use RAM, thereby limiting the amount of available RAM. The computer's RAM must be used judiciously.

Speed of computation and of disk access are very important in knowledge-based systems. This is particularly true of systems with large knowledge bases. These factors are most apparent to the user. For example, speed in personal computers ranges from about 1 megahertz to 33 megahertz. The KE is aware of access time and the users' comfort with how the program runs.

Disk drives in addition to the main hard drive may be used for database calls, graphics storage, and other programs used on an "as needed" basis by the knowledge-based system.

Compatibility concerns include the computer type, program interface, and components. The shell or language in which the knowledge base is programmed and stored must work within the computer's limitations. The KE must be aware of the available computers and the plans of the client. Even in-house development must take into account plans for future computer workstations, expansion, and other changes.

Some programs require a VAX, LISP, or UNIX environment; OS/2; or other special considerations. In addition, some environments are already established. The KE might be in a situation in which management wants to expand the use of a selected environment rather than introduce change.

Networks, whether local area or wide area, are considered for data sharing. Connectivity strategies can be valuable by promoting time and money savings. Software license restrictions are carefully addressed prior to deciding on a network strategy.

Monitor type can be a significant consideration when there is graphics or other software requiring high resolution, color representation, or video images. The KE weighs users and their requirements in light of the availability and costs of equipment.

QUESTIONS TO ASK

Armed with a general understanding of hardware, software, interfaces, and operating environments, there is a series of questions to ask or consider when selecting the appropriate system.

Hardware Questions

What hardware now exists?

The array of existing hardware may be able to support the knowledge-based system application's storage requirements, speed, RAM, user interface, and other considerations. The KE evaluates these concerns. Should there be inadequate hardware, recommendations are made for developing appropriate configurations.

Will the intended users of the application know how to operate the hardware?

Besides having the appropriate hardware for the application, the end users need to know how to operate the hardware. If the knowledge-based system application poses operational difficulties for the users, provisions are made to train the end users or accommodate their needs, e.g., those of handicapped users.

Is security needed?

Because of the nature of some of the systems constructed, there may be a requirement to address security precautions. These can range from machine location to passwords or other higher levels of security. The knowledge-based systems that are constructed have a wealth of distilled, focused knowledge that could be targeted for theft or manipulation.

Additional hardware questions include:

- Are there to be multiple users?
- How much storage space will the knowledge base require?
- Does the display require color? If so, CGA, EGA, or VGA?
- How much RAM will the knowledge-based system require?
- Do arrangements for peripheral devices need to be considered?
- What other software will the hardware be expected to run?
- Can the hardware be expanded?
- Are backup hardware systems required if there is *down-time* on the primary system?
- Processor speed?
- Number of slots?
- Number of ports?
- Physical space requirements?

Software Questions

Does the tool have the power to meet the application or project requirements?

The KE will choose between a programming language and a knowledge-based system tool (or a combination). A programming language permits flexibility, but generally results in longer development and higher cost. Tools are less flexible, but generally allow faster and less expensive development. The KE selects the language or tool based on the problem, the ability of the development team, and the cost and time constraints.

Does a shell type lend itself to the knowledge representation requirements?

Included for consideration of tools is how knowledge will be represented as rules, frames, semantic nets, etc. The ability of a shell to represent procedural knowledge, for example, may be important for designing hybrid systems.

Does the selected shell or language impact memory?

Shells and languages take storage and RAM space. The KE must be aware of the requirements of the application. This is especially true when the application is embedded or accessed using a hot key while other programs are resident in memory.

Does the reasoning strategy match the problem-solving model of the domain expert?

There are system features that can be used to conduct a search of the knowledge base. Different systems offer different search structures and different knowledge base types which, when combined, provide optimal search ability and consequently increased speed.

Is there a need for mathematical capabilities?

Sometimes mathematical computations are necessary for user input or tracking user responses. Not all tools support mathematical procedures.

Is the explanation subsystem adequate?

Not all shells offer the same features, provide the same functions, or extend the same benefits. Some applications require user explanation while others cannot take the time to offer explanation because of the nature of the decisions offered. The KE must understand the requirements of the users and the goal of the system to evaluate the explanation subsystem.

Are the text editor programs adequate for writing, forming, and editing the knowledge base?

The quality of the text editor can serve to simplify the creation and revision of the knowledge base. A helpful feature of an editor is the ability to import and export text. The KE must know the capabilities and limitations of the editor.

Can the system be linked to other application packages?

Since all of the knowledge or search strategies may not lend themselves to self-contained storage, external program calls to spreadsheets or database programs may prove beneficial. External calls can also be made to graphics or communication programs. The KE must identify and evaluate flexibility requirements of development personnel and intended end-users.

Are there adequate utilities that can be used in conjunction with the tool?

Utilities can make development easier. Common utilities include graphics capture programs, windowing programs, print screen options, report generation, code generation options, debugging utilities, and global options.

Is purchase price a consideration?

The shell price or language expense can range from as little as $50 for a PC-based workstation to over $100,000 for mainframe language programs. Price should be weighed second, after function and requirements.

Are there run-time license costs or restrictions?

In addition to purchase price considerations, most languages and shells impose a royalty or use fee on distribution copies. Another common fee is a version update charge. These fees can impact heavily on the total costs and prove to be a major expense.

Is there vendor support?

When a utility malfunctions, or a process does not seem to be working correctly, or a question arises, vendor support is necessary. If documentation is not sufficient, a vendor hot line may ''save the day.''

Interfaces

Is there a need to customize the presentation screens?

Many tools provide little flexibility for the developer to customize screen display or presentation. Display and presentation features provide such user interaction techniques as graphics, menus, and fill-in forms. The intended end-users might have experiences with, or expectations for, certain screen layouts or input routines. The KE develops an awareness of the intended users' experience and expectations for screen display. Acceptance by the users may be at risk if their perceived needs are not met.

Can the tool interact with the user through a variety of helps?

User helps ease understanding and learning for the user. Helps include function key and input descriptions, and explanations of program usage. Some tools offer hypertext abilities that can benefit both the developer and the end-users.

How is color used?

Flexibility in text and background appearance, including color, offers the KE an important set of presentation options for screen clarity. Screens can "feel" better and communicate better if planned for that purpose. The user should be readily able to read and understand the output, and provide input. The use of color can either help or hinder the users' understanding of the presentation and what is expected of them. Color can be used to highlight directions, options, and helps.

Operating Environments

The operating environment required or advisable for the application raises a number of significant questions.

What are the options for operating systems?

Currently available operating systems include PC DOS, MS DOS, OS/2, and UNIX. The KE determines the requirements of the completed system. For example, if the end product is accessed over a network, OS/2 or UNIX could be considered. There are operating environments that are machine-dependent, such as the Macintosh. The KE devises a plan based on what exists, what is needed, and what is possible.

Are peripherals needed?

Devices and architectures such as printers, modems, and LANs need to be considered and evaluated. Languages and shells do not automatically link to these devices. As a result, special interface programs or provisions may need to be investigated, designed, and developed.

Are disk drives needed?

Some applications require output of reports or access to graphics software or other data. If there is insufficient memory, or a requirement to place output or input files on a transportable disk, diskette drives will need to be considered. Current disk drive possibilities include 5.25″ double density and high density, and 3.5″ double density and high density. Each of these drive types has specific requirements, limitations, and other aspects that need to be considered.

Another class of drives uses Compact Disc (CD) technologies. These technologies include read-only (ROM), write once read many (WORM), erasable-writable, digital video interactive (DVI), and others. The CD options also have specific requirements, limitations, and other considerations that the KE focuses upon.

What are the file storage requirements?

File storage requirements vary according to the system files, knowledge base files, and other file requirements such as compilers. The KE must know the limitations of the hardware and the requirements of the application.

What are the RAM requirements?

RAM becomes an issue when the application runs concurrently with other programs. Under a conventional DOS environment, there is a 640K RAM limitation. However, there are options for extended (linear) and expanded (paged) memory. The KE considers the impact of the knowledge-based system application and any concurrent programs on the development effort.

Are there any specific requirements for monitors?

Monitors are available in a wide range of sizes, resolutions, colors, and other display options. Each of the monitor types has cost, benefits, and disadvantages associated with it. The KE considers cost, links, user requirements, language or hardware interfaces, and other features when selecting monitors or developing an application.

Are there any compatibility issues for the application?

The KE must consider compatibility with peripherals, LANs, other software programs, user knowledge, and other requirements or restrictions. Each of these requirements can impact the development effort.

KNOWLEDGE AND LANGUAGE

The representation of knowledge for a knowledge-based system also involves strategies that transform brain power into machine power. The creation of a knowledge system that can cope with a variety of knowledge types and depths is another challenge for the knowledge engineer.

The Depths of Knowledge

A conceptual view of knowledge acquisition for representation considerations focuses on knowledge depth. Knowledge can be decomposed into *surface knowledge* and *deep knowledge*. Surface knowledge applies to information within a narrow range of application, such as directory information or cursory solution applications. Surface knowledge is generally represented by declarative statements. Deep knowledge applies to an information structure that represents both the facts and the interactions among the components. Deep knowledge structures can be applied to generalized situations.

Shallow knowledge may consider that:

It barks, therefore it must be a dog.

Deep knowledge would consider:

It barks, therefore it is probably a dog. AND . . .

The animal IS about 22 inches tall and weighs about 60 pounds. It HAS a coat that is a golden color with shiny long fur on its tail and chest. It HAS ears that hang down. It HAS an overall appearance of balance and purpose. It is CONNECTED TO a variety of similar dogs. It LIKES to play in water. It HAS a kindly expression.

Typically, shallow knowledge deals with an input-output behavior or relationship. Deep knowledge considers knowledge about an object and attempts to create distinctions and discriminators. Deep knowledge tends to probe the fundamental attributes of a system.

Domain experts are inclined to discuss shallow knowledge topics as casual, simple facts. Deep knowledge is often discussed as a part of a system that influences other objects or structures. Shallow knowledge can also occur as a casual understanding of a complex subject. The KE develops an awareness of the knowledge level of the domain expert.

Within a knowledge-based system, a surface-level strategy can drive a system rapidly through a set of possibilities. This strategy is used prior to the deeper probing that takes place when a high-confidence possibility is located. Knowledge about a subject is a continuum, so the KE calculates where a logical cutoff is placed. This cutoff is established by the requirements of the knowledge structure and the purpose of the application.

The shallow knowledge example did not clearly define the situation and is subject to error. For example, if the barking were heard while near the ocean, the bark might have come from a seal. Shallow rules serve as an optimizer by helping to eliminate possibilities. If a knowledge-based system were to be used to draw conclusions about barking sounds and what makes them, the system might first ask for a location. This location question would explore the user's proximity to ocean sites.

The deeper knowledge structure institutes a probe of the underlying attributes. This deep knowledge is used to develop the rules, frames, and other knowledge representations that reflect the connectivity of the system and the nature of the relationships among attributes. The deep knowledge structure can serve to generalize the identification of objects within its base. The deep knowledge structure case of the dog could provide examples for identification of mammals. Instances in the knowledge base would include: habitat, behaviors, weight, size, color, and other factors.

Using the collected mammal attributes, the knowledge base could be elaborated to investigate beyond the simple concept of the mammal. It could be used to examine impact on the environment, desirable genetic traits, or breeding habits. These systems respectively, could be used to determine population shifts, survival of a species, and considerations for captivity.

Clearly, capturing and representing deep knowledge is difficult and time-consuming, thus expensive. The KE establishes a knowledge cutoff that considers the goal of the application and the target audience. Surface knowledge can be used in more systems than many KEs think. A system application designed to select business graphics does not need to contain a knowledge structure for the selection of instructional graphics. There are proven relationships between types of business graphics and the content to be represented. There is little need to explore the many additional considerations that apply to instructional graphics.

Both surface and deep knowledge can be represented using any knowledge representation technique.

Concept Sets Revisited

Chapter 1 introduced concept sets as a method of analyzing and organizing knowledge. This chapter focuses on the application of these concepts sets as a part of the knowledge acquisition process. In any knowledge representation effort, the knowledge is considered from a variety of perspectives that provide the attributes necessary for coding. The collective attributes that provide the representation constitute the knowledge set.

Once the domain expert and the KE have determined the major factors for knowledge acquisition, attributes and interactions are established. The following attributes and interactions define the knowledge set.

- Label
- Attributes
- Transaction
- Constraint
- Depiction

This knowledge set can serve as a guideline for establishing the attributes for any knowledge system. A KE can use the knowledge set as a knowledge diagram. The Label can be thought of as the subject of the sentence. This subject is usually a noun or a proper noun. A book can be labeled as "Hard Cover" or a component in an automobile labeled as "Battery."

The KE carefully specifies a label that is descriptive yet unique. The symbolic representation of the object can be selected in consideration of the object's function. A water storage and recreational facility might be termed "reservoir."

Attributes are addressed by a modifier or adjective. These adjectives can be descriptive as in "cloudy appearance," limiting as in "few bits," numerical as in "three pitches," or proper as in "English origin." Thus, characterization provides descriptions or principal attributes of the label.

The attributes are driven by the focus of the application. For example, an automotive repair system would not be concerned that a car is available in red, but a shopper's directory system would be. Knowledge acquisition is driven by the focus, and knowledge representation is chosen according to the intent of the application.

Transaction refers to the action type or verb that provides the link or defines the relationship. This verb is usually a transitive verb with an associated noun object. The verb-object varies as to need. For example,

- Action: A jet *breaks through* the sound barrier.
- Link: The battery *is connected* to the starter.
- Relation: A private *is subordinate* to a corporal.

Constraints are the cases or inflections that provide a relationship.

A golden retriever is a type of dog.

That relationship linked an object to a general class. A relationship may also link an object to an attribute:

A dog has a tail.

The constraints provide both a hierarchical and conceptual framework. One approach is to generalize an object into a larger group. A flower can be placed in the larger group of plants. Relationships can be established which locate or "tag" the plant under multiple headings such as green, over ten inches tall, edible, requires shade.

Hierarchical structuring can assist the search techniques of the inference system, and so increase selection speed. The hierarchy typically moves from general to specific.

Depiction refers to the operational parameters, e.g., when the temperature of water at sea level exceeds 212 degrees Fahrenheit, *it will boil* and begin to change form. The depiction is used to establish range values or an overall relationship. Typical depictions include size, age, location, values, etc. These values assist the inference system in optimizing its search. For example, if age is a factor, a question which sets a maximum of, say, 21 years can eliminate a significant percentage of the possibilities.

KNOWLEDGE ACQUISITION FOR REPRESENTATION

In order to represent declarative or procedural knowledge, knowledge is translated into structures which set out the major factors, their attributes, and what happens when certain conditions are true. The selected representation contains and uses appropriate and consistent names to describe the objects and events, and their relationships, and constraints.

The objective of representing knowledge is to support the processing required to arrive at a conclusion or to provide options for selecting a solution.

In knowledge-based systems, the knowledge engineer does research and determines what insight is available and how to acquire and represent that knowledge in a knowledge base. Knowledge representation consists of translating declarative and procedural interpretations into a form that can be interpreted by a machine.

Humans form knowledge constructs that constitute a perception network. This network starts with the perception of self and "spider webs" out through family, community, society, and the world. We humans are inclined to perceive all experiences through our personal models or knowledge constructs. Each human interaction or professional realization is evaluated, categorized, and stored based on these models. The KE studies the models of others to determine ways of representing knowledge. These knowledge constructs or models use a variety of techniques to gather and process inputs. Included among these processes are generalizing, questioning, interpreting, organizing, and predicting.

Generalizing

Generalized understanding can be exploited when a new set of inputs is encountered.

- Given: Person A has a generalized understanding about the operation of an automobile.

- Situation: There is an opportunity to drive an automobile model that has not been encountered in the past.

- Assumption: This person can drive the automobile.

In this case, there is an assumed transfer of previous experience to a new, but similar, experience.

Questioning

Humans have models that are in a constant state of refinement. There are constant probes when assumed outcomes deviate from internalized models. Refinement tends to be in two areas. One area focuses on exacting model expectations and the other focuses on a generalized set.

Interpreting

Among the drivers for questioning established models is sensory information. From sight, sound, touch, and smell, sensory input information is drawn and compared to stored models. When there is a match deviation, the questioning process begins. Each person has an internal sensory perception model of objects in the physical world. Sensory input is interpreted, matched against internal models, and an action plan is established. Recall instances when something did not seem right. One sensory input such as sight picked up no problems, but the sense of smell indicated something was amiss. Thus, questions are asked based upon interpretations measured against internal models.

Organizing

Comparing sensory input data to internal models permits a perceptual overlay that reveals similarities and differences. Organizing the interpreted data and questions allows a higher degree of synthesis and refinement of the models.

Predicting

With a solid model in mind, humans are able to predict events based on a performance or sensed trend. Often these predictions are less than one hundred percent certain. For example, trends in the stock market may cause a prediction of bull or bear behavior. The same is true for weather, medicine, and military and political strategies.

KNOWLEDGE REPRESENTATION STRATEGIES

The KE has options to consider when selecting a knowledge representation strategy. The knowledge representation system is influenced by the selected hardware and software. The selection of a knowledge representation strategy might have no limits in theory, but be limited in practice.

Given that a knowledge representation scheme is dependent on hardware and software, a KE evaluates options. There are four basic considerations for evaluation: the knowledge structures, the storage facility, the retrieval facility, and the programming environment.

The Knowledge Structures

Basic considerations for evaluating knowledge structures include the following items.

- What are the limitations of the symbolic representation in terms of numbers and types of elements, and the size and complexity of the structure which can be used to represent the domain knowledge?
- Is the knowledge structure defined by natural language statements, or does the user need to learn a programming language?
- Can portions of the knowledge structure be modified or moved within the knowledge structure with reasonable ease?
- Can portions of the knowledge structure be imported or exported to other systems?
- Are global search and replace capabilities available?

An important aspect of knowledge representation is the language used to build the structure. When natural language is used, a domain expert can review the structure for validation. If the knowledge structure requires a programming language, performance of the system is the only means of validation. This poses problems such as a requirement for translation and an inability to validate milestones. This translation effect in program language representation is akin to a person stating something in English and then representing it in another language. The accuracy of the translation is sometimes suspect.

The Storage Facility

Considerations for evaluating storage facilities include the following items:

- Can the operating system manipulate the stored files? Does each file carry a date-time stamp for latest version identification?
- Does the knowledge structure have fixed file size or field lengths?
- Does the knowledge structure require a minimum computing speed for acceptable operation?

Storage facilities vary in speed and dependability. The KE considers the flexibility and requirements of various systems. Flexibility of storage facilities can help the KE's productiveness and impact costs.

The Retrieval Facility

Basic considerations when evaluating retrieval facilities include the following issues:

- Are the knowledge base access methods and speeds acceptable?
- Do windows and overlays allow an adequate user interface?
- Are outside program calls subject to delays or unacceptable screen effects?
- Are there any provisions for browsing or quick search facilities?

The retrieval facility is seen by the developer and the end user, although transparent to both. The manner in which knowledge bases are accessed, presented, and able to handle input and output is critical to the development and delivery of a quality system.

The Development Environment

Considerations when evaluating a development environment include the following concerns.

- How does the development environment handle searches?
- How does the development environment support rapid prototyping?
- How powerful is the reporting capability?
- How easy is it to browse through the knowledge base in addition to searching by keyword matching?

- Does the size of the knowledge base affect the speed of the system beyond reasonable tolerance?
- Is source code provided so that selected utility programs can be modified?
- Can the program interact with outside program editors? With what level of difficulty?

While the development environment is a product of the selected hardware and software, there are differences in the systems. An awareness of the capabilities and limitations of various systems is needed in order to hold down development and revision costs.

In general, the KE cannot mix and match the features and function options presented in this section. However, there needs to be an awareness of the critical factors or attributes that produce the most fertile development environments.

Certainty Factors

According to Joseph Wood Krutch, ''Logic is the art of going wrong with confidence.'' In any knowledge capture method, certainty factors are used to help place confidence levels on uncertain situations. A certainty factor is a numerical or graphic indication of how confident the domain expert is in the validity of a particular rule, or how sure the user is of a fact.

Recall that many of the rules used in knowledge base systems are based on heuristics. These heuristic rules are simplifications of processes or rules of thumb used by the experts. Heuristic rules are used in knowledge-based systems because the knowledge that is represented tends to resist mathematical certainty and algorithmic solutions. Examples of systems which are resistant to mathematical certainty and algorithmic solution are medical diagnostic systems, troubleshooting systems, legal consultant systems and weather forecasting systems.

An algorithmic solution guarantees a solution to a problem, while a heuristic solution produces a viable solution most of the time. Conventional computer programs work with algorithms. Knowledge-based system programs work with certainty factors where the solution is not necessarily perfect or unique.

The KE works with the certainty of the rules and examples acquired from the domain experts regardless of the knowledge representation used. Most certainty factors are represented as a percentage of likelihood. It is the job of the KE to help the domain expert determine the degree of confidence. For example, if there are two possible outcomes, the KE may ask if either one will work. If either solution will suffice, a confidence factor of 50% is associated with each solution. However, if the domain expert states that solution A is used more often than solution B, the KE probes and arrives at an agreement such as 60%/40% or 70%/30%.

Identify the Outputs

The purpose of most consultation systems is to provide a recommendation or specific action to take under given conditions. The outcomes must be accurate and relevant to the user. A recommendation that is beyond the sophistication of the user is of no use. The design and identification of the outcomes is critical.

SUMMARY

In knowledge-based systems, knowledge is the information required by the computer to emulate human reasoning and decision making, and to behave intelligently. For a human, knowledge is the storage of declarative and procedural relationships that constitute intelligence. Humans are able to classify, organize, analyze, synthesize, index, compress, form models, and manipulate descriptions and representations of experiences.

When humans encounter a problem, they are able to perceive that problem in a familiar form that represents an operable condition which can be manipulated through established, proven techniques. Unfamiliar situations are approached through a kindred system of representation called informed common sense. Using informed common sense, novel situations can be approached with an appropriate strategy.

The knowledge used in knowledge-based systems is represented in the computer in such a way that it can be accessed for the purpose of reasoning. This knowledge is placed in a knowledge structure that permits organized storage and access. The knowledge structure in a knowledge-based system is similar to the data structures used by computer programs to store and manipulate data. The knowledge structure is the housing of the knowledge representation and varies according to the application.

PRACTICAL APPLICATION

1. You've been working with a domain expert acquiring knowledge for the knowledge base. The time has come when you feel that your understanding and grasp of the domain are sufficient to begin an exploration of a knowledge representation structure. In the process, the questions you ask of the domain expert take a slight turn and become more repetitive. The expert challenges you and claims that that information has already been provided. You need to explain the importance of knowledge representation structures and arrange for a cooperative effort on the selection of the most appropriate and reasonable structures (given the available hardware, software, etc.). Make some notes about how you will respond to these queries.

2. You have an appointment with the Management Information Systems (MIS) manager concerning current and projected company systems and software. In preparation for your meeting, anticipate some project-related questions and formulate answers to them. Remember to include responses to any objections or challenges that might be made.

3. Continue the efforts from question 9 in chapter 5. Project a schedule and project milestones for your knowledge-based application. Answer appropriate questions presented in the Definition Domain section of this chapter.

4. Complete the Software Tool Checklist presented in this chapter as it relates to your application.

5. Use the components of the concept set (label, attributes, transaction, constraint, and depiction) to help analyze and organize the knowledge attributes for your application.

6. Select a tactic to help form knowledge constructs for your application. The knowledge constructs were presented in the "Knowledge Acquisition for Representation" section of this chapter.

7
Knowledge Acquisition: Process

Nam et ispa scientia potestas est.
(Knowledge is power.)

Francis Bacon

INTRODUCTION

This chapter addresses knowledge acquisition techniques to help provide a conceptual framework for the knowledge engineer's task of codifying the acquired knowledge. Clearly, knowledge is the refined information that an expert uses to solve problems. Human knowledge is related to language and an intelligence to acquire, process, store, recall, and communicate that knowledge. To replicate human knowledge in machines, knowledge is acquired and formally represented.

Chapter 6 discussed knowledge acquisition strategies; this chapter provides information about the knowledge acquisition process. In addition, chapter 6 discussed the preliminary knowledge supplied by the team. This chapter explores the high-level rules or heuristic rules that are at the source of an expert's mental prowess.

KNOWLEDGE ACQUISITION

Let us review the structure of knowledge acquisition.

The Goal

The goal of knowledge acquisition is to obtain the detailed knowledge used by domain experts to solve problems. This knowledge extends beyond the boundaries of education; this knowledge represents years of experience. Wolfgram, Dear, and Galbraith (1987) list detailed knowledge attributes as:

- The relationships between various data and rules
- The hierarchy of rules, what rules are intermediate, and what rules lead directly to the conclusions
- The relative validity and importance of data
- The certainty of data and the relative probabilities regarding assumptions, strategies, and conclusions
- The basis for the expert's assumptions and "educated guesses"
- The priorities and order of performing tasks
- The resolution of any conflicts between rules and conclusions
- Any alternative paths and strategies for problem solving
- Any shortcuts in reasoning and the conditions under which they are used
- The alternative paths for problem solving
- The shortcuts in reasoning and the conditions under which they are used
- The tradeoffs and the implications of tradeoffs
- The "strength of belief" in different rules, outcomes, and data
- The input demands of different goals and subgoals
- The appropriate measures of performance in outcomes and data in inputs

The Process

The knowledge base in a knowledge-based system may be acquired from many sources including books, databases, reports, case studies, empirical data, and those with personal experience. Most knowledge-based systems contain knowledge acquired from a domain expert. The KE procures the knowledge from the domain expert through direct interactions. The interactions between the KE and the domain expert include discussions, observations, posed problems, toy (simple) problems, etc. This knowledge acquisition is either a manual or an automated process. The manual process will be presented first.

In general, the KE works with domain experts in solving specific problems. An obvious approach to understanding the methods and establishing the rules by which a domain expert solves problems is to ask. The difficulty with this approach is that domain experts seldom know "how" it is that they solve problems, or they experience difficulty expressing their problem-solving methods.

One reason this difficulty exists is that domain experts tend to state their reasoning in broad, general terms, which do not benefit the KE's quest. The domain expert makes complex decisions rapidly with no awareness of the decision-making process. In addition, the domain expert makes assumptions about the knowledge level of the KE and the target audience. As a result, there are many jumps and gaps in the vocalization of the problem-solving process as the domain expert articulates that process.

In order to fill the gaps and limit the jumps, the KE gains a familiarity with the content and generic problem sets. This step can be very important because the domain experts also have a tendency to construct a line of problem-solving logic that may, in fact, have little relationship to the actual problem-solving process. These experts may think that they've considered a single attribute, while they've actually considered a combination of attributes.

To overcome this fact, two heuristic strategies for the KE surface. First, domain experts require an outside reasoning assistant or sounding board. This sounding board is usually another domain expert. Second, the KE should not accept everything the domain expert says as totally accurate.

The KE has another option to handle the near-miss logic chains. A short series of rules can be assembled and matched against test cases. If the rules are validated, the series is retained; if not, it can be modified or discarded.

In support of domain experts, it must be said that many assumptions made by them regarding the knowledge of others are reasonable. This statement is predicated upon the fact that knowledge-based systems are also informed commonsense systems. Informed common sense implies that for those who have the experience, training, or knowledge, certain situations do have obvious solutions. Two surgeons can identify and remedy a malady of a patient while others in attendance may not recognize the problem or understand the solution. Because the surgeons have the knowledge and experience, what was obvious to them was a mystery to others. If the surgeons make assumptions that the problem and remedy were obvious and not worth mentioning, gaps and logic jumps occur.

The same types of assumptions are made by the automotive mechanic who just "hears" the problem, the secretary who "knows" that the copier jammed because a lighter weight paper was used, and the backyard barbecue chef who can obviously "tell" that the fish is ready. All of these experts make many assumptions about the knowledge, experience, and awareness of both the KEs and the target audience. If the KE is experienced or is aware of the assumptions made by domain experts, many problems can be avoided which, if left unnoticed, would produce a knowledge base that would completely "miss the mark." The net effect of missing the mark for these reasons is mistrust in the value or abilities of KEs at large.

In order to better understand how a KE extracts and distills knowledge, an exploration of expert processing is presented. Experts do not have an internalized memory index of knowledge that is scanned and used like a library card catalog system. The actions of many experts may seem more intuitive than knowledgeable.

Few would deny that experts possess considerable knowledge prerequisite to manifesting their skill. Experts have been found to use a type of pattern recognition match to address their heuristic index. This pattern match is a type of intuition. When an expert is confronted with a problem, the problem situation is compared to previously experienced problems and solutions. This has become evident from working with experts who, as a group, tend to state, "This problem situation is similar to . . .," and render a judgment or approach. It is also worth noting that experts tend to work by eliminating possibilities as they focus on a hypothesis.

When experts are confronted with situations unique to their experience, their problem-solving behavior changes. With new situations, the experts tend to apply their heuristic knowledge as an informed commonsense exploration tool. The consequence of this method is a deductive approach to establishing a causal link between what is known and what is perceived.

To allow for this problem-solving duality, it is beneficial to provide the expert with a variety of stimuli. Some situations are presented that are familiar and others are presented that are novel. The KE who observes the expert in problem-solving sessions can gain insight into the manner in which the expert analyzes the problem. As a result, a firm knowledge base can be constructed.

Another approach to capitalize on the diversity in problem-solving techniques is to construct a problem-solving opportunity for an expert and for an informed novice. The expert solves the problem with the pattern match logic while the novice uses an informed commonsense or deductive approach to solve the problem. In a debriefing, the KE compares the steps used by the novice and observes the logic assumptions, gaps, and jumps made by the expert.

The deductive logic approach of the informed novice can be called first-stage logic. The pattern match techniques of the heuristically endowed expert can be called second-stage logic. These two stages of problem-solving logic are to be kept in mind during the interview process.

Ever since people have attempted to formalize the acquisition of knowledge from one source for the purpose of representation and transfer of that knowledge to others, there have been taxonomies and models. Authors such as Harmon and King; Bowerman and Glover; Wolfgram, Dear, and Galbraith; Hart; and others have written about knowledge acquisition strategies that can be represented by similar models. A recent publication by James Martin and Steven Oxman provides a model that is consistent with the other listed models.

Martin and Oxman (1988) discuss the knowledge acquisition process as iterative with loops that depend upon the size of system to be built, the depth and breadth of the task to be supported, and the quality of the knowledge as it is acquired. Their view of the process is:

1. Acquire initial subject domain knowledge.
2. Prototype the knowledge data and place it in an expert system development shell for knowledge data test purposes.
3. Give the prototype system a sample task.
4. Let the expert comment on the system.
5. If the knowledge base is reasonably complete, exit.
6. Let the expert infer what is missing from the knowledge base.
7. Acquire the missing knowledge.
8. Add the missing knowledge to the knowledge base.
9. Return to Step 3.

While there is divergence in some aspects of the models, there is a consistency of message. Knowledge engineers over time, develop effective techniques that can respond to different knowledge acquisition opportunities and situations.

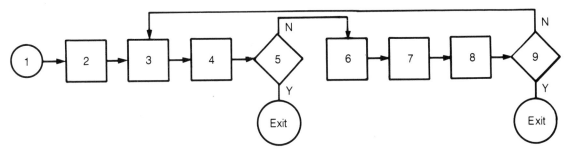

Fig. 7-1. The iterative nature of knowledge acquisition.

The model in FIG. 7-1 is a hybrid of applications and techniques derived from a composite of disciplines including computer science and psychology, experience through time, and analysis and synthesis of field data and past projects.

KNOWLEDGE ACQUISITION TECHNIQUES

This section describes six major classes of knowledge acquisition techniques in common usage: interviews, protocols, neurolinguistic programming, traits, analysis and, automated knowledge acquisition. Observation and questionnaires are two other techniques which are implicitly covered in a number of discussions elsewhere in this book.

Interviews

Interviews are the most common technique employed by knowledge engineers to acquire knowledge from a domain expert. Although the most common technique, it is not always the first, last, or best method of learning domain techniques and heuristic rules. Interviews have two basic shortcomings. The first shortcoming is a lack of direction. Merely discussing why an expert does what he does, under what circumstances, and when it is most appropriate is both inefficient and time-consuming. Secondly, unless the KE prepares for the interview by planning a definite structure for it and by gaining familiarity with the subject of the interview, the encounter can conceivably be filled with inefficiencies, frustrations, and loss of time.

Interviews do, however, contribute to the knowledge base in two primary ways. First, interviews alert the KE to the shallow knowledge aspects of the domain. This shallow knowledge elicitation also provides an opportunity to interact with the expert, establish a rapport, and evaluate the knowledge and communicative ability of the expert. This spin-off benefit verifies the team's model of the domain if the expert was not an original participant, or provides an opportunity to establish or further rapport with the expert. Secondly, structured interviews with domain experts can fill in the gaps resulting from the knowledge engineer's descent into the deeper aspects of the knowledge domain.

Preparation. To make an interview session productive, plan it with an agenda and goals. Preparing for a session requires both the KE and the domain expert to assume responsibilities. The KE reviews the subject matter to be covered in the day's session. In addition, the agenda is set, presented, and approved by the responsible parties. The expert handles business before the session and plans that there be no interruptions. He also understands what is expected by reviewing the agenda and is prepared to modify or accept the day's tasks. Any special preparation for tools or techniques, and the gathering of sample or support materials, are considered so that a mental focus can be set and maintained. The expert considers the parameters of the topic and avoids deviating from the focus. The expert should also be prepared to manage the interview when the KE takes a cursory approach or is leaving gaps.

Preparation also includes props. Props are the tools of the trade of the KE and the domain expert(s). The props used by a knowledge engineer comprise response recording devices and stimulus generating devices such as computers, whiteboards, note pads, flip charts, tape recorders, videotapes, simulations, case studies, etc. Props used by the domain expert(s) are examples of the domain including computers, models, documentation, blueprints, and a controlled environment. The location for the session should be quiet and comfortable with adequate creature comforts. These comforts include good lighting, refreshments, and comfortable seating and tables.

A final word about props. All of the participating parties need to be aware of the nature and purpose of the props to be used and their importance. The KE and the expert(s) are on the same team. The notes, real-time or transcribed, are reviewed by the expert. There are no secrets. If all parties are informed throughout all stages of the process, the sessions will be more successful. Nevertheless, the KE asks permission to use a recording device or take notes. This is common courtesy. Also, it is sometimes appropriate to suspend note taking and turn off the recording device.

The key to success for any type of interview described in this segment is preparation. The knowledge engineer, the expert(s), and the physical location(s) should all be prepared. If one of the legs of this triad is incomplete, the session will be unproductive. A part of the interview also includes the completion of the top portion of a Session Form and its distribution by the KE prior to the interaction.

In advance of the session the KE should go over an interview checklist that includes at least the following items:

- Complete and distribute Knowledge Acquisition Forms.
- Confirm room location, time, and props.
- Test the props immediately prior to the session.
- Have a supply of extra paper, pencils, pens, markers, batteries, etc.
- Arrange for breaks and refreshments.
- Eliminate or minimize interruptions.
- Sit comfortably in terms of proximity to the expert(s).
- Maintain eye contact, listen to what is said and how it is said without interruption.

- Be flexible. If schedules need to change or the best-made plans fall short, adapt.
- A little humor never hurts.

The field of psychology has devoted time and concentration to methods of questioning and the use of effective questioning techniques. Puff (1982) wrote about methods for addressing human memory. In addition to the methods discussed in this chapter, there are interview techniques common to the methods. Further there are types of questions that are worth considering.

Each interview has three basic components: a beginning, a middle, and an ending.

Beginning. The beginning of an interview has been the subject of many studies with similar results. Those results can be grouped under the general heading of *tone*.

Tone involves the ambiance of the environment, the greeting and the "feel" of the moment. The tone should be professional, low-risk, and comfortable. "Professional" relates to such factors as the organization of the environment, stating of objectives, appropriate dress and manner of the interviewer, and the demeanor of the interviewer—a smile and a handshake. "Low risk" includes small talk, status report of progress to date, and reassurance that the expert's input is valuable. "Comfort" implies a well-planned session, no schedule or time conflicts on the part of the expert, and flexibility.

Middle. The middle of the interview entails the rigors of the process outlined in the Knowledge Acquisition Form. It is important to stay on track, prompt when necessary, ask questions, make suggestions, challenge inconsistencies, clarify meaning, and attend to verbal and nonverbal cues. The topics of verbal and nonverbal communication are explored in the segment of Neurolinguistic Programming.

End. The end of the interview is used to summarize the accomplishments of the session. Most domain experts feel an obligation to invest time, not spend or waste time. Further, interview sessions can be physically and mentally exhausting. In order to satisfy the domain expert's time concerns, the KE can close the loops of the session. For example, the objectives can be paired with the results. Any action plans or "to do" commitments are restated with a time of completion associated with the commitment.

Ending an interview session is another interview technique. The end of a session may be more than clock-driven like a high school class. Sessions may end before or after the exactly scheduled instant. The KE must remember that the task is more important than the time it takes to effect the task. Most knowledge engineers have learned verbal and nonverbal closing techniques.

McGraw and Harbison-Briggs (1989) list verbal and nonverbal techniques for ending an interview session.

Verbal Closings. The following list adapts and presents some verbal closings.

Technique	Example
Scheduled end:	"Time flies when you're having a good time; it is already time to stop."
Declaration:	"Well, that seems to have been the last item on the agenda."
Appreciation:	"Thank you for your input. It will really help the project."
Milestone:	"That was our last formal item. Is there anything that I did not cover?"
Action item:	"That's it for our agenda. Let's schedule our next meeting."

Nonverbal Closings. Nonverbal closings either precede or are concurrent with verbal closings. These signals can originate from the KE or the domain expert(s). Care is taken not to offend the domain expert. Common nonverbal signals include:

- Clock watching
- Gathering of materials
- Audible sigh and change of posture
- Rising from a sitting position

Question Anatomy and Attributes. This may come as no surprise, but the dominant tool of interviewing is the question. The difference between a successful interview and an unsuccessful interview may be asking the right question at the right time in the right manner. The sciences of education and instructional design focus on two basic types of questions: open-ended and closed.

Open-ended Questions. Open-ended questions provide an opportunity for free response. Control is formally given to the domain expert upon asking an open-ended question. There is no limit on the type, level, scope, or nature of the response. The level of knowledge on the part of the domain expert and the KE may influence the use of open-ended questions.

The higher the level of domain awareness that the KEs have, the greater the depth of information their open-ended questions can produce. In addition, the purpose of the session helps to determine the questioning strategy. For example, shallow knowledge, domain familiarization, facts, concepts, and rules lend themselves to open-ended questioning.

Strengths of Open-ended Questions

- Provide associations, links, new ares to explore
- Elicit certainty or confidence in responses

Weaknesses of Open-ended Questions

- Respondent can meander, digress, add too many caveats
- Incorrect level of detail addressed
- Challenge for the note-taker, whose work may then be subjected to incorrect interpretation
- Placement of control in the hands of the respondent

Open-ended questions are characterized by key words such as: list, describe, name, associate, what, and why.

Closed Questions. Closed questions place control with the questioner. They do not imply yes or no responses. Closed questions focus on particular aspects of a domain attribute or assist in the analysis of a concept or heuristic rule. Deep knowledge, clarification of declarative and procedural statements, and range exploration are often probed by closed questions.

Strengths of Closed Questions

- Clarify, reinforce, delimit
- Not subject to interpretation
- Time effective

Weaknesses of Closed Questions

- Over simplify the choices
- Some domain experts do not volunteer more than asked
- The answer is only as good as the question

Closed questions are characterized by lead words such as: *when, why,* how much, how many, who, name, and what.

A knowledge engineer can learn to avoid salvos of questions. When confronted by a cacophony of unrelated questions, the domain expert can become confused. Analysis of the responses can net inconclusive results. With care and practice in questioning techniques, the KE can obtain informed, focused responses. As a general rule, questions spawn questions. Watch any political news conference for questioning techniques. The reporter tends to ask an open-ended or closed question with a follow-up or secondary question.

McGraw and Harbison-Briggs (1989) address the issue of primary and secondary questioning based on the work of Kahn and Cannell. Kahn and Cannell describe the secondary question as a probing question. They suggest probing questions when responses to primary questions are vague, uncertain, superficial, or irrelevant. The following adaptation lists six types of probing questions.

- Silence Probe: If the expert does not seem to have completed a response, use passive listening techniques (e.g., eye contact, body language) and remain quiet to encourage further response.

- Prompting Probe: If a nonverbal probe does not stimulate further response, use verbal techniques such as, "Is there more... ?"

- Last Chance Probe: To make sure that all relevant information has surfaced, use a probe such as "Does this close the loop on this topic?"

- Depth Probe: If the level of response is surface-level, use a probe such as, "I do not quite understand what you mean; can you explain further or give me an example?"

- Specifying Probe: If the response seems nebulous or incomplete, use a probe such as, "What do you mean by...", or throw back a key word and let it hang such as, "Delinquent... ?"

- Reflective Probe: If a statement seems inaccurate, in conflict with earlier information, or if the answer to a specifying probe falls short, use a probe such as, "Did I hear seven?"

Depending on the knowledge to be extracted, the KE will mix and sequence question types to meet the requirements of the expert and the project. Only time and practice can improve questioning strategies and effectiveness. One suggestion in this area is to observe others practicing the art including other knowledge engineers, reporters, analysts, and psychologists.

Unstructured Interviews. Unstructured interviews, by design, are led by domain experts. The experts expand on some of the concepts introduced in the domain conceptualization. Unstructured interviews are usually of limited value. The experts tend to meander through the domain or focus on "nice to know" aspects of the domain. The benefit of unstructured interviews is twofold. First, unstructured interviews allow the experts to experience the interview process. Secondly, unstructured interviews allow the experts to focus on their own views of the taxonomy of the domain.

A taxonomy is a classification system that depicts the major features of the domain. Taxonomies are used in education and training to define and classify sets. These taxonomic schemas assist in the organization of thought. In addition, the taxonomy identifies subgroups or attributes that represent the underlying structure of the major features. Taxonomies are particularly useful for the organization of declarative knowledge. The construction of a taxonomy focuses on the elements of the domain and involves tasks such as identification, definition, grouping, and comparing of the elements.

Structured Interviews. The structured interview is led and organized by the KE. It pursues the major factors and the attributes identified in domain conceptualization. The structured interview is systematic, with a focus. This focus is directed to one of the major factors that is viewed with its associations and attributes.

The KE prepares for the structured interview by reviewing notes, viewing the interview's place in the "big picture," and using terms, definitions, and jargon correctly and appropriately. Structured interviews remain on track. If issues arise that are important but not within the mission of the interview, the KE weighs the desirability of the diversion. If pursuit of the diversion seems reasonable and logical, the KE attends to the diversion. If pursuit of the diversion can be scheduled for another time, the KE makes a careful note, assigns tasks, and follows up.

Strategies. Using the interview technique, the KE poses questions to stimulate an initial response followed by introspective detailing by the domain expert. The KE prompts the domain expert by interjecting "what if's?" to maintain the focus. One useful technique for this process is to *counterpose* the actions of the domain expert. In other words, the KE looks for opposites by reasoning, "If this is what happens when A is true, what happens when A is not true?"

The interview can be conducted using a variety of structures such as two interviewers with one domain expert, or one or more interviewers with multiple domain experts. Two interviewers coupled with one expert can be intimidating to the expert, but often produces richer results, containing a greater depth and breadth of the knowledge being sought. The knowledge acquired is enriched because, like domain experts, no two knowledge engineers think or perceive exactly alike. As the interviewers draw upon their experiences, different approaches to a topic can be taken or different perceptions elicited.

A proven successful technique used in two on one interviewing is to have one interviewer initially conduct the interview while the second interviewer takes notes or begins to graphically represent the knowledge. The roles and responsibilities of the interviewers can often be reversed. It is also suggested that all interview sessions be recorded with a non-obtrusive cassette recorder. Tape recorders do not forget.

As mentioned earlier, the KE secures permission from those present for both legal and professional reasons. The recorder could be positioned as another interviewer. The tapes are erased after the information is reviewed. Some participants may be intimidated by the tape recorder and may not voice their discomfort. The interviewer should be sensitive to this situation.

The interview process can be conducted in a manner similar to knowledge-based system search techniques, that is, depth-first or breadth-first. The depth-first interview examines a facet of the expert's knowledge on a single track until it is exhausted. When there is little breadth to the topic, it is easy to focus on a single line of reasoning. However, when there is considerable breadth to the topic, it is often easier for the domain expert to present the knowledge across the range of the topic.

The thinking and recall process of the expert needs to be considered too. It proves beneficial if the expert is informed and provided with an example of each technique, and then asked which approach would be preferable.

The questioning process lasts about twenty minutes with a short break. This enables the expert to relax, and consider the questions and formulate complete responses. It also gives the interviewers an opportunity to review and reorganize the graphically represented responses. When the next session begins, the graphic representation is shared with the expert for accuracy and completeness. It is also recommended that the interviewers create and maintain a catalog system which matches the recording with its hard copy representation.

A shortcoming of the interview process is the set of knowledge assumptions made by the domain expert. This is a result of the rapid pattern matches unknowingly made by the domain experts. By using a recorder, the KE can focus on what the domain expert is saying and look beyond the words rather than recording by hand or trying to remember what is said.

One or More Interviewers on Many Experts. This situation is interesting, as time and effort are expended in order to avoid conflict and a waste of time. Interviewing multiple experts often leads to refereeing internal power and ego struggles as well as personality differences among the experts. These situations need to be avoided for the sake of production and sanity. The best solution for these situations is to anticipate and avoid them as early as possible. The potential for conflict is often evident in the preliminary meetings. A development prototype can be used to provide an insight into the completed application, and for secondary benefits as well. A development prototype provides opportunities for conflict and bringing into play the personality mix of the team. It is discussed in depth in chapter 10.

If conflict is inevitable, it can be monitored and dealt with using several techniques. First, a group leader can be appointed to resolve conflicting opinions. Using a group leader is workable, but can lead to hard feelings. Next, portions of the knowledge base can be divided among the experts. Primary knowledge can be obtained from the selected responsible expert with validation by colleagues. A third option is to use the Delphi technique discussed earlier.

The nature of the knowledge sources can be diverse when multiple disciplines are joined to produce the knowledge base. When this situation occurs, the experts are interviewed separately and the resulting knowledge compiled. This often results in an overlapping of knowledge. A knowledge overlap is graphically represented and presented to the appropriate experts for review and comment. This process may require several iterations, but is ultimately productive.

The KE concludes interview sessions by asking the expert(s), ''Is there anything that I should have asked?'', and by providing a proposed agenda for the following session.

Protocols

Wolfgram, Dear, and Galbraith (1987) discuss protocol analysis as a method of acquiring detailed knowledge from a domain expert. Their work offers three types of protocols: verbal, motor, and eye-movement.

Verbal Protocols. Verbal protocols require the expert to "think aloud" while performing a task or solving a problem. The expert's narrative is usually recorded, and sometimes quietly narrated by the KE as a sports announcer would narrate a golf pro's actions. Verbal protocols are also called process tracing, as these protocols sequentially follow the expert's progress through a task.

The KE is cautioned to prepare very carefully for a verbal protocol session. The KE must be familiar with the process, its tasks, and requirements. Further, the KE should not initiate any conversations. However, if there are silences seemingly due to the expert forgetting to talk, the KE reminds the expert to keep talking.

In a typical session, the expert starts by cataloging the extent of possible conclusions. Each time the domain expert eliminates or pursues a line of reasoning or a focus point, it is mentioned aloud. Disadvantages of observation and the domain expert's verbalization are the gaps and jumps discussed earlier.

Following the session, the KE systematically debriefs the expert on the content and process. This debriefing is generally a two-step process. During the first step, the protocol is reviewed as described. The second step involves the domain expert, the KE, and a second recording device. The expert listens to the first tape and adds a level of detail.

Motor Protocols. Motor protocols involve observation of the expert's movements as he performs physical tasks. These tasks include reaching, grasping, turning, lifting, etc. Motor protocols are generally observed by a knowledge engineer and whose description is recorded on tape.

The expert must clearly understand that the performance of the task is the subject of the observation. Motor protocols usually supplement verbal protocols. After a session, the KE debriefs the expert in a manner similar to verbal protocols.

The interview method produces crisper, higher quality results than observation. The two-way interaction between the KE and the domain expert provides a richer atmosphere and immediate feedback.

Eye-Movement Protocol. An eye-movement protocol is a record of the expert's visual focus as tasks are performed. Eye-movement protocol is another approach to the study of a domain. This approach uses one of the senses. It it likely that other sensory protocols will be used as recording and study methods become available. Sensory protocols are more accurately traced electronically than by observation. For example, the near-term future might offer means for recording values of physiological variables as inputs for evaluating task performance. Such inputs could include pulse rate, respiration, perspiration, brain activity, blood chemistry, and other recordable bodily changes.

Sensory protocols are used to identify areas of an expert's focus. As people are holistic beings, more data could be gathered about an expert's performance than current technology and practice permits. The larger the amount of data and the greater the possibility of analyzing the data to produce information and synthesizing the information to produce knowledge, the greater the ability to transfer that expertise.

In addition to the protocols previously listed, there are other protocols as well: blind problem discussion, flash questions, and mapping.

Blind Problem Discussion. Using blind problem discussion, the KE acquires a closed-loop problem set. In the problem set, one expert has established a problem-solving logic. The KE presents the problem to the participating domain expert for a comparison of methods. The object of the exercise is for the KE to interact with the domain expert and record the organization of the knowledge, the hypothesis series, the logic pathing (long—short), and the determination of the solution. This data is compared with the closed-loop set for similarities and differences. The KE is not looking for right and wrong, but for logic flow.

Questions that may be explored by the KE include:

- Is the problem within the typical range of problem types generally encountered?
- What types of information are required to place boundaries around the problem?
- What level and type of solution(s) is required to solve the problem?
- How can the problem be decomposed into subproblems?
- What types and levels of knowledge are needed to solve the problem?
- Other than demonstration, what types of documentation or proof are required to validate the problem solution?
- What level of experience is required to have an understanding of the problem?

The KE and the domain expert explore the types of information, knowledge, experience, and procedures required to solve the defined problem types.

Flash Questions. Flash questioning by the KE extracts spontaneous responses from the domain expert. The KE provides as little information as possible, thereby forcing the domain expert to ask for needed information. For example, a KE might ask a machinist "Why does that part seem so worn?" This question might not have been expected, and can produce significant information. The domain expert might reply, "Why is that important?" This can be followed by the KE saying, "That part seems to be the focus of what you do. Tell me about it."

The answer to each data request may imply or bring to the surface a major factor and/or its subordinates or attributes. Each request for clarification from the domain expert is also accompanied by a hypothesis or rationale detailing the strategies being employed. After a conclusion is reached, the KE can engage in "What if?" scenarios that explore ranges, including the thresholds and extremes that keep the solution true.

Following the conclusion of the flash questioning, a post-session discussion is held to explore each factor and attribute that surfaced. The purpose of the post-session talk is to establish the individual contributions of the factors and attributes to the overall effort.

Mapping. One type of knowledge representation technique begins with conclusions or results, identifies major factors, and then describes the attributes of the major factors. But how is this knowledge acquired?

The mind works through associations. These associations are non-linear and nondirective. They are nonlinear because sequence has little influence on memory associations. The associations are nondirective because a central topic can invoke many topical links. A nonlinear concept can be illustrated by the following example. Picture a lake surrounded by mountains and lush green trees. The initial vignette in your mind may have been of a generic lake, but shortly thereafter your own detail and associations take over. You might recall camping or hiking events from any time period in your life. Entire sequences of people and events might pass through your mind. In addition, you may recall sounds, odors, and the feel of the warmth of the sun or the chill of a breeze.

The order of recalled events may be correct in a time continuum, or digressive as one memory triggers subordinate memory clusters. A nondirective association can be illustrated as follows. Visualize a mammal. Whatever mammal you visualized, you probably thought of other mammals as well. In addition, an array of facts also came instantly to mind, such as warm-blooded, live births, fur, milk, etc. If you were to dwell on the thought, you would begin to recall other details acquired through readings, personal experience, etc.

The problem-solving techniques used by domain experts work in the same fashion. A problem can be identified for the domain expert to solve through associations, and in the process many branches and links would be identified. Because of the ability to link, a central topic could be the core focus. From this focus, a structure can emerge that branches into "thought trees." Each thought tree is a major factor of the focus. The branches on the tree represent the attributes.

The KE and the domain expert work together to identify the granularity of the knowledge decomposition. For example, let's consider the topic of transportation. The focus of the knowledge base system to be constructed is the cost of shipping. To start the map, draw a circle and write the word "transportation" within the circle. From this point, the granularity issue arises.

Transportation can be separated into land, water, and air. It can also be broken down by time and distance requirements such as next-day or three-day delivery. If the transportation needs do not require delivery via ship, then that possibility does not warrant consideration. If the goods to be shipped do not weigh excessive amounts or require large containers, trains may not need to be considered. By discussing major factors before including them as projections from the circle focus, the solution can be optimized. When the development team optimizes the focus, a clear picture of the task is obtainable. Figure 7-2 is a "first pass" map of transportation. As the need develops, the map is revised; for example, time factors are added and non-useful options removed.

Once the tactical positioning of the knowledge is established, detail can be added as required. If a line of reasoning is pursued as a branch and it appears that the relative importance is high, the branch can be established as a trunk.

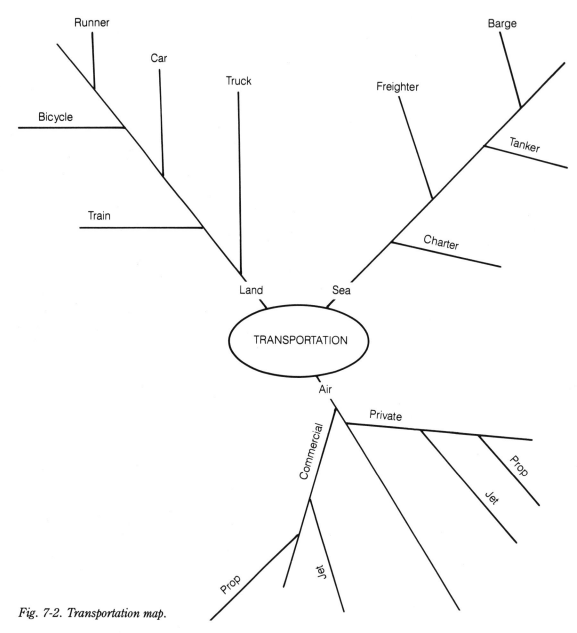

Fig. 7-2. Transportation map.

By visualizing and diagramming the visualization, the major factors and their attributes are made apparent.

Upon further exploration of the map, it may be realized that rather than focusing on transportation, a focus is targeted on each of the transportation types. Thus, the focus may be air transportation, or package size, or delivery time requirements. The skill of the KE and the communication ability of the domain expert are the limiting factors in the successful use of this method.

The Mapping Process. Since the brain works in a nonlinear fashion, conventional note taking and outlines are but weak written representations of the major factors, their attributes, and interrelationships. An approach to discussion that constantly provides the "big picture" is called mind mapping. Buzan (1983) contrasts mind mapping with linear note taking as follows.

- The center or main idea is more clearly defined.
- The relative importance of each idea is clearly indicated. More important ideas will be near the center and less important ideas will be near the edge.
- The links between the key concepts will be immediately recognizable because of their proximity and connection.
- As a result of the above, recall and review will be more effective and rapid.
- The nature of the structure allows for the easy addition of new information without messy scratching out or squeezing in, etc.
- Each map that is generated will look different from other maps. This will aid in recall.
- In more creative areas of note making such as essay preparation, the open-ended nature of the map will enable the brain to make new connections far more readily.

Mind-Mapping Strategies. While the rules are few, mind mapping is a powerful tool that is almost directly transferable into some induction-based expert system shells. As the skill of the KE increases, the personal "shorthand" grows. Some of the basic rules are:

- The focus point starts in the center and is placed inside some geometric or pictorial representation.
- Printed words are placed on lines; each line is connected to the focus or another line.
- The key thoughts on the lines are limited to as few words as possible.
- Since the process is like brainstorming, evaluation of the map is saved for a later time. The expert's thoughts will probably generate a multitude of ideas that generally surface in a hierarchical order. The major factors that support the focus tend to be first-pass knowledge provided by the expert.

After completing the map, the expert can add arrows that illustrate relatedness and sequence of dependencies. Additional shapes and colors can denote other parallel concepts or kindred concepts. Additional maps can be constructed that detail major factors or attributes noted in another location. These maps can be sorted, sequenced, analyzed, and synthesized into knowledge representations. Figure 7-3 shows the transportation map with a little more detail.

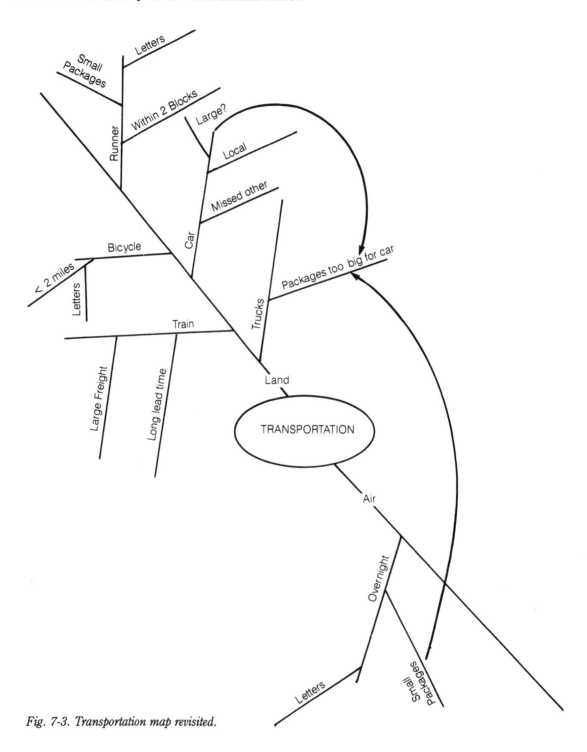

Fig. 7-3. Transportation map revisited.

Mind mapping also can be used for an initial problem-defining session. The general idea of the problem is placed in a circle. Six lines are drawn that radiate outward. The words on the lines are who, what, when, where, why, and how.

- Who: Focuses on people or objects that are affected
- What: Lists what it is about
- When: Discusses delivery schedules and milestones
- Where: Identifies locations where the problem occurs
- Why: Defines the major reasons the problem needs fixing
- How: Suggests the manner in which the problem may be resolved

The completed problem map is then subject to group scrutiny. When everyone can view the "big picture," discussions can proceed at a higher level. Often mind maps can aid in the decision-making process. Figure 7-4 provides a conceptual view of an initial problem exploration.

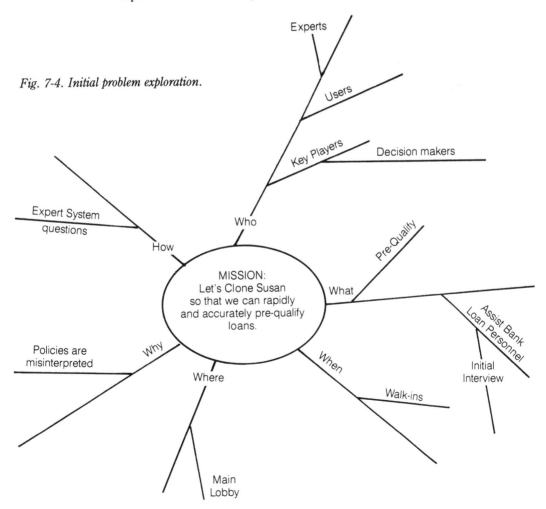

Fig. 7-4. Initial problem exploration.

Mapping provides a visual representation of the concept sets discussed in chapters 1 and 6. Figure 7-5 lists the concept set elements. These concept set elements can be used to elaborate on the major factors and attributes of an application. Figure 7-6 focuses on the loan pre-qualifier. It contains the problem to be solved in the center. Each branch of the map catalogs a concept set element matching the considerations. The KE can use color, line types, and other personalized symbols to further identify concept element members.

Maps can be used to further refine major factors or attributes. For example, the element "constraints" could be placed in the center. The major factors of income, job, references, property, and debts are independent arms. Attributes radiate from each of the factors. These maps can be constructed quickly and in real time.

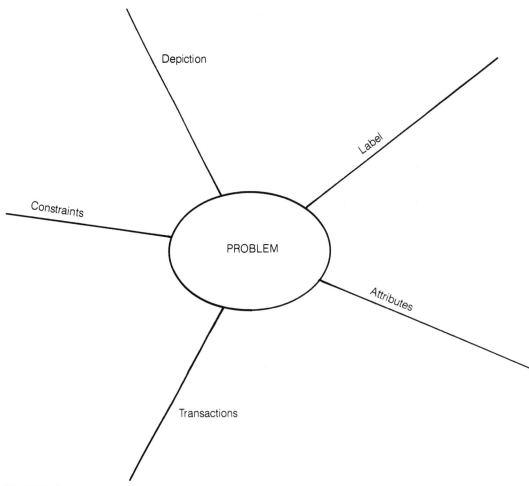

Fig. 7-5. Concept sets.

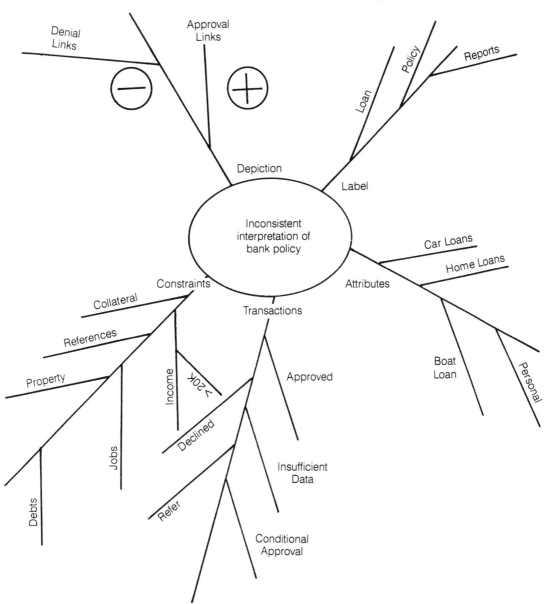

Fig. 7-6. Conceptual loan application.

Neurolinguistic Programming

To state the obvious, the ability to communicate effectively is the heart of interviewing. It does not take a great leap of the imagination to understand the benefits of being able to read the minds of others. Is the secret of mind reading about to be revealed? No. However, a window to the mind is available through neurolinguistic programming (NLP).

Bandler and Grinder (1979) wrote, "You will always get answers to your questions insofar as you have the sensory apparatus to notice the responses. And rarely will the verbal or conscious part of the response be relevant." Bandler and Grinder contend that nonverbal responses are always given. They are not, however, always received.

Individuals, such as knowledge engineers, can learn to sharpen their receptors of these nonverbal signals. Nonverbal signals are given visually by the sender. These nonverbal signals represent internalized activities that are composed of visual, auditory, and kinesthetic responses to stimuli.

Eye movements, according to Bandler and Grinder, indicate an individual's internalized processing. There are two imaging components: eidetic and constructed. Eidetic images are remembered images. Constructed images are the result of building visual representations of events, situations, or other visual model creations. There are three aspects of auditory assessment. Auditory experience is composed of auditory constructed sounds, or words and auditory recalled sounds and words. Auditory projection involves creation of a sound not previously heard. *Kinesthetic* processing involves feelings, smell, and taste.

Eye position during these internalized representations are different for right-handed people and left-handed people. The eye positions tend to be reversed. In addition, there is the issue of normalized organization. This refers to the tendency of the majority of subjects. Taking all of these heuristic rule caveats into consideration, FIG. 7-7 provides the visual cues for a normally-organized, right-handed person. This illustration is adapted from Bandler and Grinder.

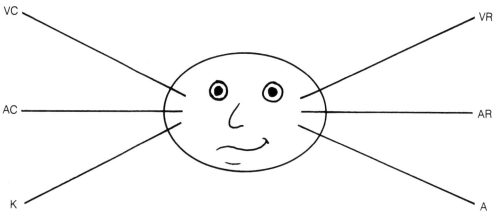

Fig. 7-7. Visual cues.

VC	Visually constructed images	VR	Visually remembered or eidetic images
AC	Auditory constructed sounds or words	AR	Auditory remembered sounds or words
K	Kinesthetic feelings, smell, and taste	A	Auditory sounds or words

In addition, visual processing is taking place when the eyes are unfocused and unmoving. This look is sometimes called the "thousand yard stare."

So what does all of this mean? Bandler and Grinder state that the words people use to describe their representation system or model illustrate their consciousness. The wording indicates which of the internalized representations is brought into awareness. The eye-scanning patterns present an entire sequence of assessing or strategy.

Knowledge engineers can use NLP awareness in two ways. First, the KE becomes in tune with a domain expert's representation system. If the domain expert is talking about how he or she feels when solving a particular problem and the KE communicates through visual representations, there will be a mismatch. For example, consider the following interaction.

KE: "Please describe your process for the steam valve changeover."

DE: "OK. When the batch is just about ready, the core structure feels different."

KE: "I understand. Are there sensory indicators that record this difference?"

DE: "No, there is a different feel in the structure."

KE: "I see. Let's focus on this difference. Can you show me when and where this change occurs?"

DE: "I just can feel the change in the core structure."

KE: "I see what you are saying, but this is not moving us forward. Can you describe what it is that you watch for?"

DE: "I am trying to tell you that the system just feels tighter—like it is almost full . . . "

This example is somewhat exaggerated; however, the domain expert has a kinesthetic orientation and the KE has a visual orientation. The conversation would have been more productive if the KE had keyed in on the expert's kinesthetic orientation.

Secondly, the KE can use the visual cues to audit the model constructs of the domain expert. As the internalized model is talked through, the various aspects of the model can be sorted out using the variety of constructs identified through visual cues. In addition, when processes are crucial to a system, the tracking of these processes can be assisted by attention to possible visual cues. Reconsider the previous interaction.

KE: "Please describe your process for the steam valve changeover."

DE: "OK. When the batch is just about ready, the core structure feels different."

KE: "I understand. Are there sensory indicators that record this difference?"

DE: "No. There is a different feel in the structure."

KE: "I see. Let's focus on this difference. Can you describe the feel? Is it physical or a type of intuition?"

DE: "There is change in the core structure that makes the valves harder to turn, and when this happens, I think that there is a slight vibration in the structure."

KE: "Do you think that a sensory instrument could be used to record the feel?"

DE: "I am not sure about that, but I can demonstrate what I mean."

Once again, this conversation is hypothetical. However the interactions and reactions between the participants seem smoother. Assuming another's visual, auditory, or kinesthetic references is like "walking a mile in his shoes." This point of reference may help the KE to better understand the domain and work more productively with the domain expert.

NLP is a young discipline in the area of human behavior and communication. An array of options can help the KE become more successful at the craft of acquiring and representing knowledge. An awareness of ongoing work in psychology and related fields is important. Knowledge engineering is a cross-domain science.

Traits

The strength of most knowledge-based systems is their ability to offer selections of options based upon traits that provide hard information, or those that provide soft data. One strategy for knowledge acquisition is to deal with similar sets of objects. The KE and the domain expert establish trait factors and attributes that are refined and then incorporated into a knowledge-based system application.

Typical applications require the user to make input decisions that distinguish among trait attributes and enable branching decisions to be made. Tied with these traits and their eventual outcomes is the degree of truth or confidence that the expert has on the outcome. This range of truth is reflected in the confidence factor, a value between 0 and 100, where 100 is absolutely true and 0 is absolutely false or without confidence. A number between 0 and 100 represents uncertainty. A confidence factor of 92 means that the result is fairly certain, while a confidence factor of 50 is the highest degree of uncertainty. Values less than 50 imply that the result is improbable.

Most experts make their decisions based upon the attributes of an object or event that enable a differentiation between it and other objects or events. The discriminators are called the characteristics or traits. These characteristics and traits are generally arrived at by careful questioning of the expert. One approach to accomplishing this is to ask the expert to think of concrete examples and conduct a trait extraction. Some of these questions might be:

- Think of three objects. How is one different from the other two?
- What does this make you think or do?
- Is there anything else that makes you think or do this?
- Is there an opposite trait to this one?
- When does this opposite occur?
- To what degree does this occur?
- Are there other alternatives?

In the following example, the objects are business suits. One suit needs to be selected for a business meeting that is three hours away by air. A domain expert—in this case, a presenter—and a KE have a dialogue for selection based on traits. For the sake of simplicity, the confidence factor discussion will be deferred until chapter 8.

KE: "Think of the three suits. How is one different from the other two?"

DE: "Two suits are dark and one is light."

KE: "Anything else?"

DE: "Well, the light suit and one dark suit are each three-piece. And the two-piece dark suit wrinkles easily."

KE: "How does wrinkling affect your selection decision?"

DE: "When I travel, I need to be concerned about how a suit looks. Sometimes there is time to have the suit dry-cleaned, so this is not necessarily a problem."

KE: "Are there any other considerations that affect your selection?"

DE: "Sure . . . time of year, the client's business culture, and the nature of the presentation."

KE: "How do these factors influence your choice?"

DE: "When it is cold, I need a topcoat. My topcoat is tan; I feel it looks better with the dark suit. This particular client is likely to want to go to dinner afterwards. They always go Italian; they always order red wine. Come to think of it, I usually drink white wine just in case it spills or drips."

KE: "When is the type of presentation a factor?"

DE: "When we sit and discuss the presentation, coats are usually taken off . . . and I, well, you know, I sweat."

KE: "OK, what seasons do you prefer for each suit?"

As this discussion unfolds, the KE learns some other factors that are summarized in FIG. 7-8. Yes, this discussion was hypothetical; yes, it explored weird tangents; yes, it was all over a decision of what to wear. By the way, the dark three-piece was selected. He did not worry about wrinkles, and this discussion did not explore shirts and ties. However, as outrageous as this example seems, a KE is likely to experience pursuits of attributes with a domain expert that will explore strange lands.

3 (3P) piece	2 (2P) piece	Wrinkles	Non-wrinkle	OK for red wine	Suit coat off	Winter	Spring	Summer	Fall
Dark Light	D	D2P D3P	L3P	D2P D3P	D3P	D3P D2P	L3P D2P	L3P D3P	D3P D2P L3P

Fig. 7-8. Traits.

A series of traits can be grouped into a trait attribute set that the expert can review and provide with a confidence value. The collection of trait attributes helps to establish the problem boundaries and primary considerations for selection. The problem boundaries provide the threshold and limits of the problem. With this information, the KE can use examples and counterexamples to help optimize the decision-making process. The primary considerations assist the KE in a system's user-questioning strategies. By asking focused questions, the system can use a breadth-first search strategy to facilitate a rapid search. Traits are used in repertory grids and example sets which are discussed in chapter 8.

Generalization. After the traits are grouped into attribute sets with assigned confidence ratings, a further refining process begins. The collection and organization of traits, attributes, and examples are analyzed to create rules. This process involves the placement of knowledge into a hierarchical framework. The process of extracting rules from the example set is an inductive process.

The nature of knowledge-based systems is to proceed with inexact knowledge and make "educated guesses" in order to move to the next consideration or outcome. The steps in the process are:

1. Identify the outcomes.
2. Identify the major attributes and traits.
3. Capture the steps, facts, and discriminators that the expert uses to arrive at a conclusion, including the confidence rating.
4. Represent the knowledge in a manner appropriate to the knowledge type and tool.

The KE prompts for and listens to key words that the domain expert uses to imply the basis of a rule. These key words and phrases include: if, then, whenever, while, during, ranging from, always, and never.

The generalization and refining process is discussed in greater detail in chapter 8. However, the KE begins thinking about how acquired information will be represented for validation and machine input. Using the four steps, a KE can both acquire and represent the information into knowledge strings, e.g., "Whenever travel is required, the season is winter, Italian food is likely to be eaten, and the suit coat is taken off following or during a presentation, the dark three-piece suit is selected. This selection has a 99% certainty factor." Expressing this knowledge string as a rule:

> IF season is winter
> AND Italian food likely to be eaten
> AND (coat may be taken off following a presentation
> OR coat may be taken off during a presentation)
> THEN select the dark three-piece suit
> CF 99

More about rules and certainty is available in chapter 8.

Topics for Decision Making

The reason for acquiring information from domain experts is to be able to place it in a knowledge base for decision making. In general, decision making is the process by which an expert arrives at appropriate selections to reach a conclusion. Generally, the expert can select from a list of alternatives. This list is usually in the form of selection options or requests for specific input. The selection process can easily be emulated by a knowledge-based system in a structured presentation format.

The first question presented to the user is designed to optimize the selection process, so that the solution is reached with the fewest possible number of questions. The idea is to have the response to the first question eliminate a high percentage of the options, and each subsequent question's response further reduce the number of remaining options.

This process provides intermediate selections and branches for related, focused questions or selections. When a system offers an optimized tree of selections, it is termed a hierarchical decision-making system. The hierarchy can be graphically represented in tree form with major factors as the branches and attributes as the twigs. Note that humans can reasonably handle only a limited number of notions, ideas, or objects at one time. Some studies place that number at seven. Thus, actual selection alternatives should number no more than seven. If there seems to be a requirement for more than seven selection options, consider splitting them into two groups. In the business suit example, the selection can be optimized by asking questions about the season and if the coat will be removed. The answers to these questions would lead to a solution.

In general, attributes are in place to discriminate among degrees of the major factors. Attributes include discriminators like young, old, dark, light, dull, shiny, etc. Attributes also include descriptors such as yellow, green, blue, white, etc. The strategy of attributes with opposites is one that KEs can use to help domain experts focus on their task.

One of the challenges of knowledge acquisition is that domain experts often do not know how they arrive at their decisions. The experts generally do not analyze their decision-making process, nor are they consciously aware of the major factors and attributes that they consider during that process. One way to help a domain expert is to focus on the attribute identification aspects of tasks.

Experts can trace their reasoning processes in specific cases and reveal the major factors and attributes used in those processes. They generally have a difficult time relating their day-to-day strategies and tactics. The job of the KE is to bring these strategies and tactics to light. The KE can piece together the decision-making processes of the experts and reveal the structures of their thinking through the use of carefully selected questions and scenarios.

The KE focuses on the truly relevant major factors and attributes. When a KE or domain expert adds "nice to know" information or "I know this, so I should include it" to a knowledge base, the KE or the domain expert is practicing techno-trivia. Techno-trivia is the unnecessary addition of "bells and whistles" to a system. Techno-trivia can be a software or hardware abuse.

In summary, two key factors in the process of knowledge acquisition are accuracy of source materials and representation of the interrelations and their associated decision-making criteria.

Knowledge Acquisition Summary

So far, we have presented a series of knowledge acquisition techniques which provide strategies for *real-time* data gathering. The interview techniques help to structure the data gathering process. Protocols were introduced as a reminder that there is more to meaning than is stated by mere words. Mapping techniques are used to provide informal representations of the interview process.

After the data is gathered, the analysis process—the conversion of that data to information—begins.

Analysis

Once the data sources have been exploited, they are analyzed, organized, and compared to the domain objectives. Each of the tapes, note sheets, and other hard and soft copy sources is tagged and organized. This process is a necessary follow-up to each knowledge acquisition session.

There is usually little benefit in transcribing an entire tape recording of a session. It is suggested that the KE listen to the tape at increased speed. The pitch of the voices is shifted upwards, but there is an immense time saving. Portions of the tape that are crucial to the project can be transcribed. Videotapes can also be run at an increased speed or slowed down as appropriate.

The review of sources is guided by the Knowledge Acquisition Form, which presents the objectives of the individual and collective sessions. It is often beneficial to review any conclusions with domain experts other than the contributing domain expert in that particular effort. It is also good practice to obtain the opinion of another knowledge engineer.

Remember that the objective of analyzing the source materials is to construct knowledge representations for validation and system construction. Representation schemes are discussed in detail in the following chapter. However, there are several strategies that knowledge engineers use to organize the knowledge provided by domain experts.

Analysis of the knowledge-based sources is used to clarify problem situations, alternative considerations, and appropriate solution sets. One effective technique used to assist in the analysis of knowledge base sources is a tabular display. This table is composed of example sets that focus on a single problem. The table lists major factors, their attributes, the result of the set, and a confidence rating about the set.

Some of the analysis tasks may be reduced or eliminated as knowledge acquisition software evolves. The future holds great promise for the automation of the knowledge acquisition and analysis processes.

Automated Knowledge Acquisition

Manual knowledge acquisition is time-consuming and expensive. The majority of time in most knowledge-based system projects is spent on the acquisition of knowledge. The costs of system applications would be reduced if the time spent on knowledge acquisition was decreased, less-skilled individuals were used to acquire the knowledge, and automation was available for selected aspects of the process.

Tools. Just as knowledge-based systems are used to emulate the decision-making processes of human experts in specific domains, *Automated Knowledge Acquisition Tools* (AKATs) will be able to emulate the knowledge acquisition techniques of a knowledge engineer. AKATs will be able to assist in reducing the costs of producing knowledge-based systems.

AKAT research has developed in two areas: knowledge elicitation and machine learning. Knowledge elicitation focuses on techniques such as repertory grids which feature descriptions of objects in terms of their properties and organizations. Machine learning provides "continuing education" for a knowledge-based system application.

AKATs are likely to develop along a path similar to the one for CASE tools described in chapter 4. They will be a series of integrated modules that perform specific aspects of the knowledge acquisition, representation, and coding generation processes. The knowledge acquisition tool will assist with or perform the following tasks:

- Determine knowledge source locations
- Organize the sources of facts, concepts and rules
- Determine the best human sources of heuristic knowledge
- Extract, catalog, and organize declarative and procedural knowledge
- Identify common sense requirements
- Determine and classify certainty factors
- Create the concept set elements of names, attributes, transactions, constraints, and depictions

- Identify the longevity of knowledge: permanent, static, or dynamic
- Create a working mental model

The knowledge representation tool will construct graphical knowledge representation schemas such as:

- Example set tables
- Production rule trees
- Repertory grids
- Frames
- O-A-V triplets

The coding generator will determine and create:

- User interfaces
- Search techniques
- Explanation subsystems
- Report generators

AKATs will have an impact on domain experts in the development of small or "in-house" applications. While some domain experts are willing to interact with automated software, most will not have the time or interest. In addition, automating the knowledge acquisition process will benefit rather than replace the knowledge engineer, as the sponsors of commercial applications are more likely to involve human knowledge engineers who employ AKATs.

Machine Learning. Machine learning starts with an established knowledge base. It then searches for new rules about the contents, rules, and relationships within that knowledge base. In this way machine learning systems will enrich the knowledge base through the generation of new rules.

Machine learning systems will evolve into self-learning systems. Human experts learn as they experience new instances and gain new perspectives about their domain. Human experts constantly reassemble models through infusions of newly introduced information. Machine learning systems will emulate this human process.

The distinctive feature of machine learning systems is their ability to add to their knowledge bases. Links into databases, electronic texts, and periodicals are established for scanning, analyzing, synthesizing, and incorporating relevant new information into the knowledge base. Thus, the knowledge bases of these systems will be dynamic.

In addition, these learning systems will track and assess user responses. An active dialogue between the user and the system will be established. The user will judge the system's recommendations and transmit that judgment to the process. The system uses its inductive reasoning processes to weigh and incorporate or not incorporate the new knowledge into the knowledge base. Add the ability to communicate with the system through voice commands, and this system will be the near-term ancestor to the HAL 9000 of Arthur C. Clarke's *2001: A Space Odyssey*.

SUMMARY

In this chapter, we discussed techniques that can be used by the KE to acquire knowledge for the knowledge base from the domain expert. The communications process involved in knowledge acquisition requires that a KE be proficient in the area of interviewing and questioning techniques, and have the ability to assess how the domain expert thinks, reasons, and solves problems. The techniques used and the abilities of the KE are closely linked—the level of expertise in one will affect the other and vice versa.

Through the knowledge acquisition process, the KE develops a growing base of knowledge and begins molding it into some type of hierarchical structure. Collected traits, attributes, and examples are analyzed to create rules. What follows is the task of analyzing and organizing the collection so that it is ready for input to the system structure.

PRACTICAL APPLICATION

A factor easily overlooked in the knowledge acquisition process is the most comfortable style of communication for the KE.

1. Prepare an Interview Checklist using the one presented in this chapter.

2. Take some time with one or more other people if possible, to determine the interview style with which you are most at ease—as an interviewer and as the person being interviewed. It is important to remember that communication is a two-way exchange; while you are interviewing the domain expert, the expert may also be "interviewing" you to assess for himself what your personality is, any hidden agendas you might have, and most importantly, the nature of the process you are conducting.

    a. Prepare for the interview by considering the three components of an interview: the beginning, middle, and the ending. Plan open-ended and closed questions.

b. Attempt a verbal protocol strategy with your expert.

c. Construct a map to represent the interview.

d. List and describe the visual cues the expert gives you. Is the expert basically a visual, auditory, or kinesthetic person? What did you do to accommodate the expert's inclination?

3. After identifying your preferred interview technique(s), consider its impact on the domain expert selection process.

8

Knowledge Acquisition: Structures

To criticize is to appreciate, to appropriate,
to take intellectual possession,
to establish in fine a relation with the criticized thing
and to make it one's own.

Henry James

INTRODUCTION

To establish knowledge bases on machines, the KE acquires and represents the knowledge of domain experts. First, initial knowledge is acquired from the domain experts and other sources, and then placed by the KE into a knowledge base. The KE uses one or more representation schemes to validate that knowledge and satisfy the requirements of the selected tool or language.

For the domain experts, these schemes are designed to provide a graphic representation of the knowledge for review. Knowledge representation structures are also used internally in knowledge-based systems; often the knowledge structures need to be re-created. Both shallow and deep knowledge are represented in these structures. For example, declarative knowledge is used to provide relationships and classify objects. This knowledge is used to provide concept awareness. Declarative knowledge uses representation schemes like production rules, semantic networks, and frames. Procedural knowledge explains how things work and how to apply declarative knowledge. Procedural knowledge is represented through scripts, examples, and production rules.

As the technology of knowledge-based systems improves, more knowledge representation schemes will emerge. This chapter presents several knowledge representation schemes. To date, there is no preeminent way to represent knowledge. Many knowledge representation strategies have been successfully in a variety of programs. Thus, the selection of a knowledge representation scheme is dependent on the knowledge being represented and the system under consideration.

The representation schemes are presented with descriptions and with generic examples. There are many variables that determine which knowledge representation scheme to use. These variables include content of the knowledge base, best communication medium for validation, final form of the knowledge base, time, and skill. The reader is encouraged to explore the exercises at the end of this chapter, which offer an opportunity to experiment with the possibilities.

KNOWLEDGE REPRESENTATION ALTERNATIVES

Knowledge representation alternatives are founded on studies and observations of human reasoning. Thus, the KE has an interesting task. The knowledge gained from the experts and other sources is gathered, organized, and represented. Ideally, it is structured in a form that can be reviewed by the expert and used by the computer. However, some tools or languages can have unnatural knowledge representation schemas which deviate too far from the understanding of the expert. As a result, the expert cannot relate to the representation. If the KE concentrates on the requirements of the expert, the representation may need to be redone to suit the parameters of the tool or language.

One way to maximize the possibilities for satisfying domain expert and machine needs is to have a KE who is well acquainted with the various knowledge representation options for knowledge-based system tools. The bottom line is to make sure that the knowledge of the expert is represented in the knowledge base of the knowledge-based system. Thus, the final knowledge representation scheme is driven by a tool or program language. Knowledge can be represented in many ways including rules, frames, semantic networks, outlines, maps, object-attribute-value triplets, logical expressions, lists, trees, schemas, scripts, and so on.

Out of all the possible options for representing knowledge, certain approaches are commonly used. These are semantic networks, production rules, frames, scripts, outlines, flowcharts, example sets, repertory grids, and object-oriented representations.

Semantic Network

One of the oldest knowledge representation schemes in AI research is the *semantic network* or semantic net. The term "semantic network" originated in the work of Quillian and others. The original use of the semantic net was for characterizing human memory in psychological models. These models attempted to represent knowledge in terms of natural memory and human memory concepts.

However, semantic nets have yet to be used as stand-alone models of human knowledge. They do not have a formalized standard for structure. In addition, the completed net is not able to be imported into any existing knowledge-based systems. Semantic nets are generally used in a visual representation of relationships. Knowledge relationships for system-importable schemes include frames or production rules.

A semantic net is a collection of nodes that contain objects, concepts, or events. Semantic networks are visual descriptions of knowledge about objects and their relationships. They are very effective at representing hierarchical declarative knowledge. Any knowledge that can be classified or categorized can be placed in a semantic net.

Semantic nets are composed of two basic units called *nodes* and *links*. Nodes are used to represent objects such as people, places, and things. Nodes can also be concepts, events, or actions. A concept could be Einstein's theory of relativity. An event or action could be the processing of information, or the flow of electricity between two points, or the filling of a swimming pool. Attributes of an object can be associated with a node. Examples are color, size, and temperature. Graphically, nodes are represented by circles or boxes.

Nodes are connected by links that show the relationships between objects. These links are also called arcs. Examples of common arcs include is-a, has-a, and made-of. Is-a links generally provide class or hierarchical relationships. Has-a links are used to show characteristics of objects. Made-of and similar links provide definitions of the connected objects. Graphically, links are represented by lines and arrows.

Semantic nets are very effective at representing any kind of object or concept. A KE can define almost any knowledge situation that can be structured with objects, links, and relationships. There are no exact procedures that can be suggested; however, there are considerations that can be explored by the KE prior to the selection of a semantic net.

The labeling convention for the nodes and links are personal to the KE. However, there are some common practices such as placing the primary node or nodes near the center with the links radiating out from the node(s). Figure 8-1 provides a semantic net representation of a popular play. Here, nodes are used to represent declarative knowledge.

Advantages of Semantic Nets. Semantic nets are based on a network structure which is visual and easy to understand. Advantages of the semantic net include the following:

- The semantic net offers flexibility in adding new nodes and links to a definition as needed. The visual impression is like that of an organization chart.
- The semantic net offers economy of effort since a node can inherit characteristics from other nodes to which it has an "is-a" relationship.
- The semantic net functions in a manner similar to that of human information storage.
- Since nodes in semantic nets have the ability to inherit relationships from other nodes, a net can support the ability to reason and create definition statements between non-linked nodes.

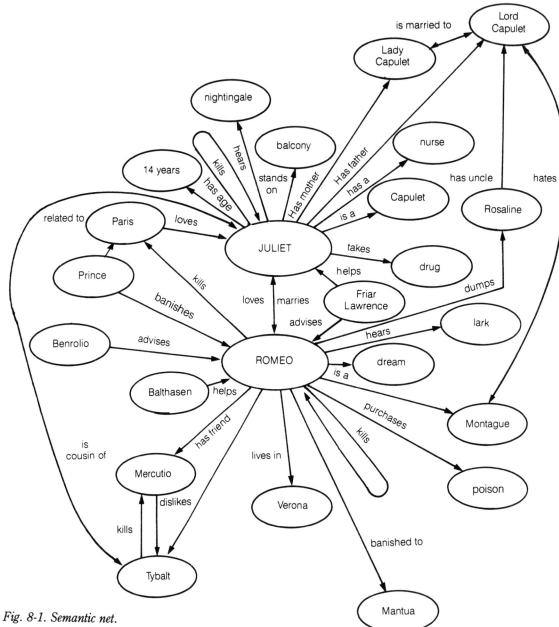

Fig. 8-1. Semantic net.

Problems of Semantic Nets. Semantic nets also have some problems.

- No standards exist for the definition of nodes, or relationships between and among nodes.
- The power of inheriting characteristics from one node to another offers potential difficulties with exceptions.

- The perception of the situation by the domain expert can place relevant facts at inappropriate points in the network.
- Procedural knowledge is difficult to represent in a semantic net, since sequence and time are not explicitly represented.

Semantic nets do not reside in a computer in display or graphic form. The semantic net's objects and relationships are stated in verbal terms using a variety of languages or tools. A program is provided with a node at which to start and searches by various techniques for desired objects and relationships.

Semantic nets offer graphic representations of knowledge, but are stored in another form for use. In a knowledge-based program, the completed network can be used for knowledge validation by a domain expert. Knowledge representation alternatives such as rules can represent knowledge structures and be used in the application. The KE weighs representation strategies for accuracy and cost effectiveness.

Object-Attribute-Value Triplets

Object-Attribute-Value (O-A-V) triplets are a common variation of semantic nets. The object portion of the triplet is either a physical or conceptual entity. Entities are represented as nodes. The attribute is a characteristic of the object. Attributes are designated by arcs. The value is associated with that attribute of that object. Valu₂s are also represented by nodes. O-A-V triplets provide structure for the semantic net. O-A-V triplets are also used in other representation structures such as frames.

Harmon (1985) discussed O-A-V triplets as having the ability to represent static objects and dynamic instances. Static objects are described as unchanging. Dynamic instances define objects that change from case to case. The example shown in FIG. 8-2 and similar examples in the semantic net shown in FIG. 8-1 represent dynamic instances. These instances are dynamic because the value portions can change. However, if only the object and attribute portions of the triplet are used as a strategy to portray knowledge, this strategy is static. For example, FIG. 8-3 shows relationships that describe an environment where the object and the attribute are constant. The domain expert or the knowledge engineer can use the O-A pairs as a form.

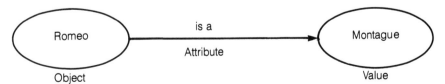

Fig. 8-2. Object-attribute-value triplet.

O-A-V triplets can be used to show order and relationships. These relationships are accomplished through a tree structure. In turn, the tree structure can be used to establish a static strategy and a dynamic structure. Consider the fol-

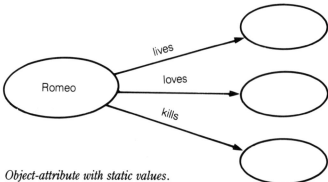

Fig. 8-3. Object-attribute with static values.

lowing two figures. Figure 8-4 illustrates a static strategy tree for an employment application. No values have been assigned for any objects or attributes. Note that this kind of structure plays for a knowledge base somewhat the same role that a schema does for a database.

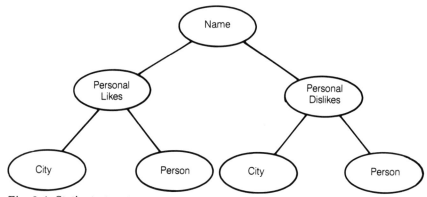

Fig. 8-4. Static strategy tree.

Figure 8-5 illustrates a dynamic tree structure. This structure uses O-A-V triplets to activate the static form. This tree does not show the exact linkage between the objects. However, the tree does show inheritance.

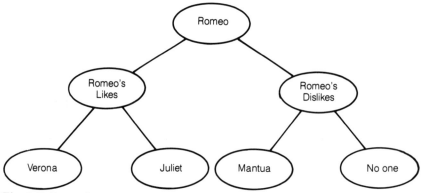

Fig. 8-5. Dynamic strategy tree.

The same illustration can be used to show linkage between objects in terms of subpart links and casual links. Subpart links are similar to major factors of the object. Casual links are similar to attributes of the major factors. Collectively, the casual links can be used to describe the root node (FIG. 8-6).

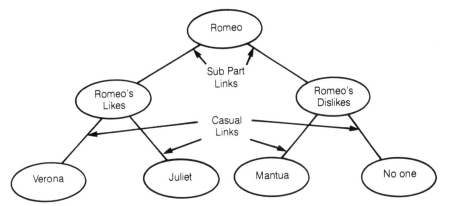

Fig. 8-6. Linkage within the tree.

Frames

A *frame*, like a semantic net, is a structure for representing chunks of declarative knowledge. Frames differ from semantic nets in that the values are grouped together into a single unit called a frame. Thus, a frame houses the composite knowledge as a single set of attribute-value pairs, whereas semantic nets require several O-A-V triplets to represent the same knowledge.

Frames offer an organization for detailing the attributes of an object. When humans recall images, the focus of the image is accompanied by the attributes of the object. In addition, some of the attributes can link to other objects so as to form the equivalent of a network. A frame is a matrix structure. All of the knowledge in a frame is interrelated. The contents of the frame include the characteristics of a concept, values of the characteristics, and related behavior.

A typical frame is divided into components called *slots* and *facets*. The slot contains an object attribute. These attributes represent a particular character-istic, specification, or other datum used to define an object or situation. A facet is an attribute associated with a slot itself, such as the maximum length of its value. The value of a slot is considered to be one of its facets. The size of a frame can vary, depending on the complexity of the represented object. There-fore, frames can be used at all levels of analysis.

The human reasoning that takes place with a frame is at two levels. At the deeper level, or level two, is the knowledge of the domain expert working in familiar situations. At this level, the established problem-solving procedure can be represented and called upon. Both the slot and values are filled in (FIG. 8-7).

Frames can also provide a structure for organizing declarative knowledge into slots and the procedural knowledge into the facets. A procedure designated in a facet can carry out a certain function whenever the contents of its slot are modified.

JULIET	
Slots	Values
Age	14
Mother	Lady Capulet
Father	Lord Capulet
Boy friend	Romeo Montague
Fiancé	Count Paris
Auditory Reference	Nightingale
Habit	Takes sleeping drug
Aversion	Sharp knives

Fig. 8-7. Frame of Juliet.

When a novel situation is encountered, attempts can be made to match familiar slots with the new information. Through this matching, inferences can be drawn about the objects or events using informed common sense.

It has been pointed out that multiple frames can be linked in a manner similar to that of the semantic net. Individual slots can be linked to additional frames in other parts of the knowledge base. When frame structures are linked, a powerful knowledge base is established. For example, a frame that addresses a computer model may look like FIG. 8-8.

In addition to the frame that represents this single computer, the KE could create frames for other models as well. The combination of these frames would constitute a knowledge base.

IBM PS/2 MODEL 80	
Microprocessor	16 MHz Intel 80386
RAM	1 MB
Color	Video Graphic Array
Interface	Parallel, serial, mouse
Hard Drive	44 MB
Diskette	1.44 MB 3.5"
Expansion Slot	32 bit microchannel (3) 16 bit microchannel (4)
Memory	32 bit capacity

Fig. 8-8. Frame of a computer.

Advantages of Frames. The principal advantage of frame-based knowledge representation is that a sound structure is provided for the data and the attributes of that data. Other advantages include:

- Generic sets of rules can be built from the representation with a lessened risk of redundancy, and consequently with economy of rules.
- A visual display of frames helps in understanding the knowledge and the interrelations of the structure.
- Frames provide a working base for adjusting and maintaining a knowledge base.

Problems with Frames. There are a limited number of tools that work with frames, and few knowledge engineers who have experience with frame-based knowledge representation. Additional problems are cited in the following list.

- Computer programs are not equipped to work with entire frames, and encounter efficiency problems caused by increasing search time.
- Knowledge engineers and others seem to experience difficulty in limiting the size and components of the frame so that they match the reasoning process or search techniques of the system.
- Frames can overlap too much for the sake of efficiency. A lack of understanding of where to stop often requires restructuring the representation, which can be costly.

Scripts

A *script* is a knowledge representation scheme similar to a frame. Rather than describing an object, as a frame does, a script describes a sequence of events. Similarly to a frame, a script depicts a generic situation, but the situation is presented in a narrower context. The script uses a series of slotlike fields that contain the declarative and procedural knowledge (FIG. 8-9).

Schank and Abelson (1977) developed scripts as a knowledge representation method. The idea behind scripts was that human behavior can be characterized in terms of familiar ways of dealing with various situations. Typical components of a script include conditions, props, roles, and scenes. Conditions delimit the situations that are to be met for a valid script. Props are the objects used in the situations. Roles are the people or prime objects in the script. Scenes provide the sequence of events as they occur in the script.

Typical scripts describe the events of a given situation. Scripts reason by anticipating what should happen next within its structure. They contain scenes that are mini-scripts within the event sequence and which represent subsets of the main theme. These scripts are useful to a KE for predicting what will happen in a given situation. However, to use scripts, the script representation must be programmed into a language readable by a computer. A script can be illustrated by a tragic love story.

```
Script:    Play
Track:     Tragic love story
Props:     Fending families
           Young lady
           Young man
           Friends
           Sharp objects
           Poisons
           Patients
           Parents
           Suitor
```

Entry Conditions	Results
Families hate families	Tension
Boy sees girl	Interest
Boy meets girl	More interest
Friends give advice	Little help
Parents make arrangements	No help
Hostilities occur	People die
Boy and girl marry	Bad timing
Boy and girl die	End of play

Fig. 8-9. Script of a tragic love story.

```
Event 1   Enter play
Event 2   Meet characters
Event 3   Anticipate problems
Event 4   See problems grow
Event 5   See problems come to a head
Event 6   Feel despair over death
Event 7   Leave play
```

Production Rules

Semantic nets and frames have their strengths as declarative or object-oriented systems of knowledge representation. They represent facts about those objects and how the objects relate to each other. Cleverly manipulated, they can address some procedurally based knowledge as well. However, when the need is to recommend a course of action based on observable events or situations, it may be more effective to use a procedural system for the knowledge representation. This procedural system contains both the situational facts and the appropriate application of those facts to effect an action.

Production rules are the most common knowledge representation used to date. They consist of a two-part statement containing a premise and a conclusion. The premises represent the conditions similar to declarative knowledge. Premises are represented by IF statements. Conclusions represent resolutions in THEN statements. The conclusions are similar to procedural knowledge or the action portion of a statement. The task of the knowledge engineer and the domain expert is to create a knowledge base that contains the smallest possible information units.

From a terminology standpoint, there are other expressions used for the two-part production rule system. Some of the most common references are:

First Part	Second Part
Antecedent	Consequent
Situation	Action
Premise	Conclusion

Rule-based systems are easy to understand and represent. Most knowledge domains can be represented in this format. Examples of rules in a rule-based system are:

> IF the fuel gauge nears empty
> THEN purchase fuel.

> IF the glass is full
> THEN stop filling the glass.

In addition to the IF-THEN statements, AND and OR statements can also be present. When an AND statement is used, all of the conditions must be true for the rule to fire. When an OR statement is used, any of the ORed conditions can activate or "fire" the rule. It is also possible to mix AND and OR statements.

More complex rules are needed for some knowledge domains.

> IF a large animal acts aggressive
> AND the animal is not chained
> AND it is focusing its attention on you
> THEN do not enter the gate.

In this example, IF begins the statement, followed by two AND phrases which further define the situation. For the conclusion to be true, all three conditional statements must be true.

In addition to, or in place of the AND statement, OR statements can be used. OR statements are used when more than one premise can cause an action.

> IF the battery is dead
> OR there is no fuel
> THEN the vehicle will not start.

In rule-based systems, the THEN statement is only true if each of the AND/OR statements is true. Rule-based systems are powerful because they are easy to update and evaluate. Each rule stands on its own merits. When rules overlap, they can be combined.

Rules are very small portions of knowledge. There may be a requirement for many, many rules to represent knowledge in a specific domain. Depending on the complexity of the knowledge-based system, the number of rules can range from a few dozen to thousands.

Rule-based system construction seems to work well for situations for which there is an abundance of evidence. Examples are classification of a plant, repair manuals, and policy decisions. Rule-based shells tend to be strong in their recommendations when they have a carefully defined set of rules. Rule-based systems are generally used when the rules are known and a confidence factor can be linked to the rule.

Heuristic knowledge is well represented using production rules. Each heuristic rule is independent, thereby enabling reordering of the knowledge base and a means for maintaining and updating the system. In order to accurately define a domain, a large volume of production rules is needed. The rules must interrelate, not be redundant, and not be contradictory. This is one of the many challenges undertaken by the KE.

Rules can also be displayed by Attribute-Value or Object-Attribute-Value representations. A previous example discussed wise behavior for dealing with an aggressive animal. It had a three-part "IF" clause and a conclusion based on a "THEN" clause. The rule is repeated here, and made a little more complex with the addition of an OR statement. In addition, a confidence factor (CF) is added to the rule.

IF the large animal acts aggressive
AND the animal is not chained
OR it is tethered with a chain of undetermined length
AND it is focusing its attention on you
THEN do not enter the gate

	Object	Attribute	Value	CF
IF	animal	behavior	aggressive	
AND	animal	chaining	(nil)	
OR	chain	length	undetermined	
	animal	focus	you	
THEN	you	action	(nil)	100

A knowledge base composed of production rules is generally large. Large knowledge bases require longer search times than smaller knowledge bases. Therefore, the KE considers the appropriate selection of languages or tools for the potential application. Selection of languages is discussed in chapter 10. Selection of hardware was discussed in chapter 6.

Advantages of Production Rules. There are several advantages of production rules.

- Communicating: By representing knowledge in a rule-based system, those who are familiar with the domain and those who are not, can read the rules and understand their meaning.

- Explanation: The reasoning for the system's recommendation is contained within the IF (cause) and THEN (action) statement.

- Modification: The rule-based system can easily be modified by adding, deleting, or altering selected rules in the system.

Disadvantages of Production Rules. In addition to advantages, there are disadvantages in the use of production rules.

- The most common problem is a control program search limitation usually due to the size of the knowledge base. Some programs have difficulty in searching for a rule and firing. Other events cause a rule to be evaluated and subsequently overlooked.
- Systems with a large number of rules can exceed the capabilities of the computer, or become unmanageable from a human maintenance and evaluation standpoint.
- Knowledge engineers sometimes try to force fit knowledge domains into rule sets rather than matching the nature of the knowledge base with a better option.
- It is sometimes difficult to assign an appropriate confidence rating to all rules in the knowledge base.

Associated with production rules is the manner in which a production system uses rules. There are two basic strategies, forward chaining and backward chaining. The KE determines the appropriate method for the knowledge base in light of the abilities of the tool that has been selected or is under consideration.

A heuristic rule concerning the selection of backward or forward chaining is: if there are more possible outcomes than there are conditions or decision states, a backward search strategy may prove the fastest. If there are more initial states than goal states, forward chaining is the best choice. This latter statement is true because multiple options for an entry point can quickly lead to a conclusion. The multiple options can be considered like doors in an auditorium. The greater the number of doors, the easier it is for people to reach their seats.

Another heuristic rule in the area of forward and backward chaining is that larger and more complex systems tend to use a bidirectional search method.

Example Sets

Example sets are similar to frames. In frames, a major factor is decomposed into statements that contain the attribute set. These sets are linked with a series of example statements leading to a solution for the given conditions. Together, they comprise a knowledge representation that is easy to see and form into a rule base. Example sets are valuable because domain experts and nonexperts alike can make sense out of them.

The use of examples to represent knowledge is generally an intermediate step in the process. After setting up the example matrix, the selected tool or KE converts the matrix into rules, or the tool works solely from the example matrix. Generally, the example method begins with a listing of the conclusion, then the support of the conclusion with major applicable factors and attributes. Several major factor-attribute combinations can lead to the same conclusion.

The example matrix provides a convenient layout of rows and columns which is easy to read and understand. Some tools provide spreadsheet style input to represent the knowledge. This input is for the developer, not the system itself. The tool that provides for input of examples converts the examples into rules. The control program then searches the rules to reach a goal state. Figure 8-10 illustrates an example set for a small loan.

Credit Rating	Years on Job	Income	Homeowner	Results
Excellent	3	35000	Yes	Approved
Excellent	2	35000	No	Approved
Excellent	1	20000	No	Denied
Good	3	40000	Yes	Approved
Good	3	20000	No	Denied
Good	3	30000	No	Denied
Poor	—	—	—	Denied

Fig. 8-10. Example matrix.

Repertory Grids

Beginning with Kelly's (1955) model of thinking called personal construct theory, Gains and Shaw (1980) conceived a theory, called *repertory grids*, that could be used in the field of knowledge-based systems. A repertory grid is a system that experts can use to represent mental problem-solving processes.

The grid houses examples of the expert's model of a problem and its primary elements. Patterns are established in the grid which help the expert to focus on the major factors and attributes of the problem. Repertory grids thus tend to benefit analysis of problems rather than synthesis of knowledge.

A KE can construct a grid with an expert as a method of representing that expert's view of objects, attributes, or values. One strategy for constructing a grid is that of selection. The selection technique establishes the values used by the expert to differentiate objects. The grid serves the dual purpose of enabling an expert to establish and then select from a set of alternatives. For example, traits for automobile selection could include: price, number of doors, maintenance requirements, insurance costs, etc.

The expert can also use traits as sort criteria. For example, some alternatives may be eliminated by clustering them around a single attribute such as the price of automobiles. A final or intermediate decision can then be made from the remaining alternatives. Additional traits can be derived from bipolar aspects of an original one, such as a trait and its opposite.

Bipolar trait aspects include:

Trait	Opposite
old	young
rich	poor
heavy	light
dark	light

Sometimes different traits use the same term, such as the term "light" in the above example. This is not an unusual situation. Terms like "light" may be recorded in the Knowledge Dictionary. In the heavy/light pair, light means light in weight. "Light" in the dark/light pair could refer to readability. Dark and light could even refer to the calories in beer. Whatever the trait pairs, the terms must have a uniform meaning among team members. In addition, trait pairs presented to users must have uniform meanings as well.

Values or attributes of the bipolar trait can be added for discrimination or clarity. For example, a scale of 1 to 5 can be used to rate the degree of trait characteristics.

Old				Young
1	2	3	4	5

Degrees of the trait can be specified for a clearer understanding of the meaning of the rating.

Old				Young
very old	old	middle-aged	young	very young

The traits can also be associated with attributes.

Attribute	Trait	Opposite
age	old	young
wealth	rich	poor
weight	heavy	light
print density	dark	light

Once a series of appropriate traits are identified, understood, and rated, the KE and the domain expert can construct a grid. The technique for this is to consider objects in threes. Trait terms are similar to the attributes of major factors which in turn, are similar to objects.

Consider three people for a position where each is equally qualified and all are known to the selector. We will name these people: Jim Smith, Jane Jones, and Chelsea Chaiseworthy. The intent is to differentiate among the three. Begin by asking, "What is a trait that is characteristic of only two of the candidates?" This selector considered the trait of typing speed. Both Jim and Jane are fast typists. In fact, Jim is very fast. He could be rated 1 and Jane could be rated 2. The opposite of a fast typist is a slow typist. Chelsea can be rated for the typing trait as appropriate. This process continues and its results are illustrated in FIG. 8-11.

PERSONNEL			
Jim	Jane	Chelsea	TRAITS
1	2	5	Typing speed
1	2	3	Promptness
1	2	2	Quality of work
2	3	1	Friendliness
5	3	1	Professional appearance
5	5	1	Goes the extra mile

Fig. 8-11. Repertory grid.

Once the grid is constructed, the KE and the expert can analyze it. The grid provides a visual comparison that can be modified, as the expert can now see the "big picture." Various statistical techniques can be used to analyze the grid. Example sets can be characterized by further analysis of the grids, and used to establish rules through inductive reasoning. By inducing a set of rules from the grid, a knowledge base can emerge.

Object-oriented Strategies

Object-oriented strategies are a type of merger between frames and semantic nets. The principal strategy is that knowledge is viewed as object sets complete with behaviors. It is hierarchically structured such that lower levels in the structure access attributes and relationships from levels higher in the structure.

Objects are similar to frames because they use description sets for characterization. Objects use attributes; frames use slots. However, both objects and frames have a hierarchically arranged structure. Objects use methods and frames use procedures. Communication between sets in objects is through messages while frames use rules. Hybrid systems are resulting from converging strategies of object and frame knowledge representation.

Objects are similar to semantic nets by reason of the hierarchical or network structure. Thus, the object sets in lower levels inherit attributes from sets in the upper levels of the structure. Object sets are situationally oriented. For example, the object of an automobile and its object set differ when used for passengers as opposed to racing. For passengers, the automobile is configured for comfort. For racing, the automobile is tailored with respect to weight and performance.

Flexibility of description is the major strength of the object-oriented system. One basic object set can be established and then replicated with appropriate situational modifications. As a result, work can be leveraged by modifying already existing states, as necessary. One state can be established with sub-states that compare or contrast with the base state. For example, the state of race car can be altered for specific sub-states such as drag racing, sports rally, or track. Each race car has attributes, some the same, and some different from the object set. An object-oriented knowledge representation can be illustrated by a tragic love story (FIG. 8-12).

Outlines

Another organizational method is that of the *outline*. Outlines are generally used when the desired outcomes, major facts, and attributes are known. The outline is used as a method of organizing the information so that rules can be constructed. The outline helps in the construction of a hierarchy for the knowledge base.

One interesting attribute of outlines is that they are generally constructed on a word processor, where it is easy to manipulate the components of the outline. The single most important or optimizing factor may be used to begin an outline. For example, the beginning of a computer hardware selection outline might look like this:

I. Clock speed over 12 MHz (Major selection factor)
    A. Manufacturer 1
        1. Model A.
        2. Model B.
    B. Manufacturer 2
        1. Model A
            a. Option 1.
            b. Option 2.
        2. Model B

II. Footprint appropriate for small office.
    A. Manufacturer 1
        1. Model A.
            a. Option 1.
            b. Option 2.
    B. Manufacturer 2
        1. Model A
        2. Model B

Some team members will better visualize the findings if presented in outline form.

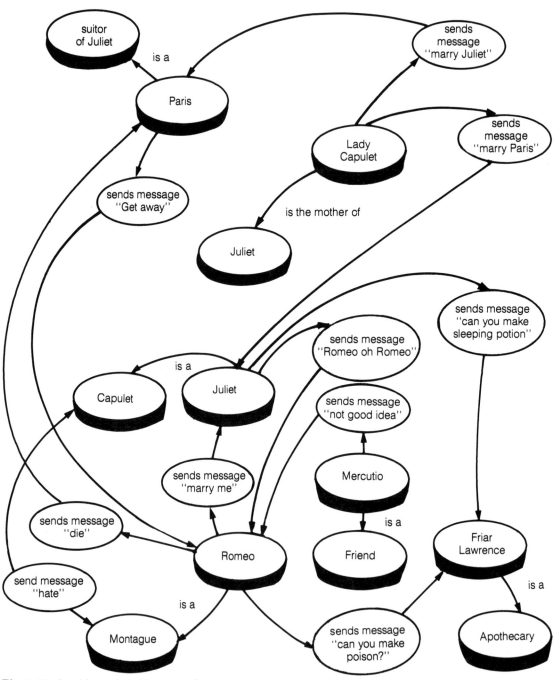

Fig. 8-12. An object-oriented love tragedy.

Flowcharts

A *flowchart* provides a sequential picture of events and decision points. The symbols used to represent processes and other events can vary. One scheme is to represent entry and exit points as circles, actions as rectangles, and decision points as diamonds. (See FIG. 8-13.)

Blackboards

A *blackboard architecture* is composed of various knowledge sources that are used in a manner similar to that of databases. These knowledge sources communicate through a central structure called a blackboard. The user of a blackboard system may store or retrieve information from any of the knowledge sources. The blackboard provides a centralized way of recording and tabulating intermediate decisions about a problem.

Blackboard architecture has three components: a global database, the blackboard; independent knowledge sources that can interact with the blackboard; and a scheduler to control knowledge source activities (FIG. 8-14).

Blackboards are generally used when a problem requires multiple experts as knowledge sources, or when a problem lends itself to decomposition. This architecture can accept any knowledge type. The physical blackboard can be as simple as notes on a wall, or as sophisticated as a specialized software system. The chief benefit of selecting blackboard architecture is the potential use of multiple experts or knowledge sources to solve a problem. An analogy of a blackboard system is provided as follows. Consider a blackboard used to plan a custom home. The knowledge sources are the various specialists who construct and finish the home. The control source is the general contractor.

The key to success in blackboard architecture is control. The focus of control is determining what is placed on the blackboard. Typical strategies for blackboard control include goal focus, model focus, and event focus.

Goal focus strategy adds elements to the blackboard that move toward the goal. Only the "need to know" sources are included. During the planning stage in the house example, the quality of the paint is a "need to know" attribute and the color of the paint is a "nice to know" attribute. During the finishing stage, the decorator and the painter coordinate on color selection. The controller needs to know the timeliness of the knowledge sources.

Model focus strategy involves the establishment, adoption, or adaptation of a model for emulation. Models can establish sequences, priorities, and characterizations about the problem and knowledge sources. In the house example, a strategy for efficiency which enables framers and electricians to work together may not be the working practice of those involved. The controller needs to either alter the model or alter the staff.

Event focus strategy is a reactive strategy to events as they occur. The overall strategy varies according to new conditions and alters its focus accordingly. In the house example, inspections, weather conditions, and materials sometimes require unplanned changes in the work plan.

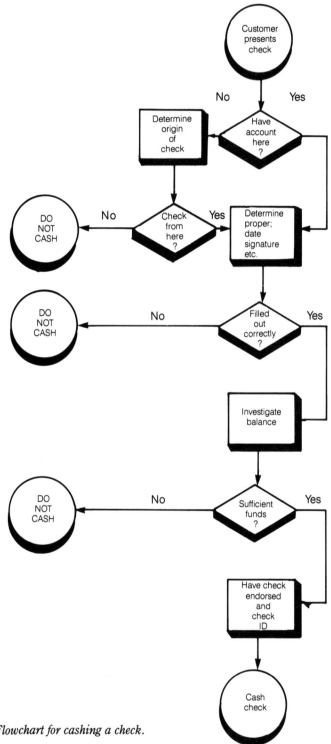

Fig. 8-13. Flowchart for cashing a check.

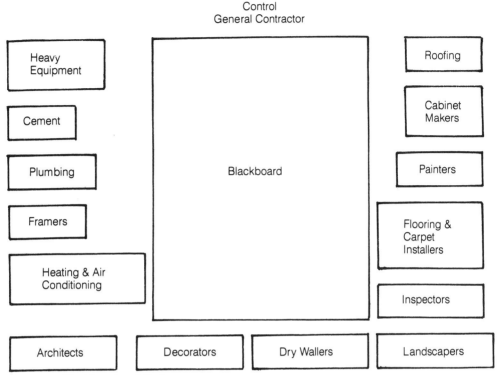

Fig. 8-14. Blackboard architecture.

The overall strategies may be driven by the blackboard objects, the knowledge source, or a combination of the two. For example, if the house building project were behind schedule, the controller could investigate the objects or the knowledge sources.

INHERITANCE

In each of the knowledge representation options, a common requirement exists. This requirement is the organization and connection of the knowledge components. The challenge is how to access and retrieve attributes from sets within the structure. For example, in a system designed to identify a class of mammals called dogs, the description of each member of the species should not include the fact that it has fur, bears live young, walks on four feet, etc. This information should be stored as properties generic to the species within the set.

The base set is used to optimize the search and serves as a base structure high in the is-a hierarchy. If a component of the base set is required by a set at a lower level (containing a higher degree of detail), the attributes are inherited.

Most KE analyses reveal logical groupings. Each of the groupings has links or inheritance properties that can be grouped and regrouped. For example, in a task analysis, tasks can be grouped as supertasks or distributed as subtasks. Consider a job analysis of the knowledge acquisition process performed by a knowledge engineer in chapter 7. *Knowledge acquisition* is a major category of task, and is near the top of the hierarchy.

Subordinate to Knowledge Acquisition is the *Interview*. This task is divided into "structured," "unstructured," etc. Thus, the task of Interview is a super-task. All of the attributes listed in a member of a task placed near the top of a hierarchy are inherited by those connected below. This structure enables a knowledge economy benefiting storage and access. Figure 8-15 is a partial job task analysis of a knowledge engineer.

Note that the job analysis of a knowledge engineer also has sets with upward links that identify relationships with parent sets on different branches. The state of inheritance of attributes from different branch sets is termed multiple inheritance.

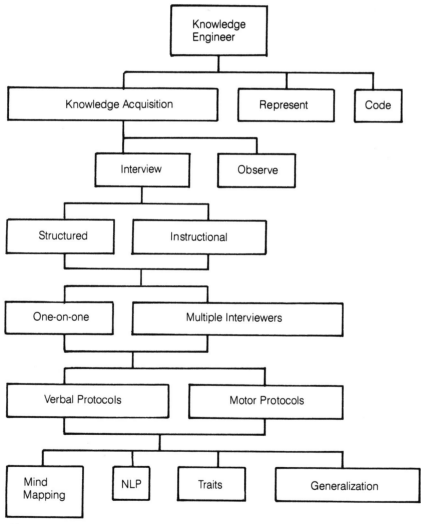

Fig. 8-15. Partial job task analysis of a knowledge engineer.

MEASURES OF CONFIDENCE

Knowledge-based systems are able to deal with ambiguity and uncertainty. Conventional programs that use algorithms to arrive at output cannot deal with uncertainty. Algorithms require specific input values in order to run. Conventional programs that are provided with expected inputs respond with expected outputs. However, when unexpected or incorrect inputs are given, an incorrect output results.

AI software, on the other hand, does not always require exact inputs to provide useful responses. Knowledge-based systems tend to ask questions or provide a menu of options for a user. In some systems, a user can request help or question a response. In other situations, a user may not have access to any form of weighing for the application's responses. With or without confidence measures, users can also question the validity of results. The experts that supply the knowledge or rules for the knowledge base require mechanisms that enable entry of degrees of uncertainty.

Certainty Factors

Every situation or conclusion cannot be 100 percent accurate, so *certainty factors* are used to handle ambiguous and uncertain knowledge. A certainty factor is a numerical measure of belief in the validity of a fact or rule. Certainty factors allow an inferencing program to work with inexact information or levels of truth.

Strategies vary for certainty factors. Some systems use scales from 0 to 1, or 0 to 10, or 0 to 100, or even -1 to $+1$. In scales of 0 through 1 or 10 or 100, 0 is rated as the low end of confidence. In the -1 through $+1$ scale, -1 is absolutely false, up to 0 is partially false, 0 is unknown, and up to $+1$ is a range of truth.

Certainty factor strategies involve or can be implemented by probability, Bayes' theorem, fuzzy logic, certainty theory, and ranking.

Probability. Probability differs from the arbitrary scale of a certainty factor. Mathematically, a probability, P, is the ratio of the number of times, X, that an event will occur to the number, N, of trials over which the event takes place.

$$P = X/N$$

Most of us have experienced mathematics classes that have expressed probability using the old reliable die-rolling example. With the die, there is a one in six probability that a die will show a given number. If a die were to be rolled and the outcomes tracked into infinity, each number would show up approximately an equal number of times. The probability of rolling a five, say, can be expressed mathematically as:

$$P = X/N$$
$$P(5) = 1/6 \text{ or } .16666 \text{ or } 16.7\% \text{ of the time}$$

An interesting consideration for using probability is that knowledge-based systems and the knowledge they contain generally do not have the benefit of sufficient data over time. For example, medical science does not have enough data to draw conclusions with certainty. As a result, using probability is a way of expressing opinion in a numerical fashion. This is commonly seen in odds for gambling. As further examples, a person might look outside and say that there is a better than 50% probability that it will rain, or survivors of a shipwreck might state that the probability of rescue is low. Thus, the KE considers the mathematical applications for probability in a system of opinion cloaked in probability.

Probability is a measure of certainty between 0 and 1 and is simply expressed by a formula. However, the probability illustrated was concerned with one type of event. Most events that occur in life occur in multiples or in combination.

The probability of event A is expressed as P(A). When two events are considered, P(A and B) expresses both, or joint events. When event A or B is considered, P(A or B) is written and indicates that one or both events will occur. Texts on mathematical probability should be consulted for further details.

Bayes' Theorem. Bayes' theorem has been used in many expert systems. This theorem is based on the concept that preceding events influence the probability of a given conclusion. Consider a police officer who spots a potential drug runner. The officer may have arrested several drug runners in a particular area who fitted the same profile. Therefore, the officer may assign a high probability to the suspect in question being a drug runner. However, another possibility is that the person may coincidentally fit the profile. Thus, the officer concludes only that the person has a high likelihood of being a drug runner, and looks for additional signs or indications. IF a stop is made for probable cause, the officer can observe the person's reactions and decide on a course of action, including none, if the person appears to be innocent.

The officer relied on personal experience about the relative probability of the person's activities to trigger action alternatives. Bayes' theorem expresses a conditional probability as:

$$P(H|E) = P(H) \times P(E|H) / P(E)$$

where | H | = hypothesis |
|---|---|
| E | = evidence |
| P(H\|E) | = probability of H, given E |
| P(H) | = probability of H, without regard to E |
| P(E\|H) | = probability of E, given H |
| P(E) | = probability of E, without regard to H |

In practice in expert systems, it is the odds in favor of a particular event that are used, not the probabilities. Bayes' theorem involves subjective opinion and mathematical probability, resulting in a method of combining inexact values.

Fuzzy Logic. *Fuzzy logic* or fuzzy truth is the use of inexact adjectives or adverbs to describe an object. Examples of fuzzy adjectives are large, small, fast, assumed, and so on. This system of logic was conceived by the mathematician and computer scientist, Lofti Zadeh. Fuzzy logic deals with relative values, expressed as a number between 0 and 1. In conventional set theory an object is either a member of a set (membership = 1) or it is not (membership = 0). In fuzzy set theory, an object can be just a little bit a member of a set (m = 0.1) or almost really totally a member (m = 0.95).

If we start with a herd of 10,000 cattle, its membership in the set of large herds is essentially 1. If we reduce its size to three, the membership is 0. How about 500? m = 0.8?

The size of the herd is relative and the descriptions of the herd are nebulous. In addition, the viewpoint of the onlooker differs based on experience. A relative quantity or quality to one person looks different to another. Fuzzy logic at this time is not widely used for confidence factors or certainty ratings because it is complex and difficult to incorporate into a system. In addition, there is no advantage over less complex systems. Fuzzy logic offers the KE an alternate approach to dealing with uncertainty in knowledge representation.

Fuzzy logic can be rated in a fashion similar to that of repertory grids. Values or attributes of the bipolar trait can be added for degree or clarity. For example, a scale of 1 to 5 can be used to rate the degree of the trait characteristics.

Nice			**Mean**	
1	2	3	4	5

An object can be considered according to a fuzzy scale. The meanings of a scale are often hard to communicate. If a common communication ground can be established among team members, fuzzy logic can work in a specific domain among informed and like-thinking groups. For example, consider "nice" and "mean" in terms of selecting personnel for public contact. If the domain expert selects these values, the KE can quantify the characterization with a few questions.

- "Nice as Sister Teresa or mean as Torquemada?"
- "Nice as the characters Doris Day plays or mean as the characters of Joan Collins?"
- "Nice as Rose Bird or mean as Roy Bean?"

In this way, the participants can set up an interpretable "nice → mean" scale, and specify a threshold point on it.

Consider a program to assist new handlers of animals in a zoo. The fuzzy scale of "nice" and "mean" might be of paramount importance. The KE could ask:

- "Nice as a rosy boa or mean as a cobra?"

Once again, the fuzzy terms and rating scales must be understood by all participants.

Logic. *Logic* is a precise system of reasoning credited to the early Greeks. Logic is used in AI programs to represent knowledge as a group of logical formulas. For example, PROLOG is a logic-based AI language that applies a set of inference rules to a knowledge base to reach conclusions.

Common systems used in AI applications are propositional calculus, predicate logic, and a restricted form of predicate logic called first-order predicate logic.

Propositional Calculus. *Propositional calculus* is a basic system of formal logic that expresses whether a "proposition" is true or false. This system is begun with a true or false statement. Propositional calculus then provides an inference system flow for proving the accuracy of chained statements.

For example, consider these statements.

A = If it is not raining, my car will start.
B = It is not raining today.
C = My car will start.

This is a simple example, but if it is assumed that statements A and B are true, then a propositional calculus rule called *modus ponens* states that statement C must be true. However, simple propositions like this example are of little use. Most problems suitable for expert systems are more complex and interrelated. In order to form more complex propositions, logical connectives are used. These connectives or operators are AND, OR, NOT, IMPLIES, and EQUIVALENT.

Through the use of propositions and connectives, sets of premises and logical conclusions can be expressed. When the connectives are represented as symbols, they can be manipulated by inference programs.

Predicate Calculus. *Predicate calculus* or predicate logic is similar to propositional calculus, but adds the dimension of specification of relationships and an ability to make generalizations. Thus, predicate calculus can represent knowledge in greater detail. This detail is at the level of components including an object, a characteristic of an object, and an action or direction the object can take.

A statement in the predicate calculus has two components, the argument(s) (object) and the predicate (assertion). The argument is the subject of a factual statement. The predicate is the verb or verbal phrase that specifies the nature of the fact. For example, a proposition could read:

The keys are in the top drawer.

This would be stated using predicate calculus as: IS-IN (keys, top drawer), where:

IS-IN   = Assertion

Keys   = Argument
Drawer   = Argument

Using predicate calculus, AI programs can be created to trigger on various relationships. There are numerous variations of logic used by AI programs, such as that found in PROLOG. The goal of logic-based knowledge is the ability to draw inferences through the knowledge base:

Advantages

Preciseness: Logic is exact. It establishes definite triggers.

Modularity: Logic chains are self-contained. Therefore, they can be modified, deleted, or created. Logic chains are similar to production rules in this manner.

Disadvantages

Clutter: As the number of facts in a predicate calculus knowledge base increases, the permutations among the facts increase dramatically.

Ranking. *Ranking* is another method that a domain expert can use to express uncertainty. Ranking is an ordering technique that provides an opportunity for an expert to compare a set of physical or conceptual objects. Ranking is desirable when there are few objects to rank. As the number of objects increases, alternate strategies should be considered.

Ranking requires an expert to make simultaneous judgments over a group of objects. While this can pose many difficulties, it can also help the experts to clarify their knowledge. Thus, ranking offers challenges and opportunities to the experts.

There are many techniques for sorting, and assessing the results. Parsaye and Chignell (1988) detail methods of ranking including ranking by selection, ranking by insertion, and ranking by exchanges.

Confidence Measure Summary. Figure 8-16 presents a table that lists the certainty and logical systems discussed, and their purposes, determinations, advantages, and disadvantages. All knowledge statements are not accurate. Most knowledge statements are given with caveats that are represented in a confidence measure. Knowledge statements are represented in knowledge-based systems; therefore, confidence measures need to be learned and used.

The selection of a confidence measure is dependent upon several factors including the nature of the content of the application, the preference of the domain expert, the capabilities of the tool, and the ability to communicate these measures to users.

After knowledge is represented with its associated measures of confidence, the KE is finished with the acquisition and representation, and is ready to code the system, right? No. There is one more technique that the KE uses to fill gaps. This technique is called Fault Tree Analysis.

	Purpose	Determination	Advantage	Disadvantage
Certainty Factors	Shows degree of belief	Arbitrary	Accepted by users	May not be accurate
Probability	Show Ratio	Mathematical ratio	Precise	Everything not measured precisely
Bayes' Theorem	Influence of previous events	Mathematical conditional probability	Accurate	Time-consuming— hard for domain experts to understand
Fuzzy Logic	Shows degree of belief	Relative truth	Derived from expert	Subject to interpretation
Logic	System of reasoning	Logical formulas	Accurate	Time Consuming
Propositional Calculus	Formal logic system	Interface system	Reasoned with KE and expert can translate into rules	
Predicate Calculus	Specifies relationships and makes generalities	Draws inference	Precise, modular	Clutter due to permutations
Ranking	Ordering	Judgment	Derived from the expert	Not directly transferable to a system

Fig. 8-16. Confidence measure summary.

FAULT TREE ANALYSIS

As a knowledge base evolves, the KE and the expert specify certainty factors for the various solutions backed by a series of events. These solutions are the results of a series of rules or examples. The IF, AND, and OR conditions for the rules and series of attributes for the example sets provide an analysis in terms of success for the system.

An analysis of the factors that promote system failure is also beneficial. For example, when an expert places an 80% confidence rating on a result, in one case in five (on the average) there is an opportunity for some factor to promote failure of the result. This measure of confidence is usually relayed to the user. A result with an 80% measure of confidence may not warrant action. If the domain expert and the KE invest more time, the confidence in a knowledge set may increase.

While every statement cannot have a 100% confidence measure, results with low measures are often meaningless. For example, a result that says that it might rain with a 12% confidence factor is not going to have much impact. A domain expert might have knowledge beyond the scope of the application and incorporate irrelevant tasks. Software and hardware are sometimes selected that perform tasks not required for the application. If there is little or no derived benefit, these tasks should not be done, and the software or hardware should not be used. Fault tree analysis can be used to identify confidence gaps or trivial knowledge base inclusion. Fault tree analysis provides a method for analyzing unacceptable events that can occur within a sequence of events.

The basic idea of the fault tree is that any failure in a system can trigger other, consequent failures, or, conversely, that it might be possible to trace backwards from a problem to its causes. These events can be arranged in a tree structure which allows their relationships to be studied.

Fault tree construction can use any conventional configuration that can show logic and dependencies such as AND and OR dependencies.

- AND: dependencies indicate that two events need to take place to produce a fault.

- OR: dependencies indicate that either of the events depicted could independently produce a fault.

- Symbols: should be established that represent event types. These symbols are any preferred geometric shapes such as circles, rectangles, and triangles. The events themselves are the primary focus. These events include terminal faults, unknown complications, and chained sequences. In addition, AND and OR conditions need to be identified.

  - First event type denotes a terminal fault. Should this event take place, the outcome is failure. This fault is represented by a circle.

  - Second event type indicates unknown complications. The presence of this event is detrimental to the outcome, but the reason or reasons are not known. This fault is represented by a rectangle.

  - Third event type is used to represent chained dependent faults. These events are low-level and have additional factors to consider that make them failure-influencing candidates. This fault is represented by a triangle.

- Arcs: are used to denote AND and OR conditions.

Additional events can be determined as needed, for a particular application and knowledge base. The KE establishes a legend to communicate the meanings of the symbols. For example, suppose that an investment advisor is under construction. After some investment rules are established, each rule is further evaluated. Consider the following rule.

CF

IF an investor needs a tax shelter
AND the investor needs inflation protection
AND the real estate market is good
THEN the investor should purchase real estate

80

Using a fault tree, the KE can further assess the rule and the 80% confidence rating. (See FIG. 8-17.)

TRUTH ABOUT TRUTH

The KE has many tasks and challenges in interacting with domain knowledge, creating knowledge representation schemes, and planning computer processing. One more task is the evaluation of truth about truth.

When problems are evaluated or the appropriate degree of granularity has been reached, a clear problem description is established. Each problem requires a clearly described initial state, goal state, and well-defined method for filling the gap between the two states with the appropriate steps. The steps to aid in this process include the following:

- Create and define a bounded problem space.
- Establish discrete initial states.
- Explicitly state the goal.
- Explore all reasonable operators. Then, explore the exceptions and list them as exceptions.
- Gain an understanding of the time constraints between initial states and goal states.

Truth about truth refers to an expert's possible delusion about why or how the state of the domain exists. These delusions can involve the use of more steps or considerations than are necessary. They can involve irrelevant information and partial truths of steps that have little or no effect on the goal state. The KE must not work in awe of a domain expert, or in a state of mistrust or disbelief, but with an obligation to ask "why?", "why not?", "what if?", "to what extent?", and other questions to validate knowledge. Sometimes a domain expert dispenses partial knowledge to protect an empire.

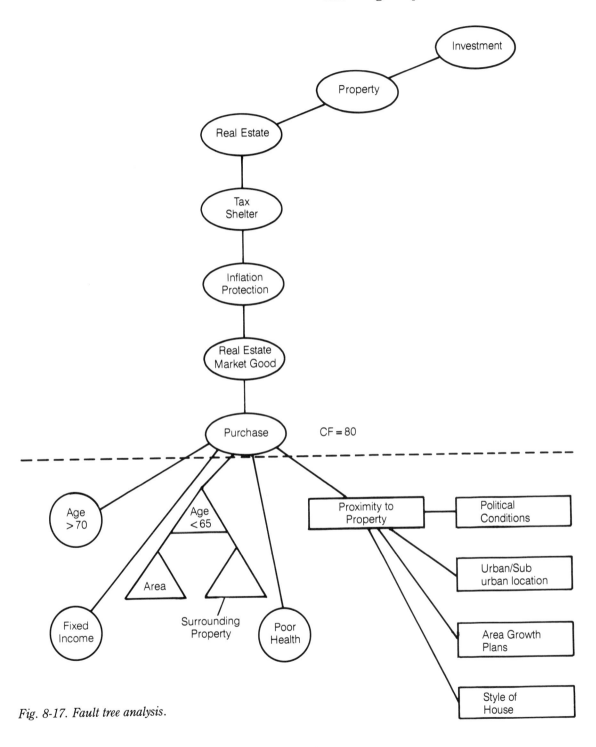

Fig. 8-17. Fault tree analysis.

One precautionary step for detection of partial truth, if suspected, is validation. This tactic provides for a review of the knowledge representation by outside experts or experts who are not directly participating in the project. Examples of partial or irrelevant truths include:

- If the computer is rebooted, the printer will work correctly. (In fact, taking the printer off-line and placing it back on-line will solve the printing problem. The reboot accomplishes the same outcome, but with more trouble and unnecessary steps and time delays.)
- Because the patients used limes in their drinking water, they did not suffer from rickets. (The vitamins supplied from the limes were also supplied from other foods and may have had little, if anything, to do with a health condition that is rare in today's world.)
- If the applicant knows someone in our company, we should hire her over other, equally qualified applicants. (Maybe yes, maybe no; there are many factors that should be considered, especially "equally qualified.")
- Seeing is believing. (Other senses and reason should be used to avoid potential illusions.)
- Discount stores offer better prices for consumers. (Considerations such as driving distance to the store, coupons offered by alternative locations, quantities to be purchased, and other factors should also be involved.)

The KE not only considers how the knowledge is represented, but also the accuracy of the state-space representation.

STATE-SPACE REPRESENTATION

State-space representation is composed of states and operators. States are unique sets of conditions in an environment. Operators are the actions that transform one state into another state. State-space representations are used to specify initial and goal conditions of a problem. These representations can be used to track the manner in which a trial and error approach is used.

The purpose of state-space representation is to represent search strategies. These strategies sometimes lend themselves to domain content and can reveal the simplicity or complexity of a solution path. When a KE has control over a search strategy such as breadth-first or depth-first strategies, state-space representation can help determine the most beneficial strategy.

State-space representation in the form of I-O-G is similar to O-A-V triplets. I is one or more initial sets, O is the set of operators that can initiate a move from one state to another, and G is the goal state. A solution path is established that provides a finite sequence of operator steps carrying out movement from an initial state to a goal state.

A common example for state-space representation is a three-coin problem. In this problem, the initial state has two coins showing heads and one coin showing tails. There are two goal states that involve three heads or three tails. The operator steps involve turning the coins to the opposite side. A tree structure (FIG. 8-18) can be used to illustrate this state-space.

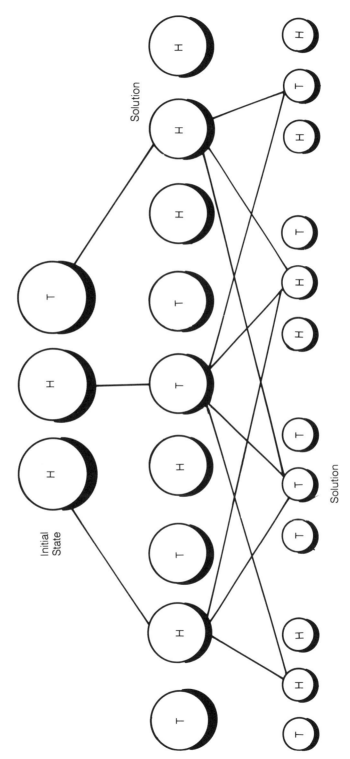

Fig. 8-18. State space representation.

Figure 8-19 illustrates how a different representation can clarify the structure of a problem. Each edge of the cube represents a single operator step.

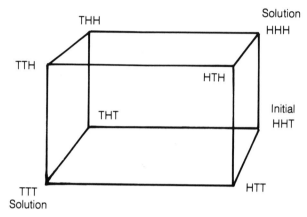

Fig. 8-19. Another representation.

PROBLEM REDUCTION REPRESENTATION

Problem reduction representation is embodied within a tree structure. The structure begins with a problem statement which is then decomposed into subproblems. Each subproblem is broken down until a solution state or primitive is reached. Problem reduction representation reduces a problem into workable chunks or subproblems and contains:

- The statement of the initial problem. The problem occupies a single node.
- Operators to connect problems. These operators consist of AND branches with an arc connector between the branches, and OR branches that have a link to a node.
- Creation of primitive problem statements as terminal nodes. These nodes can be shared.

Figure 8-20 illustrates a hypothetical problem reduction containing an initial problem statement, subproblems, and terminal nodes. The arcs denote AND conditions. The branches without arcs denote OR conditions.

Problem reduction representation is another method for considering the paths between and among states. When the KE uses tools or languages allowing control over search and structures, state-space and problem reduction representations are worthwhile considerations.

SUMMARY

This chapter focused on knowledge representation for the purposes of validation and machine intake. Many strategies were introduced. No single strategy was found to be useful in every situation. The KE matches strategies to the

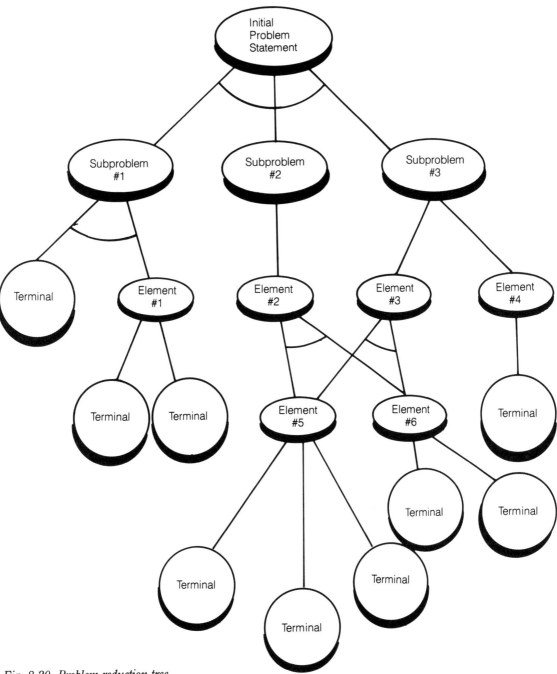

Fig. 8-20. Problem reduction tree.

need. One of the most common mistakes made is the "marriage" of a particular tool or strategy to the need and the force fitting of every encounter into that "comfortable" tool.

It must be understood that Part II does not possess all of the answers for every reader. Rather, an attempt is made to address many of the problems and to recommend resolutions. In Part II, the author strove to introduce concepts and provide some insights into knowledge acquisition and representation. Be reminded that knowledge engineering is a science requiring time and practice for proficiency.

Part III presents a model for developing a knowledge-based application. In knowledge terms, Part II provided the declarative front-end; Part III will now provide the procedural knowledge.

PRACTICAL APPLICATION

1. Construct a semantic network that represents something familiar such as the duties of a teacher, a weather pattern, or the personnel in an office.

2. Build a frame set to represent your choice in exercise one.

3. Write a script such as a trip to the dentist, a family dinner, or a record of the flow of product or materials.

4. Create a series of production rules that contain declarative and procedural components. Select something procedural such as a recipe, changing a tire, cashing a check, etc. Be sure to use statements that begin with IF, THEN, AND, and OR.

5. Assemble an example set. Select a topic such as selecting flowers for a garden, troubleshooting a bicycle, or planning a vacation. Begin with the results. Select the major factors and then supply the attributes.

6. Consider how a repertory grid can be used to express the major factors and attributes created in the previous exercise. Represent the major factors and attributes on a grid.

7. Use an object-oriented strategy to represent the example set.

8. Another way to represent major factors and their attributes is through an outline. Rewrite the example set in outline form.

9. Re-create the example set by using a flowchart.

10. Discuss how a blackboard can be used to serve as a knowledge representation visual.

11. Select certainty factors to support the result values in your example set. Write the rationale for your selection.

12. Evaluate your example set and perform a fault tree analysis.

13. Depict a problem using a problem reduction representation.

14. Which representation scheme worked best for your problem? Determine the principal reason why that representation scheme worked, such as content compatibility. What was the main obstacle to migration between representation scheme types?

PART II—SUMMARY

Part II provided a closer look at the people, process, and structures involved in the acquisition and representation of knowledge. The most critical steps in the life of a project are those that determine the project's overall design, domain, and team players. Here is where non-technical abilities are truly put to the test as the KE must maneuver through politics, budgets, personalities, and resources while maintaining a focus on the project's mission. The KE cannot operate alone and must strive to procure and work with the best resources available, all the while logging project progress and gaining continual agreement and acceptance of those supporting and financing the project.

The next step is to select the most appropriate knowledge representation structure given the hardware, software, peripherals, etc., available within the confines of the project budget, environmental space, geographical network needs (if any), audience, and so on. Once a toy system is developed and approved, detailed full-blown knowledge acquisition and representation commences.

During the development of the knowledge structure, the KE faces the most thought-provoking task. That task is to determine how the domain experts arrive at their decisions. As the structure and knowledge base are being developed, the KE must keep an eye targeted on the project goals, abide by the mission statement, maintain team acceptance, stay within budgetary constraints, and keep a fair distance away from techno-trivia.

Knowledge acquisition and representation is by far the most intense and exhausting phase of the project. It therefore behooves the KE to plan carefully and strive to "get it all and get it right" the first time.

PART II—PRACTICUM

A former associate is now in a high-level administrative position in a large firm. She is ready to invest a substantial amount of money, time, and talent in a knowledge-based system. She is concerned that her superiors and peers will challenge the amount of time and resources you have projected in your proposal and needs more detailed insight into the knowledge acquisition and representation process. Generate a response that she can present to them—among them, the Chief Financial Officer and the V.P. of MIS.

Part III

A Development Model

It is not enough to have a good mind.
The main thing is to use it well.

René Descartes

This final part presents a development model for knowledge-based systems. This model is only one of many available; however, its structure will enable a successful development effort. The development of any software project should be approached through systematic activities that constitute the software life cycle. For example, conventional software development uses a waterfall model. The waterfall model offers a structure of form and process. The purpose of part III is to present a model for developing knowledge-based system applications that have a similar form and process. The waterfall model is composed of a series of individual steps. Thus, the model is linear and seeks to produce the final product with as little backtracking as possible.

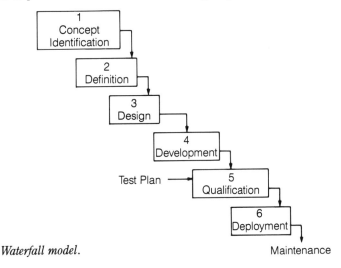

Waterfall model.

Knowledge-based system projects also require a systematic development effort. This is very important for knowledge-based developments, as the costs and resource requirements of these projects tend to be extensive. A model for the systematic development of knowledge-based applications can be thought of as an evolution of a system. The model presented in part III is designed for the business environment. It is designed to reduce risk, and support a systematic, phased, evolutionary development effort. There are six phases to the model: preliminary exploration, requirements analysis, system development, validation, implementation, and maintenance.

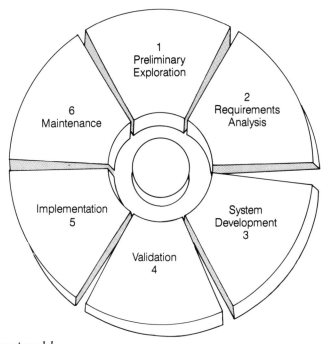

Development model.

Phase 1: Preliminary Exploration

Preliminary exploration identifies and defines the problem, the expectations for the system, alternative solutions, the resources required, and the return on investment. The identification of these elements helps to determine the suitability of the problem for a knowledge-based solution. Phase 1 is thus the concept of the system.

Phase 2: Requirements Analysis

The data gathered in Phase 1 is analyzed. The resulting information is used to create a design specification characterizing the manner in which the completed system will work. This phase is also used to determine knowledge acquisition and representation strategies. A portion of the problem is sometimes represented by the development of a rapid prototype. Phases 1 and 2 are presented in chapter 9.

Phase 3: System Development

The information learned in Phase 2 along with any new information derived from the rapid prototype, is used to produce the detailed design specification. This specification confirms or modifies the original assumptions. It lays out the milestones, deliverables, knowledge acquisition plan, and tool selection. This is the phase during which the system is actually constructed.

Phase 4: Validation

The completed system is tested against the design by qualified experts and target users. The system is examined for accuracy, ease of use, and other designated criteria. Phases 3 and 4 are presented in chapter 10.

Phase 5: Implementation

This phase is crucial for the ultimate success of the system. Users need to be informed and trained, and the system needs to be carefully documented and supported.

Phase 6: Maintenance

Maintenance of a system extends beyond fixing bugs. Often, the knowledge base needs to be expanded or revised, as knowledge is dynamic. In addition, interfaces may need modification, networks or other links may need to be changed or developed, hardware or software changes may require updates to the system or the software, etc. Phases 5 and 6 are presented in chapter 11. Chapter 12 explores the risks and safety nets for knowledge-based system development.

At the end of chapter 11, a hypothetical development effort is presented to serve as a very simple example of how the model can be used.

9

Preliminary Exploration and Requirements Analysis

"Would you tell me, please, which way I ought to go from here?"

"That depends a good deal on where you want to get to." said the Cat.

"I don't much care where—" said Alice.

"Then it doesn't matter which way you go," said the Cat.

Lewis Carroll
Alice's Adventures in Wonderland

INTRODUCTION

The purpose of this chapter is to describe a set of phases that will help ensure a successful development effort. The individual tasks within the phases are not described in great detail as this information is available in many publications. Rather a model is provided for a development effort. The basic phases of this model are consistent with most knowledge-based development applications. However, the individual steps comprising each one will vary according to the requirements of the project at hand. There are six phases in the model: preliminary exploration, requirements analysis, system development, validation, implementation, and maintenance. Each of these phases has subordinate components or tasks.

First and foremost, a plan is established which is agreed upon by the participants and followed. This is the focus of the preliminary exploration. Although subject to periodic reviews and modifications, once the plan is established and agreed upon, changes are minimized to maintain continuity and prevent rampant deviations from the focus.

PHASE 1: PRELIMINARY EXPLORATION

Early considerations for the development of a knowledge-based systems project are very important. They establish the range, functions, user interface, goals, and initial breakdown of the final product. The "Go" or "No-Go" decision is based on the data gathering efforts of this phase and considers the projected return on investment. Contract considerations are addressed in Phase 1, but are not covered in this discussion, since they are the domain of attorneys. It is recommended that contracts be used in any knowledge-based development effort.

The output of the preliminary investigation is a document of understanding that describes the problem, the knowledge-based system application solution or other solution needed to meet the problem, and the optimal environment for the completed system. This exploration is very important, as it establishes an understanding of the expectations and limitations of the recommended solution. The preliminary exploration is also referred to as a feasibility study.

The feasibility study involves a series of fact-finding interviews, discussions, and observations. It begins with the assembling of a knowledge acquisition team consisting of, at minimum, a chief knowledge engineer, a second knowledge engineer or someone familiar with the domain, and a project manager. This team may range from two to four people. The second team is the domain team which has a decision-maker, the project champion, a domain expert, and a user.

The knowledge acquisition team and the domain team prepare for the initial meeting by:

- Clearing schedules to avoid interruption
- Providing an appropriate location
- Gaining familiarity with the agenda
- Considering the proposed scope and projected requirements

In addition, the knowledge acquisition team plans the following activities at the earliest opportunity:

- Tour problem site
- Observe the facility
- Determine the general nature of the problem
- Discuss how this problem is currently solved
- Discuss the gap between the problem state and resolution state
- Observe the problem state if possible

In order to develop a knowledge-based application, it is recommended that the KE be involved in the following Feasibility Study subtasks to:

- Define the problem and the environment
- Consider the human elements

- Rule out commonsense solutions
- Qualify cognitive solutions
- Determine problem difficulty
- Consider the alternatives to constructing a knowledge-based application, such as training
- Investigate projected Return On Investment (ROI)
- Determine the focus of the knowledge-based system solution
- Specify the problem set
- Determine validation strategies

DEFINING THE PROBLEM AND THE ENVIRONMENT

The purpose of Phase 1 is to provide a central focus for later development of the application. This phase is the heart of the feasibility study in which an extensive evaluation takes place. When properly determined, the problem definition can also serve as a validation aid at the project's conclusion. This definition provides an understanding of the problem for management, target users, domain experts, and system builders. The problem definition is used to establish the development effort's mission statement.

The Problem Type

Knowledge-based system applications cannot solve every problem type. The output of a knowledge-based application may not be absolutely accurate 100% of the time. Expectations for knowledge-based system applications that can accurately predict the weather; forecast the outcome of a horse race, sporting event, or election; plan for changes in the stock market; conjecture the future price of gold; or render human moral decisions are delusionary.

An early step in the problem analysis process is to determine if the situation is clearly definable. The KE thinks in terms of cause and effect. Typical problems involve time, productivity, and people. Focusing on the actual problem is the most difficult single task and probably the most important. Sometimes, the initially identified problem is masking the actual underlying problem. For example, what seemed like a faulty battery was actually a bad diode in an alternator.

An inappropriate or incorrect problem definition can result in excessive cost, complicated usage requirements, unwieldy design problems, wasted time, and grief upon delivery. The scope of the problem interacts with the abilities of the tools, languages, and personnel available. Further, the scope defines the breadth and depth of the problem and the expected knowledge-based system solution. Both tools and languages have strengths and weaknesses. A successful effort requires a reasonable match between performance expectations of the system solution and the performance abilities of the users of the system.

Can the situation be solved through the manipulation of numbers or ideas? If the problem can be solved using an algorithm, a knowledge-based system is probably not the answer. There are simpler, less costly solutions than constructing knowledge-based systems. It is the responsibility of the KE to explore these alternative solutions.

Alternative solutions include conventional software and noncomputer solutions. An algorithm provides a precise solution when conditions are static. A knowledge-based system works best when the solution is identifiable, but the input is dynamic. If an algorithm can solve the problem, conventional computing applications can be developed. If the knowledge to be manipulated is numerical or stable, conventional software such as databases, spreadsheets, or other existing software packages are to be considered. Knowledge-based systems should not be developed if a stand-alone, conventional, off-the-shelf piece of software will suffice. However, if the knowledge is subjective, judgmental, changing, or symbolic, then a knowledge-based heuristic rule system is justified.

The problem requires the setting of boundaries. Definite solutions are defined, even if the solution has a less than 100 percent confidence rating. Besides the solution definition, the problem needs to be identified, parameterized, and decomposed. If the problem cannot be contained at the beginning of the development effort, the project is likely to be doomed to failure.

In order to make determinations of the problem, the appropriate human resources are required. These persons should represent management, users, experts, and any other group connected with the problem. Each group has its own perspective which will help define the problem. It may be surprising, but it is likely that these representatives have never met as a group to discuss the root of the problem. Questions that can be asked to help identify the problem include:

- Is there an advice bottleneck due to the lack of availability of an expert?
- Is time lost or wasted due to a recurring problem?
- Are there lost sales due to incorrect decisions?
- Is there an inconsistency of answers to recurring problems?
- Are morale and motivation suffering as a result of poor performance?
- Are decisions required that involve heuristic rule classification tasks including:

  ○ Diagnosis
  ○ Selection from a set of alternatives
  ○ Situation analysis
  ○ Risk analysis

When evaluating the problem, it is helpful to think in the direction of a solution. Conceptualize this solution given what a knowledge-based system can provide, such as:

- Control: Provides intelligent information
- Debugging: Advises corrections to faults
- Design: Details the development of specifications

- Diagnosis: Estimates defects
- Instructions: Optimizes instruction
- Interpretation: Clarifies situations
- Planning: Provides for systematic development
- Prediction: Performs intelligent prognosis
- Repair: Provides automatic diagnosis, debugging, planning and repair

These system types are members of analysis or synthesis system types as discussed in chapter 4.

The Environment

There are some basic questions that can be asked to establish two system aspects at the environment level. The first aspect is the design of the application which explores what the application system will do. The second aspect is the overall specifications that explore how the system is to accomplish the designed task. Questions addressing these aspects include:

- How will knowledge be used to solve the problem? What is the frequency of the problem, and how is it currently solved?
- What is the expected output of the system? Should the system output a single answer, or should it provide weighted alternatives?
- What types and sources of knowledge are required and available for the knowledge base?
- Who will be using the completed system? What is the range of user computer skills, attitudes, needs? What is the degree of accessibility to the system?
- What is the physical user environment of the intended application? How many users will there be? Is the environment hostile, or does it have special constraints?
- What types of application interfaces should be available to users? Should interfaces include keyboards, touchscreens, mouse devices, modems, or voice synthesizers?
- What are the requirements for interfacing with external systems? Do databases, graphics sources, or other peripheral devices require access?
- What is the availability of the domain experts who will be required to help form and later test the knowledge base?
- What is the form and format of the final deliverable?
- What is the timetable for a prototype of the system? How soon must the completed system be in place? Can there be a phased rollout? If so, will time be allocated during the rollout for modifications? (In other words, will it be a validation or strictly an implementation rollout?)

These questions explore issues related to the applicability of a knowledge-based system solution and the practicality of a knowledge-based system centered upon user knowledge, needs, and management expectations. Therefore, it is important that this portion of the study include representation from each group that will develop, use, manage, and/or pay for the application.

The outputs of these tasks are in the form of documentation that specifies the requirements, goals, and projected capabilities of the completed application. A mission statement is created to bound and direct the project.

THE HUMAN ELEMENT

Surprising as it sounds, humans are one of the most important parts of a machine system.

The Problem Solvers

Do experts exist? Since knowledge-based systems are founded on the knowledge and experience of human experts, these human experts must be identified. Somehow, the problems that are to be addressed are currently being solved by one or more experts. The solution is obtained either from in-house experts of from some other source. The knowledge base can be built using one expert as the primary source and another expert to validate the output. Multiple experts for the creation of a knowledge base can produce a challenge for the KE, but sometimes cannot or should not be avoided because of political requirements or the nature of the knowledge domain.

Considerations in this area include the extent and type of knowledge required to reach problem resolution. If a human expert can resolve the problem using personal knowledge, a knowledge-based system can emulate those problem-solving strategies. A nonexpert using the knowledge-based system can effect the same solution for problem resolution if the expert's knowledge can be captured, represented, and codified. To enable this, the expert must be able to understand the techniques and articulate them to a knowledge engineer.

The Experts

An expert is a person who does not have to think, he knows.

Frank Lloyd Wright

So, given the importance of domain experts, who are they and how can they be found?

Who is a domain expert?
A domain expert is:

- An individual with education, training, or experience in a specific area
- An individual who has efficient and effective problem-solving strategies, procedures, and heuristic knowledge

Where does one locate a domain expert?
- Consider the designer of a process or procedure
- Consider the author of a policy or concept
- Identify the source others seek for answers regarding a particular topic.

As stated many times, the knowledge-based system is only as valuable as its knowledge base. The primary source of the knowledge base is usually the domain expert. Not all experts are suited for a knowledge-based system project. The feasibility study is also an exploration of the characteristics of potential experts who may be available for the project. A profile of an expert who would be beneficial to a development effort is one who has the knowledge, is available, is supportive of the project, and can communicate.

Expert Knowledge

Experts are usually the ones that the peer group turns to for consultation or advice. They are recognized as the ones who "have the answer" or "can find the solution." They are the people who seem to "just know." These individuals usually have education, training, or experience that has afforded a variety of opportunities to view or interact with common problems in a certain area. They can "read" the signs and anticipate situations.

Availability

Knowledge interactions with a KE are time-consuming and costly. The costs are for the time invested during direct involvement as well as the loss of time from the performance of normal duties. Thus, the KE plans for quality time from the expert. In addition, the KE makes management aware of the projected time demands on the expert before a project begins. Sometimes arrangements can be made for interactions with other experts with a final review done by the primary domain expert. Whatever the case, without available time committed to the project by the domain expert, there is no project.

Utilization of multiple experts may be necessary when knowledge is dispersed among a group. Advantages, disadvantages, and strategies and tactics associated with multiple experts will be discussed later.

Buy-In

The expert must perceive the value of the project and support the ultimate benefits of the application. Without this level of commitment, the project is likely to fail. With a buy-in, the expert will be beneficial and cooperative to the effort by "going the extra mile." Without buy-in, the expert who was simply assigned by a supervisor might merely supply answers to the questions asked. If critical aspects were missed, they would not be volunteered by the expert. This is a passive-aggressive behavior that needs to be recognized and confronted.

The feasibility effort surfaces commitment, attitudes, buy-in, and other personality and professional attributes of the expert. The KE cannot expect automatic buy-in from the expert. The application could be perceived by the expert as threatening. Should this be the case, the KE sells the concept to the expert. If the KE can find a leverage that enables buy-in, everyone benefits.

Typical buy-in strategies and approaches include showing that the expert can gain through a lighter work load, prestige, a diversion from normal tasks, the focusing of knowledge for a product, the potential of a monetary award/promotion, or other personal gain. Most experts who buy into a development effort approach it differently from the KE. While the KE remains aware of the strategic impacts, the domain expert tends to approach the knowledge base tactically, focusing on its completeness and the manner in which the advice is given, along with its caveats.

Communication

The feasibility study reveals the extent to which the experts can communicate. The experts must be able to formulate declarative and procedural knowledge and then articulate the topics. Generally, the experts' thinking reflects when, how, and to what extent actions are taken, and how they ''knew'' when actions were required.

The ability to discuss is not the same as the ability to communicate at a general level. This level of communication involves jargon, technical terms, and an ability to maintain focus while setting forth the specifics. In addition, there is a need to be able to state and restate a concept or an idea, and to provide a message as often as required to achieve communication.

A final level of personnel that must have buy-in is management. There are benefits having a project champion at the level of management who expresses interest, displays commitment, and actively supports the project. From management commitment flows cooperation.

Other Human Elements

Besides the experts, there are other people to consider in a development effort. It it not uncommon for people about to enter into a project to have varying personal agendas. In addition, these individuals may have an inadequate understanding of the project, its goals, and development requirements.

Management. Management has a tendency to focus on the Return on Investment (ROI). ROI impacts initial costs, tax obligations, training when required, and other peripheral costs. The KE prepares a preliminary approach to the problem, and is ready to respond to many questions. Management is usually interested in using current equipment or reproposing an existing hardware commitment. If existing hardware is inadequate for the task, the KE is prepared with a rationale for alternatives. Some questions that help to surface some of the issues include:

- What do you see as the needs of your organization with respect to this problem?
- Do you agree with the project objectives?
- Do you feel there would be support in terms of resources?
- Are there any political factors that we should discuss?
- What is the most important aspect of the project?
- How long would you expect a project like this one to take?
- Who has budget control?
- How do you anticipate the users will respond to the system?

Developers. Developers have a tendency to champion the best in high-tech tools and software. There is a constant desire to move ahead in the exploration of new approaches or techniques. As a result, the KE focuses on the solution system as the one that is most appropriate for the job. In addition, the developer needs to act as the ''glue'' in a situation that may require mediation skills in diplomacy and an exhibition of sensitivity to politics, all the while maintaining a focus on the possible and the appropriate.

Experts

Domain experts have a tendency to preserve their knowledge and dole it out only as required. They are likely to focus on the knowledge base and the rule set, with lesser concern for user interface and operational constraints. The KE works to gain commitment and promote the enthusiasm of the experts throughout the project. In addition, the KE must feel comfortable with the experts, as the knowledge base and the success of the project may be in the KE's hands.

Target Audience

The target audience has a tendency to focus on the potential personal impacts of the application. A very careful rollout and support program are essential for a successful effort. While the KE may not be able to supervise the rollout, participation in the planning of the event should suffice.

The target audience is carefully examined. As the ultimate recipients of the system, the views and concerns of this group are seriously considered. Typical questions relating to the target population include:

- Who is the target audience?
- What skills do the potential users have?
- What knowledge do the potential users have concerning the problem?
- What is the attitude of potential users towards this problem?

- What training, if any, have the users received to resolve this problem?
- What is the age range of the target group?
- What is the average level of education of the target group?

Ask the users to respond to the following:

- Explain your job. How does it feel to work here?
- What types of problems do you encounter?
- How often do you encounter the problem?
- What do you usually do when this happens?
- What would you need to solve the problem yourself?
- What education or training would help you solve this problem?
- How much experience is needed to solve the problem?
- If a computer solution were available, would you use it?
- What do you see as your role in the development of this application?

The KE carefully considers the users' answers to these questions, as if the success of the project depends on satisfying this group, as it does.

PROCESS

There are a number of precautionary steps the KE should take.

Rule Out Common-Sense Solutions

Does the solution rely on common sense? Knowledge-based systems cannot deal with common-sense domains as they are too broad. The system needs to focus on knowledge areas that present or consider alternatives. As an example of common-sense knowledge, imagine an airport terminal radar that spots a craft at a range of 280 miles traveling at a rate of 8 mph. Common-sense knowledge recognizes an error. A knowledge-based system would probably not be designed and built to scan distance and rate tables. Another form of common sense is knowing when an answer is not available in the realm of possibilities. For example, people know what they can do with their math processing or recall abilities. People are aware of what is current and relevant, and when to give up. People have a perception of time and space, reality and image.

Knowledge-based systems cannot have knowledge bases extensive enough to accommodate all knowledge types. When a knowledge-based system begins a knowledge base search, it does not know if it contains the knowledge or not. If an individual is asked if George Washington ever flew to Europe, the likely answer is that aircraft were not invented at that time. A knowledge-based system asked the same question, would search its knowledge base, possibly request further information, and then conclude a no-data result. Knowledge-based systems are not the repositories of all the collective knowledge of humankind. If the solution requires any common sense or invention, an educational approach should be considered.

Qualify Cognitive Solutions

Does the task require cognitive skills? The stated problem must have a cognitive solution as opposed to one involving physical skills. If a human expert can solve the problem by drawing on education and experience, a knowledge-based system can also solve the problem. The knowledge acquisition team probes into the problem-solving domain. The problem-solving strategies used by the expert to solve the problem need to be discovered. The knowledge parameters can be explored through questions including:

- Is the stated problem typical?
- Can a novice solve the problem as a result of your explanation?
- How did you learn to solve the problem?
- Is this problem typical in your industry?
- Have you asked how others solve this problem?
- Who would solve the problem with the application's help?
- Are there multiple approaches to the problem or solutions?
- Do the solutions have any attached uncertainty?
- Can you think of rules or examples that you use to solve the problem?
- Do the conditions of solving the problem change or vary?
- Will this problem probably persist?
- Does the problem have subcomponents?
- What types of input do you need to solve the problem?
- What determines if the problem is adequately solved?
- Is the solution set for the problem documented?
- How should I go about learning about the problem and its solution?
- Is there anything in the corporate culture that would prevent the project from being successful?

While knowledge-based systems are primarily designed to operate in the cognitive domain, they are not without the ability to manipulate physical components. Knowledge-based systems can be linked to robot arms, servomechanisms, electronic switches, alarms, and other electromechanical devices which are triggered by out-of-range conditions defined in the knowledge base.

Determine Problem Difficulty

Does an expert require weeks to arrive at a solution? The nature of a problem that is a good candidate for a knowledge-based system is one whose solution is not too easy or too hard to find. If the problem is too simple, a job aid can probably fill the need. Another criterion is that the knowledge for the problem focuses on a narrow domain.

Broadly based problems may require a knowledge base that is too large to manage, store, and access. If the problem is large and complex, the KE finds ways to break down the problem into smaller problems. These smaller chunks can each be represented by a knowledge-based system. The larger and more complex problems are a challenge for the KE because expert(s) have greater difficulty structuring and understanding the strategies and methods that they employ to process their solutions.

Consider Alternatives

Noncomputer solutions are also explored. Because of the expense of knowledge-based systems and their recent arrival on the problem solving scene, it pays to explore these alternatives. They include the hiring of additional qualified personnel, training, job aids and documentation, and off-the-shelf conventional software.

Hiring additional qualified personnel is an alternative that was probably explored by the group with the problem. If the problem is extremely wide-spread or is so frequent that an expert's presence is critical, a knowledge-based system may be a valid option.

Another solution is that of creating additional experts through education or training. The current experts reached their knowledge level through education and experience. With a well-designed training approach, others could gain the knowledge level of the expert as well. An education solution is one that takes place over time. A training solution is costly, but has benefits when those who receive the training remain with the company. However, when there is employee turnover, or the nature of the problem is such that decisions are pol-icy-based or require sound, immediate analysis and action, a knowledge-based system is the solution.

Second to the education and training approach is that of job aids, and printed or computer-presented documentation. Each alternative has advantages and disadvantages related to time, cost, and efficiency.

Off-the-shelf software can be tailored to execute specific functions including database and number manipulation. If an existing program can be modified to fill the need, it may prove to be an inexpensive solution.

The alternatives can be individually and collectively considered. One way to carry out the examination of alternatives is by conducting an ROI series of cal-culations. After calculating an ROI, the client can embrace, and act as a cham-pion for, the development effort. The KE has options to be considered, weighed, and presented to the decision makers.

Investigate Projected ROI

Once it has been established that the problem can be clearly defined, resolved by experts using cognitive solutions, and represented in a knowledge-based system, the development justification issues are explored. The reasons that determine feasibility of a knowledge-based system may not be sufficient to warrant its development. Knowledge-based system development is expensive. The cost of an expert is measured in money, time, and talent. So how can a system be cost-justified?

One approach is to make the business case that using a knowledge-based system will save money. Expenses must be balanced by the benefits. Typical costs include: the time of the expert(s), the KE, the computer environment of hardware and software, and the time for testing and validation of the system with the associated personnel. Additional costs include loss of possible revenue by committing the time of the expert(s), required travel, and the time of the personnel for revision and maintenance of the system. The benefits of a system typically include reduced operating costs, increased productivity, a market edge, reduced risks, and preservation and leverage of knowledge. The relative costs and benefits of a proposed system determine the time it will take to pay back the development efforts. Systems that focus on problems with low risk and high payback such as bioengineering or investment systems, or diagnostic systems for human medical problems have an easier cost justification than systems involved with less tangible benefits. Systems in this latter group include those designed to reduce or eliminate loss or waste. A system could be considered cost-effective when:

- It has a high payoff
- Human experts are unable to do the job
- Human experts are scarce or unavailable
  - Needed at multiple locations
- Expertise is being lost. There is a requirement for institutional memory because of:
  - Retirement
  - Relocation
  - Job turnover

One cost analysis approach that considers cost and perceived benefit is Return on Investment (ROI) analysis. This analysis involves the projected costing of a project. ROI analysis has several approaches that can be used to arrive at a solution. Typically, it is designed to compare the development costs with the projected benefit. The objective is to obtain a result that shows a payoff in time to justify the expense. Payback can be defined as $R = B/C$, where R is the annual rate of Return, equal to the Benefit (B) divided by the Cost (C).

Example. Suppose a system is designed to save a researcher's lookup time. The knowledge-based system's design is such that it helps to focus the researcher's topic and then conducts the database search. This knowledge-based service will allow the researcher to be more productive at assigned tasks or to complete other duties. Suppose that a researcher is paid $15.00 per hour for which a company revenue of $25.00 is realized. The task is done 8 times per day by 3 researchers, and takes an average of 8 minutes. The knowledge-based system is estimated to take 2 minutes to do the same task.

The cost for the researchers is:

($.75 per minute for the 3 researchers × 8 minutes per task) × 8 times per day = $48.00 per day

$48.00 × 5 days = $240.00 per week

$48.00 × 21.66 days per month = $1039.68 per month

$48.00 × 260 days per year = $1248.00 per year

The cost of the task using a knowledge-based system:

($.75 per minute for the 3 researchers × 2 minutes per task) × 8 times per day = $12.00 per day

$12.00 × 5 days = $60.00 per week

$12.00 × 21.66 days per month = $259.92 per month

$12.00 × 260 days per year = $3120.00 per year

Direct savings is ($12480.00 − $3120.00) = $9360.00 per year

Assuming that the customer continues to be charged the same overall total, there are also indirect savings based on redirected earnings. The researchers can be producing revenue using their saved time.

Total saved time is 6 minutes for each of the researchers per task

This equals (6 minutes × 3 researchers × 8 tasks per day) = 144 minutes or 2.4 hours.

In actual savings this is (2.4 hours × $15.00 salary per hour) = $36.00 per day.

However in redirected earnings this amount becomes (2.4 hours × $25.00 revenue) = $60.00 per day

Actual savings plus the redirected earnings is

($36.00 + $60.00) = $96.00 in daily gain, or $660.00 per week, or $2079.36 per month, or $34,320.00 per year.

Considering the projected time saved using the knowledge-based system and personnel's time savings for revenue-generating activities, there is a projected $34,320 annual cash benefit. This dollar figure is the B portion of the equation:

$$R = 34,320/C$$

Should the development costs for hardware, software and labor total $60000, the ROI equation is:

$$R = 32,320/60,000$$
$$R = .572 \text{ or } 57.2\%$$

Thus, each year that the knowledge-based system is used as a lookup tool for the three researchers, there is a return on investment of 57.2 percent of the original investment.

The time in years to determine payback is:
$$Y = 100/R, \text{ where } Y \text{ is the number of years, so}$$
$$Y = 100/57.2 = 1.75 \text{ years}$$

Therefore, the initial investment would be repaid in 1.75 years.

A heuristic rule in this area is that a system should pay for itself in four to five years at the outside. Given this rule of thumb, a five-year payoff can be illustrated by solving the two equations backwards. For example, make the value of Y equal to 5 and solve for R.

$$5 = 100/R$$
$$R = 20$$

This means that the ROI needs to be 20 percent, or .20 per year for the 5-year period. In the first formula, $R = B/C$, substitute .20 for R:

$$.20 = B/C$$
$$C = 5B$$

Thus, the cost can be five times the projected benefit.

Each situation is different. In addition, many changes can take place over a five-year period. Further, there are many other methods and considerations that are gleaned from the facts at hand. The ROI is a ballpark projection.

Remember that even though a knowledge-based system will either generate income or help to prevent the loss of income, it is expensive to develop. Most knowledge-based systems have been designed to reduce or eliminate loss as opposed to generating income. By producing an ROI analysis, the KE might help to justify the development costs.

COSTING

The feasibility study reveals issues and clarifies facts from the purchaser's perspective. Part of the ROI formula is the developer's costs. The costing of a project may require input from the KE. However, it is important to have an idea of the typical considerations for a knowledge-based system development project. Each issue and almost every fact obtained in the feasibility study will have an impact on the development cost. This cost can be viewed as raw or burdened. Raw costs are actual costs. Burdened costs are raw costs plus other charges. Each costing consists of professional services, hardware and software considerations, travel-related costs, overhead costs, and a risk cost.

Cost Considerations

While every project varies, there are several costs that are constant.

- Direct staff: Knowledge engineering, programming, documentation, testing, training, travel time, and management. Considerations for time estimates include development, testing, revising, debugging, and maintenance.

- Support Staff: Accounting, typing, art, graphics, testing, duplication, and filing.

- Tools: Hardware and software tools for development and delivery, the purchase or rental of hardware, the cost and licensing of software, and shipping costs are included in this consideration.

In addition, interim and final deliverables are to be clearly defined.

Raw Costs

Raw costs are the direct costs that, among other things, do not take profit into account. Typical raw costs include labor, materials, hardware and software, overhead (mailings, telephone, insurance, taxes, lease, etc.). Another cost consideration is the time assigned to the professional staff. Experts who can spread their time across multiple projects are valuable to any organization. When an expert focuses time on a single project, there may be a financial impact on the business. The quality and quantity of the experts' time need to be considered.

There are also reimbursable costs in some projects. These costs can include special hardware; mailings; phone line costs for calls and for data transmissions with a modem or facsimile machine; and travel costs including air fare, car rental, hotel, meals, tolls, and parking.

Burdened Costs

Burdened costs are raw costs plus such charges as cost of sale, profit, etc. Typically, there is a burden on labor, materials, and travel. The rate of burden varies according to the business' policy. Considerations for burdening include dedicated personnel time and consequent unavailability of key people. There is another intangible consideration as well. That consideration is risk. Knowledge-based system projects can be on the "cutting edge" in nature and the exploration into the unknown has inherent risks to reputation. This risk may also be taken into account for burdening. Each of these costs is to be carefully considered. Remittances for costs are tied to milestone deliverables or phase completions.

SCOPING THE EFFORT

At this early stage of the project, it is important to define a system scope. This scoping effort has several considerations including knowledge requirements, a narrow domain, symbolic knowledge, no requirement for common sense, cognitive solutions, and a reasonable number of outcomes.

Knowledge Requirement

If the solution for a problem is based on a list of possible outcomes and is decided upon by a person having at least informed common sense, a knowledge-based system will do well. If experts can make correct choices more often than nonexperts, that knowledge can be captured and incorporated into a knowledge-based system.

Narrow Domain

The system's focus is narrow and precise. Present-day knowledge-based systems do not work well in broad-based subjects. These systems are too large to create, store, access and maintain. Most domains can, however, be decomposed into workable chunks.

Symbolic Knowledge

The type of knowledge best suited for a knowledge-based system is that which is represented in symbolic form. The knowledge of an expert is represented using a series of IF-THEN rules, frames, example sets, or other knowledge representation scheme. Consider that the difference between an expert and a nonexpert is the knowledge accumulated over time through practical experience. The expert establishes heuristic knowledge. It is the extent and quality of this heuristic knowledge that establishes a successful knowledge-based system.

No Common Sense Required

Common-sense knowledge is comprised of many individual pieces of unrelated knowledge. As a result, a broad-based system would be required to capture common-sense rules and examples. This ability is out of range for today's knowledge-based systems.

Cognitive Solution

Standing in opposition to common sense, active cognitive solutions are the foundation of knowledge-based systems. The primary reason that knowledge-based systems are developed is to attempt to duplicate the reasoning processes of a human expert. In these cases, the application requires solutions via thinking and reasoning.

Knowledge-based systems do not have human senses such as sight, hearing, feel, or touch. While technology has enabled synthetic capabilities in some sensory areas, sensory input and output is expensive and time-consuming. For this reason, most applications for knowledge-based systems center around the requirement for mental processing and/or external calls to determine a solution.

Reasonable Number of Outcomes

The output of a knowledge-based system is one result or several weighted alternatives. Each of the outcomes needs to be carefully considered, as each will be programmed into the system for pattern match access.

A knowledge-based system has a moderate number of solutions. If there are only a few alternatives, training or a job aid would probably suffice. Should there be hundreds or thousands of solutions, the knowledge base of the system would be too large to build, store, access, and maintain.

As a heuristic rule for knowledge-based system development, a moderately sized system consists of about 100 solutions. The number of solutions has little correlation to the number of rules in the system.

REFOCUS THE PROBLEM

In focusing on a knowledge-based system solution, the role of the completed application is considered. Typical knowledge-based system applications have systems designed to:

- Simulate a human advisor
- Select a solution set for a defined problem
- Process mental requirements, not physical
- Help in-house experts in the decision-making process
- Serve as an intelligent reference data bank

Another consideration for the knowledge-based system solution is to refocus on the problem and consider the problem in terms of:

- Character: The situation is solvable using problem-solving strategies, rules of thumb, or symbolic reasoning.

- Complexity: The situation is formidable. Problem solvers have years of experience before attaining expert status. Complexity of the problem relates to cost justification.

- Range: The situation is focused—not too broad, general, or narrow. Evaluation of the range indicates practicality.

EXAMPLES OF PROPOSED KNOWLEDGE-BASED SYSTEM APPLICATIONS

Through the years, discussions concerning appropriate knowledge-based system applications have occurred in publications, seminars, and during feasibility explorations. The following encapsulates today's thinking in terms of the current capabilities and limitations of knowledge-based hardware, software, and associated development costs.

Present a curriculum	Vague
Present a training curriculum	Too broad
Develop a strategy for a technical training curriculum	Too broad
Present a technical troubleshooting course	Better, but not quite
Design motherboards	Good
Design user screen interfaces	Good
Develop procedural guides	Good
Design job aids	Better, but not quite
Design on-line reference materials	Good
Present assessment instruments for communication skills	Good
Present diagnostic aids	Good
Develop strategies for resistor code striping	Too narrow

There are questions that can be asked to determine if an application will be appropriate. Questions to ask include:

- Is the situation clearly definable?
- Can the situation be solved by manipulating numbers or ideas?
- Does the solution rely on common sense?
- Does the task require cognitive skills?
- Do experts exist?
- Does an expert require weeks to arrive at a solution?
- Can experts articulate their strategies?
- Do experts concur on the solutions to the problems?

Once these questions are answered, the KE can begin performing additional tasks. These tasks follow.

SPECIFY THE PROBLEM SET

To specify the problem set, early discussions take place between the domain expert and the knowledge engineer. These discussions focus on conceptualizing the problem. During these discussions, concepts, relations, and control mechanisms are determined. In addition, subtasks, strategies, and constraints are discussed. Finally, the level of granularity is considered.

This process is helped along by production of a quick example set. This is a strategy that begins by listing the possible outcomes (results). Next, the major factors are listed. These factors can be compared to the major components of an analysis that decomposes the whole into logical areas of consideration. Finally, under each of the major factors, the attributes of the corresponding factor are listed.

An example of this process is a car that will not start. (This situation was examined from a different viewpoint in chapter 3.) A simple diagnostic expert system is constructed as follows:

1. The knowledge engineer and the domain expert conduct a first-pass knowledge engineering breakdown of the problem of the car that won't start.
2. They conclude that there are seven possible reasons the car will not start. These reasons are listed under Results.
3. They also conclude that there are five major factors that enable the mechanic to determine the problem area. The major factors appear as the first five column headings.
4. Beneath the major factors are the attributes that further define or provide critical information for problem determination.

Battery	<Fuel	Jump?	Noise	Weather	Results
Age	Yes	Yes	Crank	Rainy	Replace Battery
Connections	No	No	Click	Other	Clean Battery Connections
Water level			None		>Check Starter
Lights					>Check Alternator
Horn					>Clean Fuel Path
Radio					>Check Electrical Connections
					>Check Engine

Although this is not the entire knowledge base, it provides a first-pass look at the project scope. The ''>'' in front of selected results suggests that a forward chain to a new knowledge base having its own set of major factors and attributes is required. The ''<'' in front of the major factor Fuel, shows that a backward chain is needed to further explore the issue and return a value to the system. With a layout like this one, the knowledge engineer can construct a preliminary rule set for review. Following the review, the results, major factors, attributes, and forward and backward chains can be modified. This modification leads into the development of the system.

In this example, topics such as a flooded engine, security systems, dirty air cleaners, and others are considered for the diagnostic knowledge base. The first-pass system provides a strong base of operation with little time or expense. In addition, it brings to the surface some of the potential cooperation, commitment, and personality impacts between the key people involved in the development effort. Should potential conflicts surface, they could be resolved or personnel complement adjusted before a full development effort. The net gain is that rather than working with different agendas a true team will exist that can work toward common goals faithful to the mission statement established for the project.

DETERMINE VALIDATION STRATEGIES

Do experts concur on solutions? The knowledge base with its rules, frames, examples, or other knowledge representations are validated by other experts. Even though the knowledge base has not been built, a validation strategy needs to be discussed. The KEs remove themselves from a role of being judgmental about the accuracy of the knowledge base. They should not be expected to be domain experts, but rather the conduits for obtaining and representing knowledge.

Validation is generally of two types. The first validation concerns the knowledge base. Additional experts are consulted to evaluate the knowledge base using criteria of accuracy and completeness. The rule outputs are considered as a portion of the validation. The second validation involves a representative group of the target audience. This portion of the validation focuses on usability. User input requirements, interfaces, and outputs are the criteria for user validation.

There are potential liability issues for the output recommendations or actions taken by systems linked to electromechanical devices. The KEs establish a policy and a written disclaimer to make the ''powers that be'' aware that it is the experts who are responsible for the system. With this issue addressed up front, a lot of potential difficulty can be avoided later at the conclusion of the project.

Note that the KE is not without responsibility. The responsibilities and roles of the KEs and the experts are expressed at the project's beginning, and are not to be discussed in retrospect or during litigation.

PHASE 2: REQUIREMENTS ANALYSIS

Once the participants understand the problem based on the preliminary exploration, there are options available. The documented main points from the feasibility study can be represented on a whiteboard or taped to a wall to provide the overall picture of the problem. Some applications in the business environment are precariously perched on the edge of an abyss. This precarious position is usually the result of a conflict between the impatience of management who want to "see something tangible," and the developers who want to move ahead cautiously. The KE remains flexible, impartial, and prepared to move with the prevailing wind.

Out of fairness, it is sometimes the developers that are anxious to "give it a preliminary shot." Nevertheless, the first option is to use what has been learned and proceed to the demonstration prototype. The second option is to further define the requirements from the perspective of each of the groups represented by the team.

The Requirements Analysis Phase produces the "wish list" of each of the groups represented by the team. The requirements refine and focus the results of the preliminary exploration. The KE listens to each of the participants, and considers the nature of each request in terms of its practicality, political influence, and trade-offs needed to incorporate the request. The KE does what is best for the project, and "digs in his heels" when these requests begin to move the project out-of-scope.

The Preliminary Exploration Phase gathered data from the groups represented in the team, viz. management, developers, experts, and users. The data collected was predominately left-brain-guided input expressing the "need to have" feelings. The Requirements Analysis Phase explored the right brains of the participants, focusing on the "nice to have" aspects of a knowledge-based system application.

Management

Management focused on the return on investment (ROI) in the Preliminary Exploration Phase. During the Requirements Analysis Phase, management is likely to have a slight shift of view. Their focus will usually turn to the holistic aspects of the completed application. Questions generally include:

- How can we transfer the benefits of this project across divisions?
- How can we make the application commercially viable (if this was not the original purpose of the application)?
- How will the application be affected if we change our hardware or operating system?
- How will we make decisions regarding interfaces, screen designs, etc.?
- How should we implement the system?
- What can we do to limit labor costs on the project?
- Can we schedule the expert's time well in advance? What if we need the expert for something else?

Developers

The developers in the Preliminary Exploration Phase were likely to have focused on the possible and the appropriate. Their role in the Requirements

Analysis Phase is to assist in maintaining focus. It is probable that they will champion a need for state-of-the-art hardware, software, communication, and peripherals. Key questions of this group are likely to include:

- How many users will there be?
- How geographically spread out are the users?
- Can we use a host server and network the applications?
- Is there sufficient processing speed? If not, are we budgeted for an upgrade?
- Do the monitors have a high enough resolution if a decision is made to use graphic interfaces?

Experts

The Preliminary Exploration Phase probably established that the experts concentrated on the knowledge base and the rule set, with lesser concern for user interface and operational constraints. The Requirements Analysis Phase is likely to reveal that the experts want the system to seem "smart." This can be accomplished by designing mentor-type tip selection options for the users. In addition, the experts are likely to want assurance that caveats can be placed on results. This can be handled by confidence and certainty tags. Additional concerns by the experts might include:

- Are there other sources of information that can be used in place of me or us?
- What if I need to be somewhere else?
- How can we be sure that the users provide the correct input so that the results are correct for the need?
- Can we track or audit the users' names, problems, and paths through the system?

Target Audience

The target audience in the Preliminary Exploration Phase very probably had a tendency to focus on the potential personal impacts of the application. Their concerns are likely to continue along the same path. Additional questions that this group might ask include:

- What are our options in terms of interfaces and screen designs (keyboard, mouse, touchscreen, voice, text, graphics, etc.)?
- How can we create system outputs to generate reports, audits of the session, remote files, etc.?
- Will we be able to update our databases from our systems?
- Can we automate some of the decision factors that we will need to make?
- Can we customize or personalize our interfaces?

All of the collective "wishes" are categorized and prioritized. This helps the KE satisfy the requirements of the corporate culture, improving acceptance by the various groups and promoting a successful development effort.

SUMMARY

The cornerstone of any project is its mission statement, the project plan its blueprint. Like any structure, a blueprint that is incomplete, faulty, or not adhered to will result in an end product that will fail at one point or another. The excitement of moving quickly into actual development should be reined in until the plan has been developed, examined, reexamined, and documented to the satisfaction of the team. Included in the examination is an analysis of the true problem and its best solution—which may not include a knowledge-based system. This phase of Preliminary Exploration is critical to the success or failure of the project and thus demands the attention of the very best personnel. A blueprint carrying a high confidence factor could then conceivably be carried out by "worker bees" with little intervention by high-level decision makers. Additionally, the project plan serves as its own best critic—it is the plan that serves as the basis for system validation throughout the development process.

The next chapter addresses the development process.

PRACTICAL APPLICATION

Follow the model and create a knowledge-based specification. The domain of the application can be your favorite hobby or transient interest.

10

System Development and Validation

You know my methods, Watson.

Sir Arthur Conan Doyle

INTRODUCTION

There are times when a KE is called upon to develop a knowledge-based application with the purchasers bypassing the feasibility study and the requirements analysis. In addition, this same group of purchasers tends to provide the statement of the problem based upon their understanding. Rather than the System Development and Validation phases coming midway in the project, the application development effort begins with them. Therefore, we will digress to provide a flowchart to assist the KE (FIG. 10-1). This chart lists the major tasks and termination exits for the development. Sometimes, it is better to bow out gracefully than to expend time, energy, and money with failure looming over one's shoulder.

Development Steps:
A. Preliminary exploration
    1. Define the problem.
    2. Determine if a knowledge-based application solution is appropriate. If not, stop development and look for other solutions.
B. Requirements analysis
    3. Select the appropriate knowledge representation scheme and inference mechanism for the problem.
    4. Select the style of the user interface.
    5. Characterize the knowledge acquisition strategy for the system.
    6. Establish the level of explanation that will be required by the system.

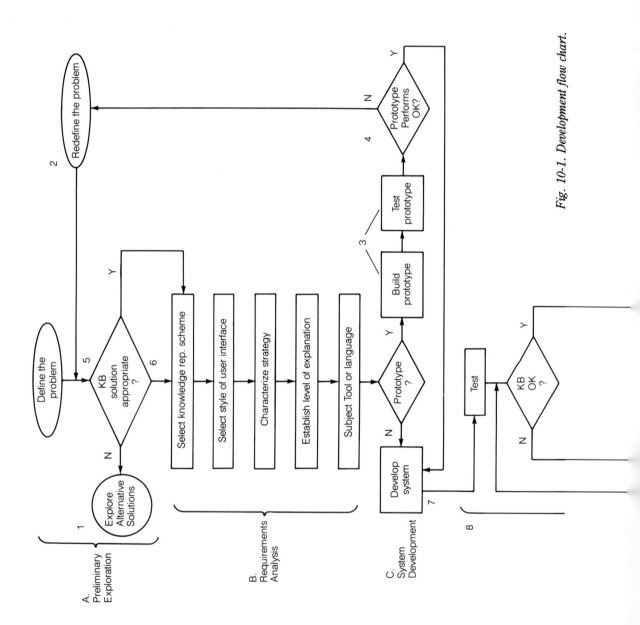

Fig. 10-1. Development flow chart.

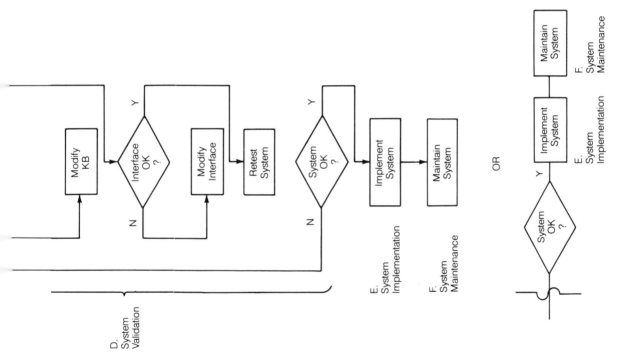

7. Using the information gathered in steps 1–6, decide if a tool or language is necessary for development.

C. System development

8. If appropriate, suggest building a prototype.
9. Acquire, represent, and codify knowledge. Build the prototype.

D. Validation

10. Test the prototype. If it performs according to expectation, continue. If not, repeat steps 2–8.
11. Assess test results from the experts, management, and users.
12. Remove or modify rules and examples in the knowledge base that are in error. Add new rules or examples as needed.
13. Make any required interface modifications.
14. Revalidate the system.

E. Implementation

15. Determine if the system is correct. If so, implement the system. If not, go to Step 12.

F. Maintenance

16. Maintain the system.

RAPID PROTOTYPE

A rapid prototype serves as a proof-of-concept system. It is a representative portion of the overall system used to evaluate the basic design of the application. Necessary components include hardware, software, selected rules and heuristic knowledge, and a test user interface. The KE has an opportunity to map key concepts, experience the information flow, interact with the domain expert(s), and establish a strategy for acquiring the knowledge and reasoning processes of the expert(s). Once this prototype is completed, it stands as a model of the planned knowledge-based application. The prototype is carefully reviewed and evaluated. This prototype could be the deciding factor for a "go" or "no-go" decision for the follow-on development effort.

It must be emphasized that a rapid prototype is an optional activity in the development of a knowledge-based application. It may not actually represent the total system. Sometimes rapid prototypes do not exhibit the efficiencies of large development efforts. In addition, prototypes can be expensive undertakings. Knowledge acquisition, representation, and system codification are completed in a prototype with the same degree of fervor as in full-scale development, with a more limited scope. Further, user interfaces, explanation subsystems, program calls, etc., are only partially included or are simulated. The KE and the buyer of a knowledge-based system application need to understand the time, effort, costs, and benefits of developing a rapid prototype.

If a proof-of-concept system is developed, there are three strategies to be considered, according to Walters and Nielsen (1988).

1. Build a prototype for the entire application, with refinements in succeeding prototype versions.

2. Build an overall skeletal prototype with one or more complete sections. As these sections are completed and tested, consider and prototype other sections.
3. Build separate prototypes for selected portions of the application. Test each portion and then integrate them into the complete application.

Walters and Nielsen contend that the strategy listed first is useful for small applications, as the entire application is reflected in the prototype. The second and third strategies are better suited for larger applications. The second strategy builds a skeleton of the major structures and adds detail as the prototype progresses. The third strategy, rather than building upon itself, uses multiple approaches, teams, and knowledge bases in the prototype development. This partition places the development at risk for inconsistencies. This strategy is best for multiple disciplines that have little overlap.

Naturally, building the prototype requires that knowledge be acquired, represented, and codified. To do these tasks, the KE will utilize techniques and procedures presented in part II.

After the prototype is built, it undergoes a rigorous evaluation. The criteria for the evaluation were established prior to building the prototype. Any other measures are out-of-scope for the exercise and are either included in the next phase or influence the entire design specification.

One key aspect of prototype evaluation is the sign-off power of the evaluator. The evaluation of the prototype is a milestone in the development process. The results of the evaluation provide clear-cut guidance for the next step or steps of the endeavor. The evaluator or evaluation team needs to have final authority or the project will remain in the evaluation twilight zone, in a constant state of flux.

The evaluation of the prototype requires a systematic process, which begins prior to the actual testing of the prototype. The prototype may have a complete-appearing interface, but possess limited functioning. It is generally treated as a nonconsumable that will remain as part of the system. The limited application is often revised and expanded based upon the test results.

Testing

Testing involves examination of the proposed system rules, design, and performance.

Rules. Test cases should have been selected and agreed upon in advance. Testing involves the evaluation of the rules or examples acquired from the domain expert(s), and a measure of system performance in the hands of a user. The method of testing the rule or example set varies. One method is verification of the rules or examples by the domain expert. Another method uses domain experts other than the one providing the knowledge. When there is a wealth of domain experts available, this latter method is desirable. Having additional experts available is called *bench strength*.

Design. A second test of the prototype involves evaluation of the design. This test is composed of four components: specification match, form, function, and crispness.

Specification match testing involves comparing the system to the design specification. This test evaluates inputs, outputs, system interfaces and clarity.

Form evaluates the manner in which information is presented or requested. The form optimizes the process so as to lead to a rapid resolution, e.g., having four questions to reach a conclusion is better than five. The user must be a controlling influence in the system input requirements and outputs. Numeric codes, for example, can confuse and frustrate a user. Numeric inputs can be required for sensor values, identification numbers, quantities, and the like. If the system expects these types of inputs, the user should know or have ready access to this data. In addition, the system should be able to recognize out-of-range inputs and possible terminology differences across functional areas. Further, the system must output understandable values whether these outputs are numeric or alphanumeric.

Function involves the evaluation of user inputs and system outputs. Domain experts are generally concerned with incorrect results because of incorrect or erroneous inputs. Function concerns the possibility of "I don't know" inputs and "no data" results. The users may not know the answer to a system-requested input with 100% confidence. While the outputs can contain a caveat that conveys a confidence level, users might not be able to place a confidence rating on their input. If the users are unsure of their inputs and the inputs are critical, the system design should respond in a meaningful way to those users. One method of handling this situation is to present an "I do not know" response selection. The system can then probe the issue further and determine its own response based on the probing.

Note that there are limits to the functionality of a knowledge-based system. The system contains but a narrow slice of the domain expert's knowledge. It is not unreasonable that situations will occur beyond the scope of the system. Problems arise when there is no provision for this possibility, particularly when results can cause catastrophic repercussions.

Crispness refers to the manner in which the system behaves interactively. Speed of execution, accessibility of helps, ease of use, and user expectations make up the issue of crispness. The holistic "feel" of the session goes beyond interfaces, specifications, and other quantitative data. Crispness involves meeting user expectations for the system. Therefore, crispness is an effective system test component.

Testing Techniques. There are many approaches that have been used to test knowledge-based applications. Most of the techniques for testing have one thing in common: the test is based on a laboratory-controlled, generic-level problem that is bounded. Test cases are often used to validate the rules, design, and performance of the application. The test cases and system conditions should be consistent with system expectations in the environment where the application will be used.

The test audience should represent the target users, irrespective of inconvenience or cost. Test case(s) should be based on reality and should require solutions that stretch the personal abilities of the users.

The testing techniques of Walters and Nielsen (1988) represent three approaches consistent with those used by many in the field. These techniques are test cases, tracing, and regression testing.

Test cases are further divided by Walters and Nielsen into the functions they perform. Thus, test cases can focus on reasoning logic, human interfaces, functionality, or the demonstration of capabilities. These test cases are focused on situations that determine if the application functions properly. Test cases may demonstrate:

- Particular portions of the logic in the knowledge base
- Selected user input requirements
- Ranges of problem types
- Ranges of problem complexity

Test cases are designed to assess the reasoning abilities of the system for users, management, and the development team of domain experts and knowledge engineers.

Tracing

Tracing is a method that audits a user session. The inputs and outputs are recorded for evaluation. This evaluation generally involves a debriefing of the user, the KE, and the domain expert. The techniques used for this debriefing are similar to those used by the KE to debrief a domain expert after a real-time problem-solving activity. These techniques were discussed in chapter 7.

The KE can trace a session by observation or by employing a debugging utility. Some shell tools have debugging utilities, while other debugging programs are commercially available. Basically, a debugging program audits user inputs, system outputs, and the branching into successive knowledge bases. The internal logic of the program is generally not subject to the audit process.

Regression Testing

Regression testing can be thought of as reevaluative testing, performed after the application has undergone a significant change. As the knowledge base is modified, rule functioning can be altered. The test case that performed admirably the first time may not work at all upon modification of the knowledge base. To guard against this, a working set of test cases is built during testing and used during the overall life cycle of the application.

One advantage of regression testing is version performance verification. If the test case set works to a point and then fails, the application can be debugged and modified. Therefore, it is important to maintain version libraries as the application evolves. In addition, the test set is expanded. The test set is used to evaluate the knowledge base at certain points in time and to assess the application for specific functionality. As the application evolves, the test cases also evolve to properly test the latest functionality. At the completion and delivery of the application, the test set becomes an archival tool group. This group can be used to test further enhancements to the system or to resolve disputes between team members regarding system performance.

Prototyping Summary

The KE carefully documents and assesses the strengths and weaknesses of all testing efforts. These findings are incorporated into the overall documentation, development plan, and weekly reports.

The prototype phase can be optional or iterative. The nature of this phase is dependent upon factors including time, budget, resources, and the size of the application. Following successful prototype efforts, the application moves into the System Development Phase. If the development phase is built on the basis of subproblems that are to merge into a final product, the prototype development cycle is iterative. This condition exists for the skeletal, and separate prototype types previously discussed.

PHASE 3: SYSTEM DEVELOPMENT

The predevelopment prototype effort produces a limited system that the KE and domain expert can look at like a used car. They can kick the tires, look under the hood, check out the paint, etc. The output of the evaluation is a good points/bad points list. At this stage, the principals on the team can establish the accuracy of the application's design.

Verify Rapid Prototype Assumptions

A KE can ask specific questions to evaluate the quality of the prototype effort. These questions include:

- Does the original mission statement stand or does it require modification?
- What is the composition of the main problem group?
- What are the subproblems?
- What data and information types are required? What data and information types are available?
- What are the important concepts being explored?
- What are the solutions, their ranges, quick fixes, early warning indications, options?

Through these and other questions, the KE and the domain expert can refine the design specification. A heuristic rule in this area is to carefully review the possible problems that are to be confronted by the system and the list of possible solutions. In order to conduct this investigation, additional or outside experts, manuals, documents, etc., may need to be consulted. It is crucial to achieve the link between the possible problems and acceptable solutions. A management sign-off should be performed to protect all parties.

Following the detailed list of outcomes is a list of required inputs necessary to achieve the outcomes. This list includes all of the choices that the user considers along with any facts, values, or other information, that a user will be required to input.

The development effort builds on findings from the rapid prototype. Any modifications of the assumptions are handled on a contractual level and in a development plan. The development effort proceeds much like the prototype effort. The main difference is in level of detail and the validation effort. The development plan includes statements that address the extent and conditions concerning each of the following:

- Reclarification of the situation
  - Discuss hardware availability
  - Identify the array of hardware components required
  - Report user awareness of the target knowledge base
  - Determine user access to the advisory system
  - Discuss the knowledge acquisition interview strategy
  - Design the user interface

- Identification of the domain experts
  - Identify all data sources to be included

- Knowledge engineering
  - Determine clusters and data reduction through analysis
  - Identify criteria to be used for analyzing interrelationships
  - Establish factors and values
  - Create the example set
  - Analyze data and examples for redundancy and inconsistency
  - Determine statistical weights for the example set
  - Construct a rule tree
  - Design the questioning strategy
  - Determine auxiliary media for user interface

- Production of knowledge engineering outputs
  - Break down the components
  - List the critical attributes
  - Discriminate between the internal structures
  - Develop an example set of potential scenarios
  - Rate each potential outcome through a confidence scale or statistic
  - Create a visible decision path from general to specific

- Determination of a strategy for easy-to-understand user interface
- Generation of a design of ancillary media for user understanding
- Development of the system

- Testing and debugging of the system
- Validation of the system
- Design of the system maintenance plan
  - ○ Review field information over time
  - ○ Review user interface data
  - ○ Review ancillary media data
  - ○ Monitor technology
  - ○ Reflect new information and technology in system updates

Select the Appropriate Tool

The selection of a software tool for use in development is one of the major decisions made. This selection first occurs during the optional prototype stage, is verified as appropriate, and is used in the development effort. If there is no prototype effort, the selection of the tool is made early in the development effort.

The implications and exposures are paramount. Software tool selection has an impact on development time and cost, system capability, licensing, user interface, maintenance considerations, and other potential risks.

There are three basic options for the tool. These options are: knowledge-based shells, knowledge-based languages, and conventional languages. Any programming effort developed under a knowledge-based system shell or language can also be programmed using conventional software languages such as C. There are advantages and disadvantages of knowledge-based shells, knowledge-based languages, and conventional languages as the tools used for a knowledge-based system solution. Therefore, careful consideration of tool selection is carried out.

A knowledge-based tool performs three basic tasks:

- Provides an interface between the developer and the output code. The developer inputs the acquired knowledge into the system to establish the knowledge base. For this, the tool needs to have editors and other appropriate utilities.
- Forms a control strategy for structuring and searching the knowledge base. The methods by which this function is accomplished varies. This function can help or hinder maintenance and updating of the knowledge base.
- Creates the user interface and explanation subsystem.

Knowledge-based System Shells. Knowledge-based system shells offer a variety of capabilities and functions. Shells do not require a programmer to serve as an intermediary in the iterative process between the domain expert and the knowledge engineer. Without a programmer in the loop, there is one less information filter through which the knowledge passes during the assembly of the knowledge base. The fewer the number of interpretations of domain expert heuristic rules, the richer the resulting knowledge base. The previous statement is a heuristic rule. While it is not true 100 percent of the time, it is true often enough to make it useful.

Maintenance of the developed program is generally easier when a shell program is used. Maintenance of the knowledge-based system shell is separate from the maintenance of the example or rule base. When the latter is done, the control program is not affected, and so there is little danger of program crash. Knowledge-based system shells are generally an excellent choice for knowledge-based system development projects.

Selection of a shell has many factors. Most of these factors have been previously discussed. However, a few of them need to be reiterated. The shell should be able to:

- Provide an interface with other applications such as databases or spreadsheets
- Communicate with other peripheral devices through modems and ports
- Supply developer utilities and a run-time program generator
- Provide an editor for debugging

In addition, considerations for a shell also include:

- Initial cost
- Licensing requirements
- System support

A final group of considerations deals with speed in terms of the time the system takes to:

- Compile the program
- Execute branches
- Make external calls

The resulting application is only as effective as the shell under which it was constructed. An application, no matter how well-built, should not be used if it does not feel right or conform to the expectations of the users.

Knowledge-based System Languages. Knowledge-based system languages are sometimes a better choice when the knowledge domain does not lend itself to IF-THEN statements or rule representation; LISP or PROLOG may be the best choice. However, most knowledge engineers are not LISP or PROLOG programmers. As a result, another layer, the potential liability of a programmer, is placed in the loop.

Once again, programmers are not a liability in themselves. The liability is in the potential for misunderstanding what the domain expert states as a pattern or characteristic. The process that occurs may include the following: the knowledge engineer and the domain expert pursue a line of thought during which time the KE takes notes. After a session, the KE meets with the programmer. The KE and the programmer discuss the implications for frame characteristics. The programmer then interprets the notes and programs the prototype. Testing follows during which the KE and domain experts view the results. Notes are taken and another iteration begins. Miscommunication can take place anytime during this process. Therefore, it is better if the knowledge domain can be refocused or rethought into a rule-represented domain, allowing use of a knowledge-based system shell program.

Conventional Languages. The use of a conventional language for the knowledge-based system development tool is generally not the best choice. Because the procedures and data in conventional programs tend to be closely interrelated, any change in either might require complete retesting. A conventional language could be considered for static programs.

In contrast to conventional languages, knowledge-based system shells and knowledge-based languages have two separate systems: the control program, including the inference engine, and the knowledge base. The control program contains the pattern match algorithms and does not change. The knowledge base can be modified without impacting the control program, so there is little danger of a program crash resulting from a modification.

Other considerations for tool selection include future growth of the development system, runtime version and licensing, vendor support, and documentation. All of these considerations impact flexibility, cost, and the potential success of the development effort.

A heuristic rule in the area of tool selection is to use a knowledge-based system shell tool that has large rule capabilities, control strategy options, and other features offering flexibility. These other features include forward and backward chaining, external program calls, number-crunching ability, rule-based and example-based sets, and others.

Another heuristic rule in this area dictates that if the extent of the knowledge base is unknown, selection of the tool should be delayed until first-pass knowledge engineering has been completed.

Develop the System

The discussion of the previously listed tasks can be expanded by referencing many of the popular books on knowledge-based systems.

There are three major component tasks for development, viz.:

- Development of the core structure
- Expansion of the knowledge base
- Design of the user interface

Development of the Core Structure Following a Rapid Prototype. If a rapid prototype was assembled, an interesting decision must be made. The prototype will either serve as the foundation of the development effort, or has served its usefulness and is to be abandoned. Because the knowledge base is separate from the system, the major factors and their associated attributes can be used in the current effort. It is the handling of the information and the structure of the knowledge base that may be modified. The experience gained from the prototype can be leveraged as an opportunity to build upon or learn from. If the prototype was on target and lends itself to the group merely expanding the knowledge base to complete the system, it beat the odds. The more likely occurrence is that the domain expert and the KE will have learned from the prototype as a level-setting device. This level-setting includes an understanding of the process, commitment, time demands and the iterative process. Level-setting will have occurred for the managers and those who pay the bills as well.

Expansion of the Knowledge Base. The knowledge base belonging to the prototype system most probably centered on the ''most common,'' ''usual,'' or ''likely'' solutions to common problems. The main development effort for the knowledge base concerns itself with a greater level of detail and the nuances of values and discriminators for branching options.

The KE and the domain expert are tasked with expanding the breadth and depth of the system. The breadth is handled by adding rules and selections that incorporate additional aspects of the problem. The depth is covered by rules providing for the nuances of the problem.

Provisions are also designed for ''no data'' results; the occurrence of these should be logged. While a solution for every problem is desired, few domain experts have all of the answers for every situation. As a result, the knowledge-based system accommodates problems that have no ready solutions. This situation can result from an incomplete knowledge base where the KE and the domain expert omitted required rules and solutions. A no-data result can also occur from incorrect input by the user resulting from a lack of experience or understanding of the problem.

In addition to providing a highly perceived value, a knowledge-based system must perform. By providing an explanation facility, a report printing capability, and a facility for capturing the user's thoughts, procedures and assumptions, a system can have greater value.

Both the domain expert and the KE must realize that once the knowledge base is established and the system has been produced, their job is not over. The system will need to be updated and maintained to accommodate change and newly realized information. One of the sources of new information is the user who records thoughts and experiences into the system.

Design of the User Interface. The user interface serves both human requirements and machine information exchange and data gathering. From the human standpoint, the system provides an explanation subsystem that offers a justification for the selection of a particular choice. One of the side benefits of a knowledge-based system is the concept of *knowledge shareware*. Knowledge shareware is a provision that helps users achieve heuristic rule knowledge that can then be transferred to similar situations. In addition, users should have the opportunity to input text that is either machine-requested or user-demanded. This text relates to views, opinions, successes, and failures from the perspective of the user. The captured data can then be reviewed by the KE and the domain expert for system inclusion or modification.

The machine interface design relates to the provision of information or the gathering of information from external sources. These sources can be computer databases, sensory sources, or various input devices that can serve as potential influences on the decision process within the system. For example, data may be required that identifies the quantity of a certain stock item. A database file can dynamically track inventory and be accessed by a knowledge-based system program call. In turn, the value may cause a system branch or secondary request.

Another external input could come from a touchscreen. A diagram is presented to a user and the system requests that the user touch the specific area of concern. From the touchscreen input, the system branches to that area or requests additional information from the user.

Acquire First-Pass Knowledge

The foregoing was designed to depict the knowledge-based system prototype efforts as vehicle for analysis. While each phase discussed may not be applicable or practical for every development effort, a prototype effort using as many of the phases as possible will pay dividends.

A competent analysis identifies time over- or under-estimates, potential monetary impacts, and potential frustrations. Further, analysis benefits the KE and the team by helping to alleviate misunderstandings in later development. As the technology of knowledge-based systems evolves, the prototype tasks and phases listed in this chapter are modified. Opportunities for future development efforts can be enhanced by exhibiting a solid track record for accurate and timely prototype efforts.

If a rapid prototype was not constructed, the knowledge gained from the Preliminary Exploration and the Requirements Analysis is used as a starting point. The knowledge sources are defined, coordinated, and tapped. After the knowledge is acquired it is represented for validation and installed into the knowledge base in its required form. The strategies and techniques for these processes were addressed in part II of this book.

Implement the Prototype

The application should be programmed with emphasis on speed and accuracy rather than on esthetic appearance. The purpose of a rapid prototype is to provide a concrete demonstration of the concepts discussed. The management of the procuring group can see a physical process in operation. The domain expert can gain an understanding of the process of knowledge acquisition in terms of the codification process.

A rapid prototype also provides the domain expert with insights as to the effectiveness of the style of acquisition selected by the KE. At this point, the domain expert can consider the level of understanding and interpretation of the KE during discussions.

It is very important to place a version number on each revision of the knowledge-based application, e.g., "Version 1.1." This version control extends to the documentation and management reports. In addition, any new or test software should be installed by a key person who assumes responsibility for the dissemination of upgrades. This key person also supplies and collects ''bug sheets'' that provide precise information for bug resolution. The culture of the organization influences the extent of, and style used in, the KE's documentation.

Test

Prototype testing follows validation of the knowledge base with its associated rules, and testing of the KB by the KE and the domain expert. It is vital to the development effort that the knowledge base is accurate. One way to accomplish this is to use another expert in a review cycle.

The KE and the domain expert test the system under simulated conditions. They test the system from the presumed point of view of the target audience. The test should be conducted with performance criteria specifying the expected output. These criteria typically contain predetermined test cases.

Present a Report for Proof of Concept

A report is assembled and presented to verify or recommend departures from the feasibility study expectations. Departures can include breadth and depth estimates for the knowledge base, user interface needs, and tool selection.

The proof of concept can also be an interim demonstration system. Differing from a prototype, this system explores the validity of the overall design as viewed at the user interface. The general ''look and feel'' of the system is presented. This aspect is the result of user interfaces, use of graphics, etc.

PHASE 4: VALIDATION OF THE SYSTEM

One way of avoiding a system that falls short of functional expectations is to follow three basic rules: test, Test, TEST. One test of the system is done by experts who use the system as if they were novice users. They follow the system's progress by noting the requested inputs and evaluating the solutions. Another test is to match a novice who uses the system with an expert, each using individual problem-solving methods. If the results are the same and the paths differ, the system is a success. Thus, a solid test plan is another of those imperative necessities for a successful project. A test plan model can be derived from the following.

Purpose

The KE states the purpose of the test plan. A typical statement of the purpose includes a list of the criteria that the system was designed to meet. The list includes statements about:

- The mission statement of the application
- Goals of the system
- Performance expectations

Assumptions

The assumptions of the test plan need to be carefully stated. Typical assumptions detail the profiles of the participants and the hardware. The list includes statements about:

- The expected target audience, in terms of number and description
- Participant preparation, if any
- Conditions of use
- Hardware/software configurations

Test Goals

The test goals are stated in behavioral terms. Typical statements include:

Given　.　.　.　, the participants will be able to　.　.　.　, in (time estimate), to an accuracy of (percent of accuracy).

These goals are approved by the KE, the expert, and the management teams.

In addition to specific test or performance goals, the application should meet requirements in the following areas:

- Surface Validity:　Does the system seem to do what it was designed to do?

- Interface:　Does the user find the system easy to understand and use?

- Outputs:　Does the system provide helpful outputs?

- Teach:　Does the system adequately explain its reasoning in such a way that the user can learn from the system?

Test Approach

The test approach defines physical conditions of the test. This includes the location and the test scenario. There is a statement about the manner in which the participants will be introduced to the test. The duration of the test, amount of guidance and intervention, and any milestones or separate exercises are detailed. If the test is to last longer than one day, a general overview of the plan is presented. Details of the schedule are presented in a later section.

Test Administrators

Test administrators are described in terms of:

- Number of administrators participating
- Functions of the administrators: train, observe, act as a resource
- Qualifications of the administrators—prerequisite knowledge
- Basic responsibilities
- Materials provided

Test administrators are given a detailed guide that supplies them with a well-organized description of their responsibilities. The guide is organized according to the logical sequence of the tasks.

Participants

Validation participants have the same characteristics as the target audience identified in the feasibility study. The number of participants is specified, as is the length of dedicated time required for their participation. Readings or other preparation that is expected of the participants is detailed. Typical participant preparation includes: reading items with a specific theme, relevant experiences in the area, and materials that the participant is to bring.

Equipment

All necessary equipment is clearly specified. In the case of a computer, the type and amounts of RAM, ROM, special cards, monitors, cabling, and peripherals are carefully listed and provided.

Facility

The facility for the test approximates real-time conditions whenever possible or practical. Any special requirements such as size, noise level, and traffic are noted.

Materials

Materials required by the participants are listed in this section of the test administrator's guide, even though they might have been mentioned previously. In this way, a quick-reference section is available for the administrators.

Data Collection and Evaluation

In general, test data is collected from three sources: questionnaires, debriefing sessions, and observations.

Questionnaires

The number of questionnaires and the times of the day that they are issued are shown. The objective of each questionnaire is presented. Samples of the questionnaires accompany the test plan.

Debriefing Sessions

The KE conducts participant debriefing sessions at logical intervals. These intervals might be at the end of a test interaction or at the end of each day. Their length might be in proportion to the criticality of the application, that is applications that are designed to provide a response calling for judgments impacting human safety or with monetary ramifications have short intervals. Applications providing noncritical advice or options can sustain longer gaps. Debriefing issues include:

- Ability to access and navigate through the system
- Completeness of system helps and explanations
- Confidence in system outputs
- Ease of system use
- Identification of bugs and usability issues
- Suggestions for system improvement

Debriefing issues also incorporate selected questionnaire items that overlap with the debriefing. Test administrators take notes or record the debriefing session for an "end of session" report.

Observations

Test administrators document their observations of participant performance and attitudes displayed during the sessions.

Data Analysis

The KE and developer review all of the data gathered from the questionnaires and debriefing sessions. A report is prepared that identifies any bugs, usability concerns, and enhancement ideas from the test. Each of the categories of issues is placed in ranked order.

Daily Schedule

A daily schedule of test events is created. The start and projected end times for each day are included as well as time for breaks, questions, and a buffer time for unforeseen problems. Each of the major events of the day is described in detail. The schedules are made available before the event for participant familiarization and are discussed during the initial presentation of the agenda.

Guided Example

For some tests, a group of guided examples is appropriate. This is particularly true when the system is a brand new one. In some applications, the target audience is not computer-skilled or familiar with all aspects of the tasks to be completed. Guided examples are generally accompanied by a carefully assembled script. This script provides a scenario and other information required to perform the needed tasks for using the system. During the guided example, the administrators supply help as it is requested by the participants.

Exercise

The exercise is carefully explained and all questions answered prior to commencement. The instructions for the exercise include the goals of the exercise and a detailed list of all tasks to be completed.

Documentation

Various phases of the development effort require different types of documentation. There are two basic categories of documentation. The first documentation type is procedural, while the second type is system-oriented.

Procedural documentation focuses on the essential procedures of the system, hints for power users, and tips and techniques. System documentation focuses on maintenance and system enhancements. It covers the internal system structures and provides information regarding the reasoning used within the system.

Procedural documentation includes select areas. The feasibility study requires a document of understanding, outlining each of the task phases. The rapid prototype effort yields a validation or modification of the time, cost, delivery, validation plan, and other elements. Development documentation includes a record of problem-solving approaches, programming flowcharts, and test case results.

Procedural documentation also includes a copy of each of the presentation screens with every branching permutation. These screens can dramatically illustrate the scope and exact content of the knowledge-based application. Commonly those who are unfamiliar with knowledge-based systems view the simple elegance of answering a few questions and obtaining an answer or recommendation option as insignificant. They then turn to the KE and say, ''So, where is the AI?'' If these individuals can see the printed outputs of each screen, their understanding may increase.

Procedural documentation describes the type of knowledge representation, such as examples, frames, etc. In addition, a rule tree is included. This documentation serves as an archive for the effort that can be consulted for clarification or modification needs. An end-of-development report is also considered. This report documents the final design specifications that are useful for maintenance purposes. It also includes notes about special circumstances that are to be considered when new people are tasked with system maintenance.

System documentation is more technical in nature. It contains information on version changes and what these changes entailed. This level of documentation also includes information such as internal structures, file organization and naming conventions, development software and operating system names and versions, test cases, etc.

A final note about documentation. The feasibility study, rapid prototype, and development phases include weekly management reports. The purpose of these reports is to communicate project status to the team. Through this reporting facility, the KE can avoid surprises about project status, progress, and risks. Information relating to producing quality documentation can be found in chapter 11.

SUMMARY

In this chapter, we discussed Phase 3: System Development and Phase 4: Validation as they pertain to the suggested development model. These phases constitute the actual building and testing of the system using the design plan or blueprint constructed in Phase 2. In some cases, Phase 2 has already been completed and the client is in need of someone to do system construction. This latter case is one in which the KE takes precautions early on. As was said in the previous chapter, a blueprint that is poorly designed, or worse yet, useless, will result in a most undesirable, flawed product.

Validation is the check and verify component of the model. The developed system is checked against its design, initial goals and objectives, and project mission statement, and is scrutinized by not only the team but also a select audience of future users. The results are analyzed and modifications with additional testing performed as needed.

The next chapter continues with the next phases of the model: Implementation and Maintenance.

PRACTICAL APPLICATION

Using the application selected in chapter 9, continue with the development considerations of the system. Outline a plan for its testing complete with forms, questionnaires, procedures, etc.

11

Implementation and Maintenance

Saying is one thing, and doing is another.

Michel Eyquem de Montaigne

INTRODUCTION

Two crucial elements of system development are often regarded as something to do only if there is adequate time and money for their support. Either of these elements can cause grief for the developers if not done.

Planned implementation is crucial for the ultimate success of the system. Users are informed and trained, and the system needs to be carefully documented and supported.

Maintenance of the system extends beyond bugs. Often the knowledge base will need to be expanded or revised, as knowledge is dynamic. In addition, interfaces might require modification, networks or other links might need to be modified or developed, hardware or software might change, etc.

PHASE 5: IMPLEMENTATION

A variety of implementation strategies are available for a knowledge-based application. The feasibility study provided user information in the form of surveys, of the development climate, critical incident surveys, and assessments of employee attitudes. The development and management team analyze the data gathered from system validation with the target users. Using this body of data, a number of strategies can be used to implement the application. These strategies include training, documentation, and support.

Training

Training of the user population may be an option or a requirement. The deciding factors for training are:

- Is it needed?
- Is it wanted?
- Are there budget provisions for training?

Some applications serve as job aids. Attributes of good job aid applications include the involvement of target users in the development phases, a focus on required user skills, and no need for heroic efforts on the parts of the users. Other applications require training to make them useful. However, neither users nor management may want training or have a training budget. If the KE feels training is required to make the application successful, he makes this known in writing.

If training is to be considered for the application, there are several questions that will need to be answered:

- How many people does the training need to support?
- How many people will need training in three years?
- Will new hires for this position have the same level of knowledge and skills as the current target audience?
- What level of performance should participants have at the conclusion of their training?
- What level of knowledge should participants have at the conclusion of their training?
- What attitudes should the participants have or project at the conclusion of their training?
- Who needs to totally accept the training to make it work?
- How will the training be conducted?
- Should the training be self-study, computer-delivered, and/or leader-led?
- When is the training expected to become available?
- What resources are there to support development and implementation of the training?

The answers to these questions provide the data required to develop a training plan or proposal. Media selection, cost, and other factors are considered and presented. If the knowledge engineer is not qualified or able to assemble a training program, a training firm is consulted.

If no formal training is required, a demonstration and workshop can be designed to implement the application. Suggestions for constructing a demonstration or workshop include:

- Approach the user learning curve deductively rather than inductively. In other words, provide hands-on training with the system rather than handing out documentation or showing a videotape of someone else using the system.

- Turn into salespersons the user group that participated in the development and validation of the system. Implementation is often a selling job.
- Distribute the system on an ''as requested'' basis. A selected ''critical mass'' is given the application. Their successful use of the application will be discussed among their peers, who are then likely to begin making demands for the system.
- Provide documentation and support.

Documentation

While documentation is indispensable, poor documentation is worse than no documentation. Poor documentation is characterized by unclear language composed for the writer rather than the user. It provides ''nice to know'' data rather than ''need to know'' declarative and procedural knowledge.

General tips for good documentation include:

- Consider the purpose of the application. Users want to know how to use the application and nothing more.
- Write to the intended audience. User terminology that the users understand. Help the users to learn the system rather than impressing them with a developer's knowledge of the system.
- Determine the logical topics that the user needs to know to do the job.
- Organize the documentation into logical clusters so that information is easy to find and update.
- Use verbs to start sentences requiring the user to perform an action, e.g., ''Press F3 to display the rule tree that was used to arrive at the results.'' Poor documentation would state, ''If you want to see how the system arrived at its decision, you can see the rule tree by pressing F3.''
- Identify and define key terms that the user will need to know. These terms are defined before they are used. Do not assume that the user will glean the meanings of terms from their context.
- Use graphics whenever possible. Include pictures of the computer screens. Use icons to provide organizers and concept reminders.
- Adhere to standards of grammar, spelling, and organization. Use short sentences; however, be clear. Do not confuse clarity with brevity.
- Distribute the documentation during a hands-on session. Have the users use the documentation.
- There is no minimum weight for documentation. Do not say in two pages what could be said in one.
- If possible, develop a *Quick Start Guide* that is a mini-version of the document. The Quick Start Guide has only the essential information needed to get into and out of the application.
- Provide a section for power users that contains such items as tips, techniques, and short cuts. For example, package the documentation in a

three-ring binder with sections and tabs. Individuals can then rearrange the sequence of the documentation to meet their needs.

Support

Whether the implementation strategy is training, documentation, or support, successful implementations have these common factors:

- Everyone has access to the proper resources. These resources include: properly configured equipment, documentation, and support.
- Hands-on experience is provided with the application.
- Users are listened to and a desire to actively consider action is demonstrated.
- Timely and specific help and feedback are provided when needed or requested.
- Everyone is kept in the information loop.
- Team and company unity are built.

Users of the application have the continuing opportunity to report bugs and operating difficulties, and make recommendations for enhancements. The following form is an example of a Bug Sheet that can be used to capture the data required for assessment of reported concerns. Bugs are reported to a focus person in the organization. Bug Sheets are reviewed, responded to if possible, and sent to the KE for consideration. By using a focus or point person at a site to screen calls, the KE can save time. A heuristic rule in this area is to establish and enforce a policy whereby a focal person is trained to be the resident expert. Problems that the focal person cannot solve are directed to the KE. If calls persist, there is either a problem with the documentation, the training program, or the focal person.

PHASE 6: MAINTENANCE

Several people, including Yogi Berra, are credited with saying "It's not over till it's over." With respect to knowledge-based applications the saying should be, "It's not over till it's done and even then, it may have a rebirth." According to the life cycle model of a knowledge-based application, maintenance is but a sunset. Maintenance can occur after successful completion of the application or start on the second day of the project. This section addresses "normal" maintenance which is maintenance that follows development. The next section addresses some problems that can occur.

BUG SHEET

Date _____

Name _____   Phone _____

Bug _____   Operating Problem _____   Enhancement _____

Program Name _____   Version _____

Nature of Concern _____

_____

_____

_____

_____

_____

_____

Suggestion for Improvement _____

_____

_____

_____

_____

_____

_____

Signature _____

Normal Maintenance

Maintenance continues until the application is no longer viable. A knowledge-based application can last for years if a well thought-out maintenance plan is put into place. This plan requires the cooperation of the development and management teams. A well designed knowledge-based application can leave a legacy of structure, approach, and portions of well thought-out, well planned knowledge-based files.

In the early stages of development, the topic of maintenance is not at the forefront. Still, the wise KE builds the application with maintenance in mind. This maintenance planning includes considerations for: library text files that are accessible by a text editor, a logical naming convention for the knowledge-based files, high-quality programming documentation, and wise selection of the language or shell in which the application was developed.

Planning ahead for maintenance can be considered preventive maintenance. It is better to plan for future system requirements than to retrofit components that result in an awkward fit. Ask those that purchased a car and then decided to have add-on air conditioning installed. Satisfaction in the results is usually low.

Maintenance considerations for a knowledge-based system include: refining, modifying, expanding, and upgrading the knowledge base, and making the system portable across hardware and software systems. Each upgrade of the system includes a version number and date, and documentation and training that reflect these changes.

In theory, maintenance is the responsibility of the purchasers of the application rather than the knowledge engineer. However, it is the responsibility of the knowledge engineer to make everyone involved in the project aware of this need. It is better to plan maintenance requirements than to be bitten by those needs.

Beginning with interfaces, there are likely to be changes in the completed application. Knowledge bases are dynamic entities; they are expected to change, grow, and have additional requirements. If possible, the KE enables the purchasers of the system to do the maintenance. This can be accomplished in one of two ways. First, the KE can train a focus person to make the majority of changes in the system. These modifications may be as simple as using a text editor to modify a library file, or as complex as learning how to program the knowledge base. If someone is to learn how to program the knowledge base, a copy of the software or a license arrangement may need to be provided. The second option is to create a maintenance agreement. Typical agreements include per-requirement agreements and retainers. A per-requirement agreement is an understanding that when a modification is required, the KE will do his best to give attention to the need. This attention is usually proportional to the nature of the need. A retainer is a monthly or annual contract that reserves a dedicated portion of the KE's time for maintenance of the application. Sometimes the retainers are a long-term commitment.

Some system changes may be beyond the abilities of the system purchaser. While the KE may be only one bidder among many, early planning will aid in system continuity. One of these system growth possibilities is in the area of portability. Portability is the movement of knowledge-based applications between systems, and has become an important issue in knowledge-based systems. Knowledge base portability is likely to be required during the life of the application, particularly as hardware and operating systems continue to evolve. If the application is written using a development shell, it is likely that the shell will evolve to offer greater functionality. Sharing knowledge bases between different operating systems may surface as a requirement that is to be met.

The KE who undertakes the maintenance effort may be a different person from the KE who developed the initial system. The maintenance KE generally has skills that include code debugging, interface enhancing, networking the system with peripheral devices or other computers, and improving the efficiency of the knowledge base.

Other Incidents of Maintenance

Maintenance can occur during the second day of development. The causes of this additional work include an unsure expert, poor planning, or afterthoughts. An unsure expert often hedges his statements by understating or underestimating a finding. When situations like this occur, the KE takes time to discuss and demonstrate confidence ratings. If the situation recurs, the KE generally takes actions to secure another expert.

Poor planning rests on the shoulders of the KE. Disjointed sessions, poor representation of acquired knowledge, or inadequate questions can render a knowledge base impotent. Disjointed questions that cause the expert to digress and become disoriented result in redundancy. Well-planned sessions, guided by the Session Form, help to avoid redundancy or digressive questions. On the positive side, redundancy on critical issues can be beneficial. For example, a single rule that decides an outcome may be reconsidered and approached from another angle.

Inadequate questions are a common cause of knowledge base reevaluation and maintenance. These questions may probe shallow knowledge or only declarative knowledge. Once the knowledge is represented for validation by the expert(s), deficiencies appear. The expert(s) identify gaps and another session is required. Some of this iteration of questioning is not uncommon. However, if these iterative meetings become the norm, there is a problem, which generally belongs to the KE. The solution is better familiarity with the domain.

On the other hand, maintenance is not a four-letter word. In a knowledge-based application, the knowledge base is separate from the control program. For this reason, required modification of the knowledge base is not a major undertaking; and about 15 percent modification is not unusual. Experienced KEs tend to plan a project time buffer which is usually expended in this area. One tip for knowledge-based modification is to plan and develop logical file names. Another tip is to have multiple small files that can be grouped into clusters. If documentation was done correctly, it is a relatively simple matter to locate the appropriate file for inspection or modification.

Additional changes will be required by an application. Some of these changes can be handled by long-term support services.

SUMMARY

It is at this point that the client is excitedly showing off the new product. This is also a point at which a costly mistake can be made—the "quick and dirty" and therefore disastrous rollout of the system. Time and care must be taken to analyze and design training, supporting documentation, and system maintenance of the new system. How often have we heard the tale of the parent staying up until the wee hours of the morning trying to put a child's bicycle together, or going from store to store looking for the right-sized batteries for the new toy?

Just as the initial design plan had to be generated and sold to the team and decision-makers, so must the implementation and maintenance plans be constructed. No matter how valuable a system might be, if it's not used, it might as well be deemed worthless. Further, the personnel who will be responsible for system maintenance and troubleshooting may be uncomfortable and apprehensive about taking on the tasks of repair, hot line servicing, and interim system updates. The enthusiasm of users and maintenance personnel is key to the successful use and growth of the system.

The client may require reminding that the system—as wonderful and near-perfect as it may seem—still needs management in terms of ongoing, careful maintenance; that users, as enthusiastic as they might be, might still need a bit of help and encouragement in their initial use and understanding of the system; and that the system's knowledge will require consistent updating to keep its knowledge base as current and exact as possible.

PRACTICAL APPLICATION

Given the system you've been working on for the previous two chapters, outline a plan for implementation and maintenance. Be sure to include forms, procedures, job tasks and responsibilities, schedules, etc.

CASE STUDY

This third part of the book, "A Development Model," probably gives the impression of an easy, fast-moving operation. Let me emphasize that knowledge-based applications take time, effort, and perseverance. In order to illustrate how the development model works, this example is offered. Note that the application example does not address each and every step or component in the model. The nature of a model is a map or a pattern. Not every nuance, twist, or turn must be negotiated to arrive at a destination. The following case study is hypothetical, simple, and totally utopian.

With caveats in place, let's consider an expert system shipping advisor as a custom development application. The expert system development company is called Applications, Inc. (AI) and the interested buyer is a training software development firm called Training 'R Us (TRU).

The vice president of operations of TRU has a problem. There is rapid turnover among personnel in the shipping department. There is a constant demand for shipping computer diskettes, paper products, and computers. Costs are out of hand. Items that could be sent by regular mail are sent overnight mail. Equipment is not properly insured. Some shipments are not received next-day because of not being ready on time. Some packages, when shipped, go to the wrong department.

Vice President Joe Smith, being a well-read person, is aware of expert systems and the reputable firm of AI. Joe contacts AI, discussions ensue, a contract for a preliminary exploration is signed, and AI sends their finest knowledge engineer, Susan Terri. A meeting is set.

Preliminary Exploration

Susan begins by touring the site. She talks with several people and learns that the problem has two basic components. First, there is little common sense involved in the problem, so it can be handled by an expert-system application or by training. Second, there might be some internal policies that need to be taken care of.

The problem type is one of analysis. Rules can be established to accommodate the shipping decisions.

Environment. After a half day of talking to project directors, shipping personnel, and Joe, Susan learned that the application could be used as an interim solution. The long-term solution is training unless the turnover rate is of little concern. The application should help the shipper determine the best carrier. Susan made the following observations:

- An expert is needed to provide the shipping rules.
- A single best carrier should be recommended.
- Knowledge sources are the carriers, past shipping personnel, and a possible consultant.

- The target user group is the shipping department personnel. Their computer skills are adequate; and a PC can be made available to the department.
- There are three people in the department. Other duties in the department are receiving, machine maintenance, office moving, and other tasks as needed. The shippers have little time for mailings, generally receive items at the last minute, and feel the task should be handled by another department.

The People. There were two individuals identified as possessing appropriate domain knowledge. The most knowledgeable person is the receptionist. The receptionist is time-burdened. The other person is in the shipping department. In addition, three carriers were contacted. Each carrier would send information.

Management has accepted the concept. They realize that there are shipping bottlenecks, cost impacts, and, more importantly, unhappy clients as a result of untimely or inaccurate shipments. The organization sees a need for a solution. There is a concern over development costs.

The target users support the project for three reasons.

1. This would be the only high-tech application in the company.
2. The application could be handed off to another department.
3. The burdens of shipping decisions are off their backs.

There is an average of six overnight mail packages per day; two computer shipments per month for shows and conferences; and miscellaneous letters, packages, diskettes, and documentation.

Process. While there is some common sense involved, the level of common sense is informed. There are declarative and procedural knowledge requirements with little performance differential between a novice and an expert. Organization and planning were defined as keys to success. Thus, it is easy to qualify cognitive solutions.

The consensus is that there is an ample supply of knowledge sources. The problem will not go away. Turnover will continue in the foreseeable future. The problem state is stable, and solutions are generally arrived at in two minutes or less. Susan identified alternate solutions such as job aids, training, and establishing procedures.

Mission Statement. The project goal is to assist the shipping department to determine timely, cost effective, and consistent modes of delivery. The mission statement follows:

The shipping advisor will enable the shipping department to determine the most expedient and cost-effective shipping medium for paper goods, diskettes, and hardware. The application will take 30 seconds or less to use and will recommend the single best solution.

ROI

Management, in this case, was looking for a techno-fix. ROI considerations were quantitative and qualitative. Quantitative ROI was underwhelming. The numbers proved to yield a payback in seven years. The qualitative payback was impressive. Missed deliverables, unhappy personnel, and irritated clients were hard to argue with. Missed opportunity was the deciding factor for management.

Solution Scope. The following shows the checklist to ensure that the application is suitable for an expert system.

- Knowledge Requirement

  The outputs are consistent. The conditions are known. The users vary in knowledge level.

- Narrow Domain:

  The domain is well-suited to a knowledge-based application.

- Symbolic Knowledge:

  The shipping advisor is well within the normal bounds.

- No Common Sense Required:

  The application can be developed with no reliance on common sense.

- Cognitive Solution:

  The system is straightforward and is cognitive in nature.

- Reasonable Number of Outcomes:

  The output for this system recommends the optimum one out of a reasonably small number of possible solutions.

Refocus the Problem. The same is done for the problem.

- Character:

  The proposed application is direct through a minimal rule set.

- Complexity:

  The proposed application has low-end complexity. It is solvable by a Level 0 system.

- Range:

  The range is within normal tolerance.

Specify the Problem Set. Susan and the most knowledgeable person in the shipping department, John, started with the results and constructed the following example set. Given the personnel involved, Susan decided a quick representation scheme that was simple and easily made into rules would prove best. The acquisition tactic Susan chose was interview.

Susan and John selected as props each of the deliverable containers and typical delivery requirements. One of the problems identified was sufficient lead time for the shipping department. John was tasked with creating a memo that

Susan would outline to him. The contents of the memo involved setting policies for lead time and preplanning.

Weight	Speed	Special Cond.	Time Rec.	Results
.5 and <	Next day	Saturday Del	N.D. 10:00	Ovrnt. ltr
.5 and <	22nd day	Registered	N.D. 12:00	Cour. pak
2 to 20	3rd day	insurance	open	Priority
over 20	< 1 week	Bulk		Exp Mail
	< 2 weeks	crate		UPS
				US Mail
				Parcel Post

Validation. Validation strategy will be through the receptionist, VP Operations, and records of past shipments.

Requirements Analysis

This list shows the attitudes of the involved personnel.

- Management: Get it done quickly.

- Developers: Political foot in door. Play it down and dirty. Be aware of shipping personnel's agenda.

- Experts: Receptionist too busy.
  John is cooperative but has a hidden agenda to off-load the responsibility.
  Records are available and adequate.
  Commercial shippers are cooperative.

- Target Audience: No problems anticipated.

System Development and Validation

Because the project was a "down and dirty" type, Susan decided to bypass any suggestions for a prototype. The problem was clear and the mission statement said it all. There were no subproblems within the system; however, Susan recommended a training component for system usage. With a little guidance, John could effectively conduct the training requirements. Also, there was to be an on-demand explanation capacity for the application.

Contracts were in place. Management freed up John's time as needed. John agreed. Susan built a work schedule with interim deliverables, indicated by " ".

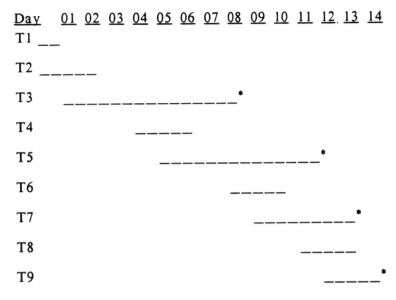

Task 1   is slated to take one day. This is the project kickoff. Susan will work with John and available records to begin the knowledge base.

Task 2   will conclude at the end of day 2. Susan will assemble an example base and talk over the phone with preidentified carriers.

Task 3   starts on day 3 and concludes at the end of day 5. Susan will deliver the completed example base for verification. She will work with John for two hours, make any needed modifications, work with the receptionist for one hour, and meet with Joe. Joe will sign off on the deliverable.

Task 4   involves a half-day brainstorming session "back at the ranch." Susan presents the findings to date. A shell is selected because of time crunch, favorable licensing, and ease of use. Susan will program the application herself. Task 4 is concluded at the end of the day.

Task 5   commences the programming effort. Susan chose to include a graphic interface. Susan is creating rules out of the example set. The task takes three days and concludes with delivery of the rule set.

Task 6   finds Susan and John verifying the rules. Susan captures John's rationale to form the explanation subsystem. This is a one-day effort.

Task 7   is the incorporation of the graphics and explanation subsystem into the application. Susan creates the validation version in two days. This version is a deliverable. Susan created the validation test cases for management approval. We are now at the end of day 12.

Task 8   is the validation. Susan, John, Joe, and four potential users are gathered in a prearranged environment. Management decides to add the day's shipments to the validation exercises. Susan loads the PCs and presents the validation plan. Validation commences. Susan takes notes and decides to add to the explanation subsystem. She also suggests that the company may benefit from a general distribution of the final run time diskettes.

Task 9   is the final delivery. Susan suggests a general maintenance plan that involves a follow-up in six months. This follow-up will evaluate any changes in the shipping practices of the company or personnel needs that would impact the application. Susan also prepares procedural documentation and system documentation.

Implementation and Maintenance

Susan's implementation plan was simple and direct. John was to conduct an information session for his company. The system would be demonstrated for the group. However, John was to announce that only selected individuals were to be given a copy of the diskette. The intent was to create a demand for the application.

The system was both intuitive and simple. The explanation subsystem was sufficient to fill the information gap. Maintenance considerations for the application were built around the explanation subsystem, which was designed to be modified as needed. Its files were created, say, by an editor and called by file name. Content changes in the subsystem would cause no impact to the application. However, any changes in the company's product line or the advent of new carriers would.

If only all projects could be so easy! Unfortunately, no knowledge-based system application is likely to be this easy.

12

Risks and Safety Nets

We have forty million reasons for failure,
but not a single excuse.

Rudyard Kipling

INTRODUCTION

Call them heuristic constructs or knowledge from the school of hard knocks, but there are potential risks that can be avoided if recognized. Risks and safety nets discussed in this chapter are tied to the six phases of the model: preliminary exploration, requirements analysis, system development, validation, implementation, and maintenance.

PRELIMINARY EXPLORATION

Results Drive Development

Risk
Sometimes the design of a project is put together too quickly in an effort to move into development.

Safety Net
The responsible party(s) for this indiscretion is usually management, but can be extended to include users, developers, and other special interest groups. These groups like to see the results, touch the final product, and avoid discussion about what will be. This group of anxious managers can be appeased by development of a rapid prototype.

Overdesign

Risk

The tighter the design, the less flexible and more option-deficient the system. A solid design effort is desirable, but knowledge-based system building is an art or craft rather than a science. Design specifications are required in order to create a plan to follow and a graphic road map to contemplate.

Safety Net

Define requirements; carefully assess all known requirements. Unknown requirements can be handled in the contract under the area of ''out of scope'' findings. It is not unreasonable to assume that a research and development effort will reveal more than the KE's and domain expert's best first efforts.

Problem Definition

Risk

The problem definition is the first and possibly most important single task of a knowledge-based application development effort.

Safety Net

If the problem cannot be defined, it cannot be solved. Questions need to be focused and addressed to the appropriate individual. Perhaps the appropriate individuals are not in attendance. Typical questions that help to define the problem include:

- What opportunities are being missed?
- What effects are surfacing as a result of the problem?
- How does the problem influence or impact other problems that are currently being solved?

Another approach is to assess what the preliminary exploration team expects from the completed application. Questions approaching the problem from this angle include:

- Which of the following will the system do?
  - Capture and distribute decision-making knowledge
  - Preserve the knowledge of selected individuals
  - Integrate the decision-making approaches of several people
  - Enable faster decisions
  - Help make better decisions based upon the inputs
  - Create a consistency of decisions
  - Reduce labor costs

Justification

Risk

A knowledge-based system may be difficult to justify in the minds select individuals among the decision makers.

Safety Net

Sometimes it is a real selling job to convince those with budget responsibility to embark on a project that uses technology unknown to the company. If possible, prepare success stories of other companies with similar problems who used these technologies. The best selling effort is for the resistant individuals to sell themselves.

If you have gotten this far, you have done well. There are questions that can be explored when appropriate, to nudge the project forward. These questions include:

- Are key people in short supply?
- Do seemingly simple tasks require too many people because no single person knows how to do everything?
- Are there too many facts about an area or a job for one person to remember?
- Is there a large discrepancy between the abilities of expert and novice workers?
- Are corporate goals falling short because of poor personnel performance?
- Is market share being lost due to decision-making problems among the personnel?
- Is a key decision-maker about to retire?
- Are there any tools currently being used to assist key personnel in decision making?
- Are key personnel spread too thin?
- Are there inconsistencies in problem-solving approaches?
- Are key personnel causing bottlenecks because of an inability to be in two places at once?
- Can processing costs be reduced through use of an application?
- Would this system generate less waste?
- Could this system improve product quality?
- Is reduced risk or financial exposure a consideration?
- Could improved product design reap benefits?
- Do decisions need to be made faster?
- Is advice needed from outside consultants?
- Do experts need to be available 24 hours a day?
- Do these experts need to be available in remote locations?
- Could such a system lower training costs?

- If such a system were available, would it help to improve user attitudes?
- Would an application like this one produce product differentiation?
- Is there some aspect of performance that this system can provide to alleviate current user or company difficulties?
- Would this system help to reduce costs?
- Could more effective production be expected with better employee support?
- Will the application result in a more cost-effective operation because workers will be able to work more autonomously?
- Will safer operations result from using an application to monitor selected processes?

Problem State: Hit or Miss?

Risk
Questions are asked that focus on how the problem is currently handled, and the possible implications for developing an application.

Safety Net
The problem of getting answers may be related to not getting what you need or want to hear. Sometimes a shotgun approach helps to disperse the mist that obscures the picture. Questions to find positive aspects include:

Identity of the Problem

- How important is it to solve this problem? Is this problem common?
- Is the problem new? Can the problem parameters be readily defined?
- Do you have people whom you would consider as experts at solving this problem?
- Do you have documentation that describes the problem and its possible solutions?
- How long does an expert take to solve a typical problem?
- What do workable solutions look like?
- Do these solutions work all of the time?
- Does the problem solver use knowledge to solve the problem? If so, how?
- Do problem solvers use references to help them solve these problems?
- Could a nonexpert, if given the appropriate questions to ask of an expert, solve the problem?

The Users

- Who do you feel would use a problem-solving application?
- Can a computer be taken into the physical environment where the problem occurs?

- What types of decisions need to be made by the application?
- How soon should a system like this one be available?

Technical Issues

- Is the solution for the problem best handled through a knowledge-based application?
- What are the considerations for the knowledge and experts, interfaces, and validation and testing?

Economic Issues

- What are the specific benefits of building this application?
- Are these benefits worth the associated costs?
- What are the risks for management, the experts, the users, the developers?

Is the problem really appropriate to a knowledge-based system application?

- Is it possible to create an algorithmic approach to solve the problem?
- Can we truly establish boundaries for the problem?
- Can we count on continuing sources of the expertise needed to form the knowledge base?
- Do the experts really have the knowledge breadth and depth to not only solve problems but also to explain their reasoning?
- Do the experts attribute their problem solving abilities to data gathering, data analysis, or both?
- Is there agreement on the approaches for solving these problems?

What do I do with the answers to the knowledge questions?

- Estimate the size of the knowledge base needed to support the knowledge required for solving the problems.
- Assess the complexity of the knowledge and problem-solving processes undertaken by the experts.
- Estimate the time needed to obtain, validate, and represent the knowledge.

Time Factors

Determine if the time needed to reason with the knowledge and react to the answers is a factor. For example, the decision on a system shut-down should occur before the start of meltdown.

Form(s) of Knowledge

Determine the form or forms of the knowledge as being permanent, static, or dynamic.

Assess important characteristics of the experts.

- Will they be available for the project?
- Do they have an interest in developing the proposed application?
- Do the experts seem to have an ability to articulate their expertise?

What considerations are there for costing the project?

- Do provisions need to be made for access to peripherals to or from the knowledge-based application?
- Does the application need to access other databases?
- Does the application need to access other computer equipment?
- Are there considerations for security or security-related issues?
- What preliminary estimates for hardware and software tools are required?
- Will a prototype be required?
- How long will the evolution from prototype to production take?
- How many prototype versions are likely to be required?
- How much of the expert's time will the application require?
- How much time and how many personnel will be needed for testing and validation?
- What are the users' training needs?
- What additional resources such as manuals or documentation need to be developed?
- Will the application require ongoing maintenance?

What are the political considerations?

- Is there a local, national, or international culture for this corporation?
- What are the recent national political influences on this type of business or industry?
- What is the current management style or management philosophy used by this company?

Are there constraints unique to this organization?

- How much flexibility is there in the selection and acquisition of hardware and software?
- Who will be responsible for fixing bugs? For how long? Can a definition for a bug be clearly formulated and agreed upon?
- What are the reporting lines for the personnel on this project?

REQUIREMENTS ANALYSIS

Inaccurate Problem Definition

Risk

The problem is much larger than anticipated and lacks clear definition. With all the start-up excitement, it is sometimes easy to miss the implications of the problem. These implications include pervasion by common sense, overzealousness by the domain expert, overselling by the marketing department, etc.

Safety Net

Involve a competent KE in early discussions of the project. Plan for a rapid prototype phase. Remember that expert systems cannot solve common-sense problems because of an inability to construct, store, or access a knowledge base large enough. An expert system cannot make social judgments, or carry out other similar functions. The rapid prototype can reveal the potential strengths and limitations of the final system. If performance expectations are not achieved, modifications in function or expectations can be made, or the project can be ended.

Defining the Users

Risk

The user group is not clearly defined.

Safety Net

Establish a form or outline that is used to answer questions that help to define the users. These questions include:

- What is the computer literacy level of the users?
- What is the user education level and familiarity with domain terminology?
- Are there any special environmental conditions or constraints under which the application will be used e.g., hands busy or dirty, input other than keyboard required, such as mouse or voice?

Management

Risk

There are risks associated with management that can impact the successful completion of the development phase.

Safety Net

Management is the responsibility of those participating in the development effort. A project of this nature is truly a team undertaking. As such, everyone succeeds or everyone fails. However, understand that each person works within an individual span of control.

Rather than focusing on all of the tasks that the managers ought to do, it is easier to show the high-risk areas that a manager should avoid. A Management Fault Tree Analysis is one approach to expressing the primary risks. This analysis lists the major mistakes that will almost ensure failure in a project. Hayes-Roth, Waterman, and Lenat (1983) offer the following as typical mistakes in project management:

- Bad evaluation of project aims and objectives
- Bad planning of times and resources
- Inappropriate choice of knowledge domain
- Imprecise objectives
- Insufficient involvement of management
- Failure to get agreement on schedule or objectives
- Change of key staff on project
- Inadequate documentation
- Purpose not clear to management or users
- No targets or checkpoints

SYSTEM DEVELOPMENT

Monster Knowledge Bases

Risk
The scope of the knowledge base can grow to unmanageable proportions, especially after full-scale development begins.

Safety Net
If there is an opportunity, conduct a high-quality problem analysis prior to starting development. Some organizations are reluctant to pay for an analysis of the problem. The company that is letting the contract assumes that they ''know'' the problem and you are there to fix it. If you operate from that viewpoint, you will fail in a large way at some time, on some contract.

There are times when the KE has no control over performing an analysis of the problem. Should this be the case, and the knowledge base begins to look like it will be immense, communicate. Tell the project champion or other management persons that the problem's influences may be larger than anticipated. Write a recommendation that a problem analysis be conducted. Carefully communicate your concerns in a weekly report. In that way, at least you tried.

Another tactic is to build the cost of an analysis into the total contract bid. In addition, a rapid prototype or proof of concept system could be recommended. If these safety nets cannot be accommodated, your most valuable commodity is at risk. That commodity is your reputation.

Form and Function

Risk
There may be many views about what the application ought to do, but little agreement on its form and function.

Safety Net

As talks progress, document the ideas and decisions discussed. Include the specific tasks that the system is expected to perform and the appropriate performance criteria. Be sure that these talks remain in a realm of expectations that can be performed by existing hardware and software.

Avoid overdesign, but be sure to include system requirements and development constraints. Also list reasonable alternatives, and restrict options for choices of components and considerations. Too many options tend to confuse rather than help in the decision-making process. These requirements and constraints include the following:

- List the proposed hardware, software, and application building tool.
- Define and describe the needed input specifications. Describe the knowledge required as well as how this knowledge will be entered into the system.
- Describe the preliminary findings of the processing specifications, i.e., how the expert system will process the information (rules, chaining, etc.).
- Describe the decision criteria—how confidence factors will be used, what edit checks will be done for verification.
- Describe the intended output specifications—what the engineering and end user interfaces will be.
- Estimate the numbers and, when possible, the names of personnel involved and duration of their commitment.
- Anticipate the areas of the organization affected by the development and implementation of the application.
- Project training and support needs and their associated costs.
- Project the application's total costs, ROI factors, and development risks.
- Project the application's development schedule.
- List the tangible and intangible benefits of the system that can be realized by the organization.
- Estimate the extent to which the projected design will accurately represent and carry out the application's mission statement.

Interfaces

Risk

There are considerations for interfaces that need to be addressed. Note that it is easy to miss some of them.

Safety Net

The role of interfaces is critical to successful application development. They determine the ease of use for users, and access methods for information input and retrieval. Considerations include the following items:

- The interface is designed to assist the user in mediating the problem.

- The use of graphical representation of the knowledge and its solution process contributes to the user's understanding of the problem and its solution.
- The interface assists the user by assisting in the user's own reasoning about the problem.
- The application does not provide commands or functions that are not useful.
- Common questions have some way to batch process simple inputs.
- The user does not attempt a search for functions that are not in the system.
- The interface has easy-to-use input strategies and screen access.
- The system is responsive to user input, and expedites productivity.
- System messages are meaningful to the user.
- The system enables users to rapidly input responses.
- System input requirements are clearly specified. This is especially important when numeric units are used, for example, 60 minutes or 1 hour, 3 feet or 36 inches, etc.
- System inputs allow for or are designed around user conceptual errors such as incorrect commands or misspellings.
- Recovery from user errors is designed in, e.g., backing up in the interaction, branching to other related screens, etc.
- An early determination is made regarding the amount and type of training necessary before a user can productively use the system.
- On-line help facilities are provided.
- The average amount of time it takes for a typical user to solve a problem is determined.
- The number of interactions required by the system of the user to solve an average problem is determined.

Tool Selection

Risk

A tool may be selected by the company that owns the development, or you yourself have one in mind.

Safety Net

Build a rapid prototype. In this way, a tool can be selected having abilities that match the requirements, and that also has the features needed for successful development. Remember what can happen when one makes too many assumptions.

Familiar Tools

Risk

The KE might select a particular tool only because it is familiar. Because it does not quite work, the knowledge is reworked or force-fitted.

Safety Net

Do not take this risk. There may be no safety net and the fall is long and terminal. Be sure that the selection of the tool is justified by objective project requirements rather than subjective bias.

Knowledge Focus

Risk

The level and focus of the knowledge for the system and the interfaces is or seems to be superficial.

Safety Net

The domain needs to be bounded in order to maintain project scope. The reasoning process needs to be conceptually described with an associated acquisition strategy. Considerations for the application's interface include explanation abilities, justification of the reasoning process, an ability to mark a current location and restart from that point, and design provisions for security of access and usage.

Nonexpert Experts

Risk

The expert might sound better than the advice given turns out to be. As a result, there might be personality conflicts and other problems.

Safety Net

Try very hard to participate in the selection of the domain expert(s). These expert(s) need to be dedicated, committed, and willing to listen and speak.

Communication is a solution. Submit weekly progress reports to management. These reports contain projected expectations for that week, the actual accomplishments, the potential exposures, and any tasks or actions that are to be completed by either party. A section about anticipated accomplishments for the following week may be helpful in setting expectations. Remember, the KE is the epistemologist on the team.

Time Shortage

Risk

The domain expert's available time may diminish for many reasons.

Safety Net

Get enthusiastic project acceptance and support from the domain expert. If the expert has an understanding of her contributions and the functioning of the system, you are one step ahead. If you tell the expert with sincerity what a good job she is doing, you are a second step ahead. If you work on-site, off-site, formally and informally, you are a third step ahead. If you can graphically show a time involvement or task chart illustrating that time is heavily loaded at the beginning, diminishes in the middle, and has a validation spike toward the end, you should be successful.

Domain Expert Takes Control

Risk
The domain expert may insist that the user needs as many choices as possible.

Safety Net
A heuristic rule in this area is that more than five choices tend to preclude reasonable selection by novice users. A group of selections that exceeds five suggests that the problem or attribute could have been decomposed into more levels.

Share some knowledge engineering knowledge and experience with the domain expert. This sharing will help build rapport and an understanding that there are heuristic rules on both sides.

Internal Politics

Risk
The development of an expert system by an outside vendor may be undermined or blocked by internal politics.

Safety Net
This is a difficult situation, one in which it is easy to expend time and effort with little return. The best cure is prevention. A predevelopment probe explores its possibility. Internal politics tend to come from groups or parties who are threatened by the development of an expert system by an outside vendor, or feel they are. A good place to start is with internal AI departments, perceptions of a system replacing human workers, interdepartmental rivals, etc.

The best heuristic rule in this area is to investigate the possibility early in the effort. If political situations are present, enlist the aid of the Project Champion or manager, or ask the problem group or individual to participate in the effort. Sometimes the problem is due to poor communication and/or poor design.

Uncooperative Expert

Risk
Sometimes the cooperation of the domain expert diminishes and places the project at risk.

Safety Net
Communication with the expert is the first approach. Tell the expert that your combined efforts are producing little. Ask if there is a problem. If this leads

to a dead end, talk with the Project Champion. In an unemotional tone, explain the problem, the steps taken to date, and the potential risks and exposures caused by the problem.

Based upon the discussions with the Project Champion, put a plan into place. Then, at a near-term review, decide if the problem has been resolved or if changes need to be made. If the expert is replaceable, this latter decision might be a good move. Internal management is the domain of the Project Champion and staff; stay out of this area if at all possible.

Too Technical for the KE

Risk

There are times when the knowledge is too technical for the KE.

Safety Net

This problem is more common than many knowledge engineers like to admit. If the problem is the result of inadequate preparation on the part of the KE, the fault and responsibility is clear. If, however, the domain is just too technical, there are options. Another person can be hired to assist the KE with the technical nature of the project. Another possibility is to use more than one interviewer. As the knowledge is captured, it is rapidly represented, and feedback and clarification are provided by the expert.

Questioning Strategy

Risk

Incorrect questioning strategy can create many problems. Ask a silly question and get a silly answer. Garbage in; garbage out. However, this problem might not be the fault of the KE, but rather of a misunderstanding between the KE and the domain expert.

Safety Net

Discuss questioning strategy with the expert. Have more than one interviewer present the questions, or review a tape recording. Avoid leading questions. Ask the expert what should be asked.

This Is Knowledge?

Risk

There are times when a KE obtains data rather than knowledge.

Safety Net

Question how the data helps, e.g., "What does this mean?", "Give me another example." Provide open-ended questions with closed-ended questions as follow-up. Mere raw data by itself will not produce a usable knowledge base.

Terms

Risk
Terminology can be misinterpreted.

Safety Net
Establish a knowledge dictionary. Define and clarify terms, acronyms, concepts, etc. Include the mission statement, personnel, tasks, responsibilities, etc.

Questions and Questioning

Risk
There are times when an expert does not answer direct questions, and tends to wander.

Safety Net
Refocus the expert by approaching the problem via additional questions. Provide examples through analogies based on problems and responses previously covered. Be sure that each session has an agenda outlining the expectations of the session. If the problem persists within a session, end the session. Express to the expert that little progress is being made. Ask for suggestions. If there is no change, approach the Project Champion and possibly change experts.

Interruptions

Risk
One quick way to lose control, time, and money is to allow interruptions.

Safety Net
Sometimes it is not possible to totally isolate the expert from others. Some approaches to minimize this difficulty include: accept only designated calls, reschedule a session, schedule short sessions, change the knowledge acquisition location to an off-site location, request help from management, discuss commitment with the expert.

PROBLEM-SOLVING

General Risks in Problem-Solving

- Difficulty in problem isolation
- Inappropriate or incorrect links
- Inaccurate perceptions
- Functional fixity (the problem of taking a familiar path)
- Myopic evaluation—a view from too narrow a perspective
- Constraints resulting from corporate culture or perceived constraints
- Selective listening, cursory attention to the viewpoint of others

- Bias-driven prognosis
- Incorrect model

Safety Nets

- Obtain the views of others
- Compare the problem to past successful models
- Assume no simple solutions
- Vary the perspective, work backwards

Unrealistic Perceived Requirements

Risk
Perceptions of reality can differ.

Safety Net
All requirements need to be considered for functionality, longevity, usability, cost-effectiveness, appropriateness, etc. Requirements can be ranked in terms of importance. A representative sampling of all of the key players should participate. Develop, post, and follow a mission statement.

Changes

Risk
Requests for redesign can get out of hand.

Safety Net
This problem needs to be eliminated at the beginning of the project, by gaining firm agreement through an understanding of the design document. The scope of the project must be clearly defined in a document produced by the feasibility study or included in the original contract. When issues move the project out of its defined boundaries, a very formal meeting needs to take place. This meeting should involve decision makers. If a task or task group is out of scope, a contract modification must be written.

One technique that can be introduced is "lockin." Lockin is a sign-off technique used to indicate the absolute finality of a milestone or interim deliverable. Lockin works best when there are many milestones established by the team before development begins. With a commitment by the team to locking in decisions, the milestones are taken very seriously. The result is a more rigorous assessment of the process and a lessened tendency to make alterations in the plan.

System Shortfalls

Risk
The feasibility study can surface system shortfalls. This is when fingers begin to point.

Safety Net

The purpose of the feasibility study is to test assumptions without total commitment of time and full-scale resources. The KE needs to make clear in writing that issues can come to light that have been overlooked to date. Weekly project reports, good communication, and client participation is a strategy that can eliminate this potential problem.

Realize that some problems are difficult to see without further study. When a problem is fuzzy, fuzzy language is appropriate. There are selected terms that can be used to frame the problem. These terms include: appears, seems, may be, tends, resembles, etc. Fuzzy words can be used as long as they communicate.

Confusion

Risk

There can be confusion over reasoning processes, causing debate among the expert and others.

Safety Net

Present general problem-solving strategies used outside of the domain. Place terms and concepts in the knowledge dictionary. These terms or concepts may include the following:

- Analysis by inductive reasoning

   Start with the solution or goal, and then try to accumulate facts that support and prove it. Attempt to reach a general conclusion by examining specific facts or premises. Reason from the specific to the general. Examples of analysis applications include diagnosis, prediction, testing, and classification.

- Synthesis by deductive reasoning

   Work with facts and attempt to build up to a solution to reach a goal. Use broad premises to draw a conclusion. Reason from the general to the specific. Examples of synthesis applications include design, planning, and configuration.

Interacting with the Expert

Risk

The KE is not always completely sure of the risk factors associated with interacting with experts.

Safety Net

There are many things that can go right with an expert. The interactions can be rich and the friendships genuine. However, there are things that can go wrong too. Thus, it is best to know the risks ahead of time.

- The expert may provide incorrect information. This situation can be the result of misunderstanding, fear of losing a job, or sabotage. It is often wise to establish an early-on knowledge validation by other experts.
- The expert may not understand the information or requirements. Establish a knowledge dictionary for terminology. Explain the objectives of the system. Show other applications.
- Explanations may wander aimlessly. Focus the sessions with an agenda. State the purpose of the session and follow the agenda.

Documentation

Risk
Documentation has critical elements that warrant careful attention.

Safety Net
Be sure that the system documentation meets the requirements for structure, completeness, and accuracy described in the last section of chapter 10.

Rollout

Risk
There are crucial elements that need to be evaluated during rollout.

Safety Net
There are many considerations requiring evaluation and monitoring. These considerations include hardware, software, interface strategies, and training. Questions that the KE considers include:

- Are any hardware changes needed for the application to meet its design goals? These goals include speedy interaction and ease of use. Solutions include modifications in the computer system such as additional memory, a more powerful processor, a better link to a host processor, and a different graphics display.
- Do any changes need to be made in the application's flow or knowledge base as a result of comments made by users about interfaces?
- Were any comments directed towards the user interface? These comments may be directed at wording changes in the displays.
- Is the training program effective?
- Are there any effective domain problems in the user community?

Trainees

Risk
The developer sometimes needs to use a knowledge engineering trainee to conduct a knowledge acquisition session. This might be in the form of a series of questions that can be asked to gather sufficient background information.

Safety Net

Everyone needs to learn sometime. However, training begins at home with guided knowledge acquisition practice sessions. There are standard questions that can be asked. The answers to these questions can then be analyzed for the next action. The apprentice also needs to understand the responsibilities of a knowledge engineer. These responsibilities include:

- Deciding the applicability of the technology used to meet the problem
- Gaining knowledge of the tool or language that is to be used
- Selecting the most appropriate tool
- Acquiring and representing the knowledge
- Programming and developing the system
- Refining the knowledge base
- Implementing the completed system
- Training target users
- Maintaining the system

The knowledge acquisition process can be started using the following questions:

- What does the novice need to know or learn about the problem in order to be proficient at solving it?
- What questions should the system ask the user in order to reach an appropriate, accurate solution?
- Does the problem include numerical manipulations that need to be performed?
- Can you provide a conceptual overview of the problem space?
- Can you think of specific procedures that relate to the problem?
- What types of inputs do you make to solve these problems?
- What types of solutions are there?
- What types of knowledge, such as declarative, procedural, commonsense, or heuristic, do you use to solve these problems?
- Can the problem be broken down into smaller units?
- Could we sketch out the interrelationships among the major factors relating to the problem?
- What types of assumptions do you make?
- What areas do you investigate that lead you to particular solutions?

Additional questions need to be asked once the problem is characterized. These questions relate to decision analysis. Hart (1986), outlined a procedure to extract the major factors relating to the decision-making process. The steps in this procedure are:

1. List all possible decisions.
2. For each decision, list all possible consequences.

3. For each consequence, assess its worth and the probability of its occurrence.
4. Calculate the expected worth of each consequence by multiplying its worth by its probability.
5. Calculate the expected worth of a decision as the sum of all of the expected values of its consequences.
6. Select the decision that maximizes the expected worth.

VALIDATION

Scope Questions

Risk
The scope of the application is sometimes questioned during validation.

Safety Net
Test prior to validation. This testing involves the evaluation of the knowledge base by appropriate experts, gaining user approval for the interfaces, conducting test cases on the prototype, and scheduling formal tests.

At each milestone there is a management sign-off. If each of the pieces is approved, the assembled application should also test and validate well. However, the end product can miss the mark in the minds of some people, but constant communication through weekly reports and frequent interactions reduces the possibility of unwelcome results.

If the KE has faithfully communicated and reported, the scope is adjusted, the project budget is modified, and the effort continues. However, there should be a stronger focus on system performance, outputs, links, and any issue raised that "missed the mark."

IMPLEMENTATION

Missing or Inadequate Planning for Implementation

Risk
It is not uncommon to learn that there is little support for projecting a need and developing a plan for implementation.

Safety Net
Relate a failure story about "all of the development went to waste because the users did not accept or use the application . . . ." Prepare and present a sketchy implementation plan that extracts some of the information during the preliminary exploration. In this information:

- Define the users
- Present the user's knowledge of computers
- Suggest a general implementation plan

- Identify the hardware
- Identify the software
- Discuss the installation of the hardware and software
- Discuss the need for training
- List the interface requirements for other databases or instruments or other hardware

Training

Risk

There are times when the KE thinks that the application will be successful if the users receive training, but is not sure of how to approach the training need.

Safety Net

Training can be critical to the success of the overall effort. Provisions for training are discussed during the Preliminary Exploration. If this phase has been passed, then there is a problem. One way to attack this problem is to enlist the help and views of the Project Champion and the users involved in testing. With a united front, management can be approached.

Inadequate Training

Risk

There are times when the company-directed training for the application does not work. As a result, the system is not used. It is generally at this late juncture that the KE is contacted and asked to resolve the problem.

Safety Net

Immediate, positive steps are needed to remedy this situation. The causes of the problem may stem from more than the training alone. User support also needs to be evaluated. Some of the questions that are asked include:

- Did the training content cover the right topics? This question is asked of the users. Find out the opinion of these users, but evaluate the program too.
- Was the duration of training too long or too short?
- Were the training sessions unstructured, too structured, or given at inconvenient times or locations?
- Was the training delivery vehicle appropriate?
- Could the problems faced by the users be handled through on-line helps?
- How frequently did user problems occur? Was the same problem a show-stopper for significant numbers of users?
- Do the users feel that the training needs improvement, modifications of on-line help facilities are required, or companion job aids need to be developed?

- Can the nature of the perceived problems be resolved through assistance provided over a telephone link?
- Is the documentation sufficient? Evaluate user manuals, job aids, and other references.
- Do the materials provide all of the information that users actually need to operate the application?
- Is documentation written in a clear, concise, and easy to understand manner? Ask the opinion of users or observe the user seeking references.
- Is the user able to find the information residing in the support materials? If not, could the materials be revised, or do they need to be redesigned and rewritten?
- Do the users feel that the system is easy to use?
- Do the users relate that system helps are indeed helpful?
- Do the users accept the recommendations made by the system?
- Does the system actually improve user performance?
- Do the users feel that the system provides the appropriate functions?
- To what degree does the system contribute to, detract from, or have no effect on user performance?
- Are the problems in the training and documentation or in the system?
- To what degree does management feel the system is beneficial?

MAINTENANCE

Maintenance Planning

Risk

Maintenance is often overlooked and more planning is needed. There are critical attributes to planning.

Safety Net

A knowledge-based system is a living, dynamic system. There are two aspects of maintenance. One aspect is update. Update involves modification of the knowledge base because of domain changes, laws, policy, practices, etc. The second aspect is extension. Extension addresses system enhancements including additional capabilities, functions, etc.

Risk

Modification of a system that has been on-line for a period of time is nightmarish. Locating the needed knowledge-based file is nearly impossible.

Safety Net

There is a very high probability that once the application is out the door, it will return. Be prepared for this possibility by planning the application for maintenance. First, design logical names for the files. Group the files into logical clusters. Utilize file extensions and dates to assist this grouping. Second, document the design. Third, carefully file the documentation for easy later retrieval.

Future Technology

Risk

Awareness of new technology requires interest and exposure. Those responsible for making recommendations in technology monitor trade journals, read books, and attend conferences. Change occurs rapidly in the world of high tech. In order to remain viable in industry, movers of technology adopt carefully considered strategic positions.

Safety Net

A model of future technology is developed and cultivated. This model is comprised of two parts: technology components and human components. Technology components include increasing processing speed, progress in user interfaces, storage capacity of optical discs, data transmission speeds, and progress in AI and related fields such as neural nets.

A model of the components provides a big picture of what is possible through technology. The human component portion of the model is concerned with people and business. The users of technology must be understood. Business is beginning to empower the knowledge worker. These knowledge workers require technology to accomplish their jobs and responsibilities. Through business trends, societal trends, ROI, and other influential attributes, a technological change agent can grasp the trends and seize opportunities.

Given this model of a monitoring strategy, a tactical plan is put into place. So, what technologies should be monitored? Neural nets for one. What are neural nets? Neural nets are computer systems modeled after the neural connections of the human brain. These connections are composed of thousands of interconnected links that attempt to emulate the connectivity of the human brain. While conventional rule-based programs execute instructions serially, neural nets process multiple action chains in parallel. As these nets operate, patterns of links are established, establishing patterns of interconnections. Are neural nets new? No. Neural nets have been around since the 1940s. What are they good for? Proponents would hazard a guess that there is insufficient data, but indications are that neural nets will control sensory functions such as vision for pattern matching, touch for robotic control, and hearing for environmental control. Each of these sensory functions requires multiple data points. Proponents of neural nets would project that neural nets will serve in closed-loop monitoring systems for industry, such as in nuclear installations, recognize aircraft or vessels at sea for military applications, analyze documents for financial institutions, or evaluate patient telemetry for the medical industry.

Critics of neural nets would point out that much has been promised, but little has been accomplished, and that there has been "much ado about nothing." These people say that neural nets will not achieve the high-level symbolic needs of AI. Perhaps the advent of faster computers will expedite the evolution of neural nets for a new generation of neural net applications.

Most technologies begin in a polarized state, complete with proponents and opponents. System versus system, and champion versus champion are common in all areas of technology. However, what tends to occur over time is the emergence of hybrid systems. There will be room for systems modeled on rules, frames, objects, semantic nets, and neural nets. My money is on neural networking surfacing in the manufacturing industry and in the military within the next few years.

What other technologies and events should be watched? Imaging, parallel processing, advances in psychology, trends in education, optical-based media, holographics, business strategic alliances, knowledge industries, changes in culture, international trends, government trends, and development in physics.

SUMMARY

Regardless of the effort, detail, and care you take in developing a system, it is impossible to foresee or even dodge every obstacle in your path. This chapter scratched the surface of possible risks that may be experienced in each phase of the development model, along with suggestions on how to prevent and deal with them. As you experience pitfalls and rise either successfully or somewhat scarred from them, add them to your personal file for future reference.

PRACTICAL APPLICATION

1. Given the issues discussed in this chapter, go back and review your hobby system plans generated in part III. What changes could you make to ward against some of the risks noted in this chapter?

2. Select one of the risks that you believe the most difficult for you, personally, to handle. Pretend that it has just happened to you during that particular phase of your project. Prepare a response and an action plan.

PART III—SUMMARY

This part of the book explored the issues and requirements associated with a knowledge-based system using a development model. Six phases of the model were explored.

- Phase 1: Preliminary Exploration—identification and study of the problem and a proposal for its resolution.
- Phase 2: Requirements Analysis—generation of a design specification.
- Phase 3: System Development—construction of the system.
- Phase 4: Validation—quality assurance testing of the system; check and confirmation against initial design.
- Phase 5: Implementation—"rollout" of the system into the user environment.
- Phase 6: Maintenance—system management to include ongoing evaluation and updating.

The final chapter provided some hints and pitfalls that correlate to each of the phases.

The concepts and practices of Knowledge Engineering are far-reaching and all-encompassing—a true challenge to one's abilities in all domains. It includes a responsibility to seriously examine one's morals, ethics, and ideals as it moves into all areas of life—from the technical to the educational, from the personal to the political.

The open society, the unrestricted access to knowledge, the unplanned and uninhibited association of men for its furtherance—these are what may make a vast, complex, ever growing, ever changing, ever more specialized and expert technological world, nevertheless a world of human community.

J. Robert Oppenheimer

PART III—PRACTICUM

Take your Part III project and review it in light of the first two parts of the book.

1. Identify the problem-solving strategies, structures, acquisition processes, etc., that you used.

2. Then look toward the future. Given that anything is possible, what improvements could be made to your system?

3. If you have not read through the first two parts, develop a marketing strategy for your hobby system. Be sure to identify your audience and keep in mind their level of familiarity with knowledge-based system.

4. Compose an article for a professional journal (that is not computer-related) about your hobby system.

Glossary

access   The process of seeking, reading, or writing data in a storage unit.

access method   A technique for moving data between a computer and its peripheral storage devices.

access time   The elapsed time between the issuance of an instruction for data access and the availability of the data for use.

address   The specific location of a stored item in a computer storage system.

algorithm   A step-by-step or systematic procedure for solving a problem. A precisely defined group of rules or processes that guarantees desired output from a given set of inputs. In computer programs, algorithms are used to define the manner in which a computer is to handle specific operations. Conventional computer languages are algorithmic languages, as they follow a predefined track. Symbolic languages such as LISP or PROLOG are not algorithmic.

anticipatory staging   The movement of blocks of stored data from one storage device to another in anticipation of need for shorter access time.

application   A computer program or system designed to perform tasks.

arc   The lines that connect nodes in a search tree or semantic network. *See* LINK.

architecture   The structure, framework, or organization of computer hardware or software.

argument   The independent variable of a function.

array   A set, group, or series of numbers, terms, or elements arranged in a logical or meaningful pattern.

artificial intelligence   The branch of computer science dedicated to the study of the manner in which computers can be used to simulate or duplicate functions of humans. AI hardware and software emulate human thinking, reasoning, decision making, knowledge storage and retrieval, problem solving, and learning.

associative storage (memory)   Storage that is addressed by content rather than by location in order to facilitate rapid access to data with specified contents.

attribute   A property "owned" by an object. One method of handling information for an expert system knowledge base is through objects, attributes, and values. This scheme of knowledge representation is used to describe Object-Attribute-Value (O-A-V) triplets. For example, in the statement, "The color of the Porsche is white," the Porsche is the object, the color is an attribute, and white is the description of the color and is therefore the value.

backtracking   A technique used in tree searches. The process of working backwards from a failed objective or incorrect result to examine unexplored alternatives. The process of backing up to a previous choice point in a search and moving to an alternative opportunity.

backward chaining   A method of reasoning that starts with the desired goal-state and works backwards, looking for declarative and procedural knowledge that supports the desired outcome. A technique used in tree searches in which a conclusion or objective is hypothesized and the system works backwards to find rules that support the hypothesis. For example, the system backs up to the "IF" clauses of a rule to determine whether these clauses are all correct. Based on what it finds, the system will either validate (confirm) or invalidate (reject) the rule containing the goal. Also known as *goal-driven* and *backward-reasoning*.

binary search   A search method for a sequenced table or file. The upper or lower half of the contents is selected based on a midpoint value examination. The portion selected is then halved in a similar fashion, iteratively, until the search is complete.

blind search   A search technique that uses no knowledge or heuristics to optimize the search process. An arbitrary search process that attempts all possibilities in searching rather than a guided process.

blocking   The combining of two or more records in a database so that they are jointly read or written by a single instruction.

bottom up   A method of reasoning, searching, or parsing that starts with a leaf in a tree or a smallest element in a string to be parsed and works toward the whole string or the root of the tree. A data-driven search approach is also called *forward chaining*.

breadth-first   A search strategy in which all the nodes on one level of a search tree are examined before any of the nodes of the next lower level.

bucket   A storage area in a database that might contain more than one record and is referred to as a whole by an addressing technique.

buffer   A storage area that temporarily holds data while it is being received, transmitted, read, or written. Buffers are often used to increase speed.

C   A high-level programming language widely used in systems and application programming.

cell   A group of contiguous storage locations. A cell is generally a track or a cylinder.

certainty   The degree of confidence in a fact or relationship.

certainty factor   A number or numerical weight assigned to a declarative or procedural statement that indicates the likelihood the statement is true. Certainty factors can be assigned in a range with 1.0 as certainly true, .5 as uncertain, and 0 as false.

chain   An organization of data linked by pointers.

cognition   The act of knowing.

cognitive model   A computer model of human thinking. Cognitive theories are derived from psychology of the human thought process. The output is a computer program that is considered intelligent.

common LISP   A dialect of the AI programming language LISP.

common sense   A knowledge base that humans form to cope with their environment. Commonsense knowledge bases contain how and why things work in various aspects of human experience.

common-sense reasoning   A decision-making system that appears to use common sense to reach its decisions.

compaction   A technique for reducing the number of bits in data storage.

compiler   A software program that converts a program from a higher-level language to a lower one, generally machine code.

computer vision   A field of artificial intelligence that focuses on emulating human vision. Optical sensors are used to scan the environment. The input from the environment is converted to binary signals. The signals are interpreted by a computer through comparison and pattern-matching.

concatenate   To link a collection of data elements (e.g., strings) together end to end.

confidence factor   A method of handling uncertainty in a production rule system. A value in a system of numbers that indicate the belief in a conclusion or conclusion option.

control strategy   A method of searching through a knowledge base or search space. For example, forward, backward, depth-first, breadth-first, heuristic, etc.

CPU   Acronym for central processing unit, the portion of a computer that handles most of the processing functions. A combination of the arithmetic-logic unit and the control section.

database   A linked collection of data stored together, independent of the programs that access the data, and capable of being modified without disruption to the existing structure.

data dictionary   A catalog of the database elements with their names and structures.

data-driven   An inference strategy used in search trees. Data-directed reasoning is bottom-up or forward chaining.

data item   The smallest unit of data described in a data set.

data management   The functions of a data system that provide control over the input and output of data.

data manipulation language   The language used by a programmer to enable data transfer between the program and the database. The data manipulation language is not a stand-alone language. It relies on a host programming language for framework and procedural requirements.

data set   A named collection of linked data items arranged in a specified manner and described by control information.

decision tree   A graphical structure resembling a tree that illustrates the nodes and arcs in a structure of alternative paths for decisions or outcomes.

declarative knowledge   Statements of fact. For example, voltage is symbolically represented as E. Current is represented as I. Resistance is represented by R.

deduction   A logical thought process that arrives at a decision.

deductive reasoning   Reasoning from the general to the specific. A logic path is selected on the basis of a premise. Known also as *consequent reasoning*.

deep knowledge   Compiled knowledge arranged into abstract and theoretical patterns.

demand staging   Movement of blocks of data from one storage device to another to shorten access time.

depth-first   A search procedure that explores each branch of the search tree in a vertical manner before moving to the right in the structure.

direct access   Storage or retrieval of data by location reference in a storage device.

directory   A table that supplies the relationships between data items in a database.

distributed free space   Planned empty storage space in a data layout to allow insertion of new data.

domain   **1.** The collection of related data items or fields in a relation or flat file. **2.** A specific field of concentration associated with knowledge and expertise. This knowledge is often associated with a human expert in a particular field. Training or procedural manuals also have domain knowledge.

dynamic storage allocation   The allocation of storage space for a procedure based on demand rather than preplanned allocation.

embedded pointers   Pointers located in data records rather than in a directory.

embedded system   A program that resides within or behind a primary program. Embedded systems are also called ShadowWare programs. Sidekick is an example of an embedded system.

entity   An object for which data is recorded.

entity identifier   A unique identifier of an entity or data regarding the entity.

environment   A general term used to describe the hardware and software products and programs which constitute a computer system.

example   A matrix used to display attributes and outcomes representing an expert's decision making. Production rules are generally inferred from examples to form a knowledge base.

example-based system   An expert system designed with rules that are induced from supplied examples. Also called an *induction system.*

exhaustive search   An inefficient search strategy used by an inference engine in which every possible combination of rules and facts is systematically searched in an attempt to solve a problem. This is a brute-force search technique.

expert system   The most successful application in artificial intelligence software. An expert system program consists of a user base, a search system, and a knowledge base. Expert systems are linked to peripherals ranging from printers to robots. An expert system contains declarative and procedural knowledge which represents an expert's problem-solving heuristics in a specific area.

expertise   Skill and knowledge acquired by selected humans as a result of performance and exceeding that of most of their peer group. Expertise is composed of information combined with heuristics and other procedures used to efficiently analyze specific problems.

extent   A contiguous area of data storage in a database.

fifth generation   A term used by those who anticipate a class of knowledge-based computers that employ high speed, parallel processing, and attributes of artificial intelligence. Fifth generation computers are a major element in the mission of the Japanese to claim computer supremacy.

file   A set of similarly constructed records in a database.

fire   To take the prescribed action when the conditions of a rule are met in a program.

flat file   A two-dimensional array of data items in a database.

FLOPS   Acronym for floating point operations per second, a term used to measure the performance of computers.

forward chaining   A method of reasoning or control strategy that uses known facts and moves forward to produce more facts to reach a conclusion. Forward chaining determines the way the expert system's inference engine draws its inferences. The inference engine determines whether the "IF" portions of a rule are true. If they are true, the "THEN" part of the rule is established as fact, and the program moves on to the next rule, and iteratively explores the process until a goal is reached or all possibilities are exhausted. Also called *data driven* or *inductive.*

frame   A knowledge representation method. A scheme to organize knowledge about an object as a collection of attributes stored in slots. Frames contain the features of a concept or situation including the objects of the concept, their actual or default values, the rules that apply to the concept or situation, the relationships between the frame and other frames, instructions for use of the frame, and instructions for out-of-range occurrences. Information components stored within the frame reside in "slots," each of which contains an information string.

functional dependence   The condition in a relation by which one attribute in a database is identified by or dependent on another.

fuzzy logic   Any reasoning technique designed to describe uncertain or incomplete information. Fuzzy logic emulates the manner in which humans approach and think about problem situations or relationships between objects. Terms such as big, fast, old, etc., are associated with fuzzy logic.

fuzzy reasoning   A method or approach to uncertainty by an assignment of a relative value. For example, fuzzy logic uses labels like true, very true, not very true, big, old. *See* FUZZY LOGIC.

goal-driven   A reasoning strategy that begins with the goal or conclusion and progresses backwards through the knowledge base to verify the goal. *See* BACKWARD CHAINING.

granularity   The level of detail to which a problem or objective is analyzed.

heuristic   **1.** Of or referring to personal or computer problem-solving methods that employ rules of thumb, shortcuts, and learned techniques to reach conclusions. **2.** A rule of thumb collection of experience and knowledge that enables a level of understanding and decision making above the norm.

hierarchy   An organizational structure in which each element at a lower level is subordinate to a single one at the next higher level.

hit rate   In a database, a measure of the number of records in a file expected to be accessed in a given run, usually expressed as a percentage.

home address   A storage location to which a data record is assigned logically; a field that contains the physical address of the data located at the beginning of a track.

hybrid system   A system of the future that merges hypertext and knowledge-based systems.

hypermedia   Data linked in logical paths that produce knowledge; it includes the integration of text, pictures, sounds, data, and knowledge. Hypermedia is thus a highly sophisticated knowledge base.

hypertext   A hypermedia application that enables the user to quickly look through existing units of text to locate ones matching the user's criteria. Hypertext has the ability of presenting stored text nonsequentially.

hypothesis   A statement that is temporarily assumed to be true. A hypothesis is generally a proposition used as a basis for an argument.

IF-THEN   A production rule technique that uses conditional rules in such a way that the rule is executed when specified conditions are met. For example, IF the symbol has a vertical line and three perpendicular lines with one at the top, one in the center, and one at the bottom, THEN it is an E. The "IF" part of the rule is known as the premise, and the "THEN" is the action part of the rule.

index   A table used to determine the location of a record in a database.

indexed-sequential storage   A file structure in a database where records are stored in ascending sequence by key.

indirect addressing   Any method of specifying or locating a storage location in a database in which the key is not the actual address.

induction shell   An expert system code-building package that allows high-level input of examples, possibly in natural English, and outputs computer code. Induction shells usually present an entry matrix for examples. The shell then generates rules.

induction system   A knowledge system whose knowledge base consists of examples. Also called an *example-driven system*.

inductive reasoning   A reasoning method that moves from the specific to the general. Also called *conditional*, or *antecedent* reasoning.

inference   The process of decision making based on reasoning from available evidence. The inference ability of a computer can lie in its ability to match patterns in "IF_THEN" type rules within an expert system.

inference engine   An expert system component that does the reasoning search function. The inference engine or search mechanism explores the knowledge base through guidance of a reasoning structure such as depth-first. It contains the strategies to solve problems, acquire knowledge, interface with other systems, and explain its reasoning to a user.

inheritance   The ability of elements in a knowledge representation system to assume the characteristics of objects higher up in the structure or hierarchy.

intelligence   The ability to acquire and apply knowledge through reasoning techniques.

interface   In a computer system, a link that provides communication between two other portions of the process. For example, a keyboard is an interface between a user and a computer.

internal schema   The physical structure of the data in a database.

interpretive routine   A routine that decodes instructions written as pseudo-codes and executes them immediately. In contrast to a compiler, the routine does not produce a machine language routine to be executed at a later time.

inverted file   A file structure in a database in which there is an index to each data element to be used as a key.

ISAM   Acronym for Index Sequential Access Method.

KE   Abbreviation for knowledge engineer.

key   A data item used to identify or locate of record or data group in a database.

key compression   A technique used to reduce the number of bits in keys. Key compression is used to make indexes occupy less space.

knowledge   A collection of declarative and procedural relationships that can be called upon in the performance of applications.

knowledge acquisition   The process of locating, organizing, and representing knowledge. Knowledge acquisition involves observation, interviews, research, and introspection.

knowledge base   An organized collection of declarative and procedural relationships designed to represent expertise or heuristics in a particular area.
The knowledge base is designed to be accessed by a search program.

knowledge-based systems   Reference systems that contain declarative and
procedural relationships referenced through a user interface. Knowledge-
based systems include expert systems and hyperknowledge systems.

knowledge engineer   A professional who administers three principal tasks:
acquiring knowledge from a human expert, representing that knowledge in a
well-defined manner, and embodying the expertise in a knowledge base.

knowledge engineering   The process of acquiring knowledge from a human
expert and representing that knowledge in a knowledge base. This is a technical skill that combines systems analysis and programming in computer system development. Knowledge engineering involves the acquisition and
transfer of knowledge from a specific area of expertise to a computer representation as a knowledge base component of the system. The accumulation
of the knowledge in the form of rules and facts in an expert system knowledge base is similar to the data in a conventional system.

knowledge representation   The structure and organization used to store
and display the declarative and procedural statements obtained from a human
expert or expert source. Examples include rules, frames, etc.

knowledge source   A repository of synthesized information. Sources
include human experts, case studies, books, empirical data, etc.

label   A symbol used to identify or describe an item, record, file, or message
in a database.

latency   A measure of the average access time required for a storage location
on a rotating surface to reach the read/write heads. The time is usually that
taken by one-half revolution of the surface.

leaf   A node with no tower-level descendants.

learning   Gaining knowledge, understanding, or skill through education and
experience.

library   The storage area for volumes such as tapes and disk packs. Also, a
library is a collection of programs, source statements, or object modules
stored on a direct-access device.

LISP   Acronym for LISt Processor, the most widely used artificial intelligence
programming language.

list   An ordered set or chain of data items in a database.

logic   A system of reasoning based on the study of propositions and their analysis to make decisions. Logic is the process of making inferences based on
known facts.

logical   A perceptual data organization scheme that describes the user's view
of the form of data organization, hardware, or system as opposed to the
actual physical scheme.

macroinstruction   A single line of source code that generates an in-line program routine, rather than one instruction.

mapping A set of associations between elements in a database.

migration The movement of data in storage for access advantage.

model The logical structure of data in a database.

module A unit of storage hardware or software instructions.

multilist organization An organization for rapid searching in which chains are divided into indexed fragments.

natural language Language used by humans in daily conversation, reading and writing. English, German, and French are natural languages. Computer programs that allow users to provide instructions to computers in English are referred to as natural language programs.

natural language interface A user interface with a computer that takes in natural language from the user or outputs natural language subsequent to internal processing, or both.

nodes The places, goals, or subgoals in a structure which represents a search space or other knowledge element.

normal form, first Data in which no element is multivalued.

normal form, second E.F. Codd's definition, by which a relation ''R'' is in second normal form if it is in first normal form and every nonprime attribute of ''R'' is nontransitively dependent on each candidate key of ''R.''

normal form, third E.F. Codd's definition, by which a relation ''R'' is in third normal form if it is in second normal form and every nonprime attribute of ''R'' is nontransitively dependent on each candidate key of ''R.''

normalization In a database, the decomposition of complex data structures into relations in a normal form.

object A physical or conceptual entity that has definable attributes and characteristics. An object can be described, defined, or qualified. Objects can be unchanging or static. Objects can also change or be dynamic.

object-attribute-value triplets The representation of factual knowledge through a collection of physical or conceptual objects. Each of these objects possesses attributes that describe or qualify the object in some way. An attribute possesses values. *See* ATTRIBUTE, OBJECT, VALUE, O-A-V TRIPLETS.

object-oriented programming A programming approach based on a hierarchy of autonomous objects, to each of which are attached the procedures for its processing.

operating system The control program of a computer system. Systems such as DOS and OS/2 contain functions that enable a user to access and manipulate the programs within a computer system.

overflow The situation when a record or segment in a database cannot be stored in its home address. It is then stored in a designated overflow location or in the home address of other records.

paging A technique used in virtual storage in which memory appears larger than it is by transferring blocks, or pages, of data into memory from external storage.

paradigm An example, model, or process used over time.

parallel architecture The use of multiple central processing units (CPUs) or other hardware to carry out the simultaneous processing of multiple programs or of different parts of a single program.

parallel data organization An organization scheme that allows multiple access to search, read, or write data simultaneously.

parsing The process of breaking down an expression in a language into components for the purpose of analysis or understanding.

path The track or direction taken through a search tree.

pattern An object, model, plan, or template that is followed or identified.

pattern-matching The automatic analysis and recognition of objects, models, plans, or templates according to a predetermined scheme.

physical Of or referring to the actual manner in which data exists in a system as opposed to the way it is perceived in logical form.

physical database A database in the form in which it is stored including pointers or other links. Multiple logical databases may be accessed within a physical database.

plex structure A relationship between records or groups in a database in which a child record can have more than one parent record. A plex structure is also called a *network structure*.

pointer The address of a record or data group in a database contained in another record for access efficiency.

predicate A statement about the subject of a proposition.

predicate calculus A logic system used to express declarative and procedural statements about objects in a domain. The system uses a rule of inference that states how symbols can be used to make formulas.

probability A mathematical ratio of the number of expected outcomes or occurrences to the number of repetitions required to achieve those occurrences.

problem solving The process of understanding an issue, forming a hypothesis, testing the hypothesis, and finding a solution. Problem solving moves from an initial state and searches through a problem space to identify the sequence of actions required to reach a goal state.

problem space A defined area representing all of the possible states that could occur resulting from interactions between the elements and operators under consideration for a particular problem.

procedural knowledge Knowledge about actions to be taken with facts and operations. For example, procedural knowledge would state the relationship between voltage, resistance and current as $E = IR$.

production rule An IF-THEN rule.

production system A problem-solving system that contains a set of rules, a control strategy, and a knowledge base.

progressive overflow An overflow handling method for a database in a randomly stored file that does not have pointers. The overflow record is stored in the first available space and later retrieved by a forward serial search from the home address.

PROLOG   An acronym for **PRO**gramming in **LOG**ic. An artificial intelligence programming language based on predicate calculus and used extensively in Europe.

propositional calculus   A logic system that reaches a conclusion from a series of statements controlled by a set of rules. Propositions are linked together with connectives such as AND, OR, NOT, and IMPLIES. The connectives used determine the truthfulness of statements.

pruning   A search technique used to expedite finding a path through a knowledge base or search tree. Pruning narrows the alternatives in a problem space.

reasoning   The mental process of arriving at logical conclusions based on facts and available evidence.

record   A group of related or linked information fields in a database that are manipulated as a unit by an application program.

relation   A two-dimensional array of data elements in a database.

relational database   A database composed of relations. This structure can recombine data elements to form different relations.

root   The base node of a tree structure.

rule   A two-part statement that consists of declarative and procedural components defining a particular conduct or behavior. An IF-THEN statement that asserts if a given condition is true, then a selected action should result.

rule-based   Of or referring to any program or system that uses a rule set to define situations and appropriate actions. Rules used in systems are called production rules. Systems that use production rules are called production systems.

rule of thumb   A heuristic based on experience in the form of a personal principle, shortcut, or method used to simplify or accelerate a process. A rule of thumb is a general guideline that is not always accurate. In early England, it was the legal size of a stick used for corrective discipline on humans.

schema   A strategy for knowledge representation that usually involves frames or scripts. Knowledge is placed in a structure that represents information about patterns of relationships.

script   A schema used for describing common sequences of events or patterns of relationships.

search   The process that explores or examines evidence for the purpose of discovery or learning.

search space   The universe of discovery opportunity based on all available states or nodes in a knowledge base. Search space is graphically represented by a search tree or graph.

search tree   A graphic illustration that resembles an inverted tree used to show the universe of the search space. A search tree is a hierarchical structure of goals and subgoals, or states, connected by arcs.

sector The smallest address portion of storage on some disk and drum storage units.

seek The positioning of the access mechanism of a direct-access storage device.

semantics The meaning, intention, or significance of a word, symbol, or expression.

semantic network A method of knowledge representation that uses nodes to represent objects, concepts, and entities, and uses arcs to represent the links that describe the relationships between the nodes.

sequential processing A processing scheme in which database records are accessed in ascending sequence by key. For example, the next record accessed has the next higher key, regardless of its physical location or position in a file.

shell A software program that allows a user to interact with a system without a programming knowledge requirement. A shell might use a natural language interface.

slot A subelement of a frame or schema. A selected characteristic, specification, or definition used in the formation of a knowledge base.

sort An arrangement of stored records in a database by a specified key.

supercomputer A mainframe computer that has superior operating speed and storage capabilities compared to other computers generally available. These computers might use parallel processing.

surface knowledge Knowledge that results from practical experience.

syllogism Deductive reasoning from the general to the specific. A structure composed of a major premise, a minor premise, and a conclusion.

symbol A designation used to represent an object, element, quantity, or relationship in mathematics, logic, or a computer program.

symbolic computing The use of symbols rather than numbers to represent and manipulate declarative and procedural relationships.

table A collection of data identified or labeled by its position in a database structure.

thinking The active reasoning process used to evaluate and render a conclusion about a subject.

tool A software package or shell that facilitates the creation of a program.

top-down reasoning A reasoning scheme that starts with the root of a tree or the largest or most general element to be analyzed, and works toward the leaves of the tree or the smallest or most specific elements.

toy problem An artificial or bounded problem used for testing knowledge-based systems.

transaction An interaction with a computer system that carries out a single defined function, e.g., a bank deposit.

tree A structure that represents objects, goals, and subgoals connected by arcs. Tree structures have roots, branches and leaves that resemble an inverted tree. The tree defines a domain or search space. In a tree, each element has only one immediate parent.

tree search   The process of exploring a tree for the purpose of problem resolution.

trigger   The activation of a rule when the predefined conditions are met.

tuple   A group of related fields in a relation; analogous to a record.

Turing test   A test designed by Alan Turing to explore machine intelligence. A subject is isolated and interrogates either a person or machine through a terminal. If the subject cannot determine if the communication is with a person or a machine, the machine is said to be intelligent.

user interface   The portion of a computer system that communicates with the user.

volatile file   A file that is often changed.

wisdom   Knowledge and understanding of what is right or just. Wisdom is good judgment and common sense combined with knowledge.

workstation   A computer, generally dedicated to a specific application and used to improve productivity. Workstations contain all of the programs and resources needed for peak production. An example is a computer system for managers that contains communications, word processing, database, spreadsheet, and other software needed to perform a variety of tasks.

write   To record information on a storage device.

Bibliography

Anderson, J.R. *Language, Memory, and Thought*. Hillsdale, N.J.: Lawrence Erlbaum Associates, 1976. [Chapter 1]

Arnheim, Rudolf. *Visual Thinking*. Los Angeles, Calif.: University of California Press, 1969. [Chapter 1]

Atre, Shaku. *Data Base Structured Techniques for Design, Performance, and Management*. New York: John Wiley & Sons, 1988. [Chapter 4]

Bacon, Francis. "Of Studies." *I Was Just Thinking*. New York: Thomas Y. Crowell Co., 1959, 10–11. [Chapter 2]

Bandler, Richard, and John Grinder. *Frogs into Princes*. Moab, Utah: Real People Press, 1979. [Chapter 7]

Bigge, Morris L. *Learning Theories For Teachers*. New York: Harper & Row, Publishers, Inc., 1982. [Chapter 1]

Bowerman, Robert G., and David E. Glover. *Putting Expert Systems into Practice*. New York: Van Nostrad Reinhold Company, 1988. [Chapter 3]

Bratton, Barry. "The Instructional Development Specialist as Consultant," *Journal of Instructional Development*, Winter 1979–80, Vol. 3, No. 2, 2–8. [Chapter 2]

Bruner, Jerome S., R.R. Olver, P.M. Greenfield, et al. *Studies in Cognitive Growth*. New York: John Wiley and Sons, 1966. [Chapter 1]

Burns, Hugh L., and Charles G. Capps. *Foundations of Intelligent Tutoring Systems*. Edited by Martha C. Polson and J. Jeffrey Richardson. Hillsdale, N.J.: Lawrence Erlbaum Associates Publishers, 1988. [Chapter 4]

Buzan, Tony. *Use Both Sides of Your Brain*. New York: Dutten Paperback, 1983. [Chapter 7]

Cram, David D. "Designing Instruction: Meeting With The SME." *NSPI Journal* (May 1981): 5–8. [Chapter 2]

deBono, Edward. *Lateral Thinking: Creativity Step by Step*. New York: Harper & Row, 1973. [Chapter 3]

DeWitt, Philip Elmer, "Fast and Smart." *Time Magazine*. Vol. 131, No. 13. (March 28, 1988). [Chapter 1]

Dreyfus, H., and S. Dreyfus. *Mind Over Machine: The Power of Human Intuition and Expertise in the Era of the Computer*. New York: The Free Press, 1986. [Chapter 1]

Firebaugh, Morris W. *Artificial Intelligence: A Knowledge-Based Approach*. Boston, Mass.: Boyd & Fraser Publishing Company, 1988. [Chapter 3]

Fischler, Martin A., and Oscar Firschein. *Intelligence: The Eye, The Brain, and The Computer*. Reading, Mass.: Addison Wesley Publishing Co., 1987. [Chapter 1]

Flavell, J.H. "Metacognitive Aspects of Problem Solving." in L.B. Resnick (Ed.), *The Nature of Intelligence*. Hillsdale, N.J.: Lawrence Erlbaum Associates, 1976. [Chapter 1]

Gains, B.R., and M.L.G. Shaw. "New Directions in the Analysis and Interactive Elicitation of Personal Construct Theories." *Internal Journal of Man-Machine Studies* (Vol. 13, 1980): 81–116. [Chapter 8]

Goodman, Danny. *The Complete Hypercard Handbook*. New York: Bantam Books, 1987. [Chapter 4]

Harmon, Paul, and David King. *Expert Systems Artificial Intelligence in Business*. New York: John Wiley & Sons, 1985. [Chapter 8]

Hart, Anna. *Knowledge Acquisition for Expert Systems*. New York: McGraw-Hill Book Company, 1986. [Chapters 1, 6, 12]

Hayes-Roth, F, D.A. Waterman, and D.B. Lenat. *Building Expert Systems*. Reading, Mass.: Addision-Wesley Publishing Co., 1983. [Chapter 12]

Hersey, Paul. *Situational Selling*. Escondido, Calif.: The Center for Leadership Studies, 1985. [Chapter 5]

Hofstadter, Douglas R. *Gödel, Escher, Bach: An Eternal Golden Braid*. New York: Vintage Books, 1979. [Chapter 1]

Johnson-Laird, P.N. *Mental Models: Towards a Cognitive Science of Language, Inference, and Consciousness*. Cambridge, Mass.: Harvard University Press, 1983. [Chapter 1]

Kelly, G.A. *The Psychology of Personal Constructs*. New York: Norton, 1955. [Chapter 8]

Leedy, Paul D. *Practical Research: Planning and Design* (Second Edition), New York: Macmillan Publishing Co., Inc., 1980. [Chapter 2]

McClure, Carma. "The CASE for Structured Development." *PC TECH Journal*, Vol. 6, No.8 (August 1988). [Chapter 4]

McGraw, Karen L., and Karan Harbison-Briggs. *Knowledge Acquisition Principles and Guidelines*. Englewood Cliffs, N.J.: Prentice-Hall, Inc., 1989. [Chapter 7]

Martin, Charles Fontaine, Ph.D. *User-Centered Requirements Analysis*. Englewood Cliffs, N.J.: Prentice–Hall, Inc., 1988. Chapter 4. [Chapter 7]

Mascaro, Juan. *The Bhagavad Gita*. Middlesex, England: Penguin Books Ltd., 1962. [Chapter 3]

Mayer, R.E. *Journal of Educational Psychology* 67, 725–734, 1075. [Chapter 1]

Michalski, Ryszard S. "Machine Learning" in Morris W. Firebaugh's *Artificial Intelligence: A Knowledge-Based Approach*. Boston, Mass.: Boyd & Fraser Publishing Company, 1988. [Chapter 6]

Minsky, Marvin. *Society of MIND*. Touchstone Edition. New York: Simon and Schuster, Inc., 1988. [Chapter 3]

Molnar, Andrew R. "The Search for New Intellectual Technologies." *T.H.E. Journal* (Sept. 1982): 104 – 112. [Chapter 2]

Newell, A., and H.A. Simon. *Human Problem Solving*. Englewood Cliffs, N.J.: Prentice-Hall, Inc., 1972. [Chapter 1]

Parsaye, Kamran, and Mark Chignell. *Expert Systems for Experts*. New York: John Wiley & Sons, Inc., 1988. [Chapters 1, 8]

Pfeiffer, John. "The Thinking Machine," as quoted in *The Unity of Prose: From Description to Allegory*. New York: Harper & Row, Publishers, 1968, 261 – 262. [Chapter 2]

Polya, G. *How To Solve It*. Princeton, N.J.: Princeton University Press, 1973. [Chapter 1]

Puff, C.R. *Handbook of Research Methods in Human Memory and Cognition*. San Diego, Calif.: Academic Press, 1982. [Chapter 7]

Rich, Elaine. *Artificial Intelligence*. New York: McGraw Hill, 1983. [Chapter 3]

Ritti, R. "Work Goals of Scientists and Engineers." *Industrial Relations* (Vol. 7) 118 – 131, 1968. [Chapter 5]

Rosenberg, M. *Educational Technology* (Vol. 18, No. 2): 50, copyright 1978. San Diego Mesa College Library Bulletins, San Diego, CA, 1983-1988. [Chapter 2]

Schank, R.C., and R.P. Abelson. *Scripts, Plans, Goals, and Understanding*. Hillsdale, N.J.: Erlbaum, 1977. [Chapter 8]

Simon, H.A. *The Sciences of the Artificial*. Cambridge, Mass.: MIT Press, 1981. [Chapter 3]

Skinner, B.F. *The Technology of Teaching*. New York: Meredith Corporation, 1968. [Chapter 4]

Walters, John R., and Norman R. Nielsen. *Crafting Knowledge-Based Systems*. New York: John Wiley & Sons, Inc. 1988. [Chapter 10]

Waterman, Donald A. *A Guide to Expert Systems*. Reading, Mass.: Addison-Wesley Publishing Company, 1985. [Chapter 4]

_____. *A Guide to Expert Systems*. Reading, Mass.: Addison-Wesley Publishing Co., 1986. [Chapter 5]

Weizenbaum, Joseph. *Computer Power and Human Reason*. San Francisco, Calif.: W.H. Freeman and Company, 1976. [Chapter 1]

Winograd, Terry, and Fernando Flores. *Understanding Computers and Cognition*. Reading, Mass.: Addison-Wesley Publishing Company, Inc., 1987. [Chapter 1]

Wolfgram, Deborah D., Teresa J. Dear, and Craig S. Galbraith. *Expert Systems for the Technical Professional*. New York: John Wiley & Sons, 1987. [Chapter 7]

Index